Colonialism, Tradition and Reform

About the Book

Gandhi was profoundly disturbed by the degenerate state of Indian society. One of his lifelong preoccupations was to explore a new moral order appropriate to India in the modern age. How he went about this task is the central concern of this widely acclaimed book on Gandhi, first published in 1989. This revised edition includes a new chapter dealing with the Marxist critique of Gandhi. It also incorporates new and hitherto inaccessible material, takes into account recent published works on Gandhi, and draws upon the author's own deeper understanding of Gandhi.

The first chapter discusses the evolution of Gandhi's own thinking and shows how he was deeply influenced by a long line of distinguished Indian thinkers. The remaining chapters discuss a variety of topics including Gandhi's understanding of the nature and causes of Indian degeneration, his conception of *yugadharma* or a new moral order; his concern to radicalise the traditional Hindu view of non-violence; his debate with terrorists about the use of violence to secure independence; his concerns about the practice of untouchability; and the mobilisation of sexual energy to attain political objectives.

Gandhi did not find it easy to challenge the traditional ways of life and thought. After initial mistakes he developed a fascinating strategy of mobilising the critical and regenerative powers of tradition. Professor Parekh analyses the nature, resources and structural constraints of the Hindu cultural tradition and explores the logical structure and philosophical basis of Gandhi's reformist discourse and praxis.

This is the first time Gandhi's ideas and actions have been analysed in this manner. The book's appeal will not be limited to those studying Gandhi but will be invaluable for all those interested in Indian philosophy, religion, history, politics and sociology.

Colonialism, Tradition and Reform

An Analysis of Gandhi's Political Discourse

Revised Edition

Bhikhu Parekh

Sage Publications
New Delhi • Thousand Oaks • London

Copyright © Bhikhu Parekh, 1989, 1999

All rights reserved. No part of this book may be reproduced or utilised in any form or by any means, electronic or mechanical, including photocopying, recording, or by any information storage and retrieval system, without permission in writing from the publisher.

First published in 1989
This revised edition published in 1999 by

Sage Publications India Pvt Ltd
M-32 Market, Greater Kailash-I
New Delhi 110 048

Sage Publications Inc
2455 Teller Road
Thousand Oaks, California 91320

Sage Publications Ltd
6 Bonhill Street
London EC2A4PU

Published by Tejeshwar Singh for Sage Publications India Pvt Ltd, Lasertypeset by Accurate Graphics, Pondicherry, and printed at Chaman Enterprises, Delhi.

Library of Congress Cataloging-in-Publication Data

Parekh, Bhikhu C.
    Colonialism, tradition, and reform: an analysis of Gandhi's political discourse / Bhikhu Parekh.
      p.   cm.
    Bibliography: p.
    Includes index.
    1. Gandhi, Mahatma, 1869–1948—Political and social views.
I. Title.
DS481.G3P346   954.03'5—dc19   1989 (Revised Edition 1999)   89–5935

Revised Edition ISBNs:
    0–7619–9382–7 (US-hb)   81–7036–851–0 (India-hb)
    0–7619–9383–5 (US-pb)   81–7036–852–9 (India-pb)

Sage Production Team: Nomita Jain, Parul Nayyar, Radha Devraj and Santosh Rawat

To
**RM
VNK
DLS**

Contents

Preface to the Revised Edition 9
Acknowledgements 12

Chapter	One	Introduction	15
Chapter	Two	Hindu Responses to British Rule	40
Chapter	Three	Gandhi and *Yugadharma*	81
Chapter	Four	Theory of Non-violence	120
Chapter	Five	Dialogue with the Terrorists	155
Chapter	Six	Sex, Energy and Politics	191
Chapter	Seven	Discourse on Untouchability	228
Chapter	Eight	Indianisation of Autobiography	272
Chapter	Nine	Gandhi and the Bourgeoisie	294

Endnotes 326
Index 350
About the Author 360

Preface to the Revised Edition

I have taken the occasion of this new edition to revise parts of the book. Most revisions are minor and either stylistic or intended to clarify the meaning. A few are substantive and necessitated by the new works on Gandhi that have appeared since I completed the text of the first edition, comments of its reviewers, and my own deeper understanding of Gandhi.[1]

Some of the most important recent works on Gandhi include Dennis Dalton's *Mahatma Gandhi: Nonviolent Power in Action*, Richard Cox's *Gandhian Utopia: Experiments with Culture*, Partha Chatterjee's *Nationalist Thought and the Colonial World*, and Judith Brown's *Gandhi: Prisoner of Hope*. Since Dalton and Brown do not directly deal with issues that are central to this book, I do not discuss them. Chatterjee's influential work raises questions that have a bearing on my reading of Gandhi.[2] I have, therefore, added a chapter dealing with the Marxist discourse on Gandhi, which discusses Chatterjee as part of a wider tradition going back to M.N. Roy and others. Having written a book on Marx myself and having gone through a Marxist phase, I am wary of essentialising Marxism and Marxists and appreciate that an adequate discussion of the Marxist interpretation of Gandhi requires far greater space than my publisher's constraints allow. I hope, however, that the chapter gives some idea of how one might go about assessing that interpretation and what I take to be its strengths and limitations. Cox's book has much to say about why the Gandhians failed to consolidate and build on their master's legacy. Since I agree with much of what he says on the subject, I refer to but do not discuss him at length.[3]

In addition to these books on Gandhi, much excellent work has also been done in recent years on the history of Indian nationalist thought and Gandhi's role in the eradication of untouchability, the two subjects I discuss at some length.[4] Although I have learned much from the literature on the former and touched up the relevant chapters in a few places, it has not led me to revise my general thesis. I continue to think that pre-Gandhian nationalists fall into one of the four groups in which I divide them, that many of them took a highly complex view of colonial rule, that Gandhi's thought was both continuous and discontinuous with that of his predecessors and both retained and lost some of their important insights, and that the nationalist thought was too multilayered to represent a unilinear direction of development.

As for Gandhi's anti-untouchability campaign, again, I have revised some parts of the relevant chapter to sharpen my argument, but see no reason to revise its general thesis. The manner in which Gandhi conceptualised and conducted the campaign was a source of both his strengths and failures. It enabled him to reach out to the Hindu masses, undermine the moral and religious basis of untouchability and give its eradication high national priority, but left its economic and social roots relatively untouched and failed to organise and make the *dalits* an effective and autonomous political force. Those who think that his campaign was ineffective, a Machiavellian diversion, a political smokescreen, or did the *dalits* more harm than good are as one-sided and mistaken as those who argue that his motives were entirely moral and religious and that he alone was responsible for eradicating the practice.

The chapter on Gandhi's experiments in celibacy has undergone considerable revision, partly in response to reviewers' comments, partly because I now realise that I had in places pushed my interpretation further than was warranted by the evidence, and partly because I have now been able to consult new material on the subject.[5] My general view of Gandhi's reasons for the experiments remains unaltered; in fact, it is confirmed by the new material, but the kind of comparison with Krishna that I had made was overdrawn.[6] Calling them 'sexual experiments', as I had inadvertently done following some writers, was misleading.[7]

Although almost all reviewers and admirers of Gandhi agreed that I had treated the subject with sensitivity and academic detachment, some asked why I discussed the subject at all. I agree that even a public figure's personal life is his or her own business. It should not be a subject of prurient interest or even idle curiosity, and that even an academic inquiry is subject to moral constraints. This was not, however, the case with Gandhi's experiments. He wrote about them openly and thought them a subject of legitimate public interest. More importantly, they were *political* acts intended to mobilise in himself a kind of spiritual power he thought he needed to control the intercommunal violence raging all around him. As a form of political praxis, they are of vital interest to a student of Gandhian politics, raising such questions as how he arrived at the idea and gave it cultural legitimacy, why he saw it as part of his larger project of spiritualising politics, and whether it made political and philosophical sense.

Since my book came out only a few months after Ayatollah Khomenei's notorious *fatwa* against Salman Rushdie's *The Satanic Verses*, some admirers of Gandhi, especially the diasporic Gujaratis, mistakenly thought that I was interested in debunking him in broadly the same way that Rushdie was allegedly deemed to have done to Prophet Mohamed. This led to some unease, earned me the sobriquet of Hindu Rushdie, and generated a few abusive phone calls and threats.[8] Thanks to the fact that Gandhians are a gentle lot who are easily embarrassed by the use of violence, and to the commendable self-disciplining power of the Gujarati diaspora, the muted campaign soon died down costing me nothing more than a few sleepless nights of soul-searching.

When this book was first written, authors were not as sensitive to sexism in language as now. Although I have made appropriate linguistic changes in several places, it has not been possible to revise the entire text. Its gender bias remains a monument to my cultural conditioning and the ethos of its provenance.

Acknowledgements

I am most grateful to my good friends Professors Upendra Baxi, Dhirubhai Sheth, Sudipta Kaviraj and Raojibhai Patel for making valuable comments on the first draft of the book. Suresh Sharma, Bharar Wariavwalla, Ashis Nandy, Ravinder Kumar, Tony Gould, Sir Peter Newsam Jaidev Sethi, the late and much-missed Umashankarbhai Joshi and R.N. Berki kindly discussed some of its central ideas and saved me from many a mistake. Discussions with Veena Das and Prakash Desai were most helpful in the composition of the sixth chapter. I must also thank Om Prakash Garkhel, Virendra Kumar Chadha, Jayshree Jayanthan, Rayaprol Shankar and Ghanashyam for their considerable help with typing, and Deepa Sharma, Surabhi Sheth and especially Jayshree Mehta for making my stay in Delhi and Baroda most enjoyable. As usual Pramila alone could decipher my increasingly illegible and arthritic writing and I owe her a special debt. I am grateful to Tejeshwar Singh for patiently suffering half a dozen deadlines to die before seeing the text of the book. He shared my hope that the *vita contemplativa* must make room for and in the end gains from periodic forays into the *vita activa*. I thank Jyoti Sharma for preparing the index.

Some of these chapters were initially tried out as lectures. The sixth chapter aroused the greatest controversy. Many welcomed it, but a few felt deeply distressed that I was 'maligning the greatest man in Indian history', as a middle-aged woman Professor in Delhi put it. I share her high esteem of Gandhi but not at all the view that his experiments in celibacy in any way diminish his moral stature. On the contrary, they were acts of extraordinary social courage and show the extent to which he was prepared to go to 'prove' a spiritual 'hypothesis' and serve the country he passionately loved.

I was associated with three institutions during the composition of the book. What I owe them cannot be adequately repaid by a formal expression of gratitude I, therefore, dedicate the book to them. And since institutions are incarnated in individuals, I dedicate it to three friends who embody the best traditions of their respective institutions and made it a joy to belong to them. They are Sir Roy Marshall who, as Vice-Chancellor of the University of Hull, created a rare spirit of freedom and humanity, Professor Vinod Kothari of the M.S. University of Baroda who was my conscience-keeper when I was its Vice-Chancellor, and Professor Dhirubhai Sheth of the Centre for the Study of Developing Societies who made sure that I asked Gandhi *his* questions and patiently awaited *his* answers.

I am grateful to the relevant publishers for their permission to reproduce some of the material used in chapters 4, 5, 7, 8 and 9.

Chapter One

Introduction

Like many of his predecessors, Gandhi was profoundly disturbed by the state of contemporary Indian, especially Hindu, society. A once creative and vibrant civilisation had become degenerate, and had as a result fallen prey to waves after waves of foreign invasions of which the British was the latest. He reflected deeply on the nature and causes of its degeneration and concluded that, unless it was radically revitalised and reconstituted on a new moral basis, India was doomed. From his early years in South Africa until his death, he devoted his entire life to the exploration of a moral order appropriate to India in the modern age, to the discovery of what he called *yugadharma*.

Gandhi's lifelong preoccupation with Indian, especially Hindu regeneration, brought him into conflict with Hindu tradition. Although he lost some battles, he also won quite a few. Hindu culture did not give pride of place to the active service of one's fellow-men; he made *sevadharma* its very essence. It was indifferent to the struggle for justice and equality; he insisted that this was the only path to *moksha* in the modern politics-dominated age. For centuries, Hindus had lived with the evil practice of untouchability; he declared war on it and shook its moral roots. Traditionally women occupied a low position in India; he not only brought a large number of them into public life, which neither Lenin nor Mao was able to do, and established their equality with men, but also articulated and attempted to live up to the extraordinary ideal of an androgynous person. The upper strata of Indian society treated the peasant with scorn; Gandhi placed him at the very centre of the political stage and gave him an unprecedented political and cultural presence. Hindu culture was callous to poverty and human suffering; Gandhi made 'wiping away every tear from every eye' the central test of morality. Hindu society glorified intellectual and spiritual activities and took a low view of manual labour; he insisted that whoever avoided it was a 'thief' and a 'parasite'. Some of these reforms did not endure, and some of them were secured by means that eventually proved counter-productive. But he at least placed them on the national agenda and sensitised his countrymen to their importance.

Gandhi was able to succeed where many others had failed for a variety of reasons. He knew how to tap and mobilise the regenerative resources of tradition. Though he made several mistakes, especially during the early years of his political leadership in India, he soon acquired a deep understanding of the nature, mode of discourse and structural constraints of Hindu tradition and instinctively knew how far not to go in order not to go too far. Thanks to his unique lifestyle, he also exercised a kind and degree of moral and political authority not available to anyone before or after him. Indeed, the very fact that he could not be fitted into any of the traditional Hindu categories baffled his countrymen and added to his charisma.

As I have argued elsewhere, Indians did not generally see him as an *avatār*, a *rishi*, a *muni*, an *āchārya* or a *sant*. Contrary to what some of his commentators have said, they did not perceive him as a 'renouncer' either for, unlike the traditional conception of the renouncer, Gandhi was intensely active, morally restless, a tireless fighter, and passionately involved in the affairs of the world. He was not above political manipulation either and had his share of human failings including obstinacy, impatience and a touch of vanity.[1] As many popular songs of the time described him, he was *na sannyāsi na sansāri*. Hindus instinctively knew who he was not, but could not figure out who he was for the simple reason that they had never in their long history encountered anyone like him. Following Tagore, they settled on the title of *mahātmā*, a term that occurs only once in the *Gitā* and not in any other classical text. As someone who totally identified himself with his countrymen and selflessly devoted himself to their service, Indians saw him as a unique and concentrated expression of some of the finest moral qualities that they cherished in themselves. It was this identification with and devotion to their *sevā* that constituted the source of his very considerable *moral* authority which he suitably converted into political authority. As a disinterested guardian of the national well-being he also acquired, once he grew old, a *social* authority and became *Bapu*, entitled to advise the national family on how to resolve its internal differences. The fact that he was for many years the unquestioned leader of the independence struggle and best equipped to judge which of their beliefs and practices helped or hindered it gave him a unique *political* authority which he skilfully translated into moral authority.

Gandhi, then, knew how to use the resources of Hindu tradition and he also wielded a unique moral and political authority. In this book, I intend to explore the manner in which he used both in his battles with his tradition. I shall examine his critical dialogue with it, his style of reform, his critique of and campaign against unacceptable beliefs and practices, and the manner in which he negotiated his way around and was sometimes defeated by its structural constraints.

I

It is a trite observation that tradition and reform are essential features of every human society. Societies exist in time and live in constant awareness of a past and a future.[2] The past is not like a distant sky, an abstract and indeterminate background to the present, but rather like the earth from which it has sprung and to which it is tied by organic bonds in the form of inherited beliefs, practices, rituals, images, symbols, language, ceremonies and institutions. These are handed down over generations and carry a measure of authority, and thus constitute its traditions. Societies vary greatly in how they individuate the past, define different levels and degrees of pastness, the kind of authority they confer on it, and in the way they relate it to the present. They also, therefore, differ in their conceptualisation of the nature and authority of tradition. For some, the past begins with yesterday's sunset and all practices existing since before then are binding; for some others, it goes beyond 'living memory', that is, beyond the remembrance of the present generation and especially its oldest living individuals; for yet others, the past properly so called begins where memory ends and only those practices originating in a remote and hazy past are invested with the prized status of tradition, the rest being mere practices, conventions or usages. In some societies, again, all past practices carry equal authority; in some others, their degree of authority varies with their pastness, the older being more authoritative than those more recent; for most, their authority depends on their place in the society's conception of itself and their role in its survival. Most societies often reserve the term tradition for practices that are deemed to be *important* and *worth preserving*. In modern society, for example, the practice of brushing one's teeth in the morning rather than in the afternoon, although of a distant and untraceable origin, is a practice and not a tradition, whereas many of those associated with birth, marriage, death and mode of governance are considered traditions.

No society is immune to change, not even the so-called timeless or primitive societies described by anthropoligists. Even if they manage to resist new inventions and modes of production, they cannot escape the interventions of nature in the form of climatic changes, disasters, variations in the rate and pattern of reproduction and diseases in plants, animals and humans. While they may studiously avoid all external contacts, other societies might not be so obliging. All this creates new problems and needs to which they must respond by suitably altering their inherited structures of practices or face extinction.

Every society, then, must find ways of preserving, transmitting and reforming its traditions, of retaining its links with the past and being ready to respond to the future, of preserving its past and safeguarding its future. Different societies rely on different mechanisms for doing so. In some, traditions cannot be reformed only reinterpreted, and change is conceptualised as altering not their content but only their meaning. Their conservative rhetoric often fools outsiders into thinking that they are resistant or opposed to change. Sometimes the opposite is the case. Societies subject to constant change often deploy a conservative rhetoric to regulate its pace and direction or to reassure themselves that they have not 'lost' their past. Again, in some societies, the headwaters of a tradition enjoy the highest authority and no reform is entertained that is not traceable to them. In others, such an appeal is considered reactionary and a reformer is expected to appeal to an immediate past, a specific turning point in it, or to an anticipated future.

Since different societies have different organising principles and differently define their identities, they are hospitable or hostile to different kinds of reform. Those whose social structures are inextricably interwoven with their 'ethnic' religions feel threatened by religious reforms, whereas those in which the two are clearly separated, as in modern Europe, feel not in the least worried by them. In some societies, such as the Hindu, belief and conduct are less closely related than, for instance, in the Muslim and the Christian, and people remain free to believe what they like so long as they continue to behave as required. Changes in beliefs there might not evoke a whisper whereas even the most minor change in a social practice might provoke a revolt. In short, different societies have different sticking points, different nerve centres, are tickled and teased differently and fight out their battles on different terrains. No society is, or even can be, *uniformly* conservative, and its response to change is necessarily differentiated and discriminating. Fiercely resistant to some changes, it is in varying degrees hospitable to others. The failure to grasp this simple point underlay much eighteenth and nineteenth century European mythology about the 'hidebound' and conservative East.

So far as Hindu society is concerned, it has its own distinct ways of conceptualising, transmitting and reforming traditions.[3] Though the vocabulary changed over time and acquired different meanings, the term *paramparā* comes closest to tradition.[4] It refers to a practice that is handed down in unbroken succession from unknown times, and binding in nature. It is binding not because of its age, nor because it is traceable to a real or mythical figure, but because it is an integral part of the established way of life, handed down by a long line of ancestors or 'elders' deserving of respect, and constitutes a sacred collective inheritance. A *paramparā* is largely a matter of memory and is orally transmitted. As the Hindus understand their history, their traditions were at a certain stage written down in the form of *smritis* or records of collective memories by such great sages as Manu, Gautama and Parashara.[5] The *dharmashāstras* are authentic accounts of traditions and set the norms against which to judge the practices and traditions that might have spontaneously developed in different communities and regions. *Ācarā* (custom) and *paramparā* are, therefore, valid only if they are *pravrittah sarvakālikah* (have existed for all times) and *srutismrityavirodha* (not in conflict with the *srutis* and *smritis*). Since traditions are anchored in the *shāstras*, debates about them necessarily take on a textual character.[6]

The *smritis* are subordinated to the *srutis* or *Vedas*. The latter are more general and have only a limited ethical and social content, and thus, leave considerable room for reinterpretations of the *smritis*. Furthermore, there are several *smritis* and their canonical status and hierarchy are subject to dispute. Different *smritis* are deemed to be relevant to different *yugas* and there is no general consensus on when what *yuga* prevails. There is, therefore, considerable room for debate on their relevance and importance. Ishwar Chandra Vidyasagar took full advantage of this when he based his campaign for widow remarriage on the argument that not *Manusmriti* but *Parāsharasmriti* was relevant in the present *kaliyuga*.

The *shāstras* draw distinctions between different kinds of *dharma* and provide principles by which to question an established practice. They distinguish between *sādhāranadharma* or *mānavadharma* (universal moral principles) and *varnadharma* (caste duties), and assign the former higher authority. They also distinguish between *sanātanadharma* (eternal principles) and *yugadharma* (historically specific principles) and insist that the latter is historically contingent and to be determined in the light of the former. As Vivekananda, who used the distinction to attack several Hindu customs and rituals, put it, 'We know that in our books a clear distinction is made between two sets of truths', one 'abiding for ever' and the other consisting of mutable 'minor laws'.

Hindu tradition is acutely sensitive to the fact that all moral situations are unique, that duties conflict, and that the general principles and duties laid down by the *shāstras* require constant and careful interpretation. Indeed, it insists that *no* moral action should be based on them alone, as that can sometimes lead to *adharma*. *Kevalam shāstramāshritya na kartavyo hi nirnayah; yuktihine vichāretu dharmahānih prajāyate* (No decision should be based on the *shāstras* alone; unintelligent conduct leads to the loss of *dharma*.)[7] The *shāstras*, therefore, are expected to be supplemented by and read in the light of the conduct of righteous men steeped and well-versed in the Vedas. *Santo digjalan,* the virtuous man is a reliable moral guide. As is said in the *Mahābhārata,* he who is *serveshām cha hite ratah* (devoted to the well-being of all) is the model of *dharma* and is to be followed in moments of doubt. *Dharmajnahpandito jneyo*: not a learned but a virtuous man is the true pandit. Indeed, it goes even further: *Chāturvedopi durvrittah sa shudrātatirichyate* (If he is not of good conduct, a man learned in the four *Vedas* is worse than a shudra).

The belief in the harmony and even identity of *satyam* (truth) and *shivam* (goodness) lies at the heart of most Hindu thought. Truth is the basis of all existence. It alone promotes human wellbeing; falsehood leads to destruction. This is generally taken to mean that if a practice leads to conflict and discord, does not promote *loksangraha* (preservation of society) and *sukha* (happiness), it cannot be true or right. The *shāstras* will never enjoin it and if they appear to do so, they should be reread and reinterpreted. The belief in the congruence of *satyam* and *shivam* has sometimes led the Hindus to subordinate truth to utility and encouraged crude pragmatism. However, in more sophisticated hands, it has led to deeper insights into their relationship and has become an important principle of social criticism.

Thanks to the space for reform provided by these and other critical resources of their tradition, many nineteenth century Hindu leaders were able to successfully challenge unacceptable social practices against their orthodox champions. If the practice was *smritivirodha,* their task was easy. If it was not, the tradition allowed them five major types of argument. They could appeal to another *smriti* or to the *Vedas,* to considerations of *sādhāranadharma, yugadharma* and *loksangraha* and to their *adhikār* as *sant* or *sistas* to reinterpret and even modify the *shāstric* injunctions. Hardly any of them satisfied the last condition, an area where Gandhi's lifestyle gave him a unique advantage. Most of them, therefore, relied on the other four. Since we cannot here analyse the fascinating ways in which Raja Ram Mohun Roy argued against *sati* and polytheism, K.C. Sen and Lala Lajpat Rai against child marriages, Ishwar Chandra Vidyasagar against Kulinism and the ban on widow remarriage and Dayananda Saraswati against image worship, we shall only note that in spite of the differences in their idioms and styles of argument, they all introduced one or more of the following four arguments. First, they appealed to the scriptures hospitable to their cause. Vidyasagar relied on *Parāsharasmriti*, the Raja on the *Upanishads* and Dayananda Saraswati on the *Vedas*. Second, they invoked *sādhāranadharma*, which they interpreted broadly to mean what they called universal principles of morality, the moral consensus of mankind or world opinion. Third, they appealed to the unique problems and needs of the prevailing *yuga*. Since the *yuga* involved colonial rule, some of them stretched the argument to legitimise adoption of European values and practices. Finally, they invoked *loksangraha* and argued that the practice in question had such grave consequences that unless eradicated, it would destroy the cohesion and viability of the Hindu social order. Vidyasagar argued that unmarried widows were turning to prostitution in Calcutta and Benares or corrupting their families; K.C. Sen contended that child marriages were weakening and endangering the survival of the Hindu 'race'; and Dayananda Saraswati argued that image worship led to sectarian quarrels and corruption of priesthood, and weakened the Hindu social order.[8]

Though the Hindu tradition was open to reform, the reform had obvious limits.[9] Since the structure of discourse left so much room for reinterpretation, it was inherently inconclusive. The nineteenth century traditionalists and reformers disagreed about such matters as their readings of the *srutis* and *smritis*, what *yuga* India was passing through, what *smriti* was relevant to it and their interpretations of the *yugadharma* and *loksangraha*. This had contradictory implications. When the reformers made out a reasonable case, they were free to reject the unacceptable practice; since their case could never be incontrovertible, the orthodox remained free to retain it and to ostracise them. If the reformers were prepared to pay the price and in a sufficiently large number, they broke away and formed a sub-community of their own as their predecessors had done over the centuries; otherwise they gave in, reached a tentative compromise, secured a limited exemption from the practice in question, or turned to the socially conservative colonial government for appropriate legislation.

II

As we saw, Gandhi's reformist programme was far more comprehensive than that of any of his predecessors. Though more conservative than some of them in certain matters, especially the social, he was far more radical in most others. He was convinced that Hindu society needed moral regeneration, a 'new system of ethics', a new *yugadharma*. He was certain that the new *yugadharma* could not be developed out of the available resources of Hindu tradition alone. Some of its fundamental values were sound and represented its great contribution to mankind. However, they had been traditionally defined in negative, passive and asocial terms and required reinterpretation and reform. Hinduism could, therefore, greatly benefit from the moral 'insights' and 'truths' discovered by other religious traditions including Buddhism, Jainism, Judaism, Islam and, especially, Christianity, and by such writers as Tolstoy, Ruskin and Thoreau.

Gandhi could not reform the Hindu tradition and open it up to the influences of others without radically redefining, that is, deconstructing and reconstructing the orthodox conception of tradition in general, and of the Hindu tradition in particular. He had so to define the latter that it allowed the kind of cross-cultural borrowing he had in mind, and so to define other traditions that he was not accused of violating their integrity by selecting specific aspects. He also needed to show that different traditions were commensurable, concerned to answer similar questions, and that they had something to offer to each other. He needed to show, too, that traditions were not monolithic wholes but internally differentiated loose structures of beliefs and practices not all of which were equally important, so that it was logically possible to abstract and combine their central values and insights. Though Gandhi executed this task with considerable originality and skill, his success did not match his ingenuity.[10]

For Gandhi, every community had to deal with the perennial problems of human existence as reflected in its specific and changing circumstances. It had no other way to find answers to them except by the method of trial and error, of conscious and unconscious experiments conducted over a long period of time. It tried out different ideas, practices and institutions, reflected on their consequences, and developed valuable insights into the nature of man and society, moral values, causes and best ways of reconciling human differences and conflicts, and the kinds of activity men found most fulfilling. These insights, which collectively constituted its traditional wisdom and cultural capital with centuries of lived experience behind them, formed the basis on which it met the challenges of the changing times and set up structures of contingent beliefs and practices. A tradition thus was not blind, a mere collection of precedents, but a *form of inquiry*, a scientific adventure, an unplanned but rigorous *communal science* constantly tested and revised against the harsh reality of life. Far from being antithetical, tradition and science were cousins. Tradition was unplanned science, and science was a tradition of planned inquiry.

According to Gandhi, the basic values and insights of a tradition were 'valid' and binding, not because of their age or certification by an individual, but because they had survived the rigorous test of lived experience and the scrutiny of their critics. Every society was articulated at two levels. Its basic values and insights, its central organising principles, had an enduring significance whereas its beliefs and practices were subject to constant revision. The former and not the latter constituted its essence. To belong to a society, to claim allegiance to its tradition, was to commit oneself to its central values not to its contingent beliefs and practices. Indeed, loyalty to it required that one should constantly evaluate and even reject prevailing practices if they appeared to betray or 'choke' the fullest realisation of its central values.

Gandhi argued that though this was true of all traditions, it was especially true of the Hindu. Unlike many traditions, it was based not on divine self-revelation placed in the charge of an accredited organisation, but on unconscious collective experimentation regularly fertilised and enriched by the moral and spiritual experiments of its great sages. Like the great scientists of modern Europe, its great minds periodically embarked upon an arduous spiritual journey and arrived at a body of insights, some of which were rejected or revised by their successors while others survived and formed its organising principles. Hinduism was a science of the spirit, an unending quest, an inherently open tradition of inquiry.

On the basis of his analysis of the nature of tradition, Gandhi argued that every tradition contained an internal principle of self-criticism in the form of its central or constitutive values. The beliefs and practices that did not conform to them required revision or even rejection. Even the values were not incorrigible. Though they had stood the test of experience and been repeatedly 'validated' and thus carried a measure of moral authority, subsequent experiences or spiritual investigations by great moral scientists might show up their inadequacies. Furthermore, a dialogue between different traditions was both possible and necessary. Since every society dealt with the fundamental problems of human existence, its insights had relevance for others. Since it dealt with them in the context of its unique circumstances, their relevance was limited. A free, equal and open-minded dialogue between traditions involving an exchange of insights was a necessary condition of their progress. It enabled each to look at itself from the standpoint of others and to gain critical self-understanding. It encouraged them to learn from and borrow eh ot others' insights. And it contributed to mankind's growing pool of moral knowledge. Both their self-interest and obligations to humanity required that every society should encourage and help others bring their best to the global conversation. That was why Gandhi thought that the European attempt to shape entire mankind in its own image damaged both. It distorted the development of non-European societies and denied Europe new moral insights and critical self-knowledge.

For Gandhi, then, every tradition was a resource, a source of valuable insights into the human condition, and part of a common human heritage. Every man was born into and shaped by a specific cultural tradition which, as it were, constituted his original family. He also enjoyed varying degrees of membership of other cultural families to whose achievements he had an unrestricted right of access. Gandhi said that as a Hindu, he was heir to its rich and ancient heritage. As an Indian, he was the privileged inheritor of its diverse religious and cultural traditions. As a human being, the great achievements of mankind constituted his heritage to which he had as much right as their native claimants. While remaining firmly rooted in his own tradition, he felt free to draw upon the cultural capital of others. To express the two central ideas of rootedness and openness, he often used the metaphor of living in a house with its windows wide open. His house was protected by walls, but its windows were open to allow winds from all directions to blow through it and to enable him to breathe fresh air at his own pace and in his own way. *Āno Bhadra ritavo yantu vishvatah* (May noble thoughts from all over the world come to us) was one of his favourite *Rigvedic* maxims.

Gandhi took full advantage of his self-proclaimed freedom and developed an ecumenical conception of *yugadharma*.[11] He abstracted what he took to be the central values of Hinduism and set up a critical dialogue between them and those derived from elsewhere. Thus, he took over the Hindu concept of *ahimsā*, in his view one of its greatest values derived from the profound doctrine of the unity of life. He found it negative and passive and reinterpreted it in the light of the Christian concept of *caritas*. He thought the latter was too emotive and led to worldly attachments, and so redefined it in the light of the Hindu concept of *anāsakti*. His double conversion, his Christianisation of a Hindu category after suitably Hinduising its Christian components, yielded the novel concept of an active and positive but detached and non-emotive love.[12] Again, he took over the traditional Hindu practice of fasting as a protest, combined it with the Judaic concept of representative leadership and the Christian concepts of vicarious atonement and suffering love, interpreted and reinterpreted each in the light of the others, and developed the amazing notion of 'voluntary crucifixion of the flesh'. It involved fasting undertaken by the acknowledged leader of a community to atone for the evil deeds of his followers, to awaken their sense of shame and guilt and to mobilise their moral and spiritual impulses for redemptive purposes. In these and other ways, Gandhi sought to combine some of the richest insights of different traditions and to develop an ecumenical view of the world. He exemplified and deepened Gadamer's idea of 'fusion of horizons' and offered an alternative conception of universalism to the post-Enlightenment ethnocentric model of the colonial rulers.

III

Gandhi's claim to reform the Hindu tradition on the basis of his conception of *yugadharma* both excited the imagination of and puzzled his countrymen, especially the orthodox. Tradition only granted the right to reform it to men who were of righteous conduct *and* well-versed in the *shāstras*, especially the *Vedas*. He satisfied the first condition but not the second. His Sanskrit was poor, he had not mastered the *shāstras*, and he had no interest in undertaking a close study of them. His moral authority, thus, was confined to their reinterpretation. Gandhi had little choice but to disown his reformist intentions. Having claimed in his early years that he intended to reform Hinduism, he later began to argue that he was only concerned with reinterpreting its central principles in the light of the needs of the modern age.

Even at this abstract level, he did not find it easy to present reform as reinterpretation. As we shall see, the traditional conception of *ahimsā* could not be easily interpreted as active love, nor *satya* as social justice, and dissolution in *Brahman* as selfless service of fellow-men. Gandhi acknowledged the difficulty but contended that he was only 'extending', 'deepening' or discovering their 'true meaning'. His countrymen had little difficulty noticing that some of these reinterpretations were forced, even false. Some gave him the benefit of the doubt; others accused him of disingenuity.

Gandhi and his adversaries knew that in the ultimate analysis he was challenging the orthodox Hindu concept of tradition and seeking to replace it with an alternative view of his own. For the orthodox, Hindu tradition was a binding structure of beliefs deriving its authority from its ancient lineage and/or *dharma-shāstras*. For Gandhi, it was a scientific inquiry whose insights deserved respect but not uncritical obedience. For his adversaries, tradition was autonomous in the sense that its authority was located within it. For Gandhi, its authority was located outside it so that a practice did not acquire authority merely by virtue of being traditional. Like that of a scientific theory, the authority of a tradition was located in its experimental validation and was subject to revision. For them, it was a well-knit structure of beliefs and practices, an organic whole. For him, it was a resource, a mine of valuable insights from which he was free to pick and choose. The traditionalists knew that even when he upheld a traditional belief or practice, he did so on non-traditional grounds and was a dangerous ally.

Gandhi's insistence on cross-cultural borrowing was another source of his difficulty. Not that the Hindu tradition was hostile to it; rather, it imposed limits on the manner and extent of borrowing which Gandhi seemed to the traditionalists to transgress. During his early years in South Africa, he was insensitive to this and made mistakes for which he continued to pay all his life. He had declared his 'profound reverence' for Jesus, his 'deep respect' for Christianity and his intention to borrow some of its central values. He had also taken over part of its vocabulary and some of its images and parables. He continued to say all this on his return to India to the consternation of many of his countrymen. He had borrowed not only Christian values, which they did not mind, but also social practices, which they did. He had borrowed the values without fully familiarising himself with the basic texts of his own tradition and, in their eyes, ran the risk of corrupting it. Above all, he had done so at a time when, under the protection of the colonial government, the missionaries were busy ridiculing and undermining the integrity of Hinduism. Not surprisingly, he was constantly accused of being a crypto-Christian trying to Christianise Hinduism. Gandhi knew that the hostility was intense and prevented him from reaching out to the masses. He thought it wise to backtrack. Not that he rejected the idea of cross-cultural borrowing or de-Christianised his *yugadharma*. Rather, he insisted that its central values were all entirely Hindu, proclaimed his undivided loyalty to his religion, and sharply criticised the arrogance and activities of the missionaries. This was a tactical retreat, not a change of mind.

In the light of our discussion, it should be obvious that though Gandhi valued tradition, he was not a traditionalist. He reduced tradition to a resource, located its essence in its general moral values which commanded respect but left room for critical evaluation, and gave every individual the freedom to draw upon the insights of other traditions. Similarly, though he stressed the role of reason, he was not a rationalist. He respected 'cultivated reason', one 'ripened' by a deep acquaintance with the wisdom embodied in tradition, especially, but not exclusively, one's own.

And though an individual remained free to revise traditional values, he was to do so only after making a 'respectful' study of them and giving them the benefit of the doubt.

Gandhi saw no hostility or contrast between reason and tradition. Reason was not a transcendental or natural faculty, but a socially acquired capacity presupposing and constantly shaped and nurtured by tradition. Tradition was not a mechanical accumulation of precedents but a product of countless conscious and semi-conscious experiments by rational men over several generations. Reason, thus, lay at the heart of tradition, fully manifest in its abiding values and organising principles and not entirely absent even in its apparently bizarre practices. As products of human choices, such practices were responses to genuine human needs and perplexities. The perplexities and needs might have been misdefined or might have long ceased to exist, but they were once real and gave meaning to the practices. The reformer's task was both to elucidate the *historical rationale* of unacceptable practices and to expose their current *irrationality*. He needed both sympathetic understanding and critical spirit, both patience and indignation. This was how Gandhi went about reforming Hindu ways of thought and life.

Since Gandhi's understanding of the nature and regenerative resources of Hindu tradition was quite different from that of his predecessors, his reformist discourse had a different logical structure. Unlike them, he was a *mahātmā* who had sincerely tried to live by the central values of his tradition. He, therefore, claimed the *adhikār* to understand it better than the 'mere pandits' and to disregard their interpretations and protests. Since he located the heart of the tradition in its central values, he also felt free to ignore the *shastras* and rarely appealed to their authority even when they supported his case. The elusive concepts of *sādhāranadharma* or *mānavadharma*, as he suggestively preferred to call it, *sanātanadharma* and the socially and politically orientated concept of *loksangraha* suited him much better.

He also found it useful to introduce a novel argument. He teased out the widely accepted justifying *principle* of an operative practice and argued that it was denied or violated by the practice he wished to criticise. For example, he argued that since the Hindus fed ants and cows because *they said* they believed in the sacredness of life, they could not consistently remain callous to human suffering. Similarly since they demanded equality with their rulers because *they said* they believed in human equality, they could not deny it to the lower castes and the untouchables.

This was not like the analogical reasoning favoured by Edmund Burke and Michael Oakeshott, in which one moves from one practice to another without the mediation of a general principle. Gandhi knew that no two practices or forms of behaviour could be deemed to be incompatible, contradictory or incoherent except on the basis of their justifying principles. If a Hindu said that he fed the cow because *it* (not all life) was sacred, or because it was meek and uncomplaining, or because he was enjoined to do so by the *shāstras*, he would not be guilty of inconsistency in ignoring human suffering. He holds the cow, and not life, sacred, he respects meekness and uncomplaining ssuffering and not the human language of claims, and he does whatever the 'divine' *shāstras* tell him. Gandhi saw that if he was to persuade his countrymen, he needed to tease out the *general principle* implicit in *their justification* of their conduct and extend it to new cases. In so doing, he hoped to show that unless they accepted the extension, their lives contained an untruth, a lie.

IV

Gandhi's critical dialogue with Hindu tradition and his struggle to reform Hindu society occurred within a colonial context making an already difficult task infinitely more difficult. A few words about it are necessary in order to understand the kind of crisis Hindu tradition faced and the range of alternatives open to Gandhi.

The British could not rule over a vast, unfamiliar and distant land in which they had chosen not to settle and in which they had made little social, economic, religious and military investment without the acquiescence of a large majority and the active support of at least a sizeable and influential minority of their subjects. This required a skilful blend of such vital ingredients as force, cunning, a subtle exploitation and creation of divisions among Indians, a better form of government than the one they replaced, a system of administration that avoided the Mughal mistake of getting sucked into the complex structure of Indian society, an assiduous cultivation of an aura of mystery and, above all, a powerful and plausible ideological legitimation of their rule. After several initial mistakes, they built up an ingenious structure of power, enabling the Raj both to last for nearly two centuries with only one major challenge which they put down with relative ease and to end in an atmosphere of relative goodwill. We shall briefly examine the nature and consequences of the way they justified their rule both to themselves and their subjects.

In the early decades, the British contended that India was a great civilisation that had fallen on bad times because their despotic form of government denied its subjects basic liberties, especially property in land, thereby drying up all sources of energy, initiative, enterprise and creativity. Its salvation lay in replacing 'Asiatic despotism' with a 'civil society' guaranteeing its subjects security of life, liberty and property, an impartial administration of justice, an honest and efficient administration and the rule of law.[13] The British said they were engaged in establishing a government based on 'liberty' and hoped in due course to arrest and reverse India's decline. From about 1820 onwards, liberalism, which had by then become a dominant ideology in Britain, generated a new mode of discourse. The British began to justify their rule in terms of the increasingly fashionable concept of civilisation largely defined in liberal rationalist terms. India was supposed to be a 'semi-barbaric' country occupying a place halfway between the 'African savages' and the 'civilised Europeans'. Its historical development had suffered an arrest not because of such *political* factors as the so-called 'Asiatic despotism' as they had earlier argued, but because of *cultural* factors, especially the absence of a scientific and rationalist approach to life. It needed not just a new form of government based on 'liberty' but also new ways of life and thought based on 'reason'. The 'reign of reason', of which Britain was deemed to be a transcendentally accredited historical agent, was to 'silently undermine the fabric of error and superstition' in economic, social, political, moral, artistic, literary and other areas of life. Even the British conservatives, who otherwise opposed liberal rationalism, preached and practised it in the case of India. For them, traditions were worth preserving only when they passed the rationalist test. The British evidently did, the Indian did not.

Once the British started to justify their rule in civilisational terms, educational metaphors began to abound. They were engaged in the enterprise of initiating their subjects into new ways of life and thought, and inculcating in them new habits, virtues and qualities of intellect and character. They were not masters but headmasters, not just law-givers but educators; Indians were not their subjects but pupils; India was a vast public school, an Eton writ large as it were, to be governed in an autocratic manner, the only mode of governance appropriate to an educational institution, and laws were designed not to oppress them but to create the necessary conditions of disciplined learning. The education was to be conducted along the 'monitorial' lines popularised by Lancaster and Bell. Britain was to train a small group of Indians who in turn would educate the rest of their countrymen in native languages.

In the early years, when the British had conceptualised their rule in terms of creating a civil society in India, they had regarded an impersonal system of laws and an impartial administration of justice as their major achievement, and used law as the primary instrument of political consolidation and social transformation. In the new civilisational phase, educational institutions became the chief instrument of social change and the central terrain of political action. Not surprisingly, the apparently innocuous phrase 'English education' became a symbol of and a coded way of referring to moral and social transformation. To 'receive' (the word itself was suggestive) English education was not merely to learn a language, nor merely to gain access to modern science and technology, but to be educated out of Indianness and into English ways of life and thought, to be transformed into a new species. Indians were keen on *education in English* as their much-needed window to the world, but deeply uneasy about *English education* which seemed to make them aliens in their own country.

Convinced of the absolute superiority of their civilisation, the British approached Indians in an aggressive and confrontational mood. They challenged them to show if they had achieved anything the British needed to learn from them. Since the answer was expected to be in the negative, they insisted that they had everything to 'teach' their subjects and nothing to 'learn' from them. It was not enough for the Indians to say that the central concerns and organising principles of their civilisation were different; they had to translate the difference and demonstrate its value in British terms, an inherently doomed enterprise. Within the absolutist colonial discourse, difference had not only no value but signified deficiency.

Under the pedagogically articulated terms of debate, Indians could only enjoy equality with their rulers under two conditions: namely, by insisting that they had nothing to learn from them, or that they had but that they also had something to teach them. To admit that they had something to learn from their rulers was to concede the latter's superiority. Ideally it implied no such thing; in the colonial context it appeared self-evident. Since they could not deny that they had many things to learn, they had to compensate for the implied inferiority by asserting their superiority in some other respects. This explains why they almost invariably talked of 'borrowing' European values and practices, implying that the 'debt' was temporary and to be repaid by teaching Europeans something of Indian values and institutions. Unless cultural exports equalled cultural imports, the moral balance of payments remained in the red. This attitude was pervasive and deep, and reflected in the writings of every Hindu leader including the most patriotic and perceptive. The following two remarks are fairly typical. First, Bankim Chandra Chatterjee who captures the mood with great poignancy:[14]

> We are particularly curious to learn what is there in Europe which would *not* be to our liking . . . . *why do we want to hear this?* I am not sure if I can explain the reason adequately. We Bengalis are considered to be a people of *no consequence* compared to the great nations like the English. In *comparison* with the English, there is nothing praiseworthy in us. *Nothing about us is commendable.* We do not know for sure if this is true. But we are beginning to believe it because we hear it every day. Such a belief does us no good. It reduces our love for our country, our regard for our own people. If we do not see in the Bengalis as *compared* to other people . . . . some *unique* excellence, we will have no love for our country. This is why we always wish to hear if we are *superior* on *any count* to the most civilized

nations. But nowhere do we hear any such thing. When we do hear such words, they come from people given to false vanity and nurtured exclusively in their own country as in a cage, not from people of balanced judgement with a concern for truth. We have no faith in these; they are no source of satisfaction.

Even someone of the stature of Vivekananda reiterated it as late as the last decade of the nineteenth century:[15]

> There cannot be friendship without *equality* and there cannot be equality when one party is always the *teacher* and the other party sits always *at his feet*.... If you want to become equal with the Englishman or the American, you will have to teach as well as to learn, and you have plenty yet to teach to the world for centuries to come.

Since Indians were constantly challenged to show what in their civilisation was worth preserving or from which their rulers could learn something, their self-esteem came to be integrally tied up with their historical performance as a people or a 'race'. They felt they had no right to love or respect themselves unless they could prove to their rulers' or at least to their own satisfaction that they were *worth* loving or respecting. They had to show that they *deserved* equal treatment before they felt justified in asking for it. They could not even press for the teaching of their languages and their history and literature without proving that these were *good enough* to be placed on a par with those of their rulers. Within the terms of colonial discourse, British civilisation was the norm and it was 'irrational' and 'reactionary' to teach or retain anything that was 'inferior' to or different from it.

Indians could take nothing for granted, not even the basic right to respect themselves and cherish their ways of life and thought. They had to *justify* themselves, including their very existence, as a collectivity in terms of their historical performance. The meaning of their personal and collective life was located in their achievements and mediated by the dubious notion of desert. Achievements were to be judged and evaluated by the criteria drawn from their rulers' civilisation. Since these were alien to them, they did not often satisfy them and developed self-pity, self-hatred and an excessive, even morbid, spirit of self-criticism. Sometimes they did satisfy them, but only after an intense personal struggle and at considerable emotional cost; and even then, they remained anxious about their future success. It was all part of the British political pedagogy to keep their pupils constantly on tenterhooks and never to allow them to relax.

The performance-centred approach to life cast Indians in a strange relationship with their ancestors. Since they were admired or criticised as a 'race' because of the achievements of their civilisation, they praised or blamed their ancestors for their current predicament. The sad consequences of this attitude were evident in the writings of many Indian leaders, of which Surendra Nath Banerjee is not an untypical example. He told his countrymen that they were 'only remembered and respected' because of the greatness of their ancestors, whom they must therefore 'approach reverentially' and in a spirit of profound gratitude. He was convinced that a civilised society had a strong sense of history and wrote about its past. Since his ancestors evidently had not written any history with the sole exception of *Rāja Tarangini*, he was in a quandary. He did not wish to feel ashamed of them and concluded that they 'must have' written history books which had alas got destroyed! As he jubilantly concluded, 'Fortunately, however, for the credit of our ancestors, fortunately for the good name of India, . . . our ancestors were acquainted with the art of historical composition.' It was not enough for him to say that his civilisation had concentrated on some areas of human endeavour and ignored others and that it should learn from Europe whatever was valuable. He could not respect his country unless it secured full marks at the British-dictated test of civilisation, and had in moments of despair to resort to lies.

Under colonial rule, Indian beliefs and practices were placed under a microscope and subjected to a close and hostile scrutiny. Indians were challenged to demonstrate their rationality as defined in instrumental and utilitarian terms. It was not enough to say that these were an integral part of their way of life and derived their rationale from their place in it. Such an argument had appealed to the earlier generations of British rulers who valued their own and others' traditions. It made no sense to their liberal successors who drew a Manichean contrast between modernity and tradition and regarded instrumentally-defined rationality as the only vehicle of progress. This placed Indians in a most difficult situation. If they did not offer an instrumental justification of a practice, they were expected to abandon it or at least feel guilty about retaining it; if they did, as many of them felt constrained to do, its authority was derived not from its traditionality but from the modernist purpose it was deemed to serve. In one case, a traditional practice was rejected; in the other, it was retained but de-traditionalised. In either case, the flow of the tradition was ruptured and reduced to a handful of isolated fragments that managed to survive the rationalist test. Wrenched from their roots in tradition, such fragments lacked vitality and became mechanical rituals. Colonialism spawned intense rationalism and undermined tradition both as a mode a discourse and as a form of knowledge.

There were several other ways in which colonial rule imposed an abstract and narrowly rationalist structure of thought on India. The British had evolved an autonomous and abstract state standing above and outside society and enjoying only minimum and formal contact with it. The legal *form* of the state was conceived independently of, and bore little relation to, the actual *content* of social life. The state, therefore, ignored the open-ended and multidimensional web of relationships that constituted the substance of Indian society, and only concentrated on those aspects that could be fitted into a framework of legal abstractions. Again, the British could not govern a country of which they knew little without collecting, classifying, organising, codifying and interpreting an endless mass of detailed information about its history, geography, customs, rituals, religion, social structure, habits and ways of thought. They could only do so in terms of principles and categories that made sense to them, that is, conformed to their notions of rationality and justice. Whatever appeared 'strange' or 'meaningless' was discarded, and most of the rest misinterpreted and condensed into an artificially coherent body of knowledge.

Thanks to the contradictory logic of colonialism, the British could not sustain their rationalism. If consistently followed, it required them to transform Indian society and to enact socially and economically progressive policies and laws. They knew that this would have provoked fierce resistance and endangered their rule. Accordingly, after 1857, they propped up feudal kingdoms and landed interests and supported their legitimising ideology and culture. What is far more important from our point of view is the way they formalised and distorted Hindu customs and traditions.[16] The complex customary law which the traditional system of administering justice knew how to interpret and enforce could not be handled by the British-established courts of law, and did not measure up to the kind of certainty, consistency and uniformity the British conception of justice required. It was, therefore, replaced by the *shāstras* and their rigid and sometimes obsolete and impractical norms. This led to excessive rigidity in the administration of justice, hindered the normal development and spontaneous adaptation of the tradition, made law a subject of endless debates and gave the pandits an unusual amount of power. The *dharmashāstras*, which hitherto had only a heuristic value in identifying and interpreting customs and traditions and were concerned with *dharma* not laws, were turned into the Hindu equivalent of the British civil code, and the pandits became the Hindu equivalent of British lawyers. The rationalistic formalism of the colonial rulers required traditionalistic formalism among the Hindus as its necessary counterpart. The colonial bureaucrats and the Brahmins struck up a sinister and complementary relationship. In the process, Indian social life, now subjected to the twin pressures of liberal and *shāstric* formalism, lost its fluidity and capacity to cope with change. The body of traditions on which every society, especially one as varied and complex as the Hindu, necessarily relies was ruptured, creating a profound triple crisis of authority, identity and confidence.

Gandhi saw this more clearly than most. As he put it:[17]

In pre-British India there was no such thing as rigid Hindu Law governing the lives of millions. The body of regulations known as *smritis* were indicative rather than inflexible codes of conduct. They never had the validity of law such as is known to modern lawyers. The observance of the restraints of the *smritis* was enforced more by social than legal sanctions. The *smritis* were, as is evident from the self-contradictory verses to be found in them, continually passing, like ourselves, through evolutionary changes, and were adapted to the new discoveries that were being made in social science. Wise kings were free to procure new interpretations to suit new conditions. Hindu religion or Hindu *shāstras* never had the changeless and unchanging character that is now being sought to be given to them. No doubt in those days there were kings and their councillors who had the wisdom and the authority required to command the respect and allegiance of society. But now the custom has grown up of thinking that *smritis* and everything that goes by the name of *shāstras* is absolutely unchangeable.

Gandhi, therefore, had an extremely difficult task. He had to protect Hindu tradition from the distortions of colonial rule and uphold its authority. At the same time, he was acutely aware that it had accumulated a lot of 'dead weight' and that the uncritical and 'mindless' traditionalism of the orthodox was both unwise and impractical. Furthermore, he had to defend the integrity of the tradition against supercilious British criticism; yet he knew that its integrity had been gravely damaged and could not be restored in its earlier form. Indeed, the tradition had to be pieced together and patiently reconstructed in a manner that took account of the rationalist challenge. Again, Gandhi had to nurture the self-confidence and pride of his humiliated and nervous countrymen. But he also had to coax, cajole, compel and, at times, coerce them into taking a critical look at themselves.

V

How Gandhi went about the task is our concern in this book. A long line of distinguished Hindu leaders from the early years of the nineteenth century onwards had wrestled with these and other moral challenges posed by colonial rule and worked out a range of responses. Gandhi was deeply influenced by these, and hence, I begin with a chapter on them. The chapter is somewhat perfunctory, goes over familiar ground and is only intended to provide a necessary background to Gandhi's thought. I concentrate on 'elite' discourse and ignore the equally, perhaps even more important, ordinary discourse in which millions of Indians, singly or in groups, daily passed spoken and unspoken judgements on colonial rule. I do so because it provides the framework within which Gandhi formulated his response to British rule and also because it grapples with issues in which I am interested in this book.

The rest of the chapters deal with Gandhi. The third examines his analysis of the nature and causes of Indian degeneration and his conception of *yugadharma*. The succeeding five chapters explore his concern to radicalise the traditional Hindu view of non-violence, his debates with terrorists about the use of violence to secure Indian independence, the practice of untouchability, mobilisation of sexual energy to attain political objectives, and Indianisation of the uniquely Western autobiographical genre of writing. In each case, I examine how Gandhi battled with the tradition, mobilised its regenerative resources, remained within and departed from it, and sometimes succeeded and on other occasions, failed to achieve his goals. The last chapter outlines and assesses the Marxist discourse on him.

Chapter Two

Hindu Responses to British Rule

Since the British took several decades to consolidate their rule over India and followed different policies in different parts of the country and with respect to its different communities, Indian responses to their rule were diverse, articulated at various levels and showed considerable regional and communal variations. For two main reasons, I shall concentrate on the nature and basis of Hindu responses between 1820, when Ram Mohun Roy was in full swing, and 1920, when Gandhi took over the leadership of the Indian independence movement. First, they provide the basic conceptual framework within which Gandhi formulated his own response. At one level he represented the culmination of, and at another a radical departure from, his nineteenth century Hindu predecessors. Second, Hindus were the first to take an early and keen interest in their rulers, interacting with them socially, offering their services to and engaging in a critical dialogue with them and, in the process, developing a rich tradition of discourse unmatched by any other community. Their conceptualisation and assessment of colonial rule is, therefore, worth studying even apart from its influence on Gandhi.

From the very beginning, the Hindu discourse displayed an unusual feature not to be found in other communities and relatively rare even in the history of anti-colonial struggles. Rather than concentrate on colonial rule and ask whether to ignore, welcome or fight against it, as the Muslims were to do later, Hindu leaders, almost to a man, located and discussed it in the wider context of their social regeneration. The British, who had never seriously encountered the Hindus before, were puzzled by them as a people and bewildered, at times even offended, by some of their beliefs and practices. Even in the allegedly halcyon days of Warren Hastings, they could not easily 'place' the Hindus who were neither like them nor like the 'noble' or ignoble African 'savages' whose descriptions were then beginning to circulate in Europe. They, therefore, asked questions, some very sharp and critical, which the Hindus could not ignore. More importantly, the British could not govern India without defining the Hindus and reducing them to manageable categories largely derived from their own ways of thought. The Hindus did not like their essentialist and inevitably biased definition, and had no other way to counter it save by providing an alternative self-definition. It is, therefore, hardly surprising that the writings of almost all Hindu writers from Ram Mohun Roy onwards were taken up not only with social reforms but also with the prior and deeper question of self-definition. Hindus could not define themselves and specify the content of their collective identity without conceptualising themselves as a single, distinct and homogenous community, something they had never done before except to a rather limited extent under Muslim rule. The hitherto diffused and vague Hindu self-consciousness, thus, began to acquire, for the first time in its history, a corporate articulation during British rule. The fact that Hindu social self-consciousness was precipitated by and developed simultaneously with the consciousness of colonial rule, each shaping and in turn being shaped by the other, meant that Hindus could not define and make sense of themselves without defining and making sense of the colonial rule and vice versa. The two modes of consciousness were not separate but interdependent dimensions of a single process. Colonial rule was not an independent and external phenomenon brought about by the British, but an expression of the inner processes occurring *within* Hindu society. It, therefore, provided not only the *context* in which the Hindus collectively defined both *what* and *who* they were, but also a *mirror* in which they caught glimpses of themselves, of their character, strengths and especially their weaknesses.

Since Hindu leaders discussed colonial rule in the wider context of the health of their society and civilisation, their responses to it were inseparable from and varied according to their analyses of the latter. Some saw little wrong with their society, and either took no interest in British rule or dismissed it as inconsequential. For convenience, I shall call them traditionalists. Most, however, were deeply disturbed by the state of their society and wondered if and how they should regenerate themselves. Since they differed in their analyses of the extent and causes of their degeneration and the possible vitalising contribution of colonial rule, their responses varied greatly and fell into three broad categories which, for convenience, I shall call modernism, critical modernism and critical traditionalism. For the modernists, Hindu society was beyond hope and its salvation lay in radical reconstruction along modern or European lines. The critical modernists or syncretists pleaded for a creative synthesis of the two civilisations, whereas the critical traditionalists preferred to mobilise indigenous resources, borrowing from Europe whatever was likely to supplement and enrich them.

In order to avoid misunderstanding, two points need to be made about our fourfold classification. First, it refers not so much to the answers given by Hindu leaders as to the *directions* in which they looked for them. Thus, modernism refers to the tendency to think that India's hope lay in emulating Europe, but says nothing about what European values, institutions and practices to adopt. And critical modernism refers to the tendency to think that India should synthesise the two civilisations but by itself says nothing about the substantive content of the synthesis. Second, the classification is designed to classify responses not respondents, structures of thought not individuals. Since Hindu leaders were all busy men lacking the time and energy to develop carefully crafted responses, were sympathetic to different, sometimes conflicting, ideas and tendencies, and had to respond to constantly changing circumstances over which they had little control, their ideas were too recalcitrant to be fitted into neat, logical categories. However,[1] these were products of considerable thought, at least in the case of the most talented among them, and reveal identifiable patterns and organising principles. While none of them falls exclusively under one category, most of them fall more easily under one rather than the others.

I

The traditionalists were content to glory in the greatness of their civilisation.[1] They were convinced that it was in good health, and either put up fierce defences of even such offensive practices as *sati*, female infanticide and child marriages, or argued that these were 'aberrations' inevitable in an old civilisation long under foreign rule and which they intended to eradicate. They did not think much of their ruler's 'materialistic' 'irreligious', 'individualist', 'selfish', 'violent' and 'greed-based' civilisation. The Europeans had roamed the world as if they were its masters and enslaved, brutally assaulted and even eliminated large groups of people in their unscrupulous pursuit of wealth and power. The traditionalist Bhudev quoted an unknown Indian as saying that 'feebler races begin to wither at the smell of Europeans', and added that the 'English beyond doubt smell stronger than all other Europeans'.[2] The English had been guilty of more cruelty than other European nations, to which they were rendered insensitive by their greater capacity for self-deception. While the Europeans at least granted full equality to their suitably 'civilised' subjects, the victims of the British were denied such a consolation prize. Some of the traditionalists even discovered that their tradition had already anticipated and warned them against the European civilisation. It was, at bottom, a manifestation of *asuri prakriti* and endowed with a self-destructive *swabhāva*. It was energy devoid of wisdom, *rajas* unregulated by *satvas*, and propelled by an inherently insatiable and self-destructive passion for power and domination.[3] It was bound one day to destroy itself in the manner of the ancient *Yadavas*, of which the European wars, especially World War I, were widely taken to be prefigurations. India had nothing to learn from Europe except perhaps its 'practical' and 'technical' skills.[4]

The fact that Britain had conquered India did not signify the moral superiority of its civilisation.[5] Might did not imply right. The British had conquered India by means of force, duplicity, mendacity, intrigue and corruption, and that hardly reflected favourably either on their national character or on the civilisation which sanctioned such means. All uncivilised people loved war and excelled at it. The ignorant Spartans defeated the wise

Athenians, the illiterate Macedonians humbled Greece, and the uncivilised barbarian tribes destroyed the Roman empire. Their victories proved pyrrhic, as their culturally superior victims eventually triumphed over them. The British conquest only showed that Indians were a gentle and peace-loving people ill-versed in the barbaric art of waging wars. India had survived many such conquests and would survive the present one as well. The traditionalists considered colonial rule morally and politically inconsequential and advised their countrymen to hold on to the traditional order. They were far more exercised about the impatient Hindu reformers than about their British rulers. And some of them were even prepared to collaborate with the latter if they agreed not to yield to the reformist pressure.

Though the traditionalist response was limited to only a few Hindus, as a mood it was shared by many more. Its self-confidence and spirit of defiance were a source of great moral and psychological strength in a confrontationist colonial context and sustained the self-esteem and cultural pride of even those better disposed to European civilisation. Ram Mohun Roy had thanked Providence for sending the British to India, arguing that it had much to learn from them in the fields of politics, science, literature and religion. When, a few years later, a missionary rebuked him for daring to make even a minor criticism of Christianity which had brought his 'ignorant' and 'effeminate' people 'rays of intelligence', the Raja shot back saying that the 'world was indebted to our ancestors for the first dawn of knowledge which sprang up in the East' and that India had nothing to learn from the British 'with respect to science, literature or religion'.[6] Bankim Chandra Chatterjee, who had once hailed the British as 'a more perfect type of civilisation', later turned full circle and spent much of his time proving the superiority of the Indian.

Though traditionalism had a polemical and psychological value, it was an untenable and impractical response to British rule. Even its most uncompromising champions could not deny that their society was in a sorry state; the ease with which it had once again fallen prey to foreign rule was a stark and daily reminder. The very fact that many of them went to the extent of claiming that ancient India had anticipated several modern inventions, including the aeroplane, showed how much their apparent defiance concealed a pathetic feeling of diffidence and inferiority. The traditionalist response had made some sense under and indeed had been largely developed as a strategy of survival during periods of Muslim invasions, but none at all under the qualitatively different British rule. Industrialisation disrupted the unity of castes and their characteristic occupations, created new castes, destroyed some of the existing ones, increased social and economic mobility, created new hierarchies within castes and brought those hitherto distant into close and unfamiliar patterns of relationship. The increasingly popular liberal ideas encouraged demands for equality, basic human rights and social justice and stimulated a rationalist critique of not only the prevailing institutions and practices but also of their traditional modes of legitimation. The colonial state was busy establishing new structures of power as the very condition of its survival and subverting the established social order, sometimes by the apparently simple device of giving old groups new names and reclassifying them. For these and other reasons, the traditional social order was and widely seen as untenable. Since Hindu morality was based on *varnadharma* and closely bound up with the caste system, Hindu society faced not just a socio-economic but a deep moral and religious crisis as well. It had either to be reconstituted on new principles or it must face extinction.

II

The vast majority of Hindu leaders freely acknowledged that the contemporary state of their society left a good deal to be desired. Though they diagnosed their predicament differently and highlighted different aspects of their degeneration, there was a remarkable consensus. They had, as a people, become 'inert', 'degenerate', and 'lifeless', and were 'fast asleep', in 'deep slumber', 'dreaming'. The louder the pressures of the world, the more tightly they drew the blankets and smothered themselves in mindless practices and beliefs. They were in 'thralldom to outworn and stale ideas', lacked initiative, energy, enthusiasm, perseverance and a sense of commitment, and had become deeply fearful of anything new. Aurobindo put the point well:[7]

If an ancient Indian of the time of the *Upanishads* the Buddhist period, or the later classical age were to be set down in modern India .... he would see his race clinging to forms and shells and rags of the past and missing nine-tenths of its nobler values ... ; he would be amazed by the extent of a later degeneracy, its mental poverty, immobility, static repetition, the comparative feebleness of the creative intuition, the long sterility of art, the cessation of science.

The lack of unity was another recurrent theme in the writings and speeches of Hindu leaders. Their countrymen were deeply divided and incapable of concerted action. They were fragmented into a large number of castes, subcastes and local communities, each a world unto itself and lacking meaningful contacts with others, with the result that they were incapable of viewing themselves as Hindus, let alone as Indians. While the castes and local communities had saved Hindus from atomisation, they had also bred a pervasive 'spirit of localism', mutual distrust and 'indifference to each other's fate'. That was why the East India Company had successfully played off different groups and communities against one another, and the leaders of the 1857 rebellion had failed to build on their initial success. Indeed, for some Hindu leaders the 'whole history' of India, at least during the past few centuries, had been a story of collaboration with foreigners against one's own people.

Thanks to their social isolation, Hindus had failed to develop a sense of mutual concern and brutally exploited their weaker compatriots.[8] As Vivekananda put it, no society 'puts its foot on the neck of the wretched so mercilessly as does that of India'. The treatment of the poor, the lower castes and the untouchables was an obvious example of this. Man was defined in terms of his caste and his humanity was exhausted in his social status. It was, therefore, hardly surprising that the lower castes had 'even forgotten' that they were human beings. In the opinion of Hindu leaders, they had become quarrelsome, factious, envious, petty and unable to sustain cooperative enterprises. Gokhale observed, 'If we are deficient in one quality more than another, it is in the instinct and habit of cooperation.' The self-willed Hindu, determined to pursue his own or his family's interest, insisted on cooperating with others on his own terms and refused to subordinate his views and interests to those of others even when this was in his own long-term interest. Since no organisation could be sustained on such a basis, Hindus failed to evolve voluntary associations based on considerations other than caste and village. Not used to the discipline of concerted action they were unable to cope with disagreement and criticism. They did not appreciate that criticism could be inspired by a genuine difference of opinion rather than jealousy and that men could disagree without being hostile to one another. As a result, no one freely spoke his mind, disagreements were not brought into the open and resolved, and there was in every organisation a false atmosphere of peace and harmony. Such an unnatural unanimity spawned the corrosive spirit of distrust, suspicion and cynicism, which eventually destroyed the organisation concerned.

Hindus were not only deeply divided among themselves but also from other communities, especially the Muslims. This question had not exercised earlier generations of leaders because they did not see its importance, were contemptuous of Muslims with whom they thought they had historical scores to settle, or because they assumed that the Muslim masses would accept their cultural leadership. After 1857 they could ignore it no longer. Such factors as the British policy of initially favouring Hindus and then Muslims, the land settlement which benefited the former at the expense of the latter, the lack of Muslim participation in the ongoing dialogue between the Hindus and the British rulers with the consequent Hindu tendency to equate theirs with Indian nationalism, and the uneven economic and social progress of the two communities opened up a deep divide between them.

Almost every Indian leader, including the most rabid Hindu nationalist, recognised that his country was doomed unless it found satisfactory ways of uniting its various communities. Their models and methods of unity and their conceptions of the cultural profile of united India varied enormously. But there was none who was not exercised about the problem. Even during his Hindu nationalist phase, Bipan Chandra Pal insisted that India needed a new 'national civilisation' based on a 'federation' of the different civilisations that has found their home in it.[9] Commenting on the aggressive Hinduism of the *Arya Samaj*, Lala Lajpat Rai observed: 'The Arya Samaj *has* to remember that India today is *not* exclusively Hindu. Its prosperity and future depends upon the reconciliation of Hinduism with the greater ism—Indian nationalism. Anything that may prevent, or even hinder, that consummation is a *sin* for which there can be *no expiation*.'[10]

Finally, Hindu leaders from Ram Mohun Roy onwards commented on the almost total absence of civic and political culture among their countrymen. Indians were only interested in their families and castes and lacked wider regional and political loyalties. They lacked the 'love of municipal freedom' and 'civil liberty', were wanting in 'civic sense' and a spirit of collective self-help, helplessly depended on the government to attend to all matters falling outside the bounds of the family and caste and took little interest in the conduct of their collective affairs. Indeed, they were not in the least bothered about who ruled over them or even about whether their country was free so long as their daily routine was not disturbed. According to the Hindu leaders, they were a profoundly unpolitical people, politically naive and childlike, ill-versed in statecraft and devoid of patriotism and a sense of national solidarity. To the extent that they had developed a sense of collective identity, it remained largely racial or ethnic and never attained a political articulation. As Lala Lajpat Rai said:[11]

> Our countrymen sadly lack the spirit of patriotism that characterises the citizens of every great and prosperous country in the world, and consequently there is no end to our troubles. Nothing short of *desh bhakti* . . . . can save us from the death and destruction that is staring us in the face. Genuine and selfless devotion (*bhakti*) for our *desh* ought to be the *dharma* of everyone of us.

Hindu leaders had no clear explanation of the causes of their degeneration and kept blaming different factors without analysing and establishing clear relations between them. For some, especially the modernists, their civilisation had been structurally flawed from the very beginning, and the causes of its subsequent degeneration lay in such factors as the oppressive inequality of the caste system, the other-worldliness of their religion, the chaotic individualism of their culture and the systematic suppression of the spirit of critical inquiry by the Brahminic champions of the dominant *advaita* tradition. Some others, such as

Bankim Chandra Chatterjee, blamed the Indian 'exaltation of asceticism', the absence of inductive method, the pervasive ethos of inequality, a lack of interest in political power and the climate. Vivekananda thought that since the Hindus enjoyed an amazing degree of religious freedom, they could only be held together by a fairly rigid social structure which under crisis, and especially under foreign rule, became excessively rigid and oppressive. Under Hegel's influence, Bipan Chandra Pal contended that almost from the very beginning, Indian civilisation had made the fatal mistake of disjoining the universal and the particular, the subject and the object, the inner and the other, the spiritual and the material, and of concentrating on the former in each pair of opposites. The result was not only that it ignored the world but also that its spirituality remained abstract and distorted.

Part of the reason why Hindu leaders did not undertake a systematic and searching analysis of the causes of their degeneration lay in the fact that most of them felt convinced that Muslim rule had played an important part in it. Some said so openly. The rest were more discreet and knew that, since they had to find ways of working with Muslims, they should avoid raking up old historical memories.[12] The tendency to blame Muslim rule is evident in most Hindu leaders, including Ram Mohun Roy, Bankim Chandra Chatterjee, Ishwar Chandra Gupta, Narmada Shankar, Ishwar Chandra Vidyasagar, Gokhale, Ranade, Tilak, Vivekananda and Aurobindo. For most of them, Muslim rulers, with such solitary exceptions as Akbar, had been tyrannical, oppressive, discriminatory, intolerant and contemptuous of Hindu beliefs and practices. They forcibly converted Hindus, destroyed their temples, insulted their religion, raped their women, plundered their property, and wantonly shed their blood. The terrified and terrorised Hindus 'naturally' turned inward, and became other-worldly, servile, timid, ritualistic and too frightened to speak their minds in public. They were afraid to make even the smallest changes in their social and religious life lest these should be exploited by the rulers or lead to their disintegration. Since the whole Hindu civilisation was under threat, the Brahmins, its traditional custodians, assumed and were allowed to assume considerable power with the rest closing ranks behind them. Its natural growth was stunted, its vitality sapped, its self-confidence shattered and its rich tradition fragmented and frozen. Writer after writer conveniently explained away such ugly practices as *sati*, the rigidity of the caste system, early child marriages, and the ban on widow remarriage as part of the Hindu society's strategy of survival under Muslim invasions and rule.

The Hindu leaders' comprehensive and often unjust denigration of Muslim rule seems to have owed its inspiration and appeal to several interrelated factors. Many of them confused Muslim invaders with Muslim rulers and attributed to the latter deeds committed by the former. Unlike the lower castes who had sometimes benefited from Muslim rule, higher castes, especially the Brahmins, generally suffered under it. Being the acknowledged guardians of their religion, they were sometimes mocked, harassed, deprived of their sources of revenue and denied a social and political role. Not surprisingly, many of them never reconciled themselves to Muslim rule. Since the low view of it was not confined to the Brahmins, it probably had deeper cultural roots. The Islamic identification of religion with the state and the use of political power to induce conversion had no parallel in their thought and puzzled Hindus. Its austere view of religion sat ill with the Hindu love of music, rituals, symbols, images and idols. Hindus found Islamic theology intellectually uninteresting and were disappointed not to find in it gods and goddesses depicting the full range of normal human emotions. Although relations between the two communities were never as bad as presented by Hindu writers and had led in some parts of the country to a creative blend of the two religions and cultures, mutual curiosity and respect were not very common. It is striking that during the several hundred years of Muslim rule, only a handful of Hindus wrote commentaries on the *Koran*, translated it into regional languages or undertook a comparative study of the two communities. The relative Muslim lack of interest in Hindu philosophy, culture and social structure, except during a few decades of Mughal rule, is just as striking. Some of the *Purānas* written in the aftermath of Islamic rule contain most unflattering references to Muslim habits, hygiene, sexual practices and modes of thought and give a fairly good idea of what some Hindu religious leaders thought of them at the time.

British historians of India also played an important part in shaping the Hindu view. Since Hindu historians had not developed a coherent discourse on their history and assigned Muslim rule its appropriate place, their past was up for grabs, and British historians filled the intellectual vacuum with their ideologically-biased history. Sir William Jones, the earliest and one of the most eminent of them, read Indian history through the distorting prism of the Enlightenment view of European history. Determined to 'know India better than any other European ever knew it', he concluded that ancient Hindus were the 'Athenians of Asia', creative and brilliant, 'splendid in arts and arms, happy in government, wise in legislation and eminent in various knowledge'. Their subsequent decline had to be explained, and Jones turned to Muslims as the Asian equivalent of the European barbarians. The British, representing the third phase of Indian history, finally put an end to the Muslim-ruled 'dark ages', rediscovered India's past and launched its Renaissance. William Robertson's *Disquisition Concerning Ancient India* and especially Thomas Maurice's two volumes of *Modern History of Hindustan* (1802–1810) explicitly spelt out Jones' low view of Muslim rule. Maurice talked about the Muslim 'perfidy', 'tyranny', 'callous insensibility', 'sordid baseness of avarice and unsanguined ambition', and remarked how painful he found it to 'give black details of and trace through desolated India their blood-stained footsteps'. The self-proclaimed imperial historian of Hindustan even wrote a tragedy entitled *The Fall of the Moghul*, giving expression to these sentiments in lurid language. In the absence of an alternative account to counter it, the British view of Indian history held considerable sway over almost all Hindu leaders, including even the most sophisticated and secular-minded among them such as Rabindranath Tagore, Jawaharlal Nehru and Jayaprakash Narayan.

Hindu antipathy to Muslim rule then had a complex origin. Although ideologically biased, British historiography created a seductive intellectual framework. It would not have been so influential if deeper cultural factors had not been at work, the history of the relations between the two communities had been less stormy, and if the leadership of the independence movement had not come from higher castes, especially the Brahmins. Similarly, the bulk of Brahminic leadership would not have so drastically marginalised and grossly misinterpreted nearly a thousand years of Indian history if the scholarly weight of British historians and the policies of British rulers had not nurtured their prejudices and if the historical experiences of the Hindus had not lent them at least some support. Whatever the explanation, the fact remained that despite their wish to live in harmony with Muslims, the bulk of Hindu leadership never came to terms with Muslim rule and seems unable to do so even now.

III

Although unclear about the causes of their decline, Hindu leaders were in no doubt that they had to arrest and reverse it. Merely tinkering with isolated customs and practices was not enough, for the 'rot' had gone much deeper and called for 'national rebirth' or 'regeneration'. India needed a 'new moral and social order', 'new principles of morality and social organisation', a new 'national civilisation', a 'new philosophy', a 'new moral consensus' and a 'new national character and culture'.[13] The search for new principles was reflected in the countless journals, pamphlets, newspapers, books, debating societies and research organisations that sprang up all over the country containing such words as truth, light, essence, search and research in their titles and names. It would seem that, in the opinion of Hindu leaders, India needed not only new truths but also a new mode of discovering and validating them. Not surprisingly, modern science became extremely popular and almost every leader turned to 'scientific research' and 'scientific method' to generate 'scientific ethics' and 'scientific principles of society'. Bengal was for a while full of Comte and found in his positivism a method of discovering new truths. Ranade advocated 'Bacon's method', Gokhale thought that J.S. Mill's 'method of empiricism' alone research in thed Aurobindo turned to a combination of Darwin and Einstein.

Despite the extensive references to science and scientific method, about which most leaders had only vague and confused ideas, none of them undertook or even attempted such an inquiry. The reason for that was simple. In the colonial context, a less exacting and more reliable method was readily available, namely, to examine how Europe, which was until recently believed to be as degenerate as India, had managed to turn the corner. Many Hindu writers accepted the dominant three-stage Enlightenment view of European history referred to earlier. Europe liberated itself from the dark 'middle' ages dominated by priesthood, blind faith, superstition and political fragmentation by turning to the original founts of its civilisation characterised by a vigorous political culture, energetic and public-spirited citizens, a climate of free and rational inquiry and a complete absence of priesthood. That resulted in the Renaissance, a period of rationalism, modern science, secularism and a vibrant political life within the framework of and under the leadership of the modern state. The Renaissance was followed by the Reformation, brought about by a similarly happy return to the central principles of original Christianity. The story of the rebirth or reincarnation of Europe underlying this fantastic reading of its history had a particular appeal for the Hindu mind.

Their highly abstract reading of European history led Hindu leaders to draw several important conclusions of which two are relevant to us. First, even as the waters of a river were pure and health-giving at its source and accumulated dirt on the way, a civilisation was pure and robust at its birth and declined over time. The remotest recorded past was the source of both light and legitimacy, and a reform based on it was at once both desirable and authoritative. Several leaders pleaded for Hindu 'Protestantism' to be brought about by a return to the *Vedas* or at least the *Upanishads*. And they advocated Indian Renaissance based on a return to their 'classical age' whose glory William Jones and others had discovered for them.[14] One would have thought that a suspiciously perfect coincidence between classical India and classical Athens, both miraculously existing during the same historical period, might have persuaded Indian leaders to check their history. Several related assumptions came in the way. It was widely held in India at the time that all great civilisations had a similar past in more or less the same way that all great religions were based on identical principles. It was this belief that inspired a long line of Indian leaders from Ram Mohun Roy onwards to undertake a comparative study of different religions in search of universal morality. Furthermore, once the researches of such Orientalists as Max Mueller and Monier Williams concluded that Indians belonged to the same Aryan 'race' as the

Europeans and that their languages and symbolisms had common roots, it was tempting to conclude, incorrectly of course, that the two civilisations had a common beginning and an identical past. Thanks to colonial rule, Indians were most anxious to look like and share familial bonds with their long-forgotten European cousins. There was also the additional attraction that the Orientalist view linked the Europeans with ancient Indians, that is, the Hindus, leaving the Muslims more or less completely out of the picture.

Second, the state or a well-organised and unified polity was the necessary basis of civilisation.[15] The classical civilisations of Athens and Rome had states of their own; the Dark Ages did not; and Renaissance Europe navigated its way out of them by means of it. The Hindu leaders found a similar pattern in their own history. They had independent polities during the Maurya and Gupta periods, the high points of their civilisation. When they declined, it suffered a severe setback and became prey to foreign invasions, especially the Muslim. Hindu leaders thought that all this was not a mere coincidence. The state held a community together, protected it from external threat, safeguarded its achievements and gave its members the security and confidence to make long-term plans and projects without which no civilisation could be built. Since its very survival so required, the state set up appropriate institutions to cultivate and foster civic and political virtues, self-discipline, patriotism and the subordination of the individual to the collective and of short-term to long-term interests. It was because Hindus did not have a state of their own and their communal activities lacked focus and support for several hundred years that their collective life became fractured, they lost interest in the world and became degenerate. A leader in the *Bengalee* of 8 July 1900 made this point with great clarity and force.[16]

> Every schoolboy knows that India's immediate past before the birth of the British Indian administration was marked by a period of political chaos, inter-racial jealousies, and all the evils of a dissolving political community. It is the tritest of maxims of political philosophy that no progress in civilisation is possible without a stable political order.

... The discipline of obedience is necessary for all political communities; but however law-abiding a people might be, the discipline of obedience is never learnt until and unless the different elements, the separate bodies, castes, and races that happen to live together in a common country learn to agree to a common Government and to place themselves under a common leader or body of leaders and render homage to the majesty of the law that emanates from the supreme political authority.

This was how the Hindu leaders explained the differences between themselves and their rulers. As individuals, they were just as good and bright, and their alleged racial inferiority was utter nonsense. When given an equal chance they had excelled in British-established schools and colleges and done well in competitive examinations. They were good on the battlefield and had given their rulers good fights which they lost not for want of military valour but because of their internal divisions and lack of political coordination. They were also just as skilful at trade, commerce and civil administration. Despite all this, they lay prostrate at the feet of a few thousand Britons. That was *only* because the latter were much better organised, sank their differences, pooled together their individual abilities and efforts, accepted collective discipline, were fired by patriotism and would not betray their colleagues or country for personal interest or out of malice and pique. The British were not always like that and only became so under the protective guidance and discipline of the state, which carefully cultivated these qualities and taught them how to act as 'one man'. The lesson for Indians was obvious.

IV

Hindu leaders were convinced that their society's salvation lay in creating a strong Indian state. Since such a state presupposed industrialisation, modern science and technology and a rationalist culture, they needed these as well. In other words, India's salvation lay in embracing modernity. Since Britain had successfully modernised itself and was indeed a world leader, India had a good deal to learn from it. As its good fortune would have it, Britain was already in India busy establishing modern institutions. Ram Mohun Roy offered 'thanks to the supreme disposer of the universe' for the British presence. The ebullient K.C. Sen thought that 'the contact of England with India was Providential and not a mere accident'. And even the sober Naoroji could not help seeing a divine hand in such an encounter at such a ripe moment.

From the very beginning of the nineteenth century, most Hindu leaders welcomed British rule and urged their countrymen to take advantage of it. The Raja contrasted the 'civilised' British with their 'tyrannical' predecessor and saw the new rulers 'not as a body of conquerors but rather as deliverers'. He went on:[17]

> From personal experience I am impressed with the conviction that the greater our intercourse with European gentlemen, the greater will be our own improvement in literacy, social and political affairs; a fact which can be easily proved by comparing the condition of those of my countrymen who have enjoyed this advantage with that of those who unfortunately have not had the opportunity!

He conceded that British rule spelt a loss of autonomy, but did not see why that mattered. Echoing the sentiments of the defenders of colonial rule and using a language remarkably free of nationalism, he observed:[18]

> National independence is not an absolute goal; the goal, so to say, of society is to secure the happiness of the greatest possible number; and when left to itself a nation cannot attain this object, when it does not contain itself the principles of future progress, it is better for it that it should be guided by the example and even the authority of a conquering people who are more civilized.

The bulk of Hindu leaders, including Dwarkanath Tagore, the early Bankim Chandra Chatterjee, Ranade, Tilak, Dadabhai Naoroji, Surendranath Banerjee, B.C. Pal, Ravindranath Tagore,

Lala Lajpat Rai, Aurobindo, the later Narmada Shankar, Tilak, Motilal Nehru and the early Gandhi, thought that British rule was both a consequence of India's degenerate state and an opportunity to turn the corner.[19] Like their rulers, they too conceptualised the colonial encounter in pedagogical terms. Indians needed to 'improve' themselves, 'sit at the feet' of their rulers and 'learn' all the skills and virtues necessary for their regeneration.[20] Although arrogant and aloof, the British were 'wise gurus' giving them useful 'political training', and if the Indians could for a while become 'apt pupils', they would one day be 'fully qualified' for self-rule. Even the reflective Bankim Chandra Chatterjee called them 'good teachers'. In his *Anandamath*, the *sannyāsis* did not follow up their successful rebellion under the divine advice that continued foreign rule was necessary for India's 'growth'. The later Narmada Shankar asked India to 'rejoice' that it was being prepared for political adulthood by Britain. Lokahitwadi even thought that as a 'child takes ten or twenty years to become educated', a country 'must require two or four hundred years'.[21] The following fairly typical remarks, which need to be read at various levels, give some idea of the way Hindu leaders thought. First, a leader in the *Hindu Patriot* of February 1872:[22]

> *There are certainly shortcomings of the British Government in India, and grave shortcomings too*; we cannot deny that there is dissatisfaction, even discontent among the people, no matter whether or not with good reasons; but nothing of the sort which lead them, as in Russia, to seek to limit the absolute despotism of the Indian Government by assassinations. They are fully sensible of the great blessings it has conferred upon them, and though they may chafe, murmur or cry, when they are pinched by this tax or that, when they are oppressed by this officer or that, or rudely shaken by this measure or that, they are still thoroughly conscious that they never had a better Government. They not only feel the might of the arms, which have *tied into a bond of political union and administrative control the diversified races and nations of India*, equal to a continent, which had been *utterly unknown in ages past*, but they are fully alive to the grave calamity which would befall the country were this mighty hand taken away.

Sankaran Nair observed in his presidential address at the 1897 annual session of the Congress:[23]

> We are well aware of the disordered state of this country when it passed, with its insecurity of person and property, under British Rule, of the enormous difficulties our rulers had to overcome in introducing orderly administration without any help from the then existing agencies. We recognise that the association of the people in the government of the country, except to a very limited extent, was then impossible. We also know that British rule cleared the way to progress and furnished us with the one element, English education, which was necessary to rouse us from the torpor of ages and bring about the religious, social and political regeneration which the country stands so much in need of. We are also aware that with the decline of British supremacy, we shall have anarchy, war and rapine. *The Mohammedans will try to recover their lost supremacy. The Hindu races and chiefs will fight amongst themselves.* The lower castes who have come under the vivifying influence of Western civilisation are scarcely likely to yield without a struggle to the dominion of the higher castes. And we have Russia and France waiting for their opportunities. The ignorant masses may possibly not recognize the gravity of the danger attendant on any decline of England's power in the East. But it is ridiculous to suggest that those who have received the benefit of English education are so short-sighted enough not to see and weigh that danger. While, however, full of gratitude for what Great Britain has done for India—for its Government which secures us from foreign aggression and ensures security of person and property—it should not be forgotten for a moment that the real link that binds us indissolubly to England is the hope, the well-founded hope and belief, that *with England's help* we shall, and, under her guidance alone, *we can attain national unity and national freedom.*

B.N. Dhar's presidential address a few years later even more clearly spelt out the 'blessings' of the Raj:[24]

> Peace, order and perfect security of life and property have been secured to us to a degree never known to the old Roman

Empire and even now not to be seen anywhere beyond the limits of the British Empire. A genuine and an active interest in the welfare of the masses, as is shown by its famine, plague, sanitation and agrarian measures, is its abiding and noblest feature. Perfect religious and social freedom it has given us unasked; and Railways, Telegraphs, Post Office and a thousand other instruments and appliances are the means by which it has added to our material comfort and social advancement. The educational system which has immortalised the names of Bentinck and Macaulay is perhaps its greatest gift to the people of India. The spread of English education, as it has instructed our minds and inspired us with new hopes and aspirations, has been accompanied by gradual and cautious concessions of political rights—the admission of Indians into the public service, the introduction of local self-government and the reform of the Legislative Councils on a partially representative basis. We have a government whose justice is exemplary and a civil service which in ability, integrity, zeal, and genuine regard, according to its own lights, for those entrusted to its care, had no rival in the world. *When I think of the dependencies ruled by other European powers*—of Algeria and Tonquin under the French, of parts of Africa under the Germans—of the large Negro populations in the United States, as the Republican Americans treat and govern them—*I thank God that I am a British subject,* and feel no hesitation in saying that the government of India by England—*faulty as it is in many respects and greatly as it needs to be reformed and renovated from top to bottom*—is still the greatest gift of Providence to my race! For England is the only country that knows how to govern those who cannot govern themselves.

Despite such encomia, Hindu leaders were under no illusion about the limitations of British rule. They knew it was racist, held them in contempt and had, after 1857, kept them at a respectable social distance. The agitation surrounding the Ilbert Bill brought home the intensity of the Anglo-Indian hatred for the 'native niggers' even to those busy ingratiating themselves with their masters. As the nationalist movement gained momentum, Anglo-Indian racism became rabid and incidents of their bad manners and violence to even middle-class Indians were quite rampant.[25] Hindu leaders well knew that for decades the British government had denied them entry to the highly prized Indian Civil Service. When it yielded under pressure it did not hold examinations in India until 1921. And even then, the Indian bureaucracy did everything in its power to make difficult the lives of the tiny minority who managed to pass them, as the widely discussed case of S.N. Banerjee showed. Ranade, Bankim Chandra Chatterjee, Gokhale, Naoroji, Rabindranath Tagore and others repeatedly complained that the East India Company had plundered their wealth in a manner reminiscent of the early Muslim invaders and that the policy of free trade introduced in the 1830s had ruined their economy. Their industrialisation was imbalanced, patchy and designed to serve British interests and had led to widespread unemployment and poverty. Thanks to the destruction of indigenous industry, agriculture had become the only source of revenue. The neglect of irrigation in favour of the railways had retarded agricultural development resulting in massive and chronic famines. The government spent very little oon education, had fostered no new industries and invested very little British capital in India. It spent vast sums of money on civil and military administration and fought unnecessary wars.

Hindu leaders were also acutely aware that their political system was an inferior and highly distorted copy of the British original and that their rulers' practices rarely matched their rhetoric. Their form of government was autocratic and 'under the iron heel of a despot', as a leader in the *Bengalee* put it in 1900, and their demands for representative institutions were constantly thwarted.[26] The government was intolerant of even mild criticism and had sunk to the lowest level of brutality in its treatment of not only the rebels but also innocent citizens in the aftermath of the 1857 rebellion. The rule of law was precarious and surrounded by vast areas of arbitrariness at the opposite ends of the administrative system. The judiciary was deeply biased in favour of British residents in India and there was no equality before the law between them and the Indians. The executive was not subject to legislative control and in certain crucial areas not even to judicial control. The press was subject to severe constraints and largely controlled by Anglo-Indians.

Despite these and other criticisms mostly expressed in a highly guarded and cryptic manner and buried in a sea of praise, most

Hindus either *genuinely welcomed* British rule or accepted it as a *regrettable historical necessity*. Only a few of them supported the 1857 rebellion and fewer still participated in it, that too in a relatively minor role. The rebellion was triggered off by different factors in different areas and the vague resentment against the high-handed British behaviour did not get articulated everywhere as an attack on their rule. As for the terrorists, most of their efforts until the last two decades of the nineteenth century were primarily directed against specific government policies or officers and at times encouraged by the moderate leaders to extract concessions. There were, of course, periodic riots and peasant and tribal agitations such as the one in the South in 1875, in Pabna in 1877 and those by the Santals and Moplas. However, some of these were directed at foolish or cruel government decisions, and only rarely at foreign rule itself except in an extremely indirect and a highly mediated manner. There is only limited evidence to show that even the anti-Partition agitation in Bengal in 1905 had a wider goal.

Most Hindus were persuaded that British rule had given them political stability, security of life and property, rule of law however truncated, a relatively impartial administration of justice, religious freedom which meant much to the Brahmins, a secular government which, though partial to missionaries, did not officially impose Christianity on the Hindus, a moderately free press, civil liberties and security from foreign aggression. It had introduced them to the English language, modern science and technology, rationalism and new forms of knowledge and given them access to the riches of modern civilisation. It had united the country not only by establishing modern means of transport and communication but also by giving them a common language and a common system of law. It had provided India with new ideals of citizenship and public virtues, examples of devoted public service and a reasonably impartial and efficient civil service. With all its limitations, British rule had 'awakened', 'energised' and 'revitalised' India and was a 'progressive' force.

Mixed motives and even more mixed reasons underlay the Hindu leaders' positive assessment of British rule. Some of them were in the employ of the Raj and had an obvious interest in flattering their rulers.[27] Nearly all of them were British educated, shared British values and had both a cultural and a material interest in continuing a system in which their skills were valued. Many of them were Brahmins who had, after initial resistance, been won over to the Raj. By skilfully manipulating the educational system, including such practices as *dakshinā*, by giving them an important role in the administration of justice, by setting up a department of temple administration, by restricting missionary activities and by remaining more or less neutral in religious matters, the colonial government turned many of them into its ardent supporters.[28] The British could not rule a vast and distant country which was only partially reconciled to their presence without creating new classes sympathetic to them. These included not only the educated elite but also bankers, money-lenders, rich peasants, managers and the urban bourgeoisie. After the bitter lessons of 1857, the colonial government propped up princes and created landed interests dependent upon it for their survival. These and other classes, whose interest were tied to the Raj, created an influential body of opinion which found its way into the writings of Hindu leaders. The government also manipulated the internal divisions among various communities and created the powerful impression that their rule alone prevented disorder and disintegration. As we saw, they canvassed an ideologically-biased reading of Indian history, especially of the period immediately preceding their arrival, thereby shaping the Hindu leaders' perceptions of their history and the colonial rule.

While all this is true, it would be wrong to dismiss the Hindu leaders as collaborators, ideologically brainwashed henchmen of the Raj or as unscrupulous men willing to support whoever served their interests. Many of them were genuinely patriotic, honourable and independent-minded men who felt convinced that the Raj *was* in India's long-term interest. As we saw, they were deeply disturbed by the degeneration of their civilisation and knew that it preceded and facilitated colonial rule and could not be blamed on it. They were anxious to do something about it and thought that British rule had both shaken them out of their inertia and released regenerative forces. That was why almost all of them discussed it in the context of and assessed it in terms of its contribution to national revitalisation. The work of British and Indian archaeologists and historians recreated their past for them and increased their sense of pride and shame. They realised how much they had fallen and why, and thought that they would turn the corner if they developed, for reasons discussed earlier, a strong and united state of their own. With all its limitations, British rule was taking them in that direction. It was, thus, a historical necessity and they could not allow their temporary personal and collective frustrations to damage their long-term interests. As a leader in the *Bengalee* put it in 1900:[29]

> The spirit of *locality* accentuating itself through the centuries, the spirit of political unmorality, as we have termed it, had grown with the lapse of years, and habits have been growing truly antagonistic to the spirit of voluntary government. Thus it is that a centralised government like the British has a value for the Indian peoples which looked at from a social point of view, is quite on a par with any other forms of culture of which they may boast. Therefore again the continuance and growth of the British connexion with India must not only be not despised, but must be valued and appreciated to a degree to which, in the *hurry of passing events and amid the disappointments of political life*, some of us may for the moment be not able to rise.

Hindu leaders also had other reasons for welcoming British rule. The traumatic memory of the dissolution of political order in the aftermath of the disintegration of the Mughal empire had become part of collective folklore which leader after leader, including Dadabhai Naoroji, invoked to popular acclaim.[30] There was also a crisis of self-confidence created by centuries of foreign rule and skilful British propaganda. The successes of the East India Company and the speed with which the colonial government put down the rebellion of 1857 reinforced deep fears of internal disunity. Hindu leaders were afraid of internecine warfare leading to internal chaos and yet another foreign invasion. Some feared the return of Muslim rule of which they took the 1857 rebellion to be a portend, whereas others shared the ill-founded and British-inspired fear of Russian invasion.[31] The Hindus were, therefore, deeply sceptical at this stage in their history of their ability to create and sustain a stable and strong polity. Even those who disliked foreign rule could not help asking what the alternatives were and concluded that on balance it needed to be continued. Historical choices are never made in the abstract but always against the background of what are judged to be realistic options by men and women whose perceptions of themselves and their abilities are deeply conditioned by their past.[32]

Many Hindu leaders were also excited at the prospect of being catapulted into world history under British tutelage and becoming members of the largest and most privileged international community. Thanks to their British connections, Indians could travel to distant lands even if only as indentured labourers and petty traders. They enjoyed access to the rest of Europe and later to America, and were able to move around there under British protection. Their classical texts were translated into European languages and their achievements admired throughout the 'civilised' world. They now had a chance to make their impact on the world at large and even perhaps to become its cultural and moral leader. While the pleasant fantasy of culturally conquering the world was only confined to a few, most Hindus welcomed their integration into the world order. It opened up new vistas and released them from the obscurity of a once-known but subsequently forgotten land.[33]

It is also worth bearing in mind that British colonialism confronted India with many faces, of which one was genuine but the rest were not completely fake. Colonialism was exploitative, despotic, racist and repressive, but it also had less inhuman facets. Many Indians saw or knew of missionary doctors serving illiterate villagers with a degree of dedication that put their Indian counterparts to shame. They had seen, heard of or had the personal experience of British teachers and college principals taking interest in their Indian pupils, sometimes financing their education in India and even in England from their own pockets and, on occasions, condemning and refusing to implement the repressive policies of their government. Some British administrators showed great kindness to their Indian colleagues and clients and their integrity and courage became legendary. Thanks to all these albeit limited encounters, hundreds of lives were changed for the better and the hope in the humanity of the Raj was kept alive.[34] Again, though the Indian bureaucracy was arrogant and brutish, several governors and viceroys were men of great honour and liberal sympathies. Warren Hastings admired and encouraged the study of Indian classics, and Ilbert introduced his anti-racist bill with the full support of the Viceroy. Although they sometimes failed or lost their nerve, Indians knew that they meant well, and this again gave the Raj a more nuanced profile.

At a different level, Indians could not avoid noticing the differences between the British at home and in India. Though treated with contempt in their own country, they often received a hospitable welcome in London. The misdeeds of the Raj were sometimes denounced in British parliament of which Burke's indictment of Warren Hastings was only one example. Several British newspapers were willing to give Indian opinion a domestic outlet. At the same time that Indians were treated as 'niggers' in India, one of them was elected to the House of Commons in the teeth of considerable opposition, an event which made a tremendous impact on them. All this must not, of course, be exaggerated. Macaulay lamented the British treatment of the rebels of 1857 but did little about it. Dyer not only went unpunished but was treated as a hero. Some of the worst Indian famines and the government's callous responses to them were glibly explained away.

In spite of all this, the opportunity to appeal, sometimes successfully, against the autocratic government of India to the government in London went some way towards reducing the harshness of colonial rule. Indians were sometimes able to embarrass Britain by citing its avowed principles and practices against it. Ram Mohun Roy gently asked how a nation 'wedded to liberty' could honourably allow its Indian agents to pursue repressive policies. When the government ignored him, he mobilised British liberal opinion with some success. A few decades later, Naoroji lambasted the ruinous economic policies of the colonial government as 'un-British' and extracted a few concessions. Some Indian leaders also worked closely with the official Opposition and especially with anti-imperialist individuals and groups in Britain and were encouraged by the thought that they were not voiceless and their rulers not a homogeneous group. Sometimes this had the paradoxical consequence of humanising and thus perpetuating the colonial rule. The Raj worked through a most ingenious network of channels and had more ways of neutralising and co-opting its critics than met their innocent eyes.

V

Most Hindu leaders, then, were convinced that India's salvation lay in embracing modernity. This created a problem. The institutions they wished to adopt were all products of modern European civilisation with a very different basis and character from their own. As they repeatedly emphasised, their civilisation was plural, rural, sociocentric, spiritual, uncentralised, based on *dharma* rather than law, on duties rather than rights, on groups rather than individuals, whereas modernity had the opposite orientation. This raised the crucial question as to whether and how modernity could be reconciled with tradition, European institutions blended with Indian values and practices and what was to be done in case of conflict. Hindu leaders answered it in one of three ways which, as noted earlier, we shall call modernism, critical modernism or syncretism and critical traditionalism.

The modernists were convinced that modernity was incompatible with India's traditional ways of life and thought, and felt that these must be rejected.[35] Some of them thought that thanks to its mysticism, other-worldliness and caste system, their civilisation had been fatally flawed from the very beginning, wheareas others argued that after a promising start it had begun to decline and reached a point when it was beyond redemption. In a civilisation that had gone on for nearly three millennia, there were bound to be some beliefs and practices which fitted in with modernity and could, perhaps, be saved. However, these were few in number and could not be revived without encouraging the spirit of 'revivalism', and hence, the best course of action was to begin with a clean slate. The modernists were not worried about the criticism that no alien institution could last without some basis in the past. As post-Renaissance European history showed, a clean break with the past was both possible and necessary. Even the recent Indian experience pointed in the same direction. British-established educational institutions had not only taken off but became extremely popular and wholly discredited the older ones. Despite the discouragement of tradition, Indians had positively responded to modern learning, including modern science, literature and technology. The longer the British rule lasted, the greater the opportunity for modernity to strike roots and to create its own past. It would, of course, facilitate the popular acceptance of modern institutions if they could somehow be linked with the ancient images and symbols. The modernist rrevolt against Hinduism was so uncompromising that it found nothing worth retrieving in its vast storehouse, and turned instead to Buddhism, idealising the rule of Ashoka, a Hindu turned Buddhist.

The modernist programme for the regeneration of India consisted in creating and using a strong, interventionist, democratic, secular and centralised state to recreate society. Indians had become divided into and defined themselves in terms of narrow social, ethnic religious and linguistic groups and never thought of themselves as members of a single collectivity. They needed to acquire a common and uniform identity as citizens and to learn to look at their problems from a common national perspective. As the European experience showed, this could not be achieved without dismantling narrow identities and creating individuals depending on the state to unite and hold them together. Obviously, such a vast country as India could not be governed from a single centre and needed to be decentralised. However, it had such a pronounced tendency towards 'regionalism' and 'localism' that the provinces should be no more than administrative units enjoying a limited degree of autonomy and under no circumstances allowed to become organic communities with a strong sense of identity.

The modernists disagreed on a number of issues, especially the economic issues where they covered the entire spectrum from eighteenth century liberalism to Marxism. However, they were all united in their Manichean and British-inspired belief that the state and society represented the opposite principles of light and darkness, respectively. The state stood for modernity, society for tradition. The state signified consciousness, society unconsciousness. The state was a realm of rationality, society of irrational beliefs and practices. Society was a nether region within whose womb lay dark and obscurantist forces, and had been the cause of Indian degeneration. Like an octopus, it had constantly expanded its tentacles and destroyed all that was creative in Indian life. The Indian state was doomed unless it transformed society in its own image, and in the meantime firmly guarded itself against its fatal embrace.

Like traditionalism, modernism was a target of constant criticism, at least until the end of the nineteenth century. Its spokesmen were frequently ridiculed as 'imitators', 'beggars without pride', 'denationalised radicals', 'traitors', 'sycophants' of colonial rulers, and 'brown sahibs'. When challenged, they had difficulty explaining how their civilisation could have lost its way for so long, whether they did not look at it through biased British eyes and why India should copy the West rather than explore an alternative model of modernisation. Despite these and other weaknesses, modernism had advantages denied to its rivals. It was intellectually coherent and had a clearly worked out answer to India's problems. It was able to point to the European experience to show that its programme had a historical basis. Its ideas connected with the new economic and political reality unfolding under colonial rule and had an air of realism about them. The prospect of moulding itself in the image of its rulers had a particular appeal for a subject country. And since modernism proposed to take India along well-trodden paths, it made few demands on political imagination and creativity.

VI

Critical modernism or syncretism, whose spokesmen included Ram Mohun Roy, K.C. Sen, G.K. Gokhale and others, occupied an unstable but popular half-way house between traditionalism and modernism. They agreed with the latter that India needed to modernise itself, but insisted that, despite all its limitations, the central principles of Indian civilisation were sound and worth preserving. Though they never specified these principles, they had in mind such things as the spiritual view of the universe and the doctrine oy agreed with than and of life; the emphasis on duties rather than rights, on altruism rather than self-interest, on society rather than the state, on the *ātmic* rather than atomic view of man and on self-sacrifice rather than self-indulgence, the centrality of the family, the regulation of *artha* and *kāma* by *dharma*; epistemological pluralism and a relaxed and non-aggressive attitude to human relations. Most of these ideas were grounded in *advaita*, which was, therefore, taken to be the 'characteristic world view' of India and ideally suited to become what Ram Mohun Roy called the 'basis of Indian unity'.

According to the critical modernists, Europeans had made the mistake of indiscriminately modernising themselves and rejecting their Greco-Roman and especially Christian heritage. As a result, their civilisation lacked moral and religious depth and a sense of meaning and purpose. It had a lot of energy and dynamism but neither wisdom nor a feel for the spiritual aspect of life. There was no reason why India should repeat their mistake. It had a unique opportunity to combine the old with the new, to integrate spirituality with modernity, and to undertake a unique civilisational experiment capable of becoming a source of universal inspiration. Unlike the traditionalists who were content to live by the values of their allegedly superior civilisation and had no interest in turning India into a spiritual laboratory of the world, and unlike the modernists who were content to adopt the (superior) European civilisation, the critical modernists aspired to synthesise the two and become world teachers. In their own way, they were India's counterpart to Britain's Christian and secular missionaries.

A number of Hindu leaders from Ram Mohun Roy onwards embarked on a massive project of 'creative synthesis'. The Raja sought to combine *Vedānta* with modern scientific culture, Indian moral values with European political values, and the Indian doctrine of the unity of man with the European ideas of liberty and equality, and had them taught in the Vedanta College which he started in 1825. His Brahmo Samaj was intended to be a 'synthesis of the doctrines of the European Enlightenment with the philosophic views of the *Upanishads*'. For K.C. Sen, India was 'sitting at the confluence of two mighty rivers' and must gather 'the product of .... ancient wisdom and modern enterprise'. His 'New Dispensation', at once 'thoroughly scientific' and 'transcendentally spiritual', was designed to 'reconcile ancient faith and modern science' and 'asceticism and civilisation'.[36] In his early years, Bankim Chandra Chatterjee wanted 'European industries and science united with Indian *dharma*'.[37] Gokhale pleaded for a 'harmonious blend' of the European spirit of science and the Hindu science of the spirit. Even Vivekananda who, as we shall see, was not a critical modernist, could not resist the idea, and pleaded that the 'strong points of that (old) India should be reinforced by the strong points of this age'. He urged the Hindu to become 'an occidental of occidentals in your spirit of equality, freedom, work and energy and, at the same time, a Hindu to the very backbone of your culture and instincts'.[38] At the political level, the critical modernists vigorously pleaded for the integration of the 'internal' and 'external' visions of the two civilisations, giving rise to new theories of man, freedom, law, state, equality, justice, rights, democracy and social reform.[39] The idea of a cultural synthesis won the sympathies of countless educated Indians. It offered them the best of both worlds, gave them an opportunity to absorb, transcend and eventually to claim superiority over their rulers, and carved out a unique historical role for India; it also fitted in with the dominant Hindu doctrine of epistemological pluralism. Furthermore, it was not an inherently implausible project as there was no obvious reason why India could not learn whatever was valuable in Europe and work out its own alternatives *to*, or at least alternative forms *of*, modernity.

The difficulty with the project lay in the fact that the Hindu leaders had no clear conception of what they meant by it, the kind of synthesis they desired and how they hoped to deal with the immensely complex problems raised by it. As they imagined it, Indian civilisation was to provide the 'foundation' upon which was to be constructed the 'structure' of Western ideas and institutions. Western natural sciences were to be 'combined' or 'integrated' with Hindu metaphysics, the Western state with Hindu society, liberal-democratic ideas with Hindu political philosophy, large-scale industrialisation with Hindu cultural values and Western moral values with the Hindu theory of *purushārthas*. This, of course, could not be done. The Hindu ethic of contentment or restriction of desires not only could not sustain but positively inhibited the pace of industrialisation. The caste-based social order militated against both individual dignity and collective action and left only a limited space for the state. Methods of natural sciences could not be synthesised with those of the 'science' of spirit. And the Hindu joint family, which all

Indians cherished, could not be easily reconciled with the liberal ideas of romantic love, privacy and individualism.

If the cultural synthesis was to be viable, Hindu leaders needed to undertake a radical critique of both their own and European civilisation and to reinterpret each in a manner compatible with the other. The old foundation could not sustain a new superstructure. Both had to be reconstructed, each in the light of the needs of the other. The Hindu leaders did not do this. They took what they liked in each and thought they could create a new civilisation by combining the 'good points' of both. They fancied themselves as happily poised between the two civilisations and freely deciding from a non-existent Archimedean standpoint what to retain from each. The naive belief that goodness, like truth, was a coherent whole and that all good things, like all true statements, were necessarily compatible is a recurrent theme in many of their writings.

The result was either eclecticism or, as was often the case, a comprehensive adoption of European institutions. Once their ritual homage to Indian civilisation and vague references to its values are removed, the political programme of many critical modernists turns out to be little different from that of the modernists. They were all for modern science and technology. They proposed no alternative path of industrialisation except to say that it should not go 'too far' and be harmonised with India's spiritual civilisation. They talked about spiritualising politics but did not go beyond advocating the familiar list of public virtues. Though they talked about the need to evolve a plural, uncentralised and sociocentric polity, the one they proposed was little different from the modern state. What basically distinguished them from the modernists was their concern to reform rather than to abolish castes, a greater stress on municipal autonomy, a higher regard for traditional practices and institutions, a deep but ill-articulated desire to give the state social roots, and a preference for cultural gradualism.

This is not to say that the critical modernists did not appreciate the need to indigenise European institutions. Rather, their approach was too mechanical and additive and their reluctance to give up many a traditional belief and practice too pronounced to produce a genuine synthesis. They glibly talked about Indianising imported institutions without asking how institutions conceived within a very different context and suffused with a very different spirit could ever be indigenised, whether their transplantation might not radically change the character of the indigenous culture, and whether they were right to assume that the two civilisations were complementary. Since the spiritual foundation was supposed to be sound and had lasted for several millennia despite brutal assaults, they uncritically assumed that it needed little attention and concentrated their energies on the superstructure. Not surprisingly, the language of synthesis remained a sincere and politically useful but practically irrelevant rhetoric. A creative cultural synthesis *was* possible, but it required greater courage than its proponents displayed and a much greater scope for uncoerced choice than colonial rule permitted.

VII

Critical traditionalism represented the third response by Hindu leaders. The traditionalists, the modernists and the critical modernists were all in their own different ways convinced that civilisations could be compared and assessed on the basis of some universal criteria. The critical traditionalists, who included the later Bankim Chandra Chatterjee, Vivekananda, B.C. Pal, and Aurobindo, rejected that assumption. For them, a civilisation was an organic whole and could not be judged in terms of criteria derived from outside it. All such criteria were themselves ultimately derived from another civilisation and lacked universality. Furthermore, a way of life was bound up with and could not be judged independently of the capacities, habits, dispositions and deepest instincts of its bearers. What was good for others might not be good for it. It, therefore, made no sense to talk about a good society in general and abstract terms.

This did not mean that every civilisation was perfect or self-contained and need not or could not learn from others. Being human creations, all civilisations were imperfect with a recurrent tendency to develop ugly practices, to lose their sense of purpose, and to decline. They could, and indeed should, draw inspiration from those that had faced similar problems, and even adopt some of their practices if they were convinced that these were good for them and cohered with their ways of life. However, no civilisation was a model for another or a source of ready recipes. Each must autonomously identify its needs and problems, assess and mobilise its resources, and *then* borrow from others whatever was likely to augment and enrich them. Accordingly, the critical traditionalists advised their countrymen to follow the method of what Aurobindo called *ātmasātkarna*, that is, 'an assimilative appropriation, making the thing settle into oneself and turning it into a characteristic form of our self-being'.[40] Rejecting the critical modernist idea of borrowing the good and rejecting the bad features of other civilisations, he set out the central principle of critical traditionalism in the following words:[41]

> But besides, these terms good and bad in this connection mean nothing definite, give us no help. If I must use them, where they can have only a relative significance, in a matter of not ethics, but of an interchange between life and life, I must first give them this general significance that whatever helps me to find myself more intimately, nobly, with greater and sounder possibility of self-expressive creation, is good; whatever carries me out of my orientation, whatever weakens and belittles my power, richness, breadth and height of self-being is bad for me.

The differences in the approaches of the critical modernists and critical traditionalists were deep and profound. Although they often advocated the same policies and institutions, their reasons for doing so were radically different. The critical modernists assumed that European and Indian civilisations could be comparatively assessed and synthesised; critical traditionalists considered the assumption preposterous. The former aspired to combine the 'best' features of both and to create a 'new' civilisation; the latter considered such an enterprise absurd and concentrated on regenerating and reforming their own. Despite their sincere search for a creative synthesis, the critical modernists implicitly or explicitly accepted the superiority of European civilisation and asked what aspects of Indian civilisation could be fitted into it; the critical traditionalists adopted the opposite approach. The former aimed to preserve what was *valuable* in Indian civilisation; the critical traditionalists were content to eliminate what was *evil*.

Since the critical traditionalists adopted a different approach to the analysis of India's predicament, one would have expected them to arrive at a different political programme for its regeneration. At one level they did, at another they did not. They were convinced that India needed modern science, a modern state and what Aurobindo called 'great effective ideas ... of social and political liberty, equality, democracy', but disagreed about modern technology and industrialisation. Dayanand Saraswati and B.C. Pal were keen on them; Vivekananda was only moderately sympathetic; Aurobindo was hostile to 'that terrible, monstrous and compelling thing, that giant *Asuric* creation, European industrialism', but felt that India was being 'forced by circumstances' into adopting it. They were all anxious that India should evolve its own appropriate forms of European institutions, but remained delightfully vague on the details. They wanted industrialisation to be 'moderate', 'gradual' and in harmony with the rural basis of Indian civilisation, but did not explain what that involved and how it was to be done. They said that the pursuit of *artha* should be regulated by *dharma* and that India should evolve its own unique alternative to the capitalist and community forms of property, but again declined to specify what that entailed. They wanted India to tease out whatever was valuable in liberalism and to integrate it into a more satisfactory spiritual philosophy of man, but again did not go beyond generalities. Aurobindo, who had thought more about the subject than the others, made out a strong case for preserving India's linguistic, religious, ethnic, regional and other diversities and suggested that it should evolve a form of polity flexible and open enough to respect and encourage them yet strong enough to hold them all together and protect them against external aggression. However, he did not face up to the difficult problems it raised and ended up recommending a federally constituted modern state.[42]

There were two areas, however, in which the critical traditionalists were more specific and significantly differed from the others, namely, the nature of the Indian state and Hinduism. The modernists and, despite their ambiguous rhetoric, even the critical modernists advocated a liberal and secular state standing above and outside society and pursuing the collectively agreed goals of national unity, prosperity, industrialisation and liberal democracy. For them, these goals legitimised it in the eyes of its citizens and gave it moral authority. The critical traditionalists disagreed. The Indian state was a custodian of its civilisation and derived its legitimacy not from its economic and political goals but from its commitment to preserve and revitalise the established way of life. In itself the state was, in Aurobindo's words, a 'mere machine', a 'clumsy convenience for common development' and had only a legal claim on its citizens. It became a moral institution enjoying moral authority when it was grounded in the 'cultural substance' of the community's way of life, that is, when it became an ethical or nation state.

Though the critical traditionalists acknowledged that Indian civilisation had been shaped by many outside influences, they were convinced that it was primarily a creation of the Hindus. The *Vedas*, the *Upanishads*, the *Gitā*, the epics, arts, culture, sculpture, the ways of life and thought—in short, all the things that composed and characterised Indian civilisation were produced by the Hindus. The Muslims and others had certainly influenced it, sometimes decisively, but these influences were all absorbed and integrated into an ongoing civilisation. The Greek civilisation did not cease to be Greek, a unique product and expression of the aspirations and sensibilities of Greek people, simply because it was later influenced by its Roman conquerors. The critical traditionalists felt that the Indian state should grant full cultural and religious autonomy to its minorities but within the framework of and subject to its central task of maintaining its essentially Hindu civilisation.

Since the Hindus were the creators, historical carriers and guardians of Indian civilisation and enjoyed an overwhelming numerical predominance, they were to constitute the cultural basis of the Indian state. All Indians, Hindus as well as others, were to be its equal citizens, but the former were to set its moral and cultural tone. The unity of the Hindus was to be the basis of the unity of the Indian state. For the critical traditionalists, India lacked the cultural and linguistic homogeneity of the European state, and its minorities, rightly jealous of their distinct cultural identities, did not wish to merge into a single cultural or ethical unit. It could not, therefore, become a nation state in the European sense of the entire state forming or becoming coextensive with a single nation. India could only be and ought to aspire to become a nation state in the sense of resting the *Indian state* on the *Hindu nation*. As the critical traditionalists imagined it, the Indian state was to be structured in terms of two separate but related principles of unity. As a legal and political entity encompassing all its citizens, it had one basis of unity. As an ethical and cultural entity, it had another. That was the only way they thought they could ensure that it would never again go under. That was also the only way they thought it could satisfy *both* the deepest and long-frustrated desire of the Hindus to have their own state and the legitimate demands of minorities for equal rights and autonomy.

The other major area in which the critical traditionalists differed from the modernists and the critical modernists related to the nature and role of Hinduism. Since they assigned the Hindus a crucial state-sustaining role, they had to radically reform their religion and social structure along appropriate lines. Surprising as it may seem, many critical traditionalists advocated a programme of reform which was substantially similar to that of the modernists and far more sweeping than that of the critical modernists.[43] The Hindus had become fragmented and were unable to act in concert. While some of the critical traditionalists were content to reform the caste system, others wanted it eradicated. High-caste Hindus had for centuries exploited the lower castes with the result that the latter had converted to other religions or collaborated with foreign rulers. The critical traditionalists advocated *sevādharma* and insisted that higher castes should expiate for their historical sins by unstintingly devoting themselves to the service of their unprivileged brethren. The horrendous practice of untouchability had long placed a substantial number of Hindus outside Hindu society. It had to be abolished and they had to be brought back into the Hindu fold. Quarrels about the nature of God and sectarianism had deeply divided the Hindus. The critical traditionalists, therefore, developed a simple and austere view of Him and reduced religion to morality. The increasingly popular notion of Indians being racially Aryans, which had been warmly embraced by the modernists and the critical modernists, was not only creating a new division between the Aryans and Dravidians but also making Indians foreigners in their own land. While Dayananda Saraswati and some other critical traditionalists fell for it, Vivekananda saw the danger and ridiculed it:[44]

> Now-a-days one hears from all castes that they are *pacca* Aryans.... And also that they are the same race as the English, in fact, first cousins.... They have come to this land from sheer kindness of heart...just like the English.... And their religion is just like that of the English. Their forebears were indistinguishable from Englishmen; only the (tropical) sun has darkened their skin.

The critical traditionalists displayed an acute sense of political realism missing in the others. For them, politics involved conflict and struggle, had its own distinct morality which was sometimes incompatible with the ordinary principles of personal morality, and *loksangraha* was its highest ideal. Human nature was frail and the use of *danda* and *bheda* was often unavoidable in social life. Political struggle was often not so much between individuals as between organised groups, and group loyalty and solidarity were inescapable and highly desirable. Not only the Hegelian Pal and quasi-Hegelian Aurobindo but also Vivekananda maintained that sometimes the hatred of other nations and violent struggles played a 'major' role in the development of a nation and should not be rejected on sentimental grounds. He was even reported to have suggested that statues of gold should be erected in honour of the Chapekar brothers hanged for murdering Captain Rand. The themes of conflict, statecraft, autonomy of political morality, political realism, courage, will power and physical strength, which were all curiously absent in the writings of the modernists and critical modernists, dominated the thought of the critical traditionalists.

Since the critical traditionalists were convinced that India could not regenerate itself without mobilising its own resources, they were merciless in their criticism of it. Their countrymen respected their motives and competence and accepted criticisms from them for which they had harassed and even threatened the lives of modernist reformers. No other leader lambasted Indians as much as Aurobindo, Dayananda Saraswati and, especially,

Vivekananda. Even as they criticised their own civilisation, they were able to admire that of their rulers without feeling nervous and inferior. Vivekananda's assessment of it was fair, balanced and even generous and steered clear of the partisan caricatures of the traditionalists and the uncritical glorification of the modernists, both of whom he treated with thinly disguised disdain. He went to Europe and America not as a pilgrim in search of holy inspiration but as a curious traveller observing and commenting with childlike delight on whatever caught his interest. Only a critical traditionalist could have had the courage and wisdom to tell each civilisation how it appeared to the other. Vivekananda observed:[45]

> Horrendous onslaughts of cholera, decimation caused by epidemics, malaria chewing into the bones and marrow, recurrent bouts of devastating famines, a battleground of disease and misery, a vast cremation ground strewn with skeletons where all hope, enterprise, joy and enthusiasm have perished and therein the *yogi* deep in meditation in quest of *moksha*—this is what the European traveller sees (in India).

> Three hundred million sub-human creatures, their souls crushed for centuries under the feet of everyone, compatriots and aliens, coreligionists and people of other faiths alike, capable of slave-like industry, listless like slaves, without hope, without any past or any future, concerned only with bare survival in the present by any means available, with the slave's proneness to jealousy, intolerant of their compatriot's success, cynical and without faith like the men who have lost all hope, stooping to low cunning and trickery like the jackal, the ultimate in selfishness, bootlickers to the powerful, verily the god of death to the powerless, weak, devoid of any moral stamina, spread all over India like maggots feeding on stinking rotten flesh—this is our image in the eyes of the English official.

> Intoxicated by the heady wine of newly acquired power, fearsome like wild animals who see no difference between good and evil, slaves to women, insane in their lust, drenched in alcohol from head to foot, without any norms of ritual conduct, unclean, materialistic, dependent on things material,

grabbing other people's territory and wealth by hook or crook, without faith in the life to come, the body their self, its appetites the only concern of their lives—such is the image of the Western demon in Indian eyes.

Like critical modernism, critical traditionalism, with which it was widely confused, was a popular response to British rule. Though it was most influential between 1870 and 1920, its appeal was not confined to that period. Its merits were obvious. It was articulated by some of the most acute philosophical minds of modern India and had an intellectual rigour and subtlety lacking in its rivals. It developed a coherent and carefully worked out political philosophy grounded in Indian reality. It understood the nature and dynamics of political life better than the others. It combined respect for tradition with an open-minded approach to modernity and was less squeamish than the critical modernists about rejecting many a traditional belief and practice.

It had, however, serious limitations. It failed to appreciate the simple fact that Hinduism covered such a wide range of beliefs and practices that none of these was shared by all its adherents, not even the belief in God, reincarnation and the law of *karma*. The Hindus could not, therefore, be religiously or even culturally united without imposing an arbitrarily selected set of beliefs upon and thereby alienating the rest. Unlike Christianity, Islam and other religions, Hinduism was not a religion to which a Hindu subscribed; rather, it was largely whatever a Hindu over time had come to believe and practise. The Hindus could not, therefore, become a nation or even an ethical unit in the sense intended by the critical traditionalists. Furthermore, any attempt to unite them inevitably alarmed the minorities so that, far from becoming the basis of the Indian state, the unity of the Hindus subverted it. It was hardly surprising that the militancy of the critical traditionalists in the early years of the twentieth century intensified Muslim separatism. Even as they misunderstood Hinduism, they misunderstood Indian history. The Muslims were not a minority in the ordinary sense of the term and had ruled India for nearly five hundred years. Islam had profoundly shaped Hinduism and not only introduced new beliefs and practices but also altered its internal structure and self-perception. It had, in turn, been so deeply influenced by Hindu culture that it was quite different from its counterparts in Persia, Turkey, Afghanistan and elsewhere from which it had initially come to India.

Thanks to all this, the identity of the Indian civilisation had undergone a profound mutation and could no longer be equated with its classical Indic basis. It was a product of the pre-Muslim past, which itself included not just Hindu but Buddhist, Jain, tribal and other influences, as well as Muslim and European cultures. If all Indians were to be able to identify with it and develop a common sense of citizenship and belonging, Indian civilisation would have to be so defined as to acknowledge its diverse origins and highlight its synthetic and plural character. The critical traditionalists were thus caught in an acute dilemma. Hindu nationalism could not form the basis of Indian nationalism, not only because it was narrow and exclusive but also because Hindu culture itself was too deeply influenced by others to be capable of being defined independently of them. One could not be both a Hindu nationalist and an Indian nationalist, and the critical traditionalists could champion either only by jettisoning the other. Their naive desire to have both involved them in all kinds of conceptual and political muddles, a predicament that continues to bedevil their contemporary successors including the Bharatiya Janata Party.

Chapter Three

Gandhi and *Yugadharma*

I

Gandhi's thought both continued and broke with the tradition of discourse developed by his predecessors. Unlike the traditionalists who blamed the conquest of India on British duplicity, cunning and superior force, many other Hindu leaders attributed it to its own weaknesses. Gandhi agreed with the latter; the 'English have not taken India; we have given it to them'.[1] It was because Indians were disunited and distrustful of each other that a small group of 'armed merchants' had been able to manipulate, divide and defeat them and consolidate its rule. 'They are not in India because of their strength, but because we keep them'. Like many of his predecessors, again, Gandhi thought that on balance British rule had been in India's interest. The British had, no doubt, exploited and drained India, ruined its traditional industries, destroyed its cultural pride, treated its people with contempt, imposed their 'materialist' and industrial civilisation, and in general distorted India's 'natural' line of development. They had also, however, energised and 'awakened' it, taught it new political ideals, introduced the scientific spirit of curiosity, restless search for truth and accuracy of thought and expression, brought Indian religions into a fertilising contact with Christianity and drawn India into a wider community of nations. He thought that from about 1919 onwards, the character of British rule began to change for the worse and reached its nadir in 1921. It betrayed its ideals, broke its repeated promises to introduce representative institutions, subjected Indians to the most humiliating indignities, including the notorious crawling orders and public floggings, turned the army into a band of 'hired assassins' and showed utter contempt for public opinion. Gandhi turned 'disloyal' and declared himself an implacable foe of the Raj. For him, as for millions of mainly middle-class Indians, the Rowlatt Acts and the Jallianwala Bagh marked the turning point.[2]

Unlike his predecessors, Gandhi's explanation and critique of colonial rule were essentially cultural. The British were a trading nation who had come to India in search of markets. And they had been able to consolidate their rule by brainwashing their subjects into thinking that their ways of life and thought were inferior to those of their rulers. The sword alone was unable to hold India; it had to be supplemented by an ideology. Had the Indians shown no interest in British goods, their rulers would have had no reason to conquer let alone stay on in India. And had they not accepted British values, institutions and practices, their rulers would not have won over their minds and hearts and acquired moral legitimacy. So long as India was 'bewitched' and 'hypnotised' by British civilisation, it was bound to remain a British colony. Even if the British political rule ended, the rule of British capital would continue. And if the latter too ended, the British 'spirit' would continue to rule over India. Colonialism was an ontological phenomenon and consisted in destroying the cultural autonomy and integrity of the subject country.[3]

Unlike his predecessors, Gandhi insisted that the colonial encounter was not between Indian and European but *ancient* and *modern* civilisations.[4] This apparently trivial reformulation gave him advantages denied to them. While their formulation was territorial and neatly divided the world into East and West or Asia and Europe, Gandhi's was temporal and allowed him to affirm the unity of mankind even within a colonial context. Since his predecessors had talked of Indian civilisation, they faced the problem of showing how a territorially specific civilisation could be universalised. For Gandhi, it embodied and sought to preserve values cherished by all pre-modern civilisations, and hence, its universality was not adventitious but inherent in it. Furthermore, by calling the European civilisation modern, he isolated it in time and space and undermined its universalist claims. It was a historical upstart and did not represent the whole of Western civilisation. And it was confined to a small section of mankind. It had neither a historical depth nor a geographical spread except when imposed by force.

Gandhi's formulation also had other advantages. He was able to remind modern Europe of its great historical heritage and to alert it to the growing danger of losing it. He was able to reassure his countrymen that they were fighting not just for themselves but for entire mankind, and thus to give them the desperately needed moral self-confidence. By detaching modern civilisation from its pre-modern past, Gandhi also made it easier for himself to borrow many central principles of Christianity.

Like his predecessors, Gandhi considered Indian civilisation spiritual and the European materialist, but defined the terms differently. Following the traditional Hindu rejection of the matter–spirit dualism, many of them had argued that spirituality referred to the spirit informing an activity. No activity was in itself either spiritual or material; it all depended on the spirit in which it was conceived and conducted. Sexual activity represented man's search for union with another person and was a form of participation in the vital task of preserving the species and the social order. As such, it was deeply spiritual provided, of course, that it was guided by *dharma* and did not overstep its limits. It became carnal and unspiritual only when based on lust and selfishness. This was equally true of such other activities as the pursuits of *artha* and power.

Gandhi's thought displayed a strange ambiguity. Sometimes he accepted the traditional conception of spirituality and the concomitant theory of *purushārthas*. For the most part, however, he drew a rigid distinction and postulated an irreconcilable conflict between spirit and body. The human being was essentially a spirit and the body was a mere appendage, a prison. It not only threw up all manner of desires that hindered spiritual growth but also, as a very condition of its survival, forced him to engage in many acts of violence. For Gandhi, sexual activity was *inherently* carnal and regrettably necessary only because there was no other way of preserving the species. He felt the same way about the pursuit of *artha*, which was primarily concerned to procure the means necessary to satisfy ever-increasing and ultimately pointless desires for bodily pleasures. For him, spirituality necessarily required self-conquest, mastery of the senses, and was incompatible with the pursuit of bodily activities and pleasures.

To avoid misunderstanding, the conflict between the spirit and the body, as Gandhi saw it, was quite different from and had nothing to do with the conflict between the spirit and the world believed by some of his predecessors to be lying at the heart of Hindu thought. Gandhi rejected this latter distinction. The cosmic spirit was identical with the totality of its manifestations and was realised by identifying oneself with them in the spirit of love and service. Dissolving oneself in *Brahman* consisted in becoming one with and dedicating oneself to the tireless service of all creation, especially living beings. Gandhi's view of spirituality was thus intensely worldly. His distinction between the spirit and the body was drawn within the framework of the *identity* between the spirit and the world, and designed to distinguish two different classes of worldly activities, devoted respectively to the pursuits of spiritual well-being and physical pleasures.

Though Gandhi's critique of modern 'materialist' civilisation was similar to that of his predecessors, it did contain novel elements. It had a strong moralistic and puritanical thrust and condemned much that they had admired. He criticised large-scale industrialisation because it disrupted cosmic harmony, took a crudely instrumental view of non-human creation, prized bodily pleasures, was propelled by greed, weakened self-discipline, involved an exploitation of fellow-men both at home and abroad, and destroyed morally self-sustaining local communities. He did not think much of the modern state either. It was highly centralised and intolerant of self-governing communities. Enjoying the monopoly of violence, it relied on the use or threat of force and did not activate the moral energies of its citizens. It was impersonal and bureaucratic, a 'soulless machine' which ruled by means of rigid rules and discouraged personal responsibility and initiative. It made a fetish of territorial integrity, thought little of sacrificing human lives in defending every inch of it and jealously demanded its citizens' exclusive loyalty. Gandhi did not think much of liberal democracy either. It was individualistic in the sense of stressing rights rather than duties and self-interest rather than altruism, and materialistic in the sense of being concerned solely with deriving its moral legitimacy from its ability to promote the material interests of its citizens. It lacked moral orientation and turned the state into an arena of conflict between organised groups. The crude adversarial system of governance on which it was based had a tendency to exaggerate differences, discourage the spirit of compromise and to rigidify political discourse. Not that Gandhi was hostile to such liberal values as liberty, equality, constitutionalism and the rule of law; rather, he felt that they suffered from the limitations of the materialist civilisation of which they were a product and needed to be differently defined and grounded.

Since Gandhi took a narrower view of spirituality than his predecessors, his interpretation of Indian civilisation differed from their's in several respects. He thought little of and was even embarrassed by its sensuality, especially sexuality. He rarely referred to the erotic tradition and its creative expressions in art, literature and sculpture. To be sure, some of his predecessors took little interest in it either, as it would have made them look just as sensuous and even 'vulgar' as their materialist rulers and denied them a moral edge. Unlike them, Gandhi did not think much of India's past commercial achievements, its trading tradition, entrepreneurial skills and preoccupation with *artha*. Nor did he share their enthusiasm for the great Maurya and Gupta empires and the Kshatriya tradition of military valour. As was his wont, he never explicitly criticised or attacked any of these. He simply ignored and marginalised them and concentrated on offering his own spiritual interpretation of Indian civilisation.

For Gandhi, India was a 'truly spiritual nation', 'predominantly the land of religion', based on a deeply held belief in the 'moral governance' of the universe. The Indian lived in constant awareness of and bore daily witness to the pervasive presence of the divine. His entire life was structured in the spirit of *yajna*, and his every activity was a grateful offering at the divine altar. The best minds of India, no less inquisitive and creative than their modern European counterparts, had devoted themselves to cultivating the 'science of the spirit' and made 'most marvellous discoveries', infinitely more impressive than the 'wonderful discoveries in things material' made by Europe. Although Gandhi nowhere listed them, he had in mind such beliefs as that the universe was structured and informed by the cosmic spirit, that all men, all life and indeed all creation were one, that man's deepest fulfilment and happiness lay in attaining unity with an increasingly wider range of human beings, that he was uniquely constituted, came to terms with himself and the world in his own unique manner and must remain free to live by his own truth, and that *satya* and *ahimsā* were the highest moral principles.

For Gandhi, Indian civilisation was essentially plural and non-dogmatic. From the very beginning, it had realised that the ultimate reality was infinite and inexhaustible and that different individuals grasped different aspects of it. None was wholly wrong and none wholly right. Everyone was, therefore, left free, even encouraged, to live out the truth as he saw it and to discover for himself its limits and possibilities. This was why, in his view, Hinduism allowed its adherents full freedom of choice between different religious texts, conceptions of God and forms of worship.

Indian civilisation was not only plural but pluralist, that is, committed to plurality as a desirable value, not just a collection of different ethnic, religious and cultural groups but a unity-in-diversity. Since it held that different men perceived ultimate reality differently and that a richer view of it could only be attained by a dialogue between them, it not only tolerated but respected and welcomed diversity and encouraged discussion between its constituent groups. It was an open civilisation with permeable boundaries allowing new influences to flow in and vitalise the old, so that the new became part of the old, the old was discarded or vitalised, and the whole civilisation renewed itself. Over the centuries, Gandhi went on, Indians 'blended with one another with the utmost freedom' and made India a microcosm of the world, a 'synthesis of different cultures', a happy family whose members, vastly different in temperaments, habits and modes of thought, enjoyed a relaxed relationship.[5] Thanks to its history of tolerance and synthesis, a unique 'spirit' had grown up in India and become an integral part of its way of life. Indeed, India had developed an arcane 'faculty for assimilation' and an 'amazing tolerance for opposite ideas'.[6] When a new religion or culture appeared, it did not have to fight for survival or claw out a quiet corner. Instead, the others moved a little and left it enough space for growth. As a result, even the most intolerant newcomers did not remain so for long. The 'dominant spirit' of Indian civilisation subtly and imperceptibly loosened their rigidity, smoothed their sharp edges and brought them in harmony with the rest. To be on Indian soil was to breathe the refreshing air of infinite diversity and to watch with admiration and delight the most ingenious ways in which individuals and groups skilfully negotiated their differences and created an integrated society without central coordination.

For Gandhi, India's epistemological pluralism provided the elusive key to its survival and to its remarkable ability to come out not only unscathed but positively richer from the three 'mighty assaults' it had faced in its history, namely, Buddhism, Islam and Christianity.[7] In each case it imbibed 'whatever was good' in the three religions and emerged refreshed 'as one would rise out of a hot bath with a warm glow'. Gandhi's assessment of Muslim rule was less hostile than that of many of his predecessors. He agreed that the early Muslim invaders and rulers had been oppressive, tyrannical and brutal, but insisted that, over time, they had been won over by the synthetic spirit of Indian civilisation. As they settled down, they entered into a dialogue with their subjects and absorbed many Hindu beliefs, values and social practices. This was facilitated by the fact that most Muslims were converted Hindus and carried the pluralist spirit to their new religion. Over time, Islam became 'Indianised' and shed some of its alien and aggressive features. Not only at the religious but also at the political level, the two communities forged common bonds of loyalty and sentiments. 'It was Hinduism that gave Mohammedanism its Akbar.' Though Hindus and Muslims had fought from time to time, these had been basically 'quarrels between the brothers', born out of simple misunderstandings and a lack of sensitivity. Their quarrels had become more frequent and vicious since the end of the nineteenth century, largely because of the British policy of 'divide and rule', and would be brought under control in independent India. Even when communal carnage raged all around him in the 1940s, Gandhi refused to reconsider his view. To have admitted that it had deeper roots would have impugned the validity of his panglossian and partial view of Indian history.

Gandhi analysed Christianity along similar lines. When Christian missionaries first came to India, their message of love and brotherhood as well as the 'pure lives' of some of them deeply impressed the Hindus, especially the lower castes. Not surprisingly, many Hindus, including some from the higher castes, converted to Christianity. Once the British consolidated their rule and the missionaries came to be seen as its spokesmen, they lost their moral authority and had to rely on force and bribes to secure converts. Gandhi thought that like the other two religions, Christianity too had stimulated internal reforms within Hindu society and religion and exercised a salubrious influence.[8]

In Gandhi's view, every civilisation had its own distinctive natural and social basis. Modern civilisation was born and could only survive in the cities, and was naturally carried all over the world by the commercial classes. Indian civilisation had, by contrast, been cradled and nurtured in the villages, and only the rural masses were its natural custodians. So long as their way of life was intact, its integrity and survival was guaranteed. If the villages were to disappear and their traditional moral and social structure were to be shattered, it would lose its socio-geographical basis and its fate would be sealed for ever. Since the civilisations that had so far come to India were all rural and thus posed no threat to it, it was easily able to accommodate and enter into a dialogue with them. Modern urban civilisation presented an unprecedented and deadly challenge and called for a most discriminating response.

II

Like his predecessors, Gandhi argued that Indian civilisation had become degenerate and developed serious 'defects' and 'excrescences'. He drew up a lengthy list of them. Most of the items on it were similar to those identified by his predecessors, but some were new. He was particularly worried about the degeneration of the Indian, especially Hindu, character. As he put it, 'The first thing we have to do is to improve our national character. No revolution is possible till we build our character.'[9] Unlike most of his predecessors, he defined Indian degeneration almost entirely in moral terms, that is, as a decline in moral character and ideals. He lamented the absence of physical, intellectual and especially moral courage among his countrymen, the pervasive spirit of selfishness, cynicism, distrust and jealousy, and the inability to sink differences, transcend self-interest and to work for a common cause.[10] Like Vivekananda, whom he read but rarely mentioned, he too regretted the absence of social conscience and the feelings of compassion and mutual concern. He agreed that India had a long tradition of *ahimsā*, but contended that it often expressed itself in 'effete sentimentalism' rather than an active and self-sacrificing love of fellow men. The Hindus strongly disapproved of killing animals, yet exploited the weak and the poor and watched thousands die without compunction.[11] 'We are all guilty of having oppressed our brothers. We make them crawl on their bellies before us and rub their noses on the ground. . . . Has the English government ever inflicted anything worse on us?'[12]

Since India's crisis was moral in nature, Gandhi argued that the process of its regeneration required *ātmashuddhi* or purification of the national soul by means of a sustained national *tapasyā*. Thanks to its *karma* over the past few centuries, its soul had lost its '*sāttvic*' tendencies and acquired *tāmasic* ones, and it needed to mount a massive national *yajna* or 'moral revolution'. Unlike a social or political revolution, a moral revolution could not be undertaken over the heads of its intended beneficiaries and entailed a personal commitment and an intense soul-searching on the part of every Indian. The programme of national *ātmashuddhi* had to be so designed that each of them was able to participate in it and 'purify' himself.[13] Gandhi thought that his *satyāgraha* and Constructive Programme achieved this objective. Unlike parliamentary and revolutionary struggles, *satyāgraha* required every Indian to suffer and make sacrifices for his country. And the Constructive Programme required him to follow a way of life involving identification with and an active service of his fellow-men.

Since degeneration had struck deep roots, Gandhi thought that the masses were unable to tackle it themselves and needed guidance. Though no Indian was completely free from the degenerate tendencies and each needed to examine his conscience and purify himself, some were more free than others and could provide leadership. Like almost all his predecessors, Gandhi was an elitist, but took a very different view of the type of elite India desperately needed. For him, English education, a mastery of modern science and technology, parliamentary skills, an intimate knowledge of European civilisation and history and so on, which were stressed by almost all of them, were at best irrelevant and at worst a grave handicap. Since India's crisis was moral, it needed moral leadership, that is, one that was 'pure' and self-disciplined, deeply rooted in Indian civilisation, familiar with the vernacular mode of moral discourse, capable of conversing in Indian languages, devoted to the service of ordinary people, willing to live and work in the villages and, for reasons to be discussed later, leading a life of *brahmacharya*. Gandhi knew that he could not attack the increasing domination of European civilisation without also attacking the power and authority of its indigenous representatives and replacing them with authentic sons of the soil.

He argued that even as an individual improved his character by mobilising his moral resources and building up his strength, a community or a civilisation had no alternative but to begin with and build on what it already had. This did not mean that India should not learn from other civilisations, including the Western. On the contrary, it should enter into a sympathetic dialogue with them and take whatever was valuable and cohered with its *swabhāva*. Since his position was often misunderstood, he observed, 'My resistance to western civilisation is really a resistance to its indiscriminate and thoughtless imitation based on the assumption that Asians are fit only to copy everything that comes from the West.'[14]

Unlike the traditionalists and even some of the critical traditionalists, Gandhi was a strong proponent of cross-cultural borrowing. As we shall see, he took over several important ideas from Christianity, Tolstoy and Ruskin without the slightest feeling of guilt, so much so that his Hinduism acquired a deep Christian orientation. In this respect, he was not very different from the critical modernists. While they borrowed heavily from modern European civilisation, he plundered Christianity and the dissenting subtraditions within modern Europe. The difference between them was not about the propriety of borrowing but about what to borrow.

Though Gandhi saw nothing wrong in learning from Europe, his major worry was that since his countrymen had no clear idea of the central principles and weaknesses of their civilisation, they did not know what to borrow and remained vulnerable to passing fashions and crude or subtle pressures of the colonial rulers. Even the most conservative Indians indiscriminately borrowed institutions and values incompatible with the central principles and ideals of their civilisation. He felt that even Tilak and Madan Mohan Malaviya were guilty of this. 'Deep down in his heart he (Tilak) would like us all to be what the Europeans are.... He underwent six years' internment but only to display a courage of the European variety'.[15] He thought even less well of such religious leaders as Dayananda Saraswati and Savarkar who had 'all too hastily' accepted some of the central values of modern civilisation, read them back into their own and subverted the very civilisation they claimed to defend. Although some of them claimed otherwise, they were all infatuated with modern civilisation and sought India's salvation in imitating it.[16]

For Gandhi, the only proper and realistic course of action open to India was to take a careful and critical look at itself in a 'discriminating conservative spirit'. For the past few centuries, India had become 'static', 'asleep', 'inert'. Thanks to its welcome contact with the West, it had both 'awakened' and gained access to the scientific spirit of inquiry. It must now turn inward, identify and critically reinterpret the central principles of its civilisation in the light of modern needs and use them as the basis of its carefully planned programme of self-purification. A dialogue with another civilisation should 'follow, never precede, an appreciation and assimilation of our own'. Once they felt convinced that some of its values and institutions were good for them and could be integrated into their ways of life and thought, Indians should courageously adopt them without feeling in the least guilty or nervous about doing so. This was not 'imitation' or 'copying' which was widely condemned as a sign of the 'de-nationalised' Indian's sense of inferiority, nor 'eclectic borrowing' widely criticised by the modernists for its lack of courage, but creative 'adaptation' to the 'needs of the age'. 'Adaptability is not imitation. It means power of resistance and assimilation.'[17] Europeanisation meant rejecting Indian civilisation in preference to another; assimilating *some* European values and practices *because* they were freely *judged* to be in its best *interest* was very different. Such as assimilation was an act of free choice and did not compromise India's moral autonomy; it was undertaken in full knowledge of what it needed and could easily absorb, and hence not inauthentic; and it was consistent with the synthetic spirit of its civilisation.

Given his manner of analysing the Indian predicament, it was hardly surprising that Gandhi was unsympathetic to the four approaches developed by his predecessors. He attacked the traditionalists for failing to appreciate the depth of Indian degradation and the gravity of the moral crisis facing it. As we shall see later, almost all his fierce social battles were fought with them. In his view, they had failed to grasp one of the central insights of their civilisation, namely, that all existence was subject to the all-destroying principle of *Kāla*. Thanks to its remorseless operations, one *yuga* succeeded another throwing up new problems and demanding new responses. *Kāla* could not be conquered by ignoring it and sticking to the *yugadharma* of a superseded *yuga*, but only by creatively reinterpreting and adapting the 'timeless' principles of Indian civilisation to the changing times.

Gandhi was no less critical of the modernists. He shared their view that the crisis confronting India was grave and unprecedented and required a radical response, but disagreed with their diagnosis of its causes and manner of dealing with it. For him, the crisis was moral in nature, one of national character and values, and called for a moral revolution. The modernists were wrong to regard it as essentially economic and political in nature, a crisis of institutions and practices that could be resolved by borrowing relevant European institutions. Institutions were formal structures only as good as the individuals who ran them. A nation's character was improved not by importing foreign expertise but by an inspiring moral leadership capable of speaking in its native idioms, activating its hidden moral nerves and creatively reinterpreting and mobilising its traditional resources. Alien institutions produced parrots who repeated what they were taught and did not generate inner or organic changes. The only way to transform a community was to revivify, revise and reform its established institutions and to link up the old with the new. This was not a matter of patriotism but common sense. Since Indians knew how to operate traditional institutions, they would not need to learn new skills. And since these were an integral part of their way of life, reforming them aroused least hostility and caused minimum upheaval.

Gandhi was sympathetic to the idea of creative synthesis advocated by the critical modernists but not to the way they understood and implemented it. Insofar as it implied a willingness to learn from other societies, he was all for it. He was, however, most hostile to its shopping list approach. Civilisations were more or less coherent wholes and could not be promiscuously combined. Besides, in any such combination, the more confident and aggressive partner invariably exercised a dominant influence, especially if it also happened to be in a position of power. This was why Gandhi thought that the project of cultural synthesis had become a vehicle of backdoor Europeanisation. He was also highly critical of its underlying assumptions that the two civilisations were on a par and that Indians were at liberty to choose bits and pieces of each. He rejected the assumptions because he thought that the Indian civilisation was superior and also because Indians who were profoundly shaped by it lacked the freedom of an abstract and unconditioned choice.

Gandhi was far more sympathetic to the critical traditionalists. In his view, they had rightly identified the Indian crisis as essentially moral in nature. They were also right to insist that a civilisation was an organic whole, that it had its own distinct *swabhāva* and that it could only be reformed in harmony with its innermost impulses. However, he was convinced that they were neither critical nor traditionalist enough. In their own way, they were dazzled by modern civilisation and unwittingly defined their own in terms of it. They had also not dug deep enough into their civilisation to see if it had the resources to cope with the crisis and how it had dealt with similar ones in the past. Crises were not new to India and it had survived them all by evolving its own distinctive manner of dealing with them. The past could never provide answers to the present, but it did suggest a *method* of finding them. Since the critical traditionalists did not appreciate this, they borrowed or indigenised European institutions rather than explore alternatives more suited to India. The alien institutions were bound in due course to subvert the very civilisation they claimed to love and wished to preserve.

III

For Gandhi, then, India was in the throes of a grave moral crisis. Thanks to the universal domination of modern civilisation, the world had entered a new age. And thanks to colonial rule, India had been ushered into it. The new age had come at a time when India had lost its old experimental vitality, become degenerate, deeply divided, effete, passive and sentimental, and lacked the courage to meet new challenges. The crisis had gone so deep that even its best minds were paralysed and looked abroad for models. It had highlighted some of the basic limitations of Indian civilisation and demonstrated beyond doubt that unless repaired and regenerated, it was doomed. At one level, British rule offered India a chance to turn the corner; at another, it created problems of unprecedented magnitude and threatened the very integrity of its civilisation.

Like his predecessors, Gandhi had no satisfactory explanation of Indian degeneration. Unlike many of them, he did not condemn the caste system and Muslim rule, and that ruled out two of the most popular explanations. Many traditionalists and critical traditionalists had blamed the doctrine of *ahiṃsā* and traced India's decline to the acceptance of Buddhist teachings. Gandhi rejected this 'fashionable' view because it was 'untrue' and impugned the validity of his own message. Sometimes he blamed such popular religious leaders as Swaminarayana and Vallabhacharya for 'robbing us of our manliness' and encouraging emotional self-indulgence. But he also said that other Vaishnavite leaders had the opposite influence, and he never explained why these doctrines and *sampradāyas* had become popular. Sometimes he blamed the unworldly orientation of Hinduism, but on other occasions he thought that it was not inherent in it and represented a biased Brahminic reading. Like his predecessors, he was also not clear about when Indian degeneration had begun. Sometimes he thought it was relatively recent; sometimes he traced it to the trauma of Muslim invasions; on other occasions he traced its roots even further back, saying on one occasion that Indian society had been in a 'rut almost since the days of Guptas', which was nearly sixteen hundred years ago. Gandhi had too little knowledge of Indian history to identify the nature and causes of its degeneration. He was far more interested in how to reverse it than in its causes, and did not appreciate that the two issues were closely related.

Gandhi was convinced that India could not tackle its current crisis without reconstituting itself on a new *yugadharma*. 'It is good to swim in the waters of tradition, but to sink in them is suicide.' He went on, 'No moral progress or reform is possible if one is not prepared to get out of the rut of orthodox tradition. By allowing ourselves to be cribbed by cast-iron social conventions we have lost'.[18] As he put it towards the end of his life, India could not escape the 'necessity and desirability of reform, discarding the old and building a new system of ethics and morals suited to the present age.'[19] Gandhi saw himself as a moral legislator or law-giver giving his country a new *shāstra* or *smriti*. Though he did not find the time to write one as he had wanted to do, he wrote quite a few *ācharsamhitās* and, in the manner of the Hindu sages, turned his life itself into a living *shāstra*.

Gandhi's lifelong quest for a new *yugadharma* began in South Africa. When he started his campaign against its racist policies, he ran into two difficulties. First, the whites launched a series of vicious attacks on Indian habits, character and civilisation, arguing that a people so corrupt, degenerate and uncivilised were not entitled to equal rights. While dismissing some of their silly and ignorant criticisms, Gandhi felt that the others, painful as they were, had a basis in facts. Second, he found it extremely difficult to activate and organise his countrymen. Rather than fight for their rights, they acquiesced, resorted to bribes and underhand dealings or expected Gandhi to do their fighting for them. He was so frustrated by their timidity, there incapacity to organise, factiousness, political naivety and lack of public spirit that he asked them to 'rebel' against themselves and sadly observed, 'If we behave like worms we should not blame others for trampling upon us.' He knew he had to do something to build up their character and self-confidence.

Accordingly, he began to write regularly in the *Indian Opinion*, advising his countrymen on matters of personal and public hygiene, social, civic and political morality, the best way to educate and bring up children, how to walk, talk, sit, sleep and behave in public and even on why it was wrong to burp and to break wind in public. Some of his concerns sprang from a sense of racial inferiority and a desire to make Indians more acceptable to the whites. However, he soon outgrew them. He also regularly reported on the latest scientific discoveries, commented on national and international events, and translated whatever books and articles happened to impress him. Almost like a father anxious for his child to grow into an adult of his dream, he was anxious that his countrymen should enjoy access to the best and the latest in the world and develop into an energetic, courageous and disciplined people.

Gandhi continued his work on his return to India. He wrote extensively and often critically about traditional Hindu morality, sexuality, duties of husband and wife, parents and children, teachers and pupils, leaders and followers, employers and employees, of neighbours, friends, widows, government ministers, citizens and those in charge of running private and public organisations. He criticised Hindu religious and social practices, the Indian lack of punctuality, the habit of not answering letters, wastefulness, the ill-treatment of the poor and the weak and social and economic inequalities and injustices. He wrote about all this in pamphlets, books, extensive private and public correspondence and especially in his weekly papers whose crucial pedagogical importance he was one of the first Indian leaders to realise.

Gandhi's concern to develop a new *yugadharma* raised the crucial question as to how to arrive at and 'validate' or justify it. Despite his vacillations, he knew that intuition, inner voice and personal preferences were too nebulous and subjective to carry conviction, especially in the 'modern age of science'. He criticised tradition and could not turn to it either. Since science represented the spirit of the age and was the only currently acceptable mode of acquiring and legitimising knowledge, he thought his best hope lay in appealing to it. That created a problem. His countrymen, especially those he was concerned to persuade, only accepted the authority of tradition, and science had no appeal for them. Gandhi hit upon an ingenious idea. He rejected the science-tradition dichotomy and insisted that all traditions, especially the Indian, were based on science.[20] There was no other way to arrive at valid knowledge than the method of 'rigorous research', 'experience' and experiment, and that is what both science and tradition did. Whenever Indian civilisation faced a moral or religious crisis, its most talented men temporarily withdrew from the world and embarked upon rigorous spiritual researches and experiments to discover new moral principles. This was as true of the ancient *rishis* and authors of *dharmashāstras* as of the Buddha, Mahavira, Nanak, Kabir, Ramkrishna Paramhamsa and countless others. In appealing to science, Gandhi said that he was doing no more than following the Indian tradition.

Though Gandhi nowhere provided a systematic statement of his conception of science, he said enough to indicate its broad outlines.[21] For him, science aimed to discover truth by means of carefully planned and controlled observations and experiments. An experiment necessarily presupposed a hypothesis, and the latter, in turn, a theory. If corroborated, the hypothesis was accepted and the theory stood confirmed; if refuted, it was rejected and the validity of the theory was at least partially impugned. Since the possibility of contrary evidence in future could not be ruled out, all knowledge was 'tentative' and subject to almost certain future revision. Until a hypothesis or a theory was disconfirmed, the scientist was entitled to act on it provided that he retained a healthy 'scepticism' about it.

Since an experiment presupposed a body of rules and procedures, a hypothesis and a theory, which were all precipitates of investigations conducted over a period of time, it presupposed a tradition of inquiry. The tradition began tentatively and was built up by a succession of talented scientists, each building on, criticising, revising and extending the work of his predecessors. Its findings, rules and procedures had authority because they had all been developed and validated in a manner approved by it. While most scientists engaged in routine investigations, the greatest among them challenged the inherited body of knowledge and gave the tradition a new turn. Such breaks were made within the context of the tradition, for a total or absolute break was inherently impossible. No scientist could embark upon his inquiry without accepting the established rules, procedures and instruments, each of which was capable of revision but not all of them at once. The scientific tradition, therefore, grew by means of discontinuities within the context of a continuing tradition, each discontinuity revising and becoming part of the tradition.

For Gandhi, scientific inquiry was co-extensive with the search for truth and not confined to the natural sciences. Human beings asked moral, religious, political and other kinds of questions, and there was no reliable way of answering them save by means of 'research' and experiment. There was, indeed there had to be, a science of the spirit analogous to the science of the material world. Even as the natural sciences sprang from the desire to understand and conquer nature, the science of the spirit sprang from man's need to understand and master himself. Like the former, the latter explored the laws of the moral and spiritual world, including the best way to activate moral energies and impulses, the kinds of life and activity in which men were most likely to find their happiness and fulfilment, and the way human beings influenced one another, built up a sense of selfhood, constructed and could deconstruct the ego. These and other questions were of utmost importance and required most rigorous research.

Gandhi argued that this was how people had for centuries gone about answering them. They tried out different rules, practices, activities, ways of life, forms of human relationships, values, principles and ideals, and distilled their findings into what was called collective wisdom or moral tradition. The wisdom was passed on from generation to generation, each adapting it to its distinct requirements and revising and enriching it in the light of new difficulties and insights. Obviously these experiments were *ad hoc*, largely unconscious and unplanned and sometimes hastily assessed. However they were not without value. Their findings had served mankind well, stood the test of time and often survived the most hostile scrutiny of modern science.

Gandhi thought that every community had a tendency to throw up, from time to time, great spiritual scientists who consciously embarked upon such experiments in search of moral and spiritual truths.[22] He had in mind such men as Jesus, Mohammed, the ancient Indian sages, Zoroaster, Moses, the Buddha, Mahavira, and the great saints of all religions. They were not deluded or victims of blind faith but great spiritual explorers who observed the lives of their fellow-men, reflected deeply on contemporary societies, lived by and, in that sense, experimented with prevailing ideals or whatever else caught their imagination, and arrived at a body of insights which either validated or reformed their tradition. It was true that many prophets spoke of divine revelation, but their remarks had to be read with care. Revelation was a cryptic way of referring to the insights they had acquired after years of intense search and research, and was really a form of inspiration. After all, great scientific discoveries were also products of inspiration. Scientific inspiration did not come to scientists at the start of their career. It required a deep familiarity with tradition, an intense effort and a touch of genius, and was only accepted after it had survived a careful scrutiny. Spiritual inspiration or so-called divine revelation was no different. It was a 'ripe fruit' of sustained *sādhana*; only a few had the courage to claim it, and of those who did, fewer still survived the test of time. The great prophets did 'see' or 'hear' certain truths, but these terms had to be understood in a scientific not a mystical sense. What they saw and heard was a culmination not a denial of a scientific inquiry.

For Gandhi, every religion was a tradition of spiritual inquiry begun by a spiritual genius. His followers were inspired by his example to conduct similar researches according to prescribed rules and procedures, and confirmed, deepened and revised his insights. Over time a religious tradition grew up whose truths were accepted as such by its adherents, not on the basis of the personal authority of any individual including its founder, but because they had been repeatedly validated by the research of a number of people over a period of time and were capable of being validated by anyone prepared to undergo the required training and perform the necessary experiments.

Even as vested interests had sometimes tried to arrest scientific inquiry and hindered the growth of scientific knowledge, men with narrow visions had sometimes tried to prevent spiritual researches and to reduce the discoveries of a spiritual genius to rigid dogmas.[23] In Gandhi's view, this had happened to such organised religions as Islam and especially Christianity. The church, whether Protestant or Catholic, had reduced Christianity to a rigid body of beliefs and practices no Christian was allowed to question. Religion, a self-critical tradition of inquiry, was reduced to theology, a scholastic and apologetic exegesis of old truths. For Gandhi, the distinction between theology and religion corresponded to that between *jñāna* and *vijñāna*. *Jñāna* referred to bookish knowledge; *vijñāna* consisted in living by it, letting it 'sink into experience' and validating or revising it. Since Christianity and Islam tended to freeze spiritual knowledge, they insisted on blind faith and turned their founders into infallible superhuman beings. Gandhi thought that this did grave injustice to the prophets, perverted the true spirit of religion and paved the way for its eventual decline.

Hinduism was in this respect unique.[24] It never lost sight of the central fact that religion was an unending quest, not a body of dogmas but a science of the spirit, not a matter of faith but a tradition of inquiry. That was why it did not believe in a one-off and final revelation, set up a church or required specific beliefs. Its history was a story of new insights constantly gathered by great spiritual adventurers. It was constantly cultivated and fertilised by courageous men rejecting the straitjacket of established practices and daring to try out the unconventional. Some of their experiments were bizarre and even offensive, but that was the price every scientific tradition had to pay. Some of them came up with different truths, thereby giving rise to new sects within the catholic and ever-widening Hindu tradition. Hindus who knew the great value of their work honoured them, fed them, exempted them from social conventions and cherished their memories.

Since Gandhi saw religion as a science, he saw scriptures as scientific texts containing profound but corrigible wisdom.[25] Prophets were not pandits used to weighing every word, and the ordinary language could never carry the full weight of their deepest insights. Just as scientific tradition was ultimately embodied not in scientific theories and books but in the manner of thinking of eminent scientists, religious tradition was fully manifest not in its scriptures but in the lives of its best men. Their lives, parables and sayings, therefore, had hermeneutic priority over the scriptures. Even as only those suitably trained had the right to interpret scientific texts, only those who had sincerely tried to understand and live by their religious tradition had the *adhikār* to interpret its scriptures.

Gandhi's interpretation of the religious tradition in general and of Hindu tradition in particular gave him several advantages not available to his predecessors. Since Hindu tradition had allegedly always relied on experiments to arrive at new truths, he said that he not only had the *adhikār* but also *dharma* to conduct new experiments to determine a new *yugadharma* and that his scientific inquiry was not an alien import but enjoyed the legitimacy of tradition. He was also able to secure its sanction for some of his most untraditional experiments, especially in the field of celibacy. Since tradition had exempted its creative explorers from social conventions, he asked for a similar freedom.

IV

For Gandhi, then, the desperately needed new *yugadharma* could only be discovered and validated by means of extensive scientific research and experiments. The task was too vast to be executed by one man alone and required a team which Gandhi could lead but never replace. Accordingly, he built up a group of what he called his 'fellow-seekers' or 'co-researchers' and invited them to conduct their own experiments and share their findings with him and with one another. He also set up *āshrams*, his laboratories as he called them, in which he trained researchers and conducted experiments in such diverse areas as intermediate technology, diet, self-discipline, *brahmacharya*, new modes of communal living and new principles of social organisation.

Gandhi conducted various experiments in his personal, professional and political life. He experimented with the best way to acquire a complete mastery over the senses and 'discovered' that none of them could be conquered in isolation from the rest. Since he found that the life of self-discipline was not easy, he experimented with the practice of taking vows to build up his will power and concluded that they were indispensable. He discovered that the first step on the road to self-conquest was the most difficult, but that once it was taken each subsequent step was progressively easier and generated a 'relish' for a disciplined life. As we shall see, he conducted unusual experiments in the field of sexual self-discipline and concluded that a simple diet of fresh fruits and nuts, periodic fasting, the control of the palate, a cold bath, absorption in socially useful work and chanting the name of God were most helpful. Again, since a non-vegetarian diet involved violence to sentient beings, Gandhi experimented with various kinds of vegetarian diet and concluded that fresh fruits, vegetables, nuts and milk supplied all the bodily requirements. He discovered that milk was a sexual stimulant and probably involved violence, but could not discover a 'fruit substitute' for it. He thought that the aggressive modern medicine violated the autonomy of the body, prevented it from developing its own internal resources and involved violence to animals. Accordingly, he decided to dispense with it and found that if left alone, the body had the capacity to overcome several diseases by its own indigenous strength, that sexual self-control protected man against most diseases and that nature cure was often the best remedy.

Determined to live a life of absolute honesty, Gandhi decided that as a lawyer he would never lie, mislead a judge, tutor his clients, plead a false case, or outwit his opponents. He took up only those cases in which his clients were innocent, tried to settle them by conciliation, fully cooperated with his opposite number in collecting and presenting all the facts of the case, and told the judge all he knew about his client. When he ran into difficulties, he explored ways of overcoming them. Over time, he found that it *was* possible to lead the life of an absolutely truthful lawyer. As a political leader, his greatest experiments related to the method of *satyāgraha* for which he turned the entire country into his laboratory. He tried it out in different situations and against different types of opponents. When he failed, he introduced new modes of action. He said that he was like a scientist charting a wholly new terrain, that his science was 'still in the making' and that his research was 'not yet complete'. He wrote about these and other experiments in his autobiography appropriately entitled *My Experiments with Truth*.

Under his inspiration, some of his colleagues set up their own 'laboratories' dotted all over the country. They conducted experiments in different areas of life and met regularly at the national level to compare their findings in something resembling a national seminar under Gandhi's chairmanship. His weekly journal took on some of the features of a scientific periodical in which he and others described and commented on each other's experiments. A large number of Indians in no way associated with him tried out little experiments in their personal lives and sometimes exchanged their experiences. Indeed, the language of experiment became quite fashionable and Gandhi presided over a vast *vijñānayajna*.[26]

Gandhi claimed to have arrived at his conception of *yugadharma* on the basis of his own and his colleagues' experiments as well as the moral insights of the great spiritual explorers of different religious traditions, especially Hinduism and Christianity. He said that his own experiences had confirmed the 'truth' lying at the heart of all religious traditions that the universe was not merely material but spiritual in nature and was informed and structured by the cosmic spirit. Apart from the familiar cosmological and teleological arguments which had nothing experimental about them, he cited the unexpected divine guidance he claimed to have received in moments of despair. Gandhi's *yugadharma* spelt out the implications of this belief. Since man was a spiritual being, his happiness and fulfilment lay in identifying himself with the cosmic spirit. The cosmic spirit did not exist independently of but was identical with the totality of creation. Identification with it, therefore, consisted in identifying oneself with all creation, especially all humans and all life. Since love was the highest form of identification, this involved universal love. Negatively, love implied non-injury; positively, it implied the active promotion of others' well-being. True religion or identification with God thus consisted in an active and unstinting service of fellow men.

Every age and every country had its own distinctive forms and sources of suffering, and hence, the nature and content of social service varied.[27] In the earlier ages when India was a 'happy and just' society, the *rishis* were perhaps justified in retiring to the forests. Since modern India was deeply scarred by acute poverty, vast social and economic inequalities, foreign rule and extensive moral degeneration, the active service of its people consisted in removing these evils. In the modern age, all aspects of individual and social life were directly or indirectly organised and administered by the state. Its presence was ubiquitous, and all human relationships were politically mediated. This was particularly the case in India and other colonies. Since politics was pervasive, it was the central terrain of action and no one could hope to serve his fellow-men and eliminate social and economic ills without active political engagement. If political life could be spiritualised, Gandhi argued, it would have a profoundly transformative effect on the rest of society. In every age a specific area of life was the unique testing ground of religion and morality and offered them a unique opportunity to retivalise themselves. In the modern age it was politics, and no religion could be taken seriously that failed to address itself to its challenges. Political action was, therefore, the only available path to *moksha*. As he put it:[28]

> Every age is known to have its predominant mode of spiritual effort best suited for the attainment of *moksha*. Whenever the religious spirit is on the decline, it is revived through such an effort in tune with the times. In this age, our degradation reveals itself through our political condition ... Gokhale not only perceived this right at the beginning of his public life but also followed the principle in action. Everyone had realised that popular awakening could be brought about only through political activity. If such activity was spiritualised, it could show the path of *moksha*.
>
> .... In this age, only political *sannyāsis* can fulfil and adorn the ideal of *sannyasa*; others will more likely than not disgrace the *sannyāsī's* saffron garb. No Indian who aspires to follow the way of true religion can afford to remain aloof from politics. In otherrds, one who aspaspires to a truly religious life cannot fail to undertake public service as his mission, and we are today so much caught up in the political machine that service of the people is impossible without taking part in politics. In olden days, our peasants, though ignorant of who ruled them, led their simple lives free from fear; they can no longer afford to be so unconcerned. In the circumstances that obtain today, in following the path of religion they must take into account the political conditions. If our *sadhus, rishis, munis, maulvis* and priests realised the truth of this, we would have a Servants of India Society. In every village, the spirit of religion would come to prevail all over India, the political system which has become odious would reform itself.

For Gandhi, then, every Indian had a duty in the modern age to become politically involved and to help regenerate his country. Political involvement took a number of forms and occurred at a variety of levels. Although participation in the struggle for independence was obviously important, it was not the most important and could itself take different forms. Since independence was merely formal and had no meaning without national regeneration, 'true politics' consisted in revitalising Indian society, culture and character by working in the villages, fighting against diseases, hunger and local injustices, helping ordinary men and women acquire courage and self-respect, building up local communities and people's power, and in general devoting oneself to creating an energetic, courageous, cooperative and just country. Every activity that contributed to the realisation of this goal was political in nature. Politics was not necessarily connected with, let alone exhausted in, the state. Indeed, the fact that it should be so understood showed the extent of degeneration both in India and elsewhere. The state had become the sole arena of political activity because modern citizens had surrendered all their moral and social powers to it. Their regeneration consisted in retrieving them and evolving non-coercive modes of settling disputes. True politics involved removing the 'addiction' to the state and necessarily occurred outside it. *Sevādharma*, or wiping away every tear from every eye in a spirit of universal love, was the new *yugadharma* and the central goal of all human activities.

Gandhi's view that politics was a spiritual activity was not novel and had been advanced by a large number of his predecessors such as Gokhale, Tilak, Ranade, B.C. Pal and Aurobindo. Gandhi himself said that he had borrowed the phrase 'spiritualisation of politics' from Gokhale, his 'political guru'. Several important differences, however, separated him from them. While many of them separated politics and spirituality and talked of spiritualising politics, for Gandhi the two were identical. Politics was itself a spiritual activity, and all true spirituality culminated in politics. For most of them spirituality largely meant morality, and politics was spiritual in the sense of being a moral activity. Hardly any of them saw it as a vehicle of *moksha*. Indeed, they would have been horrified by such a view. Again, many of them generally defined morality in social terms and equated politics with social reform. Gandhi was one of the first to define morality in political terms, and politics in terms of active struggle against injustice and oppression.

V

Since Gandhi's *yugadharma* differed in several crucial respects from Hindu religious tradition, he could not get it widely accepted without radically reinterpreting the latter. Accordingly, he redefined all its major categories in activist and social terms and established novel relations between them.[29] He urged other religious leaders to undertake similar reinterpretations of their religions so that all Indians could share a common moral and political culture based on a shared conception of *yugadharma*.

Gandhi redefined the concept of *moksha* and almost equated it with *dharma*. It did, of course, mean to him what it meant to the tradition—namely, the dissolution of individuality into *Brahman*. However the dissolution consisted not in a mystical unity with it but in losing oneself in the active service of mankind. Indeed, as we saw, he made politics the only adequate path to it in modern India and gave *karmayoga* a wholly new orientation. By defining *moksha* in this way, Gandhi was also led to redefine the state of mind traditionally associated with it. Traditionally, it implied *ānanda* or a state of supreme joy. For Gandhi, it involved not only *ānanda* but also *dukha* or suffering, for to identify oneself with all beings was to suffer for and with them and to make their suffering one's own. *Mokṣha*, therefore, meant not so much avoidance of or freedom from suffering as finding joy in sharing and ceaselessly striving to relieve it. As he said, 'Joy comes . . . out of pain voluntarily borne'. It is hardly surprising that he should have described his fasts as sources of both supreme peace and intense agony.

The Hindu philosophical tradition had stressed the central importance of *tapasyā* in attaining self-purification. Gandhi agreed, but totally redefined it. '*Tapasyā* does not simply consist in betaking oneself to the forest and sitting down there surrounded by fires. That *tapasyā* may even be the height of folly.'[30] Gandhi's amusing and unkind description of it barely conceals his contempt for it. In his view, true *tapasyā* consisted in suffering in the service of one's fellow men and included *satyāgraha*, voluntary poverty and even fasting. Gandhi contended that *sannyāsa* too meant renouncing not the world but the self. 'A *sannyāsi* is one who cares for others. He has renounced all selfishness. But he is full of sleepless and selfless activity.' He was not a recluse but a selfless worker 'burning with agony' and actively fighting against the injustices of his society. 'A *sannyāsi*, therefore, to be true to his creed of renunciation, must care for *swarāj* not for its sake but for the sake of others.'[31]

Gandhi also redefined the doctrine of *yoga*. Patanjali had elaborated several *yamas* and *niyamas* to be observed by a spiritual aspirant. Gandhi reinterpreted them all and added a few of his own so as to increase the individual's capacity for sustained social service. He replaced the traditional repertoire of spiritual exercises with a wholly new set of his own, including cleaning latrines, living and working among the untouchables and nursing the sick. Cleaning latrines was, in his view, a better way of acquiring self-discipline, 'reducing oneself to a zero' and learning the dignity of labour than some of the traditional methods. And living and working among the untouchables was a far more effective way of realising the unity of mankind than meditation.

Again, to Gandhi, *samādhi* meant not leaving the world and engaging in intense meditation for days on end, but temporary withdrawal from the daily routine in order to compose one's thoughts and to reflect on the meaning and significance of one's actions. It did, of course, require the temporary 'shelter of a cave'; however, 'I carry one about me if I would but know it'.[32] Like *samādhi*, *dhyāna* meant periods of silence in the midst of and as a preparation for intense involvement in the world. They were not 'like jewels to be kept locked in a strong box. They must be seen in every act of ours'. Gandhi also changed the traditional concept of *āshram*. Unlike the ancient and modern *rishis*, he located his first *āshram* in India on the outskirts of a major industrial city and used it to conduct experiments in education, spinning, weaving and other productive activities as well as to train a cadre of committed social workers and *satyāgrahis*.

Even as Gandhi redefined the central categories of classical Hinduism, he radically reinterpreted many of the beliefs and practices of folk Hinduism. God did not exist in heaven, heaven and hell were metaphors describing conditions in the world, and He was to be found not in temples but in the huts of the poor. Prayer did not consist in chanting hymns and devotional songs but in serving other men as a way of serving God. *Yajna* consisted not in concluding formal *karma-kānda* and rites but in seeing the entire life as one continuous offering at the altar of mankind. The true worship of God consisted not in visiting temples but nursing the sick, helping orphans and improving the conditions of the poor and the untouchables. Spinning as a way of identifying with the poor was 'the greatest prayer, the greatest worship'. For Gandhi, wearing khadi was more sacred than wearing beads and saffron robes. Not the so-called holy rivers and towns but the places where the poor and the untouchables lived were truly holy, and working and living among them in the spirit of a pilgrim was a true pilgrimage.

In these and other ways Gandhi not only reinterpreted and reformed but reconstructed Hinduism on a new foundation. He rationalised it and reduced it to a set of such basic principles as truth, love and *ahimsā*. He marginalised the countless gods and goddesses and, although he defended them against ill-conceived criticisms, he made it clear that he did not think much of them and that they were little more than a ladder for those in need of one. He de-theologised Hinduism and dismissed scholastic debates about the meanings and canonical status of the *shāstras*. When asked which *shāstras* were central to Hinduism, he replied that every Hindu had to decide it for himself! He de-scripturalised Hinduism and turned it into a living tradition of critical and unending inquiry, the *shāstras* being little more than guideposts. He opened up Hinduism to the influences of other religions and re-established the Hindu's traditional right to borrow from them whatever he considered valuable. In the ultimate analysis, Gandhi reduced Hindu tradition to a valuable resource: it was not a mere mass of raw material to be combined as one pleased nor a rigid and inviolable structure of beliefs and practices, but a cluster of important and carefully collected insights demanding respect but not blind obedience. Not beliefs and practices, which were products of changing circumstances, but moral insights and ideals, which had a perennial significance, constituted the core of a religious tradition including the Hindu. To belong to a religious tradition was to share allegiance to its central principles, not to be committed to upholding its historically contingent practices and beliefs.

VI

As we observed earlier, Gandhi's conception of *yugadharma* required that India should evolve its own appropriate alternatives to modern institutions which his countrymen were anxious to adopt and of whose limited value he was himself convinced. India had its own civilisation, rich in insights, ideas, institutions, skills of survival, resourcefulness and a long historical experience of adapting to change. It should explore ways of revitalising it by critically teasing out and adopting the central *insights* of modernity while rejecting its alien and ill-suited European *forms*.

In the modern age, no community could survive without a centrally coordinated structure of authority capable of uniting and enforcing its will on its citizens. For centuries, India had neglected this and paid a heavy price. The highly centralised modern state was one way of doing so. While it might suit the relatively homogeneous European society, it did not make sense in India which was really a society made up of scores of cohesive groups proud of their traditions of self-government and long united by diffused civilisational ties rather than an overarching political order. Instead of reproducing the state, India should become a whole made up of wholes. It should set up a loosely united, minimally centralised and federally constituted polity based on long-established regional, religious and local units running their affairs according to their customs and practices within the framework of and subject to the discipline of a minimum body of general laws. The unity of the Indian polity should be neither purely formal, as proposed by the modernists, nor based on the substantive unity of beliefs, as advocated by the critical traditionalists. Rather, it should be grounded in the organic unity of its constituent units. The central government should encourage the self-governing communities to maintain order, to negotiate their relations with one another and to undertake welfare and other activities, and should do little more than facilitate and coordinate their work.[33]

Gandhi realised that his proposal carried no conviction with his countrymen. It would seem that he himself thought it impracticable under present conditions. A loosely knit polity would be unable to stand up to powerful economic and religious groups, nor could it reduce India's vast social and economic inequalities and regional disparities. As he acknowledged at the 1931 Round Table Conference, independent India could not improve the conditions of untouchables without a massive programme of compensatory discrimination. And that called for a centralised and strong government. A weak polity could not deal with the recurrent outbreaks of inter-communal violence either.

Gandhi was not prepared to give up. Even if India was unable to evolve an alternative to the modern state, it should at least try to work out an alternative model of it. As independence drew closer, he proposed that the Indian National Congress be dissolved and turned into a *lok sevak sangh*, a national organisation of *samagra grāmsevaks* scattered all over the country and acting as all-purpose local leaders. They were to educate the masses about their rights, duties, proper methods of cultivation, family planning and habits of hygiene and sanitation. They were also to reconcile the various communities divided by deep differences, to campaign against and mount *satyāgrahas* against local injustices, to mobilise local moral energies against evil social and religious practices, and in general to help construct vibrant local communities and build up 'people's power'. As Gandhi imagined it, the new Indian polity was to rest on two pillars, the 'official state' wielding legal authority and the reconstituted Congress exercising moral authority over the citizens. They were to cooperate in the massive task of national *ātmashuddhi*, but also to remain distinct and to confine themselves to their respective spheres of work. Though Gandhi himself did not put it this way, he saw the new polity on the model of the traditional Kshatriya-Brahmin alliance. The state would perform the Kshatriya function of ruling over society; the reconstituted Congress would play the traditional Brahminic role of safeguarding and regenerating the Indian civilisation and guiding, advising and, when necessary, opposing the state. Whatever one might think of Gandhi's ingenious proposal, it showed what he meant by creatively reinterpreting and mobilising the cultural resources of tradition.

Gandhi explored alternatives to other modern institutions along similar lines. The spirit of modern science was most valuable and worth adopting. It consisted of intellectual curiosity, a restless search for truth, exactness in thought and expression and carefully planned research and experiments. Modern Europe did not know how to use it and allowed it to dictate its own logic and momentum. Accordingly, it used science to develop faster and faster modes of transport and communication, increasingly more luxurious lifestyles, lethal means of destruction and huge machines, with the result that science ended up subverting the European ways of life and thought. There was no reason why

India should go that way. It should bring the spirit of science in a critical dialogue with tradition and use it to refine and enrich rather than to replace its long-established way of life. Instead of repeating the European mistake of letting science dictate its own agenda, it should place it at the service of society and use its intellectual resources to improve traditional methods of agriculture, cooking, spinning and weaving, to reinterpret and reform old customs and practices, to improve traditional medicine rather than invent new ones and to evolve intermediate technology. Gandhi thought that India should similarly develop its own alternative to the imported capitalist and communist forms of property along the lines of his theory of state-regulated trusteeship.

VII

We have outlined Gandhi's conception of *yugadharma* and the manner in which he arrived at and validated it. It shows how much he both remained within and moved away from the Hindu religious tradition. At one level he was a product of it, and most of his central categories, such as the cosmic spirit, the unity of man, of life, and of all creation, *moksha*, rebirth, *ahimsā*, *satya*, *nishkāma karma*, epistemological pluralism and moral individualism, were derived from it. However, he redefined and established new relations between them and introduced several others drawn from other religious traditions or developed by him. Not surprisingly, his view of Hinduism bore only a limited resemblance to its traditional conception.

. Some of Gandhi's ideas had no parallels in Hindu tradition. His emphasis on the dignity of manual labour was new and is not mentioned by any of his nineteenth century predecessors with the limited exception of Vivekananda. When he took it to its logical conclusion and advocated cleaning latrines as a way of identifying with the untouchables and dissolving all traces of egoism, he frightened away even Gokhale's Servants of India Society. His equation of religion with social service had been anticipated by only a few nineteenth century leaders, and his view that a total and lifelong commitment to wiping away every tear from every eye was the *only* path to *moksha* was almost entirely new. His insistence that every man was a publicly accountable trustee of his time, talents and wealth, that he should only use them for socially beneficial purposes, and that lack of punctuality and failure to answer letters represented violations of a moral trust finds no echo in the Hindu tradition. His emphasis on struggles against injustices, his intense concern for personal integrity, his fierce loyalty to his conscience, his acute sense of personal responsibility for the actions of his countrymen, and the notions of vicarious atonement and redemptive power of suffering love underlying his fasts had no analogues in the Hindu tradition either.

As we shall see, he took over and so radically redefined many traditional concepts that most Indians had difficulty making sense of them. Thus, while for them, *ahimsā* meant non-injury and non-destruction of life, for Gandhi it meant positive love and doing all in one's power to promote human well-being. The Hindus and Jains who fed ants and animals but exploited their fellow-men or did nothing to alleviate human suffering were practising *ahimsā* in their own eyes but *himsā* in his. His concept of *satyāgraha*, too, bore only a limited resemblance to the traditional Hindu forms of protest. Unlike *trāga, dhārnā* and *hijarat*, *satyāgraha* was based on love, relied on the power of uncomplaining suffering and sought to mobilise the opponent's moral energies. Gandhi's fast too had only a limited basis in the traditional Hindu conception of it. It was not merely an act of self-purification or moral pressure, but involved taking upon oneself the burden of others' guilt, mobilising their moral energies and redeeming and uplifting them. Like his conceptions of *ahimsā* and *satyāgraha*, Gandhi's concept of the redemptive fast was based on a creative combination of some Hindu ideas and practices with the Christian concepts of vicarious atonement and suffering love. They were all new to both traditions and owed their origins to his creative synthesis of them. What he said of Ram Mohun Roy was just as and perhaps even more true of him:[34]

> He made a deep study of Hinduism . . . and then allowed himself to be influenced by the essential principles of Christianity and Islam. As a result, he saw that there was for him no

escape from inaugurating a new movement to liberalise the existing Hinduism which had been overgrown with superstitious weeds.

While a good deal of what Gandhi says about the new *yugadharma* makes a lot of sense and badly needed to be said, it is open to two serious objections. First, its content is inadequate and fails to connect with the character of the modern *yuga*. Second, it is poorly grounded. Let us take each in turn.

By definition, *yugadharma* must be relevant to and practicable within the context of a specific society within a specific *yuga*. If the analysis of the *yuga* is faulty, *dharma* based on it cannot be otherwise. This was the case with Gandhi. With great foresight he realised that India had entered an age the like of which it had never seen before, that British rule was qualitatively different from the earlier Muslim rule and that India faced a crisis of unprecedented magnitude and intensity. He saw more clearly than most of his contemporaries some of the central limitations of his civilisation, both in general and in the context of the modern age. He rightly stressed that it was oppressive, unjust, unequal and lacking in social conscience and compassion, and that its central values, largely defined in negative and passive terms, left a good deal to be desired. Since Gandhi's diagnosis was correct in these respects, those parts of his *yugadharma* that were based on it were persuasive and rightly caught the popular imagination. His emphases on *sevādharma*, moral and social equality, an active concern for the poor and the oppressed and a respect for animals and nature were all well taken.

Gandhi was, however, too hostile to some of the basic tendencies of the modern age to understand, let alone enter into a sympathetic dialogue with it. Since he opened up himself to the influence of Christianity, Islam, and the dissident strands within modern Europe, his moral philosophy greatly benefited from his dialogue with them and acquired an unusual depth and breadth. Had he similarly entered into the spirit of modern civilisation, he would have realised that it was not only about bodily pleasures and selfish accumulation of wealth. It also had its spiritual side expressed in its love of knowledge, search for truth, refinement of sexuality, concern for the poor, self-discipline, and respect for human dignity and rights. What was more, modern civilisation had produced all these not by accident but as necessary consequences of its inner logic, and they were as much a part of it as those Gandhi rightly condemned.

Since Gandhi was antipathetic to modern civilisation, he could not understand the deepest hopes, fears and aspirations of his countrymen. Contrary to what he thought, its influence was not confined to the so-called 'English educated' elite and had begun to permeate the consciousness of ordinary men and women—for Gandhi the authentic vehicles of Indian civilisation. They were beginning to value and demand the right to make their own choices, organise their lives, choose their occupations, to see western films and read western romantic novels, to see the world, travel abroad and to enjoy life without a sense of guilt. Gandhi's self-sufficient village communities, hereditary *varna* system, disapproval of desires beyond the bare minimum, intense moralism, *brahmacharya* and anti-intellectualism had, therefore, little appeal for them. To the extent that Gandhi's *yugadharma* frowned upon the burgeoning ambitions and aspirations of his countrymen and ignored the economic and cultural changes occurring all around him, it invited rejection.

This is evident in his proposed alternatives to or rather alternative modes of responding to modernity sketched earlier. The kind of industrialisation Gandhi had in mind would have made sense if India was beginning its historical journey with a clean slate. After over a hundred years of British rule, its patchy and uneven industrialisation had begun to generate forces of which his plan took no account. Furthermore, Gandhi's alternative was based on the naive belief that industries would remain confined to the spaces neatly earmarked for them, that machines would obey the moral laws laid down for them and that even his limited industrialisation would not penetrate human consciousness and generate greed, aggression, competition and conflicts of organised interests. The well-planned and balanced industrialisation he advocated involved restrictions on the movement of labour and capital, central coordination and strong administrative structures, all of which sat ill at ease with his view of the state.

Gandhi's theory of the state runs into similar difficulties. As we saw, he moved away from the model he had sketched in *Hind Swarāj* when he realised the magnitude of the task facing India.

His proposal to disband the Congress came too late and it is doubtful that it would have produced the results he expected of it. The new state would have been helpless without a well-organised political party and remained even more at the mercy of bureaucracy than was and is still the case. The danger that the reconstituted Congress might have constantly carped at and immobilised the state and denied it the opportunity to consolidate itself and acquire moral legitimacy in the popular mind could not be ruled out either. It would seem that Gandhi himself saw this. That was why perhaps he did not press his proposal and kept urging his impatient followers not to interfere with the deliberations of the Constituent Assembly and the policies of the new government. Gandhi, thus, was left with neither an alternative *to* nor an alternative Indian model *of* the modern state.

This was not because his proposal lacked sense and cogency. He rightly saw that the liberal democratic practice of building opposition within the state in the form of opposition parties concentrated all political energy within the state and deprived society of political power. He was also right to argue that his proposal fitted in with India's sociocentric tradition and offered the country a unique opportunity to experiment with a non-statist organisation of collective life. The difficulty with his proposal was twofold. First, it took little account of the acute economic and political problems facing post-independence India which could not be tackled without a strong and at least moderately centralised state. Besides, it encouraged a deep suspicion of the state and could not but prevent it from striking moral roots in a culture traditionally inhospitable to it. Since India needed a state, as Gandhi himself came to appreciate, and since a state cannot grow in a climate of hostility, which he did not, his proposal had a contradictory thrust. Having been a rebel all his life, he only saw the state from the outside and appreciated its dangers but not its importance and conditions of growth. Second, Gandhi overestimated India's political and cultural resources. For centuries India did not have a public space, a vibrant political culture, a body of active citizens and channels of organised self-expression, and lacked the capacity to sustain the kind of disbanded Congress he had in mind. Even under Gandhi's leadership, it remained a weak and rather passive organisation largely welded together by his charisma and only springing into action in times of crisis. Furthermore, thanks to industrialisation and colonial rule, such self-governing communities as did once exist and which Gandhi idealised were fast disappearing and losing their vitality. In the absence of adequate cultural, economic and political underpinnings, Gandhi's otherwise sound suggestion remained utopian.

VIII

Having so far discussed some of the strengths and limitations of the content of Gandhi's *yugadharma*, we should briefly consider his mode of validating it. As we saw, he claimed a scientific status for it and argued that it was based on his own research and experiments as well as those of the great 'spiritual scientists' of the past. A good deal of what he says makes sense. He was right to reject the dominant positivist view of science and to replace it with a broader, softer and more humane alternative. He rightly insisted that experiments were not confined to laboratories, that facts were of many different kinds, that not all evidence was or need be 'hard', 'objective' and quantifiable, that conclusions were related to premises in ways which could not all be reduced to the naive induction-deduction dichotomy, and that not all knowledge was amenable to a propositional form. In taking this view, Gandhi denied science the monopoly of knowledge, and the scientists the monopoly of science. He affirmed the dignity of common sense against scientific arrogance, of individual and collective wisdom against narrow-minded professionalism, of lived experience against contrived experiments, of life against the laboratory. He was right to reject the non-cognitivist ethics of the positivists and to insist that values were grounded in and had to be tested against human experiences.

While all this was well-taken, Gandhi's science of the spirit remained deeply flawed. As he himself said, experimental science was the 'spirit of our age'. He was, therefore, wrong to universalise it and anachronistically extrapolate it to the premodern ages. There is no evidence, and he produced none, to show that any of the great prophets were engaged in, or saw themselves as engaged in, spiritual experiments. His view had some support in Hindu tradition but only to a very limited extent, and none outside it. To see religion as a *tradition of inquiry* rather than as a body of dogmas was certainly an illuminating conceptualisation of its nature and a highly original way of protecting its autonomy against aggressive and crude positivism. However, to see it as a *science* was to undermine the integrity of both. It raised expectations about religion and subjected it to criteria it could never meet. And it led to an unacceptably loose view of science, more or less equating it with mere experience.

This becomes clear if we examine the 'scientific' basis of Gandhi's *yugadharma*. It ultimately rests on a belief in the existence of the cosmic spirit, from which he derives the principles of the unity of man, life and creation and the ethics of universal love and social service. His case for the belief is unconvincing. The limitations of teleological and cosmological arguments are too well-known to need reiteration. And Gandhi's limited personal experiences are hardly enough to validate it and they can in any case be explained differently. This is not to say that the cosmic spirit does not exist, only that it might not, and that is enough to endanger his moral edifice. It might be argued that its existence is not and can never be a matter of proof and involved faith and personal commitment. Such a fideist option, however, is not available to Gandhi because of the scientific status he claims for religion. Gandhi was right to argue that human interests were intertwined, that in harming and degrading others individuals also harmed and degraded themselves, that the whites who treated blacks and Asians as subhuman ended up behaving as subhuman beings themselves. And he was right to contend that the implied doctrine of human interdependence and solidarity was not based on faith but born out of experience. However, there was nothing scientific about this, and it rested on a number of hidden assumptions about how men ought to live.

It is striking that not many of Gandhi's experiments generated new moral and political 'truths' or led to conclusions much different from the conventional moral and political beliefs of a middle-class Hindu. Most of the 'truths' he discovered, for example, vegetarianism, the importance of vows, sexual discipline, matrimonial fidelity, non-injury to living beings, truthfulness, control of the senses and a simple and austere way of life, have for centuries been an important part of Hindu moral tradition.

His *satyāgraha* experiments were certainly original and interesting, but they did not warrant his rather large claims. They did not always work against the British, and he had to resort to such methods as social ostracism, economic boycott and fast unto death, none of which was 'purely moral' in nature and thus a *satyāgraha* in the strict sense of the term. They did not work against the Muslims either and, despite Gandhi's assertion to the contrary, probably would not have made any impact on Hitler or Stalin.

Prima facie it is puzzling that Gandhi's sincere and carefully planned experiments only ended up endorsing and conferring spurious 'scientific' legitimacy on many a traditional Hindu belief. I suggest that the explanation may perhaps be found in their two basic features. First, although Gandhi thought otherwise, he was not so much experimenting with truths as with living according to *already accepted* truths, an important distinction blurred by the English expression 'experiments with truth' as well as its Gujarati original (*satyanā proyogo*). He took a good deal of Hindu metaphysic and morality for granted. He accepted that *Brahman* alone was real, all life was one, selfhood was an illusion, and so on, none of which was a truth based on his own or anyone else's experiments. And he uncritically accepted such principles of middle-class Hindu morality as vegetarianism, truthfulness, non-violence and matrimonial fidelity. He was not interested in trying out different values or ways of life and making a comparative assessment as, for example, John Stuart Mill had proposed. Rather, he was only concerned to live by one set of values, and his experiments were designed to ascertain if he could do so, what difficulties he encountered and how to overcome them. His experiments were, thus, intended not to discover new truths but to try out old ones, and formed part of the technology of moral conduct rather than a science of moral principles. As he himself once admitted, they were little more than 'various practical applications' of certain general principles.

Second, Gandhi's experiments were not only born in faith but also sustained and limited by it. He could have confined himself to a specific way of life and yet made important discoveries if he had not approached it with a largely uncritical mind. Take, for example, his *satyāgraha* experiments. A few of them succeeded, but others failed. When they failed, he did not reconsider them, or moderate his claims. Instead he blamed himself, his followers and his methods and contended that if only they could all become morally perfect they would be able to 'melt even the stoniest heart'. Since man can never be God, Gandhi put his claim beyond empirical verification. He assured the Jews that if they practised *satyāgraha* against Hitler, the latter would be won over. When a sceptic doubted his claim, he remarked that Hitler might initially slaughter a few thousand Jews but was bound eventually to get satiated! If the Jews 1 ad followed Gandhi's advice and failed, he would almost certainly have said that the number of dead was not large enough or they were not sufficiently pure! Gandhi's claims far exceeded his experiments. They had little experimental support and were ultimately based on faith.

This is not at all to say that his experiments were without value. Since they were conceived within and designed to try out a particular way of life, they explored its potentialities and deepened and enriched it. They also yielded a wealth of useful material on how to cope with the difficulties attendant upon living up to high moral ideals. And his determination to live by his chosen ideals whatever the obstacles was itself a source of moral inspiration. Gandhi was not content with this and went on to claim a scientific status for his *yugadharma*. As we saw, his experiments were too culturally limited and dogmatic to justify such a claim, and more generally the very idea of a moral science that Gandhi's project presupposed is inherently suspect.

Chapter Four

Theory of Non-violence

Though it was deeply influenced by the Hindu, Jain, Buddhist and Christian theories of non-violence, Gandhi's theory was in a class by itself. It differed from them not only in its basic assumptions and concerns but also in its manner of origin and logical character. He considered *ahimsā* one of the highest moral values and sincerely endeavoured to live by it. In the course of doing so, he encountered difficult situations and painful dilemmas. He wrestled with these, conducted bold and imaginative experiments, reflected on their results and systematised his insights into a theory of *ahimsā*. As the theory was born out of his experiences and tested against the reality of life, Gandhi claimed that it was not an abstract intellectual construct but 'scientific' in nature and represented his contribution to the hitherto undeveloped 'science of *ahimsā*'.

Since Gandhi lived a public life in the sense of leading his entire life in public, his experiments in *ahimsā* became public property. He described them and their results in his weekly paper and invited comments. Numerous readers commented on them, sometimes agreeing but more often disagreeing with his views. Some also wrote him agonising personal letters describing the difficulties they had faced in the course of living by the principle of non-violence and asking for his guidance. Some others sought his responses to hypothetical situations and proposed alternative ways of defining and applying non-violence. Gandhi patiently dealt with every query, either by private communication or through the columns of his paper. When his decision, advice or action was controversial, the correspondence went on for weeks. Since his correspondents belonged to different cultural and religious traditions and came from all over the world, the columns of his paper took on the character of an ecumenical forum of debate between conflicting points of view. Sometimes Gandhi admitted an error of judgement; sometimes he argued that a different decision would have been just as correct; more often he offered an elaborate defence of his decision, and when the subject was of considerable importance to him or to his critics, he kept returning to it, looking at it from a different angle each time. Gandhi's theory of *ahimsā* bore the marks of its provenance. It was broadly based, open, loosely structured, richly suggestive and poorly coordinated.

I

Although Hindu religious tradition is extremely complex and diverse and includes several different systems of thought, certain basic ideas are common to most of them. The universe is generally taken to be eternal, and hence the question of its creation has never dominated the Hindu mind. It is permeated, structured and regulated by a variously described cosmic power, generally conceived not as a static substance but as an active principle informing or 'flowing through' everything in the universe and manifesting itself in different forms in different species of beings. Since all human beings embody the cosmic power, they are not merely equal but one. At a different level, all life is one; at the highest level all creation is suffused with the divine and, therefore, one. The cosmos is an internally articulated and ordered whole whose constituents are all its 'co-tenants' and equally legitimate members enjoying the right to exist and avail themselves of its resources.

Hindu religious tradition enjoins on man the duty of universal *maitri* or friendliness and goodwill.[1] He is expected to respect the integrity of the other orders of being and to recognise them as his equal partners. Rather than grudge their existence and destroy them in the pursuit of his narrowly defined species-interests, he is advised to cherish them and to take delight in the infinite beauty and diversity of the universe. A remarkable *mantra* in the

Sukla Yajurveda prays to gods: *Maitrasyāham caksusā sarvāni bhutāni samikse* (May I look upon all living beings with the eyes of a friend). In *Taitreya Samhitā*, the author wishes 'peace' to earth, trees, plants, waters and indeed to all sentient beings and prays that he may not unwittingly injure even the root of a plant. In a beautiful passage the *Mahābhārata* describes *abhayadānam*, the gift of fearlessness or security, as *sarvadānebhyah uttamam*, the noblest of all gifts. According to it, the highest gift a man can bring to his fellow-men and indeed to all living beings is the assurance that he poses them no threat, that they can depend on him never to hurt them and can relax and be at ease in his presence. *Ahimsā* is the highest expression of *abhayadānam*. It means not merely abstention from harming others but also the absence of a wish or desire to harm them and involved *veratyāga* (renunciation of feeling of enmity) or *avera* (an attitude of non-enmity). As Vyasa defines it in his *Bhāsya*, it is *sarvathā sarvadā sarvabhutānām anabhidroha*, absence of malice or hostility to all living beings in every way and at all times.

Hindu thinkers disapproved of violence on four grounds which were differently stressed by different writers. First, all life was a manifestation of *Brahman*, and hence sacred. Second, all living beings were rightful members of the cosmos and entitled to respect and autonomy which were to be interfered with only when they transgressed their naturally ordained boundaries and threatened to harm others. Third, violence involved strong passions, especially anger and hatred, and disturbed the equanimity and inner balance of the soul. Fourth, it corrupted consciousness, defiled the soul and hindered spiritual progress. While the first two arguments rejected violence for what it did to *others*, the last two were primarily concerned with what it did to the moral *agent*. To be sure, all Hindu thinkers insisted that in harming others, the moral agent harmed himself as well. However, the emphasis varied considerably, some preferring to concentrate on the harm done to the victim, others on that done to the agent.

While emphasising the spirit of cosmic friendliness and goodwill, Hindu thinkers fully appreciated that some interference with the non-human world was an inescapable feature of human existence. *Jivo Jivasya Jivanam*: life is the life of life. To live was to kill. If a living being refused to kill, it ended up killing itself.

Whatever they did human beings were guilty of violence. Not only their biological survival but also their social existence involved violence. People had to be deterred from interfering with one another, criminals had to be punished, and the social order had to be preserved against actual and potential invaders by means of war.

Causing harm or destruction to living beings, then, was evil but necessary and sometimes unavoidable. Though Hindu thinkers were deeply anguished by the human predicament, most of them took a fairly tough-minded attitude. The tender-minded among them formed the *sramana* tradition which eventually flowered into Buddhism and Jainism. For the Hindus, if causing harm or destruction was inescapable or required to maintain cosmic or social order, and not born out of ill will or malice, it was fully justified. Indeed, they argued that it was only harm or killing and not *himsā* or violence. Men killed millions of germs everyday in the course of breathing, eating, walking, sitting and so on. Since that could not be helped, it was a fact of life, neither to be regretted nor rejoiced, and did not constitute violence. Ideally men should live on a vegetarian diet. However, if that were for some reason impossible, killing animals was justified. Similarly, if the propitiation of gods required sacrifices of animals, that too was not violence. It was needed in the interest of cosmic harmony, and in any case, the gods who required it and not the men who carried out their instructions were ultimately responsible for it.

Punishing evil-doers too was not *himsā*, for one punished them not out of ill will or hatred but in the interest of *loksangraha* or preservation of the social order. Hindu thinkers drew a fairly rigid distinction between man and his deeds, the agent and his actions, and insisted that it was perfectly possible, indeed necessary, to punish an action while remaining well-disposed to its agent. It was because one wished him well that one did not want to see him perpetrate evil deeds. And one could punish criminal deeds with clinical moral precision only if one was not swayed by the distorting emotions of hatred, anger and ill will. In a remarkable sentence, the *Mahābhārata* called killing an evil-doer *vadha* but also *ahimsā*, an act of killing but not of violence, that is, an act of non-violent killing. Society had a duty to protect itself and so long as its punishment was not motivated by hatred and ill will, it did not constitute *himsā*. In several *Purānas* too, *asādhuvadha* (killing an evil man) was called *ahimsā*. The *Bhāgavata Purāna* went even further and maintained that killing those violently disposed to other men (*nir-anukrosa*) and deserving to be killed (*vadhya*) was not only *ahimsā* but also *avadha* (non-killing). Etymologically and in its standard usage, the term *himsā* means a *wish* to kill or harm and implies ill-will; conversely *ahimsā* implies not just refraining from causing harm or destruction but the absence of a wish to do so. Killing without ill will and out of a sense of duty was, therefore, considered *vadha* and not *himsā*.

For Hindu thinkers, then, not all harm or destruction amounted to *himsā*. If it was inescapable or socially and religiously necessary and thus justified, it was not *himsā*. *Himsā* referred to unjustified harm and *ahimsā* to both justified harm and non-harm. Buddhist and Jain thinkers were most critical of the Hindu view. According to them, it encouraged casuistry, blinded people to several forms of harm and destruction, and used the authority of religion to sanction unacceptable violence. They preferred to define all harm or destruction as *himsā* and then to distinguish between justified and unjustified *himsā*. For them, justified harm and destruction was *himsā*, not *ahimsā*. *Ahimsā* referred to absence of harm and destruction.

For most Indian thinkers, the ultimate objective in life was to seek liberation from the world of sorrow. This involved withdrawal from all forms of worldly involvement and cultivation of an attitude of total detachment. Love was a form of attachment which tended to become addictive and entangled the agent in the affairs of the world. Both Bhishma and Krishna warned against it in the *Mahābhārata*, and in a remarkable dialogue in *Shāntiparva*, Medhavin gave similar advice to his father. The Puranic Bharata or Jada Bharata fell from his high spiritual stage because he was once seized with a strong feeling of compassion for a young deer. The Jains disapproved of both *shubharāga* (attachment to good or noble things) and *ashubharāga* (attachment to bad things) and recommended *veetarāga* (absence of all attachment). The Buddha stressed *karunā* or compassion, but it too largely meant uninvolved, detached and non-emotive kindness to all living beings. For him, as for Hindus and Jains, *ahimsā* was not so much a virtue as a discipline, one of the five major *yamas* or moral exercises designed to help the individual cultivate detachment and spiritual purity. Given their attitude to the world, it was hardly surprising that Indian thinkers generally defined *ahimsā* in negative terms. It meant not active love or service of all living beings, but largely abstention from causing them harm or destruction.

With some exceptions, Indian thinkers argued that though all life was sacred, not all living beings had equal worth. Despite some reservations, they were all agreed that human life was higher than the animal. For most Hindu writers, all animals had equal worth whereas that of men varied according to their caste. The bulk of Jain thinkers took the opposite view—that all men had equal worth whereas that of the animal varied according to the number of its senses and capacities. For the most part, the Buddhists drew a general distinction between man and animal and did not consider it necessary to establish a further hierarchy within each category.

There was considerable discussion but no general consensus among Indian thinkers concerning the conceptual and moral relationship between harm or injury on the one hand and killing on the other, and at a different level, between pain and death. For some, death was a form of harm; for some others, harm was partial death; for yet others, the two concepts were incommensurable. They also disagreed about whether the alleviation of pain or the preservation of life was a higher moral principle. Some thought that life could be terminated if unbearably painful; others felt that it must be preserved at all cost.

Since some form of *himsā* was inherent in human existence, Indian thinkers defined *ahimsā* not as total absence or avoidance of violence, but as *alpadroha* or minimum possible violence. When some measure of participation in evil was considered unavoidable such that the relevant virtues and vices only differed in degree, there was a common tendency in Indian thought to formulate the virtues involved in negative terms. *Ahimsā* was one example of this; *asteya* and *aparigraha* were others. This is why non-violence is an inaccurate translation of *ahimsā*. *Ahimsā* permits some *himsā* and means minimum possible violence. As the *Mahābhārata* put it: 'Who is there who does not inflict harm? Can anyone in the habit of deep reflection claim to be free from the charge of violence? Even the ascetics devoted to non-violence commit violence and only by the greatest of efforts can they reduce it to the minimum'.

Indian thinkers declined to lay down a universal and uniform standard by which to decide what constituted minimum violence, for the standard was deemed to be relative to the individual's occupation, circumstances and way of life. The minimum violence possible for and expected of a warrior was different from that expected of a trader or a priest, and a *sannyāsi* could not be treated on a par with a householder. Almost all Indian thinkers laid particular emphasis on the fact that by virtue of being a custodian of the integrity of his society, a king could not be judged by the same criteria as a private individual. *Loksangraha* was the absolute principle of political life and justified the kind and degree of violence impermissible in personal life. Most Hindus did not even call it *himsā*. And even the Buddhists and Jains, who were finicky about violence in personal life, tolerated wars, prisons and even some gruesome forms of punishment.

II

Although deeply influenced by the Indian traditions of non-violence, Gandhi departed from them in several significant respects, Indeed he had little choice. They were developed within the metaphysical context of non-involvement in the world; Gandhi considered worldly involvement to be the *sine qua non* of *moksha*. They did not assign active love an important place in their moral theory; for Gandhi, it was the highest moral value. Not surprisingly, he took over the concept of *ahimsā* and defined it in a radically novel manner.[2]

Gandhi acknowledged that traditionally, *ahimsā* meant non-injury and non-killing. However, he could not see why it should be defined in such 'negative' and 'passive' terms. Non-injury or non-killing did not by itself constitute *ahimsā*; it was such only when born out of compassion. A thief stabbing a man was guilty of *himsā* whereas a surgeon using a knife on a patient was not, the reason being that the latter's action was motivated by a desire to alleviate pain. A man refraining from hitting back a much stronger assailant was not non-violent, but one refusing to retaliate against a weak opponent was, the reason being that, unlike the former, he was guided by a desire not to cause harm. In Gandhi's view, it was the wish not to cause harm or destruction, that is, the 'element of conscious compassion' that constituted the 'essence' of non-violence. 'Where there is no compassion, there is no *ahimsā*. The test of *ahimsā* is compassion'.[3] He thought that even as compassion led to avoidance of harm, it could and indeed ought to lead to a positive desire to help others. And just as it was a virtue not to injure others, it was also a virtue to help those already injured and to prevent injury being done in the first instance. To restrict *ahimsā* to non-injury was, therefore, an 'arbitrary' and 'unjustified' restriction of its meaning. Accordingly, Gandhi distinguished its two senses. In its 'narrow', 'literal', 'negative' or 'passive' sense, it meant refraining from causing harm and destruction to others. In its 'broad', 'positive' and 'active' sense, it meant promoting their well-being. In both senses, it was grounded in compassion or love; in one, love was expressed negatively, in the other, positively. Gandhi concluded that *ahimsā* was really the same as love: it was 'active love'.[4]

Gandhi arrived at his broad definition of *ahimsā* by means of three crucial steps. He equated it with compassion and the latter with love, and defined love in worldly and activist terms. Hindus and Jains generally rejected all three, and the Buddhists the last two. For Hindus and Jains, *ahimsā* was born out of either indifference to or passive goodwill towards the world, and even the latter was not the same as compassion. Furthermore, for all three traditions, love was an emotion and hence suspect. Like all other emotions, it led to worldly attachments, tended to become addictive and compromised the agent's autonomy. Even if the Buddhist *karunā* and *dayā* were to be interpreted as love, the love involved was quite different from Gandhi's which sought passionate identification with all living beings, took worldly suffering seriously and entailed active social service. In other words, the largely negative meaning given to *ahimsā* in Indian traditions was logically required by their view of man. Gandhi was at liberty to give it an activist and positive meaning, but wrong to present it as a 'natural' and 'legitimate' extension of the old.

Gandhi was well aware of how much his view of *ahimsā* diverged from the traditional Indian view, and made that clear on a number of occasions. He observed:[5]

Complete non-violence means complete cessation of all activity. Not such, however, is my definition of non-violence.

The first sentence indicates how he understood the traditional conception of non-violence; the second asserts his self-conscious departure from it. He went on:[6]

Non-violence is not a cloistered virtue to be practised by the individual for his peace and final salvation, but a rule of conduct for society if it is to live consistently with human dignity.

The first half of the sentence indicates what Gandhi took to be the central assumption of the traditional conception of non-violence, and the second his attempt to give it a wholly different orientation. He distanced himself yet further from Indian tradition, especially the Hindu:[7]

The religion of non-violence is not meant merely for the *rishis* and saints. It is meant for the common people as well.

Gandhi here makes non-violence obligatory on all, not just the ascetics, and calls it a religion. Since religion meant to him a way of life involving total transformation of all human relationships, his remark had a radical social thrust. He observed:[8]

Yours should not be a *passive* spirituality that spends itself in *idle* meditation, but it should be an *active* thing which will carry *war* into the enemy's camp.

In this remarkable sentence, Gandhi shows his impatience with Indian traditions and contrasts their 'passive' spirituality and 'idle' meditation with an active war, a veritable *dharmayuddha*, against social and economic injustices. He went on:[9]

Our non-violence is an unworldly thing. We see its utmost limit in refraining somehow from destroying bugs, mosquitoes and fleas, or from killing birds and animals. We do not care if these creatures suffer, nor even if we partly contribute to their suffering. On the contrary, we think it a heinous sin if anyone releases or helps in releasing a creature that suffers. I have already written and explained that this is not non-violence. Non-violence means an ocean of compassion.

Gandhi had in mind here the view of non-violence prevalent in contemporary India. However, he was convinced that the seeds of it lay deep in the essentially negative and passive orientation of Indian traditions. Referring to Tolstoy's equation of non-violence with active love, Gandhi observed:[10]

> Tolstoy was a great advocate of non-violence in his age. I know of no author in the West who has written as much and as effectively for the cause of non-violence as Tolstoy has done. I may go even further and say that I know no one in India or elsewhere who has had as profound an understanding of the nature of non-violence as Tolstoy had and who has tried to follow it as sincerely as he did.

Gandhi suggested that India had a great deal to learn from Tolstoy. He agreed that it had made great discoveries in the past in the sphere of non-violence, but insisted that these were inadequate and needed to be supplemented by the insights of other religions. In effect, he told his countrymen that, contrary to their frequent claims, they not only had no monopoly of the understanding of non-violence but also that their view of it was partial and limited. Gandhi thought that it was his historic task to integrate the profoundest insights of the Indian and non-Indian traditions of non-violence and to develop a more satisfactory view of it.

Gandhi's definition of *ahimsā* as active and energetic love leading to dedicated service of fellow-men represented a radical departure from Indian traditions. Not surprisingly, his countrymen felt deeply disturbed. They not only had great difficulty coping with the new definition and its moral demands but also resented being told that they did not know what *ahimsā* meant and had been practising only a negative and pale version of it. Some of them openly chided him for creating a great and unnecessary 'moral confusion' and corrupting Hinduism by introducing the Christian doctrine of love.[11]

Gandhi was aware of the intensity of their feelings. His distinction between the negative and positive senses of *ahimsā* was intended to reassure them that he knew and respected the traditions and was only 'broadening' them to meet the 'needs of the age'. He also argued that the meanings of basic concepts were necessarily subject to the 'process of evolution' and that there was no harm in redefining them in the light of the insights of other cultures. As usual, he said, too, that he was trying to capture the 'true spirit' of the Indian doctrine of *ahimsā*, and quoted isolated supportive sentences from the scriptures. He also flattered the Indian pride by suggesting that such an extension of meaning was India's greatest contribution to the world.

Gandhi could have easily avoided upsetting his countrymen by using the term *ahimsā* in its traditional negative sense and employing another to refer to active and positive love. His reasons for refusing to do so are not entirely clear. As we saw, he seems to have genuinely believed that its positive meaning grew out of and was a legitimate extension of the old.[11] It was also his practice to take over terms familiar to his audience and to define them in the way he thought proper without much worrying about their conventional meanings; for example, his definitions of *satya, swarāj, swadeshi* and *brahmacharya*. It would also seem that since the concept of active love was relatively new to India, Gandhi's best chance of getting it widely accepted lay in attaching it to the long-established and deeply cherished concept of *ahimsā*.

III

For Gandhi then, *ahimsā* meant both passive and active love, refraining from causing harm and destruction to living beings as well as positively promoting their well-being. *Himsā* was the opposite of *ahimsā*. Since ancient Indian thinkers took *himsā* to be a positive concept, they defined *ahimsā* in terms of it. Gandhi equated *ahimsā* with the positive and self-contained concept of love and adopted the opposite approach of defining *himsā* in terms of it.

In Gandhi's view, love implied identification with and service of all living beings. Its opposites were malevolence and selfishness. Malevolence implied ill will or hatred towards others, a wish to harm them even when they posed no threat to one's interests and simply because one enjoyed seeing them suffer. Contrary to what some of his commentators have said, Gandhi distinguished between self-interest and selfishness. Self-interest consisted in securing those conditions without which no man could live a fully human life. Since the earth provided 'enough for everybody's needs but not enough for anybody's greed', Gandhi thought that there was no conflict between the self-interests of all men. By contrast, selfishness meant putting oneself *above* others and pursing one's interests *at their expense*. It was inherently aggressive and limitless, and necessarily led to conflict. While the pursuit of self-interest was morally legitimate, selfishness was not.

For Gandhi, then, *himsā* meant inflicting harm or destruction upon another living being out of selfishness or ill will. As he put it, it consisted in causing 'suffering to others out of selfishness or just for the sake of doing so'.[12] A surgeon's use of a knife was *ahimsā*; a thief's and a sadist's use of it were respectively motivated by selfishness and malevolence and constituted *himsā*. In the Indian traditions harm was defined widely to include not only physical but also psychological, moral and other forms of *pidā* or *klesa* (pain). Gandhi accepted this broad definition. In his view, physical harm or destruction was the most familiar form of violence and could be caused in different ways. One might harm or kill a man by shooting him or by denying him the basic necessities of life. Whether one killed him 'at a stroke' or 'by inches', the result was the same and the individuals involved were guilty of violence.[13]

Insulting, demeaning or humiliating others, diminishing their self-respect, speaking harsh words, passing harsh judgements, anger and mental cruelty were also forms of harm. They might, and generally did, result in physical harm, but it was not necessary that they should in order to be considered acts of violence. A lack of punctuality was also an act of harm as it caused anxiety to those involved and deprived them of their time. Not answering letters was also a form of mental cruelty and even torture, and thus an act of violence. For Gandhi, violence was a property not only of conduct but also of thought. The thought of harming another was a form of violence for, had not the social conventions, absence of opportunities and considerations of long-term interest stood in his way, the agent would have acted on it.[14] Thoughts, further, were the building blocks of character, and a man tended to become what he thought. If he got into the habit of 'living with' certain types of thought, over time they tended to appear natural and self-evident to him, blunted his sensibilities and both disposed him to act in a relevant manner and legitimised his action in his eyes. Thoughts of violence paved the way for acts of violence, and were just as bad. Like most Indian thinkers, Gandhi refused to draw a qualitative distinction between thought and action. Thought was potential action or, rather, action in its early and embryonic stage, and action was operative or active thought. The two were integral parts of the same process and constituted a continuum. A thought was, therefore, never a 'mere' thought.

Ancient Indian thinkers had argued that a man could be guilty of violence by committing it himself (*krita*), aiding and instigating it (*karita*) or by watching it being committed without protest (*anumodita*). Gandhi went further and contended that a man also committed violence by participating in or benefiting from a harmful practice. Since agriculture involved violence, the Jains avoided it. However, they could not survive without its products and depended on others to engage in it. For Gandhi, this was profoundly hypocritical. It implied encouraging others to engage in violence in order that one could practise non-violence oneself, and involved enjoying the benefits of violence while disowning all responsibility for it. He observed:[15]

> The very idea that millions of the sons of the soil should remain steeped in *himsā* in order that a handful of men who live on the toil of these people might be able to practise *ahimsā* seems to me to be very unworthy of and inconsistent with the supreme duty of *ahimsā*. I feel that this betrays a lack of perception of the inwardness of *ahimsā*. Let us see, for instance, to what it leads to if pushed to its logical conclusion. You may not kill a snake if necessary, according to this principle, you may get it killed by somebody else. You may not yourself forcibly drive a thief away but you may employ another person to do it for you. If you want to protect the life of a child

entrusted to your care from the fury of a tyrant, somebody else must bear the brunt of the tyrant's fury for you. And you thus refrain from direct action in the sacred name of *ahimsā*! This, in my opinion, is neither religion nor *ahimsā*.

Gandhi observed that a similar situation occurred at the political level. Many votaries of non-violence condemned the institutionalised violence of the state, but enjoyed the order and security provided by it. And though they did not themselves fight in wars, they happily paid soldiers to do so for them. For Gandhi, this too was hypocritical. The violence of the state did not disappear merely by shutting one's eyes to it, and one did not become non-violent by conveniently transferring the moral burden of inescapable violence upon the shoulders of others.[16] Such non-violence fed off and was made possible by the violence of others, and did not absolve the individual concerned from his responsibility for the violence involved. Indeed, insofar as his conduct added hypocrisy to violence, it was doubly reprehensible. Like salvation, non-violence was indivisible. Either all were non-violent, or none was. It simply could not be practised by running away from the world, only by entering and changing it. Gandhi's departure from Indian traditions could not have been more radical and decisive.

Although Gandhi vacillated on the subject, he seems to have thought that self-inflicted or self-directed harm was not violence. Indian traditions contained scattered references to *ātma-himsā* (violence to oneself) and *ātma-ahimsā* (non-injury to oneself), but they generally defined violence as injury to *para* (another being). Gandhi shared this view and remarked on several occasions that violence meant 'causing injury to another'.[17] For Gandhi, a suicide was guilty of cowardice, not violence. If a man inflicted harm upon himself in order to force another to meet his demands, that was violence only because he caused psychological harm to the latter. It would seem that Gandhi was inconsistent in taking this view. As he defined it, infliction of harm or destruction was violence when motivated by selfishness or ill will, and it is certainly possible for a man to be guided by either in his relation to himself.

For Gandhi, then, *ahimsā* meant active love and involved both refraining from causing harm to others in the broad sense in which he used the term, and helping them grow and flourish.

Himsā meant harming others out of ill will or selfishness. Harm caused to others in the course of pursuing one's legitimate or just self-interest was *not himsā*. Although Gandhi broke with Indian traditions in several crucial respects, his break was not complete. His view of non-violence retained a subjectivist orientation characteristic of them, as he too defined it in terms of the motives of the agent. For them, as for him, *himsā* involved *ill will*, a *wish* to harm others, and hence harm did not constitute *himsā* if the element of malevolence was absent. Since human motives are largely opaque to others and sometimes even to the agent, Gandhi's definition was not easy to apply. Again, the Hindus had argued that harm caused in the interest of *loksangraha* and the maintenance of *dharma* was not *himsā*. Gandhi came close to sharing this *dhārmic* view of violence, as he too argued that harm caused in the pursuit of legitimate or just self-interest did not amount to *himsā*. The dividing line between self-interest and selfishness is thin and not easy to draw. And, as for the concept of legitimate or just self-interest, it is normative and open to dispute. Not surprisingly, like the Hindu view, Gandhi's definition left room for considerable disagreement and even casuistry.

IV

Insofar as Gandhi departed from the Indian traditions of *ahimsā* in significant respects, many of his opinions and actions surprised and bewildered his countrymen. One relatively trivial incident acted as a catalyst and brought home to both the radical novelty of his doctrine.[18] A calf in his *āshram* was badly maimed and in acute agony. All possible medical treatment was given to it. When a surgeon whose advice was sought declared it past hope, Gandhi asked him to administer it a lethal injection. His action provoked a storm of protest, some accusing him of senility and some even wishing him death.[19] The Jains who, like many of his commentators, had made the predictable mistake of taking his theory of *ahimsā* to be substantially similar to theirs, were most bitter; the Hindus only a little less so.

Gandhi's critics raised four objections. First, according to the Indian doctrine of *ahimsā* life was sacred and inviolable and the deliberate killing of a living being was never justified. Second, although Gandhi talked about love, his action betrayed a lack of love for the calf, for love could never kill. Third, if we were consistent, he would have to kill a human being under similar circumstances, and that would be most immoral. Finally, he was under 'Western' influence in thinking that the alleviation of pain was far more important than the preservation of life.

Gandhi was deeply hurt and, judging by the tone of his reply, angered by the criticisms. Not surprisingly, he used the occasion to launch a scathing general attack on the three Indian traditions, especially the Jain. He rejected the view that killing was never justified and that all killing was violence. His critics had 'wrongly' assumed that death was always worse than life, for sometimes life was so painful and unbearable that death was preferable. When a living being was in unbearable and incurable agony, not to kill it was an act of *himsā*. Gandhi said he had killed the calf in its own 'interest' and for its own 'benefit'. He had tried to nurse it and soothe its pain. When it was found to be past hope and help, he was left with no choice. 'There is violence when the intention is to give pain, otherwise it is only an act of killing'.[20] If he had killed the calf because *he* could not bear to see it suffer, his action would have been motivated by selfishness and amounted to violence. In fact he had killed it because *it* could not bear its pain. His was thus an act of 'non-violent killing'. For Gandhi's critics, as for the Indian traditions, *ahimsā* meant non-killing, and hence Gandhi's was *not* an act of *ahimsā*. For Gandhi, it meant active love, and hence it *was* an act of *ahimsā*.

Gandhi rejected the charge that his act betrayed a lack of love for the calf.[21] Love implied care and concern for others and a desire to do all one could to relieve their suffering. He had killed the calf because he loved it and wanted it to meet its certain death without any more pain. The 'horror of killing' displayed by his critics was not *ahimsā* but effete sentimentality. Indeed, since they would not end the calf's pain because they could not bear to see its life terminated, they were acquiescing in its pain for selfish reasons, and not he but they were guilty of violence.[22] They made a 'fetish' of non-killing, and this had so 'drugged' their conscience that they did not even know what 'true' *ahimsā* was. To equate *himsā* with killing and *ahimsā* with non-killing was to be 'blind' to the whole range of activities which, though apparently non-violent, were in fact violent. His wealthy critics, Gandhi argued, paid their workers substandard wages and did nothing to relieve widespread poverty and degradation. Since they did not kill anyone, they assumed that they were non-violent. In fact they 'committed violence on a large scale in the name of non-violence' and were guilty of 'crass hypocrisy'. There was 'far more violence in the slow torture of men . . . and wanton humiliation and oppression of the weak and the killing of their self-respect . . . than in mere benevolent taking of life'.[23]

As to whether he would have acted in exactly the same way if the calf had been a human being, Gandhi answered in the affirmative with the important qualification that 'natural differences' between man and animal ruled out 'a complete analogy'. Unlike the animal, man was able to express his wishes, and hence others were at liberty to decide for him only if he was unable to do so himself. Furthermore, a human body was 'much more manageable in bulk', and therefore easier to nurse. Even if he was past hope, a critically ill man was often not past help and could be nursed and soothed until his death.[24] If, however, one was convinced after disinterested reflection that nothing more could be done to relieve his pain and that his death was inevitable, one was at liberty to end his life. Gandhi proposed the following guidelines.[25]

> To recapitulate the conditions the fulfilment of *all* of which alone can warrant the taking of life from the point of view of *ahimsā*:
>
> 1. The disease from which the patient is suffering should be incurable.
> 2. All concerned have despaired of the life of the patient.
> 3. The case should be beyond all help or service.
> 4. It should be impossible for the patient in question to express his or her wish.
> 5. So long as even one of these conditions remains unfulfilled the taking of life from the point of view of *ahimsā* cannot be justified.

In a different context, Gandhi took the hypothetical case of a man whose half-slashed head was hanging loose from the neck and who was in excruciating pain. At his request or out of compassion, a passerby decided to terminate his life. Gandhi argued that this was not an act of violence. The passerby did not wish to cause him harm; on the contrary, he intended to relieve his pain. On another occasion Gandhi was asked for his comments on an actress who had killed her lover suffering from an incurable disease and in unbearable pain. He replied that hers was not an act of violence as 'understood and defined' by him.

Gandhi went on to argue that preservation of life at all cost had no sanction either in the Indian traditions of *ahimsā* or in the general principles of morality.[26] *Ahimsā* ruled out all forms of selfishness, including 'blind attachment' to life.[27] If the death of a man suffering from an incurable disease was only a matter of time, it was morally wrong of him to wish to delay it at all cost, not so much because it caused hardship, suffering and expense to those looking after him as because it showed 'cowardice' and 'sordid egoism'.[28] Since his death was certain, he should be prepared to let go of life with courage and dignity. If he was unwilling to do so, he should be persuaded to accept the inevitable. Although Gandhi was convinced that others had no moral duty to 'nurse his longing for life in all circumstances', he insisted that no life should be terminated without the consent of the individual concerned.[29]

Gandhi's critics had accused him of being under 'Western' influence in preferring death to pain in certain circumstances.[30] Throughout his life he was unusually sensitive to the charge, both because he loathed cultural parochialism and because he had absorbed a number of Western ideas and did not want orthodox Hindus to be unduly alarmed or alienated by them. He rejoined that though he saw nothing wrong in learning from the West, in this particular case his views were derived from Indian traditions. He contended, without offering any evidence, that the relief of pain had always been the first priority in the Indian, especially the Hindu, tradition of *ahimsā*. No doubt killing living beings was bad. However, if it was designed to eliminate pain in the context of certain death, the tradition not only sanctioned but required it. Gandhi conceded that the Jains might disagree, but thought that they were wrong. He observed:[31]

> The concept of non-violence in our religion is framed from the standpoint of the pain that we may cause another individual. Why should there be any outcry where death is caused either

accidentally or deliberately but without any thought or causing pain? If there is not the fear of death behind that outcry, what else is it?

Gandhi was perhaps aware that he was putting a dubious gloss on the Hindu tradition. The following remark beautifully captures his mood of defiance and reassurance, and illustrates his strategy of using the authority of tradition when he approved of it and rejecting it when he did not. He observed:[32]

> I have arrived at my views independently of any authority, though originally they may have been drawn from various sources, and I submit that they are in perfect consonance with *ahimsā* even though they prove contrary to the teaching of the philosopher.

Gandhi here insists that although his views have been inspired by Indian traditions, they are products of independent thought and must be judged on their own merits and not in terms of their conformity to a specific tradition. At the same time, he does not hesitate to assert that his views are in 'perfect consonance' with the Indian traditions, and hence binding on his countrymen! Aware that this might not be the case, he skilfully pre-empts a counter-attack by insisting that he is not interested in any of the Indian philosophers whose writings might be cited against him!

V

The cases discussed so far were relatively simple and Gandhi had little difficulty dealing with them. Political life confronted him with many difficult situations and stretched his ingenuity to the fullest. Here he was concerned not with individuals but with collectivities whose inescapable conflicts of legitimate interests raised extremely complex moral issues. We shall analyse one such situation by way of illustration. In the course of the Non-cooperation Movement of 1920, Gandhi successfully urged a boycott of British textile goods, as a result of which many workers in Lancashire mills lost their jobs and suffered considerable hardship and some even starved. Since it was his boycott that had inflicted the harm, many of his British and even some Indian critics accused him of violence. Gandhi could have admitted the charge and pleaded that it was a case of justified violence. Instead, he insisted that it could not 'by any law of morals be held to be an act of violence'.

First, he bore no ill will to the Lancashire mill-workers and did not intend to cause them harm.[33] He was only concerned to assert India's right not to cooperate with the government it loathed, and the hardship caused to Lancashire workers was its unintended and incidental consequence. When told that he could have easily foreseen the harm and must, therefore, be deemed to have intended it, Gandhi rejoined that anticipating or foreseeing consequences was not the same as intending them. Intention implied a *desire* or a *wish*, and that was clearly absent in his case. Though he had foreseen the hardship, he positively regretted it and was prepared to do all in his power to alleviate it. Since every action had infinite consequences, many of which were unspecifiable or only became manifest after a long time, it should and indeed could only be judged on the basis of those desired or wished for and in that sense intended by the agent.[34]

Second, like Britain, India had a 'right and a duty' to protect its 'just and legitimate interests' and could not be expected to acquiesce in the unemployment and starvation of its people brought about by the destruction of its indigenous industries. In protecting its industries, India was not being selfish, only pursuing its legitimate self-interest.

Third, India might be required to sacrifice even its legitimate interests if it had 'bound' itself by an implicit or explicit agreement, and thus acquired a 'duty' to protect those of the Lancashire workers at all cost. In actual fact it had never done so. Being imposed and maintained by violence, the trade agreements between the two countries could never generate a moral obligation.

Lest his reasoning should appear to be a case of special or specious pleading, it should be emphasised that Gandhi advanced similar arguments in other contexts. If men stopped visiting brothels and their inmates starved, he did not see how they could be accused of violence. Or if they stopped borrowing money from money-lenders who were thereby put out of business and suffered acute hardship, he did not see how they could be accused of violence either. However, Gandhi thought that they could be so accused if they 'transferred their custom from one money-lender to another through ill will or spite or without just cause', as the harm they then caused was intended and wished for and not required by the legitimate pursuit of their self-interest. An American critic put to him a fascinating hypothetical case. Suppose van drivers in charge of delivering milk in New York were paid starvation wages. Having exhausted all peaceful means they decided to strike, as a result of which some young children were deprived of milk and died. Gandhi argued that the van drivers' strike was 'certainly not an act of violence'. First, it was 'not designed' to cause the deaths, which were in fact deeply regretted. Its sole purpose was to secure higher wages, and the municipality, not the children, was its target. Second, the van drivers had a right and a duty to promote their 'just' and 'legitimate' interests. If they had struck because they disapproved of the way the municipality was run and intended to put pressure on it, they would have been guilty of a 'crime against humanity'. This was, however, not the case. Third, they had not 'bound' themselves and incurred an obligation to supply milk to the children at all cost and under all circumstances.

Though the van drivers were not guilty of violence, they were guilty of causing harm. However, Gandhi thought that only *minimal* blame attached to them. Like all human beings, they had a general duty not to cause harm to their fellow men. Since the duty devolved upon all men and not just them, the extent of their responsibility was reduced. Further, the New York municipality was officially responsible for ensuring the regular supply of milk to the children under its care. It had, therefore, an obligation to ensure that all those involved in the long chain of supply were reasonably contented and willing to discharge their duties. A collective enterprise required the cooperation of a number of people and depended upon each to do his share. The municipality could not consistently ask the drivers to discharge their duties while neglecting its own duties to them, and it could not legitimately expect them to be mindful of the interests of its clients while itself remaining insensitive to theirs. Had the drivers gone on strike for reasons unrelated to their legitimate interests, their case would have been very different. In fact, they were only asking for decent wages and their strike was a desperate and defensive measure. Although as moral beings they could not be totally absolved of the responsibility for the consequences of their strike, responsibility must primarily be laid at the door of the municipality.

Gandhi's discussion of these cases was informed by the crucial distinction between harm and violence noted earlier. As a lifelong fighter against all manner of injustices, he had come to feel that the distinction was central to every critical social theory. The oppressed and the exploited could not by definition pursue their just and legitimate interests without altering the established pattern of relationship and thereby adversely affecting the interests of their masters. Almost everything they did to improve their lot harmed the later. If harm were to be equated with violence, they could always be morally disarmed and blackmailed into accepting the *status quo*. For Gandhi, the harm caused *by* them was qualitatively different from that done *to* them by their masters. First, it was wholly defensive. Second, unlike the harm done to them, it was incidental to the legitimate pursuit of their interests and not born out of ill will or exploitative intentions. Third, their actions resulted in harm only because they had to function within an unjust system forcibly imposed upon them. As Gandhi put it, if a man threw off another accustomed to riding on his back, he could not be held responsible for the latter's minor bruises. Finally, the oppressed did not deny their masters' equal right to pursue their legitimate interests and only challenged their right to do so at others' expense.

Since the two kinds of harm were morally asymmetrical, Gandhi insisted that they should not be given the same name. To do so was to be guilty of moral blindness and to do a grave injustice to victims of oppression. Even to call the harm caused by them justified or defensive violence or counter-violence was to imply that it was basically of the same kind as the harm done to them. According to Gandhi, when there was no moral equivalence there should be no linguistic equivalence either. As a political activist, he well knew that disputes about words were never merely verbal.

VI

Gandhi shared the poignant vision of life characteristic of much of the Indian, especially Jain philosophy, and deeply regretted that fact that human existence was impossible without violence.[35] Men destroyed millions of living organisms in the course of breathing, walking, eating, drinking, cultivating land, using insecticides and disinfectants, lighting fire and building houses. Gandhi never defined life, a serious omission in a theorist of non-violence, and tended to equate it with a capacity for spontaneous growth rather than consciousness. In his view, there was life in 'each grain of food' men consumed and even in fruits and vegetables. The body was a 'house of slaughter' and compelled man to 'drink a bitter drought of violence' every second of his life. Gandhi observed:[36]

> The world is bound in a chain of destruction. In other words, *himsā* is an inherent necessity for life in the body. This is why a votary of *ahimsā* always prays for ultimate deliverance from the bondage of flesh.

He vacillated on the question of whether human life was superior to the non-human.[37] Sometimes he argued that all life was equally sacred. Sometimes he said that as a human being, he was biased in favour of human life and would like it to be preferred although he could not find a convincing justification for his view.[38] More often, however, he argued that since humans were rational and moral beings they had a greater moral worth.[39] This did not give them an 'absolute' superiority over animals and a right to do with them what they liked, for animals too were legitimate members of the cosmos. Rather, men *may* take animal life and subordinate animal interests to theirs only when absolutely necessary for their survival and under clearly-defined conditions.

Not only man's physical survival but also his social existence was characterised by pervasive violence. Wittingly or unwittingly, men harmed one another in the ordinary course of life and needed the coercive discipline of law. The strong tended to exploit and oppress the weak and had to be fought. Criminals had to be punished and bullies restrained, and that required the institution of prisons. Organised life was impossible without the state, which was nothing but concentrated violence. States threatened one another and needed to protect themselves.

Human existence then seemed impossible without some measure of violence. Gandhi argued that this inescapable fact had been used over the centuries, and especially in the modern age, to justify almost every kind of violence. The fact that men might legitimately do violence to nature in the interest of their survival was taken to imply that they enjoyed absolute lordship over it and were free to do with it what they liked. The fact that the state had to maintain order and restrain criminals was taken to justify a vast coercive apparatus consisting of inhuman prisons, brutalising punishment, torture and the heavily armed police. Its right to defend its way of life was taken to imply that it had a duty to defend every inch of its territory whatever the cost to its way of life and to resort to wars involving a massive destruction of life. The moral duty to fight against injustice and oppression was used to legitimise most horrendous forms of revolutionary violence. The fact that sometimes victims of oppression understandably lost their patience and resorted to violence was used to justify all their violent deeds. Gandhi was deeply worried about the way in which the limited legitimacy of violence in human life was so easily turned into its general justification, and the range of its permissible uses so extended that violence became a rule rather than an exception. He thought that this happened because once violence was considered morally justifiable, men kept taking advantage of the exceptions and made no attempt to find alternatives. In his view, the only way to avoid this recurrent human tendency to emasculate moral ideals was to adopt the opposite approach of insisting on the possibility and desirability of a *completely* non-violent life and placing the onus of justification on those seeking to make exceptions. Rather than ask when violence was justified, we should ask when a breach of non-violence may be forgiven. Gandhi's view was derived from his general approach to moral life. A few words about it will clarify the point.

Gandhi understood moral life in the image of Euclidean geometry. Euclid's straight line, circle and triangle could never be drawn, but that did not in any way limit the value of his definitions of them. Being freed of all human limitations, they acted as unchanging lodestars inspiring a search for more refined instruments. If Euclid had taken human limitations into account and defined a straight line and triangle accordingly, they would perhaps have been drawn a long time ago and the highly sophisticated modern instruments of measurement would never have been invented. His inherently unrealisable definitions were necessary conditions of scientific inquiry and progress.

Gandhi saw moral life in similar terms. By their very nature, moral ideals made most exacting demands. There was, therefore, a common human tendency to circumscribe their scope, introduce exceptions, lazily accept the limitations imposed by the established social order and the accustomed way of life, and to enjoy the satisfaction of leading a moral life without sacrificing any of the usual comforts. Over time the exceptions multiplied and all but subverted the moral ideals. Gandhi was concerned to combat such a moral and 'spiritual inertia'. At the same time, he acknowledged that like the Euclidean definitions, moral ideals could never be fully realised and that to ask men to live 'beyond their capacity' was to burden them with an unbearable sense of guilt and to destroy their moral self-respect.

It was to meet this dual requirement that Gandhi introduced the absolute–relative distinction in moral life. Moral ideals must remain absolute and intolerant of exceptions, and their votaries must be expected to live by them. The obvious limitations of their capacity, circumstances and accustomed lifestyles would naturally prevent them from doing so, and hence they must be expected constantly to explore how they should change these in order better to realise the ideals. Since they would have done their best at any given point of time, they had no reason to torment themselves and feel demoralised. Since, however, they would have failed to live up to them, they had every reason to feel dissatisfied and to strive yet harder. For Gandhi, such a creative but non-debilitating sense of discontent was the only possible source of moral progress and had three advantages. First, it did not compromise or 'relativise' ideals, which thus continued to act as 'permanent lodestars' in the moral navigation of life. Second, it surrounded the inevitable failure to live up to their full rigour with a sense of dissatisfaction and encouraged creative experiments. Third, by not demanding more than what the moral agent could do at a given time, it did not destroy his self-respect and self-confidence.

Applying this 'Euclidean view' to violence, Gandhi contended that, although its use was pardonable, excusable or understandable, it was never *justified*. He observed:[40]

> Therefore, when I say that the use of force is wrong in whatever degree and under whatever circumstances, I mean it in a relative sense. It is much better for me to say I have not sufficient non-violence in me, than to admit exceptions to an eternal principle. Moreover my refusal to admit exceptions spurs me to perfect myself in the technique of non-violence.

Gandhi went further and argued that just as every science rested on certain unquestioned postulates or axioms, the 'science of non-violence' rested on the 'postulate' of its 'absolute efficacy'. A sincere votary of non-violence must commit himself to the belief that it never failed and that it overcame *all* violence, including that of the wildest animals and lunatics. Only such a belief guarded him against taking a lazy recourse to violence in difficult situations and inspired him to conduct bold and imaginative experiments. Gandhi was ambiguous about the logical character of the postulate. Sometimes he thought that it was, like Euclid's axiom, a statement of logical possibility. More often he thought that it was a scientific hypothesis based on evidence. Asked if one should use physical force to restrain a lunatic going about murdering people, Gandhi replied:[41]

> I will excuse it for all time. But I would not say it is justified from the non-violent standpoint. I would say that there was not that degree of non-violence in you to give you confidence in purely non-violent treatment. If you had, your simple presence would be sufficient to pacify the lunatic. Non-violence carries within it its own sanction. It is not a mechanical thing. You do not become non-violent by merely saying, 'I shall not use force'. It must be felt in the heart. There must be within you an upwelling of love and pity towards the wrong-doer. When there is that feeling, it will express itself through some action. It may be a sign, a glance, even silence. But such as it is, it will melt the heart of the wrong-doer and check the wrong.

Gandhi was convinced that wild animals attacked human beings only when they apprehended threats unwittingly conveyed by a gesture, a stare or a movement of the body. He said he had heard of cases of them having been calmed and won over by love. He also pointed to several mythical characters in Indian religious literature who had conquered the intense hatred of their enemies and the ferocity of wild animals by the sheer power of their love. Gandhi's view, largely based on mythology and hearsay and supported by no evidence, was not unique to him. It went as far back as Patanjali who had averred that all violence ceased in the presence of pure non-violence, a remark frequently quoted by Gandhi. And even in modern times, such religious men as Ramkrishna Paramhamsa, Raman Maharshi and Jai Krishnamurti claimed to have 'proved' the all-conquering power of love. None of them offered any evidence for their inherently unfalsifiable assertion.

Having postulated the ideal of a completely non-violent existence, Gandhi went on to discuss different areas of life to explore why and where they required exceptions and how these could be minimised.

As we saw, man's very survival entailed considerable violence to non-human beings.[42] Since it was 'unavoidable', Gandhi called it 'less sinful'. It is not entirely clear what he meant by this. Sometimes he said that since it was not a matter of choice, it was *less of a sin*; on other occasions he said that it remained just as sinful, but that its unavoidability rendered man less *responsible* for it. In any case, Gandhi was convinced that it could be considerably minimised by restricting and refining human wants. Man had a right to lead a moderately comfortable life in order to realise his full moral and spiritual potential. All wants beyond that point were superfluous and morally illegitimate. Their restriction was doubly beneficial; it spared the lives of millions of non-human beings and increased one's powers of self-discipline. Although he advocated vegetarianism, Gandhi was prepared to concede that a non-vegetarian diet was perhaps justified in countries with a cold climate or a limited supply of fruits, vegetables and arable land. Eating more than necessary for survival, constructing large houses, wearing silk, sporting pearls, unrestrained use of insecticide, environmental pollution, extensive cultivation of land, large-scale industrialisation, pointless accumulation of wealth, and so on were all avoidable causes of violence.[43] Since considerable violence was entailed even by a life of restricted wants, Gandhi proposed that we should compensate for it by taking tender care of nature and animals and by doing all in our power to alleviate human and non-human suffering.

Protection of human life was the second frequent source of violence.[44] When Gandhi frightened away and injured monkeys interfering with crops in his *āshram*, he was criticised for adopting the 'Western utilitarian attitude' to life. He agreed that his was an act of violence and asked his colleagues and correspondents to help him explore non-violent alternatives. When snakes appeared in his *āshram* from time to time, he asked that they not be killed but caught and released in safe places. When asked what should be done if a child was attacked or a man lynched by a mob, Gandhi replied that one should interpose oneself between them, reason with the people involved and, if need be, give up one's life. If this seemed unlikely to work or if one lacked the required courage, then violence was pardonable. Gandhi observed:[45]

> God would not excuse me if, on Judgement Day, I were to plead before Him that I could not prevent these things from happening because I was held back by my creed of non-violence.

During communal riots, his advice was constantly sought by victims of rape. He advocated non-violent and, if that did not work, violent resistance. Not that women were to carry knives and pistols rather they were to use their 'nails and teeth' and whatever other physical resources they could muster. He thought that if some of the dishonoured women were to die in the course of resisting their assailants or to commit suicide afterwards, deep moral nerves would be touched and a new climate created in which men would be ashamed to commit rape.

Preservation of organised social life was yet another source of violence. Gandhi thought that although the state was created to minimise and even eliminate violence, it often failed to do so in practice and gave rise to new forms of violence. It made a fetish of its boundary and without the slightest compunction killed thousands in defence of a few acres of land. It saw every act of disorder as a challenge to its majesty and sought to forestall it by establishing a system of terror. It treated armies as symbols of national honour and political virility, and spent vast sums of money equipping them with the latest and most lethal means of destruction. Like a child with a dangerous toy, the state's ready access to concentrated violence was a standing invitation to governments to misuse it.

For Gandhi, the answer lay in redefining the nature of the state and appropriately restructuring its institutions.[46] The state was a cultural rather than a territorial unit concerned with safeguarding an established way of life. A way of life was not a monolithic unit but a confederation of sub-cultures and ways of life, each more or less open and subject to constant change. Every society consisted of long-established communities which gave its members roots and a sense of meaning and purpose. Rather than feel threatened by them and replace them with one over-arching and all-embracing association as the modern state had hitherto done, it should protect them and encourage the creation of new ones. The state should become not a collection of isolated individuals with nothing to unite them save their abstract citizenship, but a community of communities, a loosely structured federation of lively and organic social units.

In such a plural polity, moral ties, pressure of public opinion and enlightened self-interest could go a long way towards reducing the incidence of violence. Since men and women would have to resolve their differences themselves and since they would know that they had to live together and rely on each other's goodwill and cooperation, there would be less conflict, and such conflict as did occur would be less intense and easily resoluble. Order would be easier to maintain when embedded in a cooperative way of life and grounded in a climate of mutual trust and goodwill. Self-governing local communities and associations could take over many of the functions currently monopolised by the government and, thus, increasingly reduce the role of law and coercion. The police could be replaced by social workers enjoying the respect and affection of their fellow-citizens and trained in the arts of moral leadership and non-violent peace-keeping. The standing army could be replaced by citizens trained in the methods of non-violent national defence and prepared to lay down their lives rather than live under foreign rule.

Gandhi was convinced that a good deal of the external and internal violence of the state grew out of the need to maintain an unjust and exploitative economic system. He did not share the view that a revolution was the best way to achieve a just and humane society. It replaced one system of injustice with another, invested the state with enormous power and stifled the moral energies of society. It treated men and women as passive objects and did nothing to win over the dominant groups. Gandhi felt that *satyāgraha* was the only effective and moral way to tackle the problem. Every oppressive and exploitative system ultimately depended on the cooperation of its victims, and it would not last a day without their active or passive material and moral support. If they refused to cooperate with it, launched a *satyāgraha* and suffered with love and determination whatever punishment was meted out to them, they would eventually win over their erstwhile masters and restructure the system along desired lines. Gandhi was realistic enough to recognise that weak and disorganised men and women did not always find it easy to resist the use of violence, especially when confronted with determined and ruthless opponents. Although such violence was regrettable, it was 'understandable' and 'pardonable'. In 1942, he gave several important interviews to Louis Fischer in the course of which he discussed the likely peasant movement in independent India.[47]

Gandhi: In the villages the peasants will stop paying taxes. This will give them the courage to think that they are capable of independent action. Their next step will be to seize the land.
Fischer: With violence?
Gandhi: There may be violence. But then again the landlords may cooperate.
Fischer: You are an optimist.
Gandhi: They might cooperate by fleeing.
Fischer: Or they might organise violent resistance.
Gandhi: There may be fifteen days of chaos, but I think we could soon bring that under control.

The struggle for human dignity and freedom in general and political independence in particular was of special and immediate interest to Gandhi. He was convinced that the reign of violence could not be ended by adding to it and that non-violent struggle was the only answer. However he realised that non-violence did not come easily to those not fully trained in and committed to it, and that most ordinary men and women resorted to violence when provoked 'beyond endurance'. Although morally unacceptable, such violence was 'understandable'. While all violence was 'bad and must be condemned in the abstract', it was important to distinguish between its different forms and contexts. Defensive violence was morally superior to the offensive, as it was largely reactive and provoked by the opponent. Spontaneous violence was a result of accumulated frustration and superior to premeditated violence.[48] The violence of long-suppressed groups lacking the capacity for concerted action was more 'understandable' than that of those with an opportunity to participate in political life and to develop organised strength. Though regrettable, the violence of those who had been humiliated and brutalised for centuries was not 'senseless' and served the useful purpose of helping them acquire a sense of power and dignity. Desperate violence by isolated individuals and groups in the face of an overwhelming violence by their oppressors was often the only available way to preserve their human dignity. Indeed, since it was largely symbolic and 'unequally matched', it was 'really' or 'comparatively' non-violent. The Polish resistance to German invaders during the Second World War was, like the resistance of a mouse to a cat, 'almost non-violent'.[49] Although it was 'thoughtless', the violence committed during the 'Quit India' Movement of 1942 was born out of 'sheer desperation' and 'provoked by the government'. When Gandhi came to know that prisoners were tortured in some of the princely states of India, he advised them that if they could not do so non-violently, they should 'resist the tortures with all the violence they can summon from within and die'.

Finally, Gandhi argued that although non-violence was far superior to violence, the latter was 'infinitely' better than cowardice. A coward lacked 'manliness' and was commited to nothing more elevated than sheer survival. By contrast, a man prepared to use violence had pride and self-respect and was prepared to die rather than surrender what he held dear. Forgiveness was certainly better than vengeance, but the latter was 'any day superior to passive, effeminate and helpless submission'. Furthermore, a violent man might one day be won over to non-violence, whereas a coward was beyond hope. 'We do want to drive out the beast in man, but we do not want on that account to emasculate him.'[50] Gandhi also thought that violence had at least some deterrent effect and might reduce its future incidence whereas cowards only fed the voracious appetite of the bullies.[51]

VII

In the earlier sections we outlined and commented on different aspects of Gandhi's theory of *ahimsā*. Before concluding the chapter, we might comment on one of its striking and paradoxical features. On the one hand, he carried *ahimsā* much further than any other theorist of it had ever done. Unlike most of them, he did not merely attack wars but also the institution of the state, including armies, the police and prisons. And unlike almost all of them, he showed a remarkable sensitivity to the non-human world and insisted on the 'absolute efficacy' of *ahimsā*. On the other hand, he permitted or condoned violence in many more types of situation than most of them had done. He drew fine, sometimes too fine, distinctions between different forms and levels of violence and even called some of them 'almost' or 'comparatively' non-violent. He freely used the vocabulary of violence and called *satyāgraha* 'non-violent warfare' or 'war without violence', his followers non-violent 'soldiers' or an 'army for swaraj', and himself their 'general' or 'dictator'. He also borrowed some of its organisational tools and modelled some of his *satyāgrahas* after the army requiring oaths, pledges and unquestioning obedience. His Indian and Christian critics were not entirely wrong to suggest that his non-violence had an air of militancy about it and shared far more in common with violence than he realised or cared to admit.

The apparently paradoxical character of Gandhi's theory is traceable to several sources of which two are relevant to our discussion. First, for him, non-violence was not the only or even the highest value and had to be reconciled with such other values as truth (which he defined broadly to include justice and integrity), national independence, courage, human survival, self-respect and dignity. He knew that these values sometimes conflicted and that non-violence could not always be given moral priority. Second, Gandhi's theory was developed in the context of and intended to guide political action. Unlike most theorists of non-violence who were religious men primarily concerned to preserve their moral integrity in the face of evil, Gandhi led a great national movement aiming to liberate and regenerate a long-subjugated and diffident people. He had, therefore, little choice but to adjust his theory to the inescapable constraints of political life and mass action. He knew that a principle which took no account of the logic of its context was doomed to impotence. Having condemned all acts of violence early in his political career in India, he began to appreciate that a complete embargo on it was neither realistic nor desirable. Desperate and oppressed people unused to disciplined non-violent action and provoked beyond endurance were bound, at times, to lose patience and to resort to violence. Setting them an impossible ideal not only demoralised them but also discredited the doctrine of non-violence. A calculated use of violence as a matter of deliberate policy was one thing; a spontaneous recourse to it under intense provocation was altogether different. Gandhi thought that no inconsistency was involved in condemning the former and reluctantly acquiescing in the latter. He knew that he stood a better chance of regulating, reducing and eventually eliminating violence by acknowledging and finding a limited and clearly defined moral space for it in his political theory than by abstractly condemning or shutting his eyes to it.

While Gandhi was right to recognise moral plurality and to adapt his theory to the intractable world of politics, the way he went about his task created acute difficulties. He knew that his ideal of a completely non-violent society was unrealisable and that violence was necessary, unavoidable or understandable when used in the pursuit of such values as individual and social life, justice, the assertion of human dignity and the development of courage or when provoked by unbearable oppression. However, he did not show how these values were grounded, why they were desirable, what was to be done when they conflicted, how much moral weight to assign to each of them and how they were related to the principle of non-violence. Nor did he clarify whether his list was exhaustive or whether there could also be other values limiting the scope of non-violence. Since the values were not *internally* related to non-violence, Gandhi's resolution of their conflict lacked a guiding principle and remained *ad hoc* and a matter of his personal preferences.

Since Gandhi's moral theory contained a mass of disparate and internally unrelated values, it remained extremely loose and open-ended and was unable to offer much guidance to his followers. For example, they could not decide whether they were justified in launching a *satyāgraha* when there was a risk of violence. Gandhi's *theory* pointed both ways. His *practice* did not help much either. He disapproved of peasant *satyāgrahas* in the thirties on the ground that they were likely to lead to violence. Yet he approved of them in his interview with Louis Fischer and launched the Quit India Movement in 1942 in full knowledge that some violence was bound to occur. Take another rather trivial case. He said that his *ahimsā* ruled out a non-vegetarian diet, especially when fruits, vegetables and agricultural products were available in plenty. But he also said that if a man was used to it and likely to be hurt when denied it, he should be provided with a non-vegetarian diet as the violence involved in denying it to him was greater than that of killing an animal! Accordingly, he served meat to such visitors to his strictly vegetarian *āshram* as Louis Fischer and Maulana Azad. Many of his Jain and Hindu followers were puzzled and some were deeply offended by his behaviour. They thought that he could have persuaded his guests to refrain from a non-vegetarian diet while they were in the *āshram* and that, while he was solicitous about their needs, he did not much care about the sentiments of his fellow-*āshramites*, especially the women. Since Gandhi's *ahimsā* could be interpreted in several different ways, it led to confusion and casuistry.

Gandhi often remarked that it was not his job to tell people how to organise their lives and that each of them should sincerely decide for himself how best to practise *ahimsā*. This obviously would not do, for sincerity by itself is too vague a guide to the complexity of life and too feeble a protection against conscious and unconscious self-deception. Furthermore, Gandhi was not and did not see himself as a private individual living his life as he pleased. He was a moral 'scientist' engaged in conducting moral 'experiments' with a view to discovering a new *yugadharma* for his countrymen. Those attracted to his ideals were, therefore, entitled to expect a guiding framework other than his own practice. In its absence they felt lost and invoked his authority to sanction contradictory modes of conduct.

Traditionally Hindu moral theory has oscillated between providing, on the one hand, an elaborate code of conduct regulating the minutest details of life, and, on the other, a set of highly abstract ideals with the minimum possible rules to guide their practice, for the most part recommending the former for ordinary men and women and the latter for the moral elite. This has often led to unthinking conformism at one end of the social spectrum and limitless freedom lacking crucial navigational devices at the other. Gandhi's moral theory not only failed to solve this traditional Hindu dilemma but accentuated it.

Chapter Five

Dialogue with the Terrorists

I

Though India's struggle for independence was largely non-violent, it was constantly shadowed and vitalised by a relatively small but vocal and, at times, highly effective terrorist movement.[1] The movement began in the 1870s as a reaction against the way in which the colonial government set about responding to the political trauma of 1857. As we saw elsewhere, most Indians thought that the government in London was sympathetic to their aspirations, but that its good intentions were systematically frustrated by its narrow-minded representatives in India. Queen Victoria's proclamation seemed to them to indict previous Indian governments and to promise better times. The Raj's subsequent failure to satisfy the legitimate expectations it had itself aroused led to bitter disappointment. Furthermore, the new style of government in India intensified the growing trend towards a bureaucratic rule. The Indian administrative system was a closed corporation, proud of its professionalism, supremely convinced that it knew how to rule and civilise the country, and held together by a fierce sense of mutual loyalty. It was remote, arrogant, unbending, and in no doubt that it was devoted to the pursuit of the interests of its subjects. It fancied itself as their protector and guardian, and in close touch with their hopes and fears. As such, it was impatient of the criticisms of the western-educated Indian leadership whom it contemptuously dismissed as 'self-serving', 'unrepresentative' and 'out of touch' with its countrymen. Its arrogant claim to know 'real Indians' better than their own countrymen and its subtle attempt to drive a wedge between the two naturally aroused strong resentment. Indian leaders also bitterly attacked it for reducing the 'art of ruling' to an 'inhuman and impersonal science' and 'mechanically' imposing a strait-jacket of abstract rules on a highly diverse reality.

The brutal British treatment of those involved in the rebellion of 1857 and even of innocent citizens aroused strong feelings of revulsion and gave a glimpse of the ruthlessness of the 'civilised' Raj. Captured rebels were generally blown away by the cannon to which they had been securely strapped and entire villages near Kanpur were put to the torch. Bahadur Shah's sons were murdered in cold blood by a Captain Hodson who was determined to ensure the 'total extinction of a dynasty'. Many ordinary British residents went mad and wantonly attacked innocent villagers and even their faithful domestic servants. The liberal Macaulay, now retired in London, expressed the widespread feeling in England:[2]

> The cruelties of the sepoys have inflamed the nation to a degree unprecedented within my memory. Peace Societies, and Aborigines Protection Societies, and Societies for the Reformation of Criminals, are silenced. There is *one terrible cry for revenge*. The account of that dreadful military execution at Peshawur—forty men blown at once from the mouths of cannon—their heads, legs, arms flying in all directions—*was read with delight by people who three weeks ago were against all capital punishment*. Bright himself declares for the vigorous suppression of the mutiny. The almost universal feeling is that not a single sepoy within the walls of Delhi should be spared; and I own that it is a feeling with which I cannot help sympathising.
>
> ... *But it is painful to be so revengeful as I feel myself*. I, who cannot bear to see a beast or bird in pain, could look on without winking while Nana Sahib underwent all the tortures of Ravaillac. And these feelings are not mine alone. Is it possible that a year passed under the influence of such feelings should not have some effect on the national character?

Thanks to the fear of Indians generated by the rebellion of 1857, and thanks also to the opening of the Suez Canal which brought British women to India in large numbers and generated a climate of sexual jealousy and emotional insecurity, the colonial rulers isolated themselves from their subjects and displayed morbid forms of personal and institutional racism. Educated Indians, who had staked much on becoming Westernised, were insulted, mocked, made to feel small and denied positions commensurate with their proven abilities. The phrase *Jati-vairita* or racial animosity, first used by Bhudev Mukhopadhyay in 1864, caught the dominant mood and became popular.[3] The British insisted that they were separated from their subjects by an 'unsurpassable' racial divide; the latter reciprocated by developing what Bankim called this 'evil yet necessary sentiment' of racial animosity. As Pennel, a district and sessions judge, put it in his summing up of an important case:[4]

> Assaults by Europeans upon natives are unfortunately not uncommon. They are not likely to cease until the disappearance of real or supposed racial superiority.

The agitation surrounding the Ilbert Bill was an important milestone. Exposed for the first time to the unrestrained expression of the most violent racist invectives, Indians were left in no doubt about what the Anglo-Indians really thought of them. They also saw that it was possible for a small but determined and well-organised group to force the government to withdraw a measure behind which it had thrown all its weight. An anonymous letter in the *Hindu Patriot* drew the obvious lesson when it advised Hindus to 'return hatred for hatred' and to 'learn to help themselves'.[5] The weekly *Charuvarta* put the point more strongly: 'No one ventures to oppress where there is power. Endurance renders oppression easy; opposition produces power. The people of India should depend entirely on their own power.'[6]

The tragic consequences of the government's economic policies, especially the free trade introduced in the 1830s, became evident in the 1860s and 1870s. Destruction of indigenous industries, the commercialisation of agriculture, the increasing loss of autonomy of the Indian economy, the increase in land rent and taxes to meet the expensive civil and military administration, among others, led to large-scale unemployment, acute poverty and long and chronic famines. The appearance of an extensive body of critical economic literature during the 1870s, Ranade's 'doctrine of the relativity of economic laws', Naoroji's highly popular 'drain theory' and the spread of the *Swadeshi* movement were all reflections of the growing consciousness of economic exploitation. During the late 1870s, the themes of arrogant and remote bureaucracy, contemptuous rejection of the representative claims of the educated elite, racism and economic exploitation dominated the national agenda and became subjects of much heated discussion in the English language and vernacular literature. Lacking legitimate channels of protest and pressure, the frustrated Indians, especially the urban, middle class, educated and largely unemployed youth, reared on the heroic stories of 1857 and the bitter memories of the Raj's brutal response, began to think of violence as the only available mode of action. Terrorist groups and secret societies sprang up in Bengal and Maharashtra and, a few years later, in the Punjab and the United Provinces. Their literature was widely circulated and eagerly devoured even by those unsympathetic to their methods. *Akhārās* and gymnasia were set up in several parts of the country to provide martial training. Landlords in Bengal allowed terrorists to use secluded parts of their lands to store their equipment and to organise training camps. Money was raised to send young Indians abroad, initially to France to make contacts with Russian revolutionaries, and later to the Soviet Union to learn 'advanced methods' of terrorism. The terrorists were fascinated by the bomb and saw this 'Russian method' as the only effective answer to British rule. As the presiding judge at Tilak's trial observed several years later, the 'advent of the bomb in India' was in the eyes of many a terrorist a 'great historical event'. One of the interesting books to be produced by the terrorists was appropriately called the *Philosophy of the Bomb*.

The terrorist movement enjoyed some measure of support among overseas Indians in Canada, the USA, South-East Asia and especially Britain.[7] Shyamji Krishna Varma, a Cambridge graduate, started the India Home Rule Society in London. Valentine Chitrol of the *Times* described it as the 'most dangerous organisation outside India'. It recruited young Indian activists, collected money and arms, and maintained close contacts with its counterparts in India. It published a weekly called the *Indian Sociologist*, a title chosen to convey its founders' conviction that the 'new scientific discipline of sociology' founded by Comte and popularised by Spencer should form the ideological basis of the Indian struggle for independence. Not surprisingly, it carried quotations from Spencer's writings on its masthead. The authority of the two sociologists was invoked to justify a biologically orientated world view with its emphases on struggle, violence, national solidarity and subordination of the individual to the needs of the 'national organism'.

By the end of the nineteenth century, the terrorist movement had become too important to be ignored. Though not powerful enough to threaten colonial rule, it was strong enough to be a source of some concern. It had resulted in the deaths or attacks on the lives of nearly forty government officials and several raids on ammunition factories and public buildings. The colonial government was worried and so were many national leaders. Allan Octavian Hume apprehended a 'terrible revolution' and wrote in his memorandum to the government that the ranks of young terrorists were now joined by the 'lowest classes' who chose to fight rather than 'starve and die'. 'They were going to do something and stand by each other, and that something meant violence.'[8] He proposed a constitutional organisation as a 'safety-valve for the escape of great and growing forces generated by our action'. Along with a group of Anglo-Indian and Indian liberals, he helped set up the Indian National Congress in 1885, and even Lord Dufferin, the new Viceroy, hoped that it would emerge as 'Her Majesty's Opposition' in India.

The Congress became and for years remained a forum of debate rather than an instrument of action, and scrupulously avoided issues likely to offend the government on the one hand and orthodox Hindus and Muslims on the other. Even Hume's memorandum mildly warning the government of the political consequences of growing poverty created a stir in Britain and India and was disowned by Dadabhai Naoroji and several other Congress leaders. Being constantly subject to pressures from below, the Congress could not remain totally inoffensive and moderate. From time to time it spoke up against the colonial government's policies, only to be accused of being secretly sympathetic to the terrorist cause. For nearly a quarter of a century it remained little more than a debating society of upper class Indians. Not surprisingly, it carried little weight either with Indians or with the government. Its president sometimes had great difficulty even securing an interview with the Viceroy. Hyndman put the point well in a letter to Naoroji:[9]

> I cannot help feeling contempt for the Indians here and in India who, instead of taking up their own cause in a serious way, pass such a silly resolution of congratulation to the Queen as was passed at the Indian National Congress the other day. Congratulations for what? For having ruined India for two or three generations to come? It is pitiful. Men in high positions have said to me, 'Where is the evidence of discontent, Mr. Hyndman? Where is the cry for justice from the people of India themselves? If the people are so poor and oppressed, as you say they are, surely we should hear a little more of it than we do hear.

The impotence of the Congress was exposed in the way it dealt with the Partition of Bengal, first mooted in the 1890s, formally proposed in 1903 and effected in 1905. Though perhaps administratively defensible, the Partition aroused the deepest fears. It showed a radical shift in the hitherto pro-Hindu British policy and appeared to be part of a larger design to give Muslims an independent territorial and political base and build them up as a counterweight to Hindus. It coincided with the move to grant Muslims a separate electorate and was unfolded by Curzon in a manner that aroused strong and legitimate suspicions. It also looked like both a reprimand to the Congress for its mild but growing militancy and a gesture of defiance against the terrorists. Public reaction to the Partition all over India, and especially in Bengal, was immediate and fierce. Since it was perceived by the Hindus as a threat to their political aspirations and interests, it provided a rallying point for their growing self-consciousness and self-confidence and generated a highly influential Hindu nationalist ideology and movement. Thanks to the distinction between political and social questions informing Congress deliberations, Hindu self-consciousness had grown up outside its ranks. Hence, when it took a political form, it threw up an independent parallel movement interacting with but largely outside of the Congress. The Congress leadership was unable even to understand the deeper causes of Hindu anger and fears, let alone give them political articulation and leadership. Predictably, the emergent Hindu nationalism, the first phase in the evolution of the so-called political Hinduism, initially linked up with the terrorist movement and later attempted to take over the Congress itself. The terrorist movement now acquired a new dimension. It had hitherto drawn inspiration from European positivism and attacked colonial rule on political and economic grounds. It now began to turn to Hindu philosophy, especially the *Vedanta*, and stressed the moral and cultural consequences of colonial rule. Though militant Hindu nationalism was not necessarily terrorist and only some of its leaders engaged in terrorist activities, most of them were in varying degrees convinced that terrorist violence was unavoidable.

Once the Partition of Bengal ceased to dominate the political agenda, the terrorist movement went into a relative decline. Thanks to the increasingly high-handed and repressive methods of the colonial government, of which the Jallianwala Bagh massacre was a poignant example, it re-emerged in the 1920s. Many erstwhile terrorists had hitherto supported the Congress which had, under Gandhi's leadership, become an activist organisation articulating and giving effective expression to growing popular discontent. Gandhi's nationalism, however, was neither secular like that of the Congress, nor Hindu like that of the militant Hindu nationalists, but intercommunal and based on amity and accord between the major religious communities. As such, it did not wholly satisfy either group. His insistence on non-violence created further difficulties highlighted by the Chauri Chaura incident. Many religiously minded as well as secular young radicals, who had enthusiastically joined the Non-Cooperation Movement, were deeply angered and frustrated by his unilateral withdrawal of it. Gandhi's decision was motivated by several considerations, one of them being his determination to make it clear at the start of his political career in India that *he* was the leader of the independence movement and that he would have no truck with violence. Many secular radicals and Hindu nationalists, who thought that the choice of the method of struggle for independence was a matter of tactics rather than moral principle, got the message and parted company with him. Until India's independence, many of them continued to engage in terrorist activities. They were drawn from different political parties such as the Hindu Mahasabha, the Congress Socialist Party, the Communists and even the Congress. They did not form a coherent group sharing a common ideology. Different groups operated independently of each other and their only common bond was the belief that Indian independence was unattainable without violence.

II

By international standards the Indian terrorist movement was sober and restrained. It was never attracted by the doctrine glorifying violence as a law of nature, a uniquely authentic form of self-expression, a 'blood bath' that in Marx's words cleansed away the psychological and moral mud of the ages or as the highest expression of human energy and freedom. It saw violence in instrumental terms and as a regrettable method of last resort. Though, as we saw, the terrorists articulated their justification of it in different idioms at different times, two arguments remained constant. First, the colonial government was racist, repressive, exploitative and contemptuous of Indians and their culture. It ignored public opinion, provided no or largely ineffective channels for constitutional pressure, disregarded the rule of law and crushed expressions of dissent and dissatisfaction. Since it ruled the country by terror, it could only be influenced and eventually dislodged by counter-terror. As Madame Bhikaji Cama put it quoting the widely popular figure of Mazzini, 'Let us stop arguing with people who know our arguments by heart and do not heed them'.[10] Aurobindo expressed a similar view:[11]

> Liberty is the life-breath of a nation; and when the life is attacked, when it is sought to suppress all chance of breathing by violent pressure, any and every means of self-preservation becomes right and justifiable,—just as it is lawful for a man who is being strangled to rid himself of the pressure on his throat by any means in his power.

Second, thanks to centuries of foreign rule, especially the British, the only one in India's long history to disarm its people, the latter had become 'effeminate', 'cowardly', 'passive', 'lifeless' and paralysed by a deep sense of inferiority, fear and powerlessness. They had been systematically brainwashed into despising themselves and their civilisation and deprived of pride and self-respect. As Madame Cama said, 'We do not want to imitate British civilisation.' Indians needed to be energised, taught to fight and given a collective sense of power. Violence by a courageous and committed few was the only way to do so. It demonstrated the fragility of the colonial structure of power and convinced Indians that they were not as powerless as they thought and that the British were not as invulnerable as they pretended. It also inspired Indians with a common sense of purpose, forged between them the deepest bonds of common sacrifice and gave them a sense of involvement in the struggle for their independence. When told that a few bombs would not drive away the British, Barin Ghose, a terrorist leader in Bengal, said, 'We did not mean or expect to liberate our country by killing a few Englishmen. We wanted to show people how to dare and die.'[12]

Despite their advocacy and use of violence, the terrorists seem to have felt deeply uneasy and defensive about both 'shedding blood' and doing so in 'cowardly secrecy'. On occasion after occasion, they expressed their abhorrence of violence and insisted that they would have preferred to use the slow methods of constitutional agitation and pressure had these been available to them, and that they would have liked to fight an 'open war' had the British not disarmed them. Madame Cama confessed that she thoroughly loathed violence but that 'owing to the heartlessness, the hypocrisy and the rascality' of the government and the Indian liberals, 'that feeling is now gone'. Even the Bombay government's confidential report in 1933 noted 'some fairly strong natural resistance' to terrorist violence. In the United States, where all Indians were called Hindus, they were considered poor terrorists because of, among other things, their poor training and inability to finish off their targets. In the course of covering the trial of Ram Chandra, the editor of *Hindustan Gadar*, *The New York Times* observed that unlike the Germans, the Hindus belonged to a 'race from which nothing at all is expected in the way of rapid and accurate pistol practice'.[13] The remark was intended to draw attention to several incidents in which Indian terrorists had displayed a strange loss of nerve at critical moments. Madanlal Dhingra, a member of the London branch of

Abhinav Bharat, who shot dead Sir Curzon Wyllie, said in his statement:[14]

> I admit, the other day, I attempted to shed English blood as a humble revenge for the inhuman hangings and deportations of patriotic Indian youths. I believe that nation held in bondage with the help of foreign bayonets is in a perpetual state of war. *Since* open battle is rendered impossible to a disarmed race, I attacked by surprise; *since* guns are denied to me, I drew forth my pistol and fired. The war of Independence will continue between India and England so long as the English and Hindu races last (if this present unnatural relation does not cease).

Dhingra's views were echoed by Savarkar:[15]

> We feel *no special love* for *secret* organisations or surprise and secret warfare. We hold that whenever the open preaching and practising of truth is banned by enthroned violence, *then alone* secret societies and secret warfare are justified as the inevitable and indispensable means to combat violence by force. Whenever the natural process of national and political evolution is violently suppressed by the forces of wrong, then revolution must step in as a natural reaction and ought to be welcomed as the only effective instrument to re-enthrone Truth and Right.
>
> ... You rule by bayonets and under those circumstances it is mockery to talk of constitutional agitation when no constitution exists at all. But it would be *worse than a mockery, even a crime* to talk of revolution when there is a constitution that allows the fullest and freest development of a nation. *Only because* you deny us a gun, we pick up a pistol. *Only because* you deny us light, we gather in darkness to compass means to knock out the fetters that hold our Mother down.

III

The terrorist movement could not survive let alone flourish under the vigilant colonial eye without a significant measure of popular support, especially among Hindus. Hindus vastly outnumbered the rest, and most of the terrorists were drawn from their ranks. Unlike the Sikh and Islamic traditions, both classical and folk Hinduism were ambiguous on the legitimacy of violence, especially when used *against* the established government by those lacking the *adhikār* to do so. When Gandhi appeared on the scene and preached non-violence, most of his critics were also Hindus. For these and other reasons we shall concentrate on the way terrorist violence was legitimised in the eyes of the Hindu masses.

In order to secure the support of and mobilise the Hindu masses, terrorists needed to do two things. First, they had to show that not just violence *per se* but *terrorist* violence had the sanction of the Hindu tradition and that it did not involve *adharma* or *pāpa*. Second, in the colonial context, they needed not just acquiescence but the active moral, emotional and financial support of the Hindu masses. They had, therefore, to mobilise the latter, to instil in them a sense of collective responsibility for terrorist violence and to show them that it was positively their *dharma* to support it. In order to attain these objectives, the terrorists and their sympathisers needed to reinterpret Hinduism in active, collectivist and political terms.

In Maharashtra, Tilak and his colleagues reinterpreted and collectivised the worship of Ganesh, a god who straddled both classical and folk Hinduism and combined the former's asceticism and wisdom with the latter's hedonism and devotionalism. Unlike Vithal, the popular regional god who was tied to the apolitical Bhakti tradition, Ganesh had close links with Siva, was a lord and protector of *gana* (community) and enjoyed the reputation of being a 'conqueror of all obstacles'. Though worshipped for several centuries, his worship had been largely a private affair, at best involving friends and neighbours. From about 1894 onwards, Tilak began to collectivise his worship and give it an unmistakable political orientation. 'Why shouldn't we convert large religious festivals into mass political rallies?', he asked in 1896.

Thanks to Tilak's able leadership, Ganapati societies sprang up all over Maharashtra and soon spread to other provinces.[16] By 1905, they were flourishing in nearly a hundred towns. They had their own choirs, songs, festivals, and drama societies that staged allegorical plays which promiscuously combined different gods and their legends. Revolutionary *shlokas* and songs were recited on the occasion of Ganesh worship and collected into widely popular booklets. The legend of Ganapati slaying the demon Gajasura became highly popular and was given a suitable political interpretation. He was adopted as a patron god by schoolboys and college students who, once drawn into the movement, were organised into athletic clubs of which the Abhinav Bharat was one of the most famous. Tilak suggestively compared Ganapati celebrations to the Olympic Games in ancient Greece and expected them to play a similar inspirational and unifying role.

Ganapati celebrations had been quite popular during the Peshwa regime before the extinction of Maratha rule. Their revival brought with it the memory of Shivaji, the glorification of whose deeds came to be added to the celebrations. The strange fact that Ganesh and Shivaji should have been run in a tandem and the latter turned into a *national* hero and an inspiration for a new *rājasuya yajna* shows how much Hindu religion was being politicised and politics religionised. The first Shivaji celebrations began in April 1896 and were distinctly political. Like the Ganesh celebrations, which were partly inspired by a desire to find a Hindu alternative to the Muslim Tazia, Shivaji celebrations too were distinctly communal and designed to affirm Hindu identity against both the British and the Muslims.

In Bengal, the suitably reinterpreted Durga, the goddess of *Shakti*, played an important political role, especially in the form of Kali.[17] Initially a helper of Durga and an expression of her wrath, Kali had gradually developed into an independent deity and the mistress of the universe. The public worship of her in Bengal began in the seventeenth century. Like Ganesh and Shivaji in Maharashtra, she was closely associated with the protection of Hinduism in general and the Brahmins in particular. Described as the 'Mother of Mother India', Kali became the guardian of her honour and the two mothers were bonded in a fascinating symbiotic relationship. Her anger, energy and vengefulness received particular emphasis and she came to be interpreted as a goddess who loved secrecy and mercilessly punished all violations of it. Secret societies sprang up all over Bengal requiring vows to be taken in her presence. The one required by the Decca Anusilan Samiti, the most rigidly organised of all, was by no means untypical:[18]

> In the presence of God, fire, mother, preceptor and the leader (making them witnesses) I swear that I will do all the work of the circle staking my life. If I fail to keep this vow, may the curse of Brahmans, of the mother, and of the great patriots of every country speedily destroy me.

Kali was supposed to demand the blood of 'wicked intruders'. Following the influential *dhārmic* view of violence discussed elsewhere, it was widely argued that assassinations executed in her name did *not* amount to violence. As one of the terrorists put it.[19]

> The Mother is thirsting after the blood of the Feringhees who have bled her profusely. Satisfy her thirst. Killing the Feringhee, we say, is *no* murder. Brother, chant this verse while slaying the Feringhee white goat, for *killing him is not murder*.

In the Punjab the Arya Samaj, which was initially an elitist and reformist movement, came to be interpreted along political lines. It inspired secret societies advocating violence against high government officials and dissuading peasants from joining the army. Shyamji Krishna Varma, who later set up a secret society in London and started the *Indian Sociologist*, was for many years a member of the Arya Samaj and a trusted lieutenant of Dayananda Saraswati. Apparently he found much in common between Dayananda and Spencer and made an easy transition from militant reformism to 'scientific' terrorism. Lala Lajpat Rai, described by the Viceroy as the 'head and centre' of the Arya Samaj, defended terrorist violence and made an effortless transition to some form of Marxism on which he built up the best library in the Punjab. Mahatma Munshi Ram, who later became Swami Shraddhananda, wrote the influential *Arya Samaj: A Political Body* freely using the basic principles of the Samaj and several Hindu scriptures to justify militant nationalism.

Throughout India, the two epics and the *Purānas* were reinterpreted in activist and collectivist terms. Those *Purānas* which described violent conflicts were given prominence, their central characters and episodes were interpreted in political terms, and some of their gods and goddesses were presented as proto-terrorists. The *Rāmāyana*, an essentially moral treatise with a large social and only a limited political content, was read in oversimplified Manichean terms. Since the violence it sanctioned was that of a ruler to whom a grave injustice had been done, it did not serve the terrorist cause and was generally ignored in favour of the more political *Mahābhārata*. To be sure the latter, too, posed considerable difficulties. The Pandavas had lost their land in a game of dice to which they had freely agreed. War became unavoidable only because the Kauravas refused to return the land even after their enemies had completed the required period of exile. Violence occurred within the context of a war. And it caused such massive destruction of human life that even the victors felt cheated of their victory. Since the Indian political reality did not quite fit this pattern, advocates of violence had to resort to highly convoluted interpretations of both the epic and the Indian situation. They described Indians as Pandavas and the colonial rulers as Kauravas. The latter had 'deceived' Indians by pretending to be interested only in trade and taking 'unscrupulous' advantage of their innocence and hospitality. Indians were only fighting for their rights and their struggle for independence was really a *dharmayuddha*. Their use of violence was not only justified but really a form of *yajna* or religious sacrifice. The *Appeal*, issued in Bengal shortly after the murder of Shams-ul-Alam, put the point well:[20]

> When God has so ordained, think ye not that at this auspicious moment it is the duty of every good son of India to slay these white enemies? ... *shāstras* are our guide for discrimination between virtue and vice. Our *shāstras* repeatedly tell us that the killing of these white fiends and of their aiders and abettors is equal to a great ceremonial sacrifice (*Aswamedh Yajna*). Come, one and all. Let us offer our sacrifice before the altar in chorus, and pray that in this ceremony all white serpents may perish in its flames as the vipers perished in the serpent slaying ceremony of *Jammajog*. Keep in mind that *it is not murder but yajna*—a sacrificial rite.

The terrorists found the *Gitā* especially useful. As it satisfied a number of disparate demands, it had begun to enjoy considerable popularity since the middle decades of the nineteenth century. It was concise and self-contained and could be presented to the supercilious missionaries as the Hindu equivalent of the Bible. Being highly philosophical, it could even be shown to be superior to the 'moralistic' and 'story-telling' Bible. Since it was eclectic and contained doctrines acceptable to different Hindu sects, it was capable of uniting them all. It was set in the context of a war and no less a personage than the Lord Himself sanctioned violence. Above all, it provided the Hindus engaged in a momentous struggle against the colonial government with a much-needed theory of action. Not surprisingly, there was hardly a national leader who did not study and write about it. Since they turned to it for different reasons, they naturally offered different and sometimes conflicting interpretations of it.

The terrorists and their sympathisers gave the *Gitā* unprecedented importance and thought that it summed up the essence of Hinduism. Many of them read it daily, some carried copies of it, a few wrote extensive commentaries on it, and nearly all of them invoked it in self-justification. Khudiram was hanged with a copy of the *Gitā* slung across his neck. During his incarceration, Tilak turned to the *Gitā* for guidance and wrote a massive treatise on it. More than a dozen copies of it were found among the effects of the Decca Anusilan Samiti when its premises were searched in 1908 and there was evidence to show that special *Gitā* classes were regularly held there. *Jugantar*, a paper sympathetic to the terrorist cause, had *yadā yadā hi dharmasya* as its motto. Several secret societies required their members to take oaths with a sword and a copy of the *Gitā* on their heads.

Terrorist writers read the *Gitā* in political and activist terms. Though their interpretations of its philosophy differed in several important respects, there was a broad consensus on its moral and political message. *Moksha* was the highest ideal of life and could only be attained by discharging one's *dharma*. *Dharma* held society together and *adharma* led to its disintegration. Social life was characterised by a constant conflict between good and evil or *dharma* and *adharma*. Since social order was the *sine qua non* of *dharma*, *loksangraha* or preservation of organised social life was the highest *political* value. Every individual, thus, had a duty to fight evil and to uphold and ensure the victory of *dharma*. The life of action or *karmayoga* was higher than *jnānayoga* and *bhaktiyoga*. In this imperfect world the fight against *adharma* sometimes required painful choices and apparently amoral actions such as taking life, breaking promises and telling lies. Though regrettable these were all fully justified. Krishna's remark, *ye yathā mām prapadyante tām tathaiv bhajāmyaham* was interpreted by Tilak to mean that 'tit for tat' of *shatham prati shāthyam kuryāt* was an inescapable principle of political life. The fact that Krishna himself had to tell a few lies and to ask Arjuna to resort to massive violence showed that even God could not function in this world without occasionally bending rules. Tilak spoke for most when he wrote:[21]

> Let us even assume that Shivaji first planned and then executed the murder of Afzal Khan. Was this act of Maharaj good or bad? This question which has to be considered should not be viewed from the standpoint of Indian Penal Code or *even smritis of Manu* or even the principle of morality laid down in the Western or Eastern ethical systems. The laws which bind society are for the common man like yourself and myself.... *Great men are above the common principles of morality* .... Did Shivaji commit a sin in killing Afzal Khan? The answer to this question can be found in *Mahābhārata* itself: Krishna's advice to Arjuna to kill his Guru and kinsmen for the sake of the conquest of *Dharma* over evil. No blame attaches to any person if he is doing deeds without being actuated by a desire to reap the fruits of his deeds. Shivaji did nothing with a view to fill the small void of his own belly from interested motives. With benevolent intentions, he murdered Afzal Khan for the good of others. If thieves enter our house and we have not sufficient strength in our wrist to drive them out, we should, without hesitation shut them up and burn them alive.
>
> Do not circumscribe your vision like a frog in a well: get out of the Penal Code, enter into the extremely high atmosphere of the *Bhagawat Gitā* and then consider the actions of the great men.

It was true that a sensitive moral agent often felt anguished and depressed by the need to use violence and preferred instead to withdraw from the world or acquiesce in injustices. Indeed, the *Gitā* itself was the story of how Arjuna, a lifelong warrior, felt paralysed by the very thought of violence. It required all the philosophical acumen of the Lord Himself, capped by *Vishwaroop darshan*, to get him out of his moral despair. As Krishna showed, the maintenance of *dharma* was the highest good and the violence used in pursuit of it was fully justified. Indeed, such a *dhārmic* violence was morally innocent and a matter of sacred duty. Krishna had himself announced in the *Gitā* that whenever *dharma* was threatened, he incarnated himself on earth to destroy the wicked. Violence could not have a greater legitimation.

The terrorists and their sympathisers, thus, derived not only a theory of violence but also a wider, quasi-Machiavellian theory of political morality from the *Gitā* in particular and the *Mahābhārata* in general. In order to show that their reading of the epic was not an aberration but represented the mainstream Hindu thought, they read other Hindu classics in similar light and concluded that the dominant image of a non-violent and unworldly Hindu, assiduously cultivated by colonial rulers and uncritically accepted by many national leaders, was a myth. He was well-versed in and fully equipped to cope with the duplicitous and violent ways of the world. The terrorist literature claimed to give the Hindu a true image of himself, his religion, history and cultural heritage, which every successful terrorist act was used to reinforce and popularise.

IV

Gandhi was deeply worried about the growing influence of the terrorists. He thought that their limited successes and brilliant propaganda had convinced their countrymen of the inevitability of violence. As he wrote to Lord Ampthill during his visit to London in 1908, 'I have met practically no one who believes that India can ever become free without resort to violence'.[22] Gandhi had to undermine that belief if he was to persuade his countrymen to give serious consideration to his alternative method of political struggle. He was even more worried about the influential and, in his view, thoroughly mistaken and extremely dangerous terrorist reinterpretation of Hinduism. He felt that the terrorists and their sympathisers were dazzled by modern civilisation and desperately anxious to mould India in its image. To say so openly or even to admit it to themselves would reinforce the painful sense of inferiority. Consciously or unconsciously, they therefore retrojected modern Europe into India's past and created the image of a once strong and militarily powerful country it was the duty of every patriotic Indian to recreate. Since the terrorist violence sprang from an 'infatuation' with modern civilisation, he thought that his best hope of undermining its moral and emotional appeal lay in subjecting the latter to a searching critique. This was why his first book, *Hind Swarāj*, was both an 'answer to the Indian school of violence' *and* a 'severe condemnation of modern civilisation'. For Gandhi, the two were inseparable. Evidently, the British shared his view for they banned both the terrorist movement and Gandhi's book.

Gandhi also had another reason for taking the terrorists seriously. Though he profoundly disagreed with their interpretation of Indian civilisation, he shared their view that Indians had become passive and lifeless, that they needed to be energised and organised and that this could only be done by a cadre of committed and courageous men. And though he disagreed with their methods, he greatly admired their bravery and high spirits. As he said on many occasions, violence was morally superior to cowardice, and those willing to fight and kill or be killed were better than those content to acquiesce and survive. Gandhi seems to have thought that if he could win over the terrorists to the cause of non-violence, he would solve two problems at once, namely, eliminate his rivals and recruit energetic lieutenants. This was why he sought them out during his crowded visit to London, attended their meetings, spent long hours discussing large issues with them and cultivated their friendship.[23] After his return to India, he continued to seek them out and kept up a long correspondence with them. Though critical of him, many of them trusted and confided in him, sought his advice in difficult situations and saluted his courage and patriotism.

Gandhi's dialogue with the terrorists was conducted at two levels.[24] He strongly disagreed with their advocacy of violence, and he also questioned their interpretation of Hindu religious and cultural thought, especially the *Gitā*. We shall take each in turn.

Gandhi rejected violence on four grounds: the ontological, the epistemological, the moral and the practical.[25] Being a manifestation of *Brahman*, every living being was divine. Taking life was, therefore, sacrilegious and a form of deicide. Furthermore, as a spiritual being, every man was amenable to moral persuasion. Even when he was blinded by narrow self-interest and prejudices, it was always possible to awaken his spiritual nature, appeal to his sense of dignity and fellow-feeling and to activate his moral impulses. Obviously, such 'spiritual surgery' required patience, persistence, suffering and a heart free of hatred and ill-will. *Qua* spiritual being, one owed it to oneself and to his fellow-men to cultivate these qualities. The use of violence in search of instant solutions reflected 'moral indolence' and 'spiritual inertia' and was unworthy of him. It also implied that some men were so degenerate that they had ceased to be spiritual beings. Gandhi considered this an impertinent assumption for which he found no evidence whatever.

Unlike many other critics of violence, Gandhi advanced a novel epistemological argument against it.[26] It was a fundamental and inescapable fact of human life that all knowledge was partial and corrigible. Differently endowed and situated persons saw the world differently, each grasping only a specific aspect of it. Their knowledge, further, grew over time and benefited from new experiences and discussions with others. In Gandhi's view, violence denied these fundamental facts. In order to be justified in taking the extreme step of harming or killing someone, one must assume that one is *absolutely* right, that the opponent is *totally* wrong and that violence will *definitely* achieve the desired result. The consequences of violence are irreversible in the sense that a life once terminated or damaged can never be revived or easily put together. And irreversible deeds require infallible knowledge to justify them. Since such knowledge was beyond human reach, Gandhi contended that violence rested on a false epistemological foundation. He acknowledged that, taken to its logical extreme, his theory of 'relative truth' undermined the very basis of action, for no man could ever act if he constantly entertained the nagging doubt that he might be wholly mistaken. However, Gandhi thought that one must at least acknowledge one's fallibility and leave ample room for reflection and reconsideration. Violence did not allow this. It generated feelings of anger, hatred and insecurity, none of which was conducive to critical self-reflection. It also required an investment of enormous emotional energy and commitment, and made acknowledgement of mistakes and graceful retracing of steps exceedingly difficult. Violence was doubly flawed: it assumed infallibility and ruled out corrigibility.

Gandhi also rejected violence on moral grounds. Morality consisted in doing what was right *because* one believed it to be right, and required unity of belief and conduct. Since the use of violence did not change the opponent's perception of truth, it compelled him to behave in a manner contrary to his sincerely held beliefs. By disjoining his belief and conduct, it created an untruth at the very heart of his being, violated his integrity and diminished his status as a moral being.[27]

Finally, Gandhi argued that violence could never achieve lasting results. An act of violence was deemed to be successful when it achieved its intended immediate objectives. However, if it were to be judged in terms of its long-term consequences and the kind of society it created, our conclusion would have to be very different. Every apparently successful act of violence encouraged the belief that it was the only effective way to achieve the desired goal and encouraged the habit of using it every time one ran into resistance. Society became used to it and never felt compelled to explore an alternative. Gandhi thought that violence also had the propensity to generate an inflationary spiral. Every successful use of it blunted the community's moral sensibility and raised its threshold of violence, so that over time an increasingly larger amount of it became necessary to achieve the same results. Initially, throwing a stone might be enough to draw the government's attention to a grievance; soon the assassination of an officer and later that of several of them became necessary. Every act of violence led to a vicious circle of mutual fears from which neither party was able to extricate itself. Each armed itself to the teeth, and not truth but superior force carried the trophy.

Gandhi acknowledged that since the terrorists did not share his philosophy of life, there was no point in debating with them the immorality of violence. He was, therefore, prepared to 'forget his philosophy of non-violence', examine violence 'only as a method' and to argue solely on the basis of 'hard facts'. They justified violence on the grounds that it alone was capable of 'driving away' the British and energising and regenerating the Indian people. Gandhi rejoined that it was capable of achieving neither.

Gandhi asked the terrorists how their violence was likely to drive away the British.[28] Ending colonial rule meant three things for him. First, getting rid of the British and securing India's political independence. Second, putting an end to their economic exploitation of India. And third, liberating the country from the cultural and moral domination of British civilisation and making it genuinely autonomous. For Gandhi, the three levels of domination were closely connected. The British had come to India in search of markets and colonised it in order to exploit it more effectively. Their political rule, therefore, had an economic basis. Furthermore, the British could not rule over such a large country without the latter's willing cooperation and support, which they could only obtain by getting Indians to believe that British civilisation was far superior to their own and that their initiation into it under colonial tutelage was in their long-term interest. If the Indians had not been a willing party to their moral indoctrination, the British would not have been able to consolidate and maintain their rule with such ease.

In Gandhi's view it was perfectly possible to end British rule while leaving intact the other two levels of domination. The British might leave India and yet their 'capital' might continue to rule with or without the collaboration of indigenous capitalists. And even ending their economic exploitation did not guarantee an end to their cultural and moral colonisation. India needed to end all three forms of domination, not just the political. As Gandhi put it, India must aim at *swarāj*, not just independence.

Unlike independence, a negative and legal concept, *swarāj* was a positive and cultural concept signifying full autonomy or self-determination. Every community had a distinct *swabhāva* or moral and spiritual constitution consisting of its deepest instincts, temperament, disposition and ways of thinking and doing things. It had acquired it during the course of its long history and was constituted and distinguished by it. It could, no doubt, change its *swabhāva*, but slowly, only in parts and in harmony with its inherent tendencies. *Swarāj* was a form of collective integrity, a community's mode of being true to itself and running its affairs in harmony with its deepest truth. For Gandhi, *swarāj* was the ultimate ideal of every territorially organised society. Independence was its necessary but by no means sufficient condition and was desirable only because a country forced to live by its ruler's truth remained untrue to itself. Every subject country, therefore, had a right and a duty to fight for its independence, and to do so in a manner that both cohered with its *swabhāva* and did not damage its larger goal of *swarāj*

Gandhi argued that the terrorists did not understand the complexity and deeper roots of colonialism. They were obsessed with political domination and ignored the two far more disturbing forms of colonial rule. Since they had not even thought about the latter, their method was incapable of ending them. Gandhi could not see how violence by itself generated hostility to foreign economic domination or alerted Indians to the dangers of invidious alliances between foreign and indigenous capitalists. Indeed, he thought that since the terrorists wanted to make India a strong industrial and political power, they were bound to tie its economic system even more closely to the metropolitan economy.

Gandhi was even less convinced that terrorist violence could ever end cultural and moral colonialism. The values of the terrorists were all of the 'European variety'. They admired physical bravery and not the apparently passive but really resolute and tenacious courage of the traditional Indian variety; material and not spiritual strength; self-assertion not self-abnegation, self-interest not self-sacrifice; uniformity rather than plurality of beliefs and value systems; the centralised state rather than a loosely structured traditional polity; affluence rather than a simple life. Gandhi thought the terrorists could not, therefore, avoid turning India into a 'mere copy' of Europe. Their nationalism thus, had a deep anti-national thrust, and their patriotism was subversive of the 'soul' of the country they claimed to love.

In Gandhi's view, violence could not achieve the limited terrorist goal of independence either. The colonial government enjoyed a measure of legitimacy in the eyes of its ideologically indoctrinated subjects and had little difficulty mobilising their support. It was heavily armed, highly efficient, firmly entrenched and prepared to be ruthless, and it had every economic reason to retain India. Indians presented a pathetic contrast. Many of them had no tradition of fighting, and those who had stood disarmed. They were deeply divided on ethnic, linguistic, religious and cultural lines and found it exceedingly difficult to unite. As the 'whole history' of India showed, collaborators and informers were available in plenty. That was why the terrorists remained few in number and were often betrayed by their colleagues. What was more, every act of terrorism gave the government an excuse to increase military expenditure and to curtail civil liberties. This further impoverished and weakened the morale of the already demoralised masses. Gandhi concluded that terrorism was 'suicidal at this stage of the country's life at any rate, if not for all time to come in a country so vast, so hopelessly divided, and with the masses so deeply sunk in pauperism and so fearfully terror-struck'.[29]

The terrorists insisted that their violence energised and regenerated their countrymen and developed their courage, pride and capacity for organised action. Gandhi totally disagreed. Having argued in *Hind Swarāj* that the violent agitation during the Partition of Bengal had 'awakened' the country and given it a sense of power, he later changed his mind, perhaps because he thought that he had found in his *satyāgrahas* a better way of achieving the objective. In his view, violence was necessarily restricted to a few and did not actively involve the masses who passively idealised terrorist deeds and basked in their vicarious glory. Instead of energising them, terrorist violence only reinforced their 'effete sentimentalism'. In the absence of active participation and personal sacrifices, Gandhi could not see how ordinary men and women would develop the qualities the terrorists wished to encourage. Indeed, terrorist violence had the opposite effect. Every time the government severely punished or hanged a terrorist, it so terrified its nervous subjects that they became 'more cowardly than . . . before' and withdrew into their private worlds.

Gandhi also questioned the terrorist equation of violence with courage. Violence required physical bravery but not necessarily political and moral courage, and implied that one was not afraid of *death*—not that one was not afraid of one's *opponent*. It was easier to shoot a man or throw a bomb at him in the dark than to stand up to him and challenge him to do his worst. Indeed, Gandhi thought that violence was often a product of cowardice. Afraid to look at a man straight in the eye, one took the easy way of killing him. As he put it: 'If I could be persuaded that revolutionary activity has dispelled cowardice, it will go a long way to soften my abhorrence of the method, however much I may still oppose it on principle.' He was not convinced that it did so.[30]

In Gandhi's view, building up the pride and self-confidence of a diffident and long-oppressed people, *ātmashuddhi* as he called it, was an immensely complex and protracted task calling for great patience, hard work and skilful organisation. It required living in the remotest villages, educating illiterate people, organising them, teaching them sanitation, hygiene and habits of cooperation, building up their economic strength, reconciling those long divided by deep cultural, religious, linguistic and other differences and healing wounds inflicted by centuries of oppression. The 'pilgrimage to *swarāj* is a painful climb' and required a 'patient, intelligent and constructive effort of tens of thousands of men and women, young and old'. It was not 'like the magician's mango' that could spring up from nowhere merely by engaging in heroic deeds.

Gandhi went on to argue that the terrorist did not see all this because he was far more interested in personal glory than in national regeneration. He was 'intoxicated with the thought of his bravery' and eager to die a highly visible, heroic death likely to yield him and his family worldly acclaim. Gandhi thought that this was a profoundly selfish and self-indulgent approach. Though not 'spectacular enough', a slow, painful and anonymous death suffered in the course of nursing the sick in a malaria-infected area or in fighting against evil social customs and local tyranny was far 'more heroic than the death on the scaffold under false exaltation'. Violence was not necessarily heroic or patriotic, and not all heroic action necessarily deserved admiration and encouragement. Since terrorism derived much of its appeal from the 'glamour' associated with such terms as heroism, courage and patriotism, Gandhi called for their 'new valuation' and 'definition'.

V

Gandhi had considerable difficulty refuting the terrorists' interpretation of Hindu thought and practice. They did not deny that

Hinduism held *ahimsā* in high esteem but insisted that it sanctioned violence in certain situations, a view they supported by citing sacred texts, especially the *Gitā*, and that Hindus had never hesitated to use violence when necessary.

Gandhi admitted that the terrorist reading of Hindu thought and history had a point. The ancient practice of animal sacrifice, the Hindu treatment of Buddhists, the small and large wars fought by Hindu kings, the Hindu treatment of *shudras* and *atishudras* and the gruesome forms of punishment recommended in the *Dharmashāstras* were all proof of this. Indeed, he had once though of writing a history of India from a non-violent standpoint and was struck by its conflicting traditions.[31]

> When I was in detention in the Aga Khan palace, I once sat down to write a thesis on India as a protagonist of non-violence. But as I proceeded with my writing, I could not go on. I had to stop. There are two aspects of Hinduism. There is, on the one hand, the historical Hinduism with its untouchability, superstitious worship of stocks and stones, animal sacrifice and so on. On the other, we have the Hinduism of the *Gitā*, the *Upanishads* and Patanjali's *Yoga Sutra* which is the acme of *ahimsā* and oneness of all creation, pure worship of one immanent, formless imperishable God. *Ahimsā*, which to me is the chief glory of Hinduism, has been sought to be explained away by our people as being meant for *sannyāsis* only. I do not share that view.

While conceding that the terrorist reading of Hindu thought and practice had some basis in facts, Gandhi went on to challenge it on two grounds. First, it was only partially true and ignored some of the deepest tendencies of Hindu thought. Second, the texts upon which the terrorists heavily relied, especially the *Gita*, were amenable to the opposite and more plausible interpretation.

Although it was true that Hindus justified and practised violence, it was no less true that they also described *ahimsā* as the highest value. Not only the *Upanishads* and Patanjali's *Yoga Sutra* but also the *Mahābhārata* called it *paramo dharma*. Hinduism believed in the doctrine of the unity of all life and even all creation and encouraged 'cosmic friendliness'. Over the centuries, some of the greatest Hindu sages and seers had endeavoured to live by these principles, conducted bold experiments, and left behind a rich tradition of inquiry into the nature of non-violence. Ever since the beginning of their civilisation, even the ordinary Hindus had thought of non-violence as its central organising principle and distinguishing feature, Gandhi argued.

According to Gandhi, *ahimsā* had not just remained an ideal but formed the basis of Hindu life. Hindus had established a non-conflictual and non-competitive social order based on *varnas*. Their habit of feeding ants and animals was a limited but significant indication of their recognition of the principle of the unity of life. And although they took a negative and passive view of non-violence, they did practise it in that form. It was because violence outraged their deepest instincts and aspirations that they never felt comfortable with it and confined it to the Kshatriyas to use it for clearly defined purposes. It was, of course, true that the Hindu state had frequently relied on violence in the form of prisons, gruesome forms of punishment, armed police and wars. However, the fact that it *practised* violence did not necessarily imply that it *believed* in it. Hindus acquiesced in the violence because they could not find an alternative manner of organising and running the state. For Gandhi, this was evident in the fact that when he invented the method of *satyāgraha*, they 'instinctively' responded to it both in South Africa and India and that no other community had welcomed it as much as the Hindus. He found it striking, too, that though Hindu kings had used violence as freely as their counterparts elsewhere, only a Hindu king abandoned it at the height of his power and spent the rest of his life administering his vast empire on non-violent lines. In Gandhi's view, all this demonstrated the abiding appeal of non-violence to the Hindu mind and its deep cultural roots. A civilisation as ancient and as subject to foreign invasions as the Indian was bound to develop cruel and ugly practices. However, a civilisation had to be judged not by the lowest depths to which it had fallen but by the greatest heights to which it had risen, not by its contingent social practices but by its deepest and abiding aspirations. As he put it:[32]

> The most distinctive and the largest contribution of Hinduism to India's culture is the doctrine of *ahimsā*. It has given a

definite bias to the history of the country for the last three thousand years and over, and it has not ceased to be a living force in the lives of India's millions even today. It is a growing doctrine, its message is still being delivered. Its teaching has so far permeated our people that an armed revolution has almost become an impossibility in India, not because, as some would have it, we as a race are physically weak, for it does not require much physical strength so much as a devilish will to press a trigger to shoot a person, but because the tradition of *ahimsā* has struck deep roots among the people.

Though Gandhi's interpretation of Hindu religion and history had some basis in facts, it was highly selective. He was right to argue that non-violence was a central value in Hindu thought, that rare individuals had practised it to the highest possible degree and that even the ordinary men, in their own limited ways, endeavoured to live by it. However, as we saw elsewhere, Hindus have generally taken a fairly tough-minded attitude to violence and were for that reason attacked by Buddhists and Jains. They did not even call it violence if it was required by human survival, religion and *loksangraha*. They fought many wars, some horrendous, and built up repressive political systems not because they did not find alternatives but because they saw nothing wrong in them. There is no evidence that, with isolated exceptions, any major Hindu thinker or ruler was deeply perturbed by political violence and interested in exploring an alternative to it. As Gandhi himself argued on other occasions, a social order that condemned a large number of people to subhuman existence could hardly be said to exhibit much non-violence. And the *varna* system he idealised involved a considerable amount of state violence to the lower castes.

Gandhi's interpretation of Hindu thought and practice was less coherent and persuasive than that of the terrorists. On occasions, he himself conceded that he had abstracted and romanticised one strand within it. Surprising as it may seem, he did not think that this required him to reject or even modify his thesis. The reasons for that lay in his attitude to history.[33] He was highly sceptical of the possibility of historical truth and objectivity. All interpretations of the past were partial and biased and there was no point in quarrelling about them. Even if historical truth were attainable, it was for him only one value and by no means the highest. The past had many uses and could be approached in several different ways, the historical being only one of them. For Gandhi, the historian did not have a monopoly of it and was wrong to feel possessive about it. The past was collective cultural capital, a vital moral resource, which a community had painfully built up over a long period and which it remained free to use to meet its present and future needs. The historian was really a parasite depending on his community to furnish him with his material. It was not open to him to tell it what it should do with the material let alone require it to conform to his norms. The past belonged to the community and he could not be allowed to hijack it or to deprive the community of its control over it.

For Gandhi, the historian's attitude to the past was necessarily different from that of his community. For the historian, the past was dead; indeed, this was the necessary precondition of his discipline. For the community, it was alive, potentially immortal, and subject to the cycle of rebirth, each generation reviving, reinterpreting and drawing new inspiration from it. The historian was concerned with the past; a moral community was concerned with the future and necessarily saw the past in terms of it. Its past was the basis of its future, and its hopes and memories, moral aspirations and historical recollections were necessarily intertwined. Again, the historian was interested in history *as it had* occurred; a community was primarily interested in *making* history and was at liberty and indeed had a duty to use its past for that purpose. So long as its interpretation had some basis in facts and was not wholly fanciful, a community was free to reconstruct its past in a manner that inspired its members to *make* history along desired moral lines. This did involve an element of myth-making, but that did not matter, for every individual and every community required myths and even an allegedly objective historian was never wholly free from it.[34] Moral truth was higher than historical truth, if not in general then at least from the standpoint of a human community. The two were subject to different criteria. And if moral truth involved *some* violation of historical truth, that was fully justified. Since non-violence was the only way forward for mankind and since India alone had cherished and experimented with it, Gandhi thought that he was entitled to stick to his interpretation. It was not totally wrong and had the great moral merit of inspiring his countrymen to give the violence-weary world a new lead.

We cannot comment here on the large philosophical issues raised by Gandhi's approach to the past and shall only make two points. First, it was derived from the traditional Hindu view of history and shared much in common with the treatment of the past characteristic of the *Purānas* and especially the epics. Second, Gandhi's view was widely shared by many of his contemporaries. As we noted elsewhere, Indians felt threatened by and had to find ways of coping with the historical approach to the past. They could not reject it altogether, both because that would have carried no conviction with anyone as also because they knew that history played a vital role in creating national self-consciousness. For reasons discussed earlier, they saw that it was a supremely *political* discipline with the state as its primary subject and subject matter and that it not only *described* its activities but also *defined* and *created* it in the very course of describing them. From about the middle of the nineteenth century, they therefore settled upon the Gandhian type of demarcationist approach which left the historian and his community equally free to deal with the past in their own different ways. Since the two were supposed to be interested in different kinds of truth, there was believed to be no conflict between them any more than there was between science and religion.

VI

The terrorists had argued that the *Gitā* not only sanctioned but enjoined violence under certain circumstances. Gandhi could have denied that it was a canonical text or enjoyed equality with the *Vedas* and the *Upanishads*. Since, for his own different reasons, he shared the terrorist view that it summed up the central principles of Hinduism, that answer was not available to him. He could have said that the *Gitā* was not an ethical but a metaphysical treatise advocating surrender to the will of God rather than a life of action. This was how Aurobindo had read *sarvadharamān parityajya māmekam sharanam vraja*. Like the terrorists,

Gandhi was a *karmayogi* and looked to the *Gitā* for a philosophy of action, and hence, that answer was not available to him either. He was left with no other alternative than to debate with the terrorists on their own ground.[35]

Gandhi's interpretation of the *Gitā* underwent an important change. Since it was an integral part of the *Mahābhārata*, he argued that the proper way to read it could only be decided on the basis of a prior determination of the nature of the wider text. In his view, it was generally agreed that the *Mahābhārata* was not an *itihās*, nor a fiction, nor a *kathā*, but a *dharmagrantha*. It was not an *itihās* because that was an essentially Western form of writing neither popular nor much developed in ancient India.[6] It was not a fiction because it centred around real persons and events and had a moral purpose. *Kathā* was history told with a view to conveying a message, a morally informed narrative. Since the historical basis of the *Mahābhārata* was thin and unimportant, it was not a *kathā* either. It was basically a *dharmagrantha*, an ethical treatise using suitably redefined historical situations to analyse moral dilemmas and to show how to deal with them. It did not discuss moral principles in the abstract and aimed to cultivate moral skills, sensibilities and intuitions by discussing general principles in concrete and realistic situations. As such, it was a 'story of the human soul', an allegory on life describing man's internal struggles in a quasi-historical manner.

Gandhi argued that the allegorical character of the *Mahābhārata* was evident in the way its author told the main story. The names of the majority of its central characters stood for 'personified qualities'. *Duryodhana* meant a man difficult to defeat in war and *Yudhishthira* meant one who remained unperturbed in situations of conflict. Again Vyasa ascribed most fanciful origins to many of the heroes. *Bhishma* was a son of the Ganges, *Karna* of the sun, *Dharma* of the God of death and *Bhima* of wind. The Pandavas were described as sons of *Dharma*. The hundred Kauravas were said to have been all born at the same time. And *Sanjaya*, who was supposed to describe the great war, was born blind. Gandhi contended that Hindu writers introduced most fanciful and implausible material in a text they did not want to be taken literally. This was evident in the case of *Rāmāyana*, the *Purānas* and countless popular legends. The *Mahābhārata* was not an exception.

Since the *Gitā* was an integral part of it, it too was meant to be read as an allegory. That was why its author used Arjuna's simple question to open up a wide range of philosophical and moral issues. The battle in it was not between two armies but between good and evil, spirit and flesh, forces of light and darkness; Kurukshetra stood for the human soul; the Pāndavas and Kauravas symbolised, respectively, the good and the far more numerous evil tendencies in man; Arjuna represented the individual ego; and, Krishna was the cosmic spirit 'dwelling in everyone's heart'.[37]

Gandhi's allegorical interpretation of the *Gitā* was untenable as he himself came to realise later. If the *Mahābhārata* was a *dharmagrantha* discussing man's social obligations, the *Gitā* could not be concerned with his internal struggles, at any rate not with them alone. Furthermore, its manner of discussing moral problems rendered Gandhi's interpretation wholly implausible. As Aurobindo pointed out in a conversation with Ambala Purani:[38]

> So Sri Krishna says to Arjuna, 'You may kill the bad passions or evil tendencies, but do not be sorry, really they are not going to be killed! Who kills whom?' Thus the whole thing is an allegory. But is it? . . . . Non-violence is not in the *Gitā*. If as some people, including the Mahatma, say the *Gitā* signifies a spiritual war or battle only, then what of *Aparihāryerthe* and *Hanyamāne śarire*—'inevitable circumstance' and 'body being killed'? What of *Shoka*—sorrow—for those who are dead? To me such a reading seems the result of a defect in their mental attitude.

Gandhi's interpretation was untenable on other grounds as well. It was dualistic, almost Manichean, and did scant justice to the *Gitā's* subtle moral theory and to his own well-considered moral insights. The Pandavas and Kauravas were both disciples of the *same* teacher, a poetic way of making the point that good and evil overlapped and had a common source. Again, some of the closest associates and fellow-fighters of the Kauravas were men of outstanding moral virtue. As Gandhi himself admitted, this was intended to show that evil flourished in the world by aligning itself with good. This meant that evil was never wholly evil, a view denied by his interpretation of the *Gitā*.[39]

Increasingly, Gandhi began to appreciate that the *Gitā* dealt with the moral dilemmas thrown up by social and political life and that the violence it discussed was *political* in nature and not that between good and evil impulses. He now contended that even when seen as a social and political text, the *Gitā* did not justify, let alone advocate, violence. His arguments were ingenious and original but somewhat muddled. He distinguished two levels at which it was written and needed to be read. At one level, it was a philosophical text enunciating general moral principles. At another, it was a historical text applying the principles to a specific context. Its 'principles', 'overall teaching' and 'general thrust' advocated non-violence. In the historical context of a specific individual living in a specific society and facing a specific situation, it sanctioned violence.

Far from advocating violence, the *Gitā*, in Gandhi's view, preached its futility[40]. The *Mahābhārata* war ended in a colossal disaster. All the Kauravas and their associates died in it; only 'seven victors' out of thousands survived; the Yadava race was almost entirely annihilated; and the deeply distressed and dejected Pandavas preferred to leave the world rather than rule over the kingdom for which they had valiantly fought. All this was 'surely' not a celebration but an indictment of violence and designed to convey the message that war was 'a delusion and a folly'.[41]

Gandhi went on to argue that *anāsakti* or non-attachment was the highest ideal according to the *Gitā*. Attachment led to worldly involvement and to the cycle of rebirths and was a major obstacle to *moksha*. It sprang from desires of which such passions as anger, hatred, greed an ambition were different forms. The aspirant of *moksha* must, therefore, cultivate a state of total desirelessnesss and act not out of a hope of reward but as an instrument of God's will. As the *Gitā* put it, *Karmanyevādhikāraste mā phaleshu kadāchan*. Men engaged in violence either because they were motivated by anger and hatred or because they were passionately concerned with attaining specific worldly goals. A man aspiring to live up to the *Gitā's* highest ideal knew neither anger nor hatred and had no desire for worldly possessions either. He had grasped the fundamental fact of the unity of man and was *samadarshin* towards friends and foes. Since the very concepts of friendship and enmity, mine and thine, made no sense to him, no human being was an enemy to him. He had, therefore, no reason ever to engage in violence. As Gandhi said, '*Himsā* is impossible without anger, without attachment, without hatred, and the *Gitā* strives to carry us to... a state that excludes anger, hatred, etc'.[42] The moral theory advocated by the *Gitā* thus, ruled out violence.

Gandhi conceded that 'a few of the verses' pointed in the opposite direction and that Vyasa perhaps 'intended' to justify violence. However, what really mattered was not his intention but the objective message of his poem. 'When a poet composes his work, he does not have a clear conception of all its possible implications. It is the very beauty of a good poem that it is greater than its author'.[43] In a 'moment of inspiration' a poet grasped a 'truth' whose full significance often eluded him and even contradicted some of his settled beliefs. It is not entirely clear what Gandhi meant by this. He could be attributing contradictory intentions to Vyasa, or he could be saying that Vyasa sought to justify violence in terms of principles which, when properly interpreted, had opposite implications. In any case, Gandhi was convinced that the *Gitā*'s doctrine of *anāsakti* undercut the moral and psychological basis of violence. He insisted that though his interpretation was 'new' and 'extended', it was 'natural' and 'logical' and based upon the 'whole teaching of the *Gitā* and the spirit of Hinduism'.

Although Gandhi's reading of the overall message of the *Gitā* is plausible, it is unconvincing. While it is true that the *Mahābhārata* war caused massive destruction of life, it is also true that in the end good triumphed over evil. One could, therefore, argue that the epic intended to show that violence helped a just and harmed an unjust cause. Besides, since Vyasa allowed the war to go on in spite of massive destruction, his basic message could be that some causes were so just and noble that they must be pursued irrespective of their consequences. It could also be argued that the *Mahābhārata* condemned a total, not a limited, war, and that it had nothing to say one way or the other about the kind of limited violence used by the terrorists.

Gandhi had argued that violence was incompatible with the *Gitā*'s doctrine of *anāsakti*.[44] It is difficult to see why this should be so. The use of violence need not necessarily be motivated or even accompanied by anger and hatred. One might use it out of a sense of duty and in a spirit of complete detachment. Indeed, as Gandhi himself interpreted the *Gitā*, that was exactly how Krishna had asked Arjuna to fight. He assured Arjuna that if he acted as a mere *nimitta* and regarded his actions as offerings to God, they would not 'blind' him. The relation between *anāsakti* and violence was extensively discussed by almost all twentieth century commentators on the *Gitā*, and none of them saw any conflict between the two. Characteristically, Gandhi neither read them nor dealt with their arguments. Furthermore, the term *anāsakti* could be understood in one of two ways. It could either mean total indifference to the consequences of one's actions or, more correctly, accepting them in a spirit of detachment after taking every precaution to ensure that they were good. In its first sense, it certainly ruled out violence, but it also ruled out a life of action. In its second sense, it enjoined a life of action but permitted violence when there was no other way to attain the desired consequences. Gandhi rightly understood *anāsakti* in the second sense, but drew conclusions that could only follow from the first.

We have so far discussed Gandhi's thesis that not violence but non-violence was the central message of the *Gitā*. We shall now turn to his second thesis that it only sanctioned violence in a specific historical situation. He agreed with the terrorists that Krishna did ask Arjuna to fight, but insisted that they were wrong to interpret this as a *general* justification of violence. The *Gitā* did not discuss violence in general but only in the specific and limited context of Arjuna's puzzle. It was a 'limited discourse' aimed at answering the specific question as to why Arjuna, a Kshatriya who had lost his nerve at the thought of having to kill his relations and close friends, should pull himself together and fight a just war.

According to Gandhi, Arjuna had been a warrior all his life and had fought many battles. He was eager to fight the *Mahābhārata* war as well and had, with that end in view, sought Yudhisthira's blessings and Indra's powerful weapons.[45] When he entered the battlefield of Kurukshetra, he asked Krishna to drive his chariot towards the centre so that he could see his enemies (*kairmayā saha yodhavyam*). It was only when he saw his kinsmen and his close friends arrayed against him that he lost his nerve, felt sick and questioned the morality of violence. Gandhi argued that Arjuna was not opposed to killing as such but only to killing his friends and relations. His aversion to violence was, thus, not born out of 'love of man or the hatred of war' but 'weakness of heart' (*hrdaya durbalyam*), and 'ignorant attachment'.[46] His condition was like that of a judge who, after years of sentencing criminals to death, felt troubled about the morality of capital punishment when confronted with his criminal son. Arjuna was not involved in a moral or spiritual crisis; rather, he was simply 'confused' and his reason was 'darkened' by understandable but morally irrelevant sentiments.

When, therefore, he asked why he should fight and cause massive bloodshed, Krishna had little difficulty giving him a satisfactory answer. He told him that since he had never before questioned the morality of violence, he was not entitled to do so now that his relatives and friends were involved. Moral principles did not admit of convenient exceptions based on personal attachments. He was a Kshatriya and it was his *swadharma* to fight. Furthermore, whether he liked it or not, he was a prisoner of his nature. All his past actions, training and social conditioning had made him a particular kind of being with a specific *swabhāva* and self-image. If he yielded to his temporary sense of gloom, he would deeply regret it later and would not be able to live with himself. As Krishna put it, *Prakritim yānti bhutāni nigrahah kim karishyati*. He went even further and warned Arjuna that the compulsions of his nature were inexorable. *Mithyaisha vyāvasāyaste prakritistvām niyokshyati*. Arjuna had no alternative but to fight. A grave injustice had been done to his family by his enemies and needed to be redressed. If he had another effective method available to him, he would have been exempted from the use of violence. Since there was none, he had no choice. Finally, Krishna reassured Arjuna that he was wrong to consider himself guilty of grave *adharma* in committing violence. That would have been the case had he killed his enemies out of hatred, malice, ill will or self-interest. Since he would kill them out of a sense of duty and as a way of preserving *dharma*, his violence was not *pāpa* and did not 'taint' him. As Krishna put it, *Hatvāpi sa imān lokān na hanti na nibhashyate*.

Gandhi contended that when carefully analysed, the *Gitā* justified violence only under specific conditions, namely when the agent involved was a warrior and had a socially prescribed *dharma* to fight, had never before questioned the immorality of violence, was seeking to redress a grave injustice, did not wish to make unjustified exceptions, was not guided by ill-will, hatred and personal gain and when no effective alternative to violence was available to him. Gandhi could not see how such a limited sanction could be taken to entail a general justification of violence in the pursuit of such causes as social transformation and national independence.

Gandhi was right and the terrorists were wrong. The *Gitā* was designed to answer a limited question put by a specific individual in a specific historical context. It discussed violence in the context of a major war and had little relevance for the kind of violence in which the terrorists were engaged. The difficulty with Gandhi's position, however, was twofold. First, his insistence on the historical integrity of the text and his concern to read it in its context sat ill at ease with his persistent tendency noted elsewhere to disregard the historical approach and dehistoricise Hindu classics. He could not consistently ask the terrorists to do what he rarely did himself, and remained vulnerable to the charge of playing hide-and-seek with the historical method. Second, while insisting on the historicity of the *Gitā*'s discussion of violence, Gandhi continued to argue that its moral and social doctrines, including *varnadharma*, were of universal validity. This meant that while its political message was historically specific, its moral and social message was not. Gandhi could not consistently plead historicity for some parts of it and not for others, at least not without offering adequate reasons. Since he offered none, he remained open to the legitimate charge of emphasising its historicity only in order to explain away its embarrassing theory of violence.

Chapter Six

Sex, Energy and Politics

As we saw earlier, Gandhi was deeply distressed by the state of contemporary India. Over the centuries, a once rich and creative civilisation had become corrupt and degenerate, and its bearers passive, lifeless and dull. Not surprisingly, they had fallen an easy prey to waves of foreign invaders, the British being the latest. Gandhi was convinced that India was doomed unless its civilisation was revitalised and its people 'energised' and 'activated'. 'Moving' a vast and 'inert mass' was a Herculean task requiring an enormous amount of *shakti*. He felt he had to find ways of generating it in himself and in a committed cadre of young men and women prepared to fan out into the remotest parts of the country and mobilise the masses.[1]

Shakti, an old and evocative Hindu concept, had begun to gain political currency since the second half of the nineteenth century. Indians knew that they had no hope of extracting concessions from the colonial government and eventually dislodging it without building up an effective power of their own. A whole new action-oriented political vocabulary centred around the concept of *shakti* began to be developed, and such terms as power, energy, will, will-power, vigour, strength, struggle, conflict, *karmayoga* and *rajas* came to be used with great regularity. The vocabulary was particularly common among the terrorists and the critical traditionalists. Gandhi took it over and suitably redefined it. As he understood it, *shakti* was the opposite of *jada* or inert, and referred to both energy and power. Though he nowhere clearly distinguished the two and occasionally used them interchangeably, he seems to have thought of power as concentrated and well-directed energy. All power was derived from energy, but the latter did not generate it until it was mobilised, organised, focused and directed at a clearly specified goal. The 'inert' Indian masses lacked energy and hence power; the terrorists had plenty of energy but, since it lacked focus, organisation and direction, it got diffused and dissipated and failed to generate power. Throughout his political life, Gandhi kept exploring ways of 'releasing', 'conserving' and 'mobilising' popular energy and 'converting' and 'transforming' it into power.

I

Since power consisted in 'moving' people or setting them in motion, Gandhi thought that there were as many forms of it as there were human susceptibilities or ways of being moved.[2] In his view, they fell into two broad categories. Some forms of power, which he called material, were based on appeals to 'base' impulses or exploitation of human weaknesses, and in one form or another involved manipulation and violence. The others, which he called spiritual, appealed to 'higher' impulses, relied on willing cooperation and were basically non-violent. For Gandhi, economic, political and physical power belonged to the first category. Economic power moved people by the carrot of material reward and the stick of starvation, and secured their cooperation by manipulating their self-interest, greed or ambition. Employers knew that workers had no alternative but to work for them. For their part, the latter were well aware that they had no hope of securing better wages and healthy working conditions without hitting their employers' profits at a time they were most vulnerable. Political power was even cruder and ultimately relied on the fear of punishment. The state maintained order by means of a coercive apparatus of prisons, police and the army, and relied on a skilful manipulation of fear and self-interest in a pervasive climate of intimidation and thinly concealed terror. Although the government did appeal to its citizens' patriotism, loyalty and public spirit, Gandhi thought that such appeals were episodic and largely rhetorical and did not constitute the organising principles of the state. Physical power, such as that of a bully, a thief or a robber, was the crudest of the three and relied on threats of blatant and unauthorised violence.

Spiritual power consisted in moving humans by appealing to their higher or *ātmic* nature. Since they were manifestations of *Brahman* or the cosmic spirit, they were sacred and ultimately one. *Qua* spiritual beings, they were endowed with a sense of dignity and worth and feelings of fellowship and mutual concern, and were capable of being moved by appealing to these higher impulses. Under the influence of *avidyā* or ignorance, their awareness of their spiritual nature was sometimes eclipsed. However, even as a cloud could only temporarily veil the sun, it was always possible by appropriate moral and spiritual appeals to awaken them to their true nature. Spiritual power consisted in energising and mobilising them by activating their higher impulses.

Gandhi argued that of the two types of power, the spiritual alone was consistent with human dignity and autonomy. Material power was necessarily manipulative and coercive, was based and thrived on fear, and morally diminished those who used it as well as those upon whom it was used. Spiritual power differed from it in all these respects. It was based on uncoerced consent and willing cooperation. It brought out the best in both parties and strengthened their bonds of fellowship. It uplifted those over whom it was exercised, built up their inner resources and strengthened their sense of autonomy. Indeed, unlike the material, spiritual power was not exercised 'over' others. It consisted in releasing their latent energies and reinforced the relationship of equality and mutuality. Unlike material power, which was inherently limited and could only be possessed by some at the expense of others, spiritual power was limitless and paradoxically increased the power of those 'over' whom it was 'exercised'. The spirit was indomitable, and those fully awakened to their spiritual nature were neither terrorised by the fear of death and pain nor could be bought by the offer of all the riches of the world.

Gandhi claimed to be a spiritual scientist deeply interested in exploring how spiritual power could be generated and mobilised. Even as the world had hitherto devoted its energies to developing ever more potent instruments of material destruction, he said he had done 'researches' and conducted 'experiments' in new ways of mobilising moral and spiritual impulses, awakening the human spirit and performing the 'surgery of the soul'. He was convinced that like the material world, the spiritual world too had its own distinct laws and modes of interaction. Verbal appeals and arguments addressed the intellect and failed to reach the spirit lying beyond it. The intellect had the power to move the intellect alone and lacked the ability to activate moral and spiritual energies. Only a spirit could make contact with and move another spirit. And those who had succeeded in generating spiritual energies in themselves were capable of activating them in others. Gandhi pointed to the examples of the ancient Indian *rishis*, Jesus, Mohammed, the Buddha and other great spiritual leaders. None of them was a man of great intellect or a powerful speaker. Yet they had brought out the best in their followers and inspired them to heroic sacrifices.[3] Their appeal was undiminished by time and moved millions even today. This was so because their words were not 'hollow' and 'empty', that is, 'mere words' like those of an ordinary person or a 'learned professor', but 'charged with the power of the spirit'. Since they lived the truth they preached and were whole and unfragmented men with tremendous moral and spiritual depth, they exuded enormous force and vitality. Their every word, movement and gesture sprang from the innermost depths of their personality and was 'lit up' by their vast spiritual energy. For Gandhi, the more spiritually developed a person was, that is, the more he had mastered his senses and purified his spirit, the greater was his capacity to tap and mobilise the higher impulses of his fellow humans.

Gandhi was unclear as to how such a person influenced others and offered two different explanations. Sometimes he advanced the plausible view that human beings generally responded to the appeals of those they respected and admired. As moral beings, their self-respect and self-esteem were bound up with their ability to live up to their ideals. When they failed to do so, they could be embarrassed, shamed and inspired by those who in their view had succeeded in living or were sincerely endeavouring to live by these ideals. On other occasions Gandhi advanced the mystical view that a spiritually developed person exercised an unusual and unique kind of power over others. Like the world of nature, the spiritual world had its own structure and modes of operation and its own equivalents of physical force and laws of gravitation. Just as material entities were subject to the law of gravitation, the spirit was subject to the 'quiet' but 'irresistible' force of a more powerful spirit. Gandhi insisted that 'spiritual force' was not a figment of his imagination or a metaphor but 'real', and that its existence was amply 'testified' by the 'undying' influence of the great religious leaders mentioned earlier. He acknowledged that it was 'mysterious' and worked in 'strange' and 'incomprehensible' ways, but thought that further experiments and research by earnest seekers would one day render it intelligible.[4] Though he did not spell it out in detail, he seems to have thought that a spiritually developed person was really a vehicle through which the cosmic spirit or God worked in the world.

The cosmic spirit was ultimately nothing but infinitely powerful and intelligent energy, which a spiritually developed person was able to harness. Gandhi observed:

> If I was a perfect man, I own I should not feel the miseries of neighbours as I do. As a perfect man I should take note of them, prescribe a remedy, and *compel* adoption by the *force* of unchallengable *Truth* in me.

He went on:[5]

> When the mind is completely filled with His spirit, one cannot harbour ill will or hatred towards any one and, reciprocally, the enemy will shed his enmity and become a friend. It is not my claim that I have succeeded in converting enemies into friends, but in numerous cases it has been my experience that, when the mind is filled with His peace, all hatred ceases. An unbroken succession of world teachers since the beginning of time have borne testimony to the same.

The belief in spiritual power is a recurrent theme in the Hindu religious tradition. Though all religious traditions have some notion of supernatural power, at least in the form of what are called miracles, Hindu tradition stresses them more than others and takes an unusual view of them. Since infinite power is one of the attributes of *Brahman* and since *ātman* is not a particle but the whole of *Brahman*, in principle every person enjoys access to infinite energy. As an embodied being subject to material constraints, obviously they cannot do *all* that *Brahman* can do; however, they can acquire a substantial measure of divine power by undertaking the requisite spiritual training and penance. According to Patanjali's *Yoga Sutra*, for example, a man who has successfully gone through the eight stages of spiritual development knows the past, the future and the time of his death, possesses all the virtues, apprehends situations in a flash, exudes unusual lustre, tames even the wildest animals and wins over the most implacable enemies. For Patanjali and the mainstream Hindu tradition, these and other powers accrue to the realised individual as a matter of course and do not constitute either the goal of his spiritual pursuit or even a test of his success in it. Indeed, the tradition views them with great suspicion lest they become a source of moral arrogance and worldly involvement. It, therefore, requires their bearers not to talk about and display them in public, or use them to attain worldly objectives.

In this respect, Gandhi's relation to the mainstream Hindu tradition was ambiguous. He shared its belief that a spiritually evolved person possessed *vibhutis* or unusual powers, but he did not think much of most of them and only valued those involved in influencing other men. Again, following tradition, he insisted that their acquisition should never be the goal of spiritual pursuit. However, unlike all its previous adherents, he was a man of action desperately anxious to acquire the enormous power he needed to change his society. It was, therefore, not enough for him to posses the powers naturally resulting from self-realisation. He had to be *sure* that he had them, he had to *transform* them into political power, and he had to deploy them consciously to secure the desired political and social objectives. Here, as elsewhere, Gandhi was involved in the paradoxical situation of using the resources of his tradition to achieve objectives disapproved of by it.

II

Though Gandhi was unclear about the exact manner in which one spirit influenced another, he was convinced that only a spiritually developed person had the power to activate and mobilise the spiritual energies of his fellow-men. In order to regenerate India, he had to become as pure a spirit or as perfect a man as he possibly could. This involved mastering all the senses, especially sexuality. His theory of sexuality was integrally connected with his search for *shakti* and formed an integral part of his theory of politics.

Gandhi took a highly puritanical view of sexuality and almost declared war on it.[6] His reasons for doing so were varied and not always carefully thought out. He shared some of them with the Hindu tradition, others were unique to him.

For Gandhi, sexual activity was the most energy-consuming and enervating of all human activities. It led to the loss of semen, in his view the sole source of energy in the human body. He accepted the widespread Hindu belief that food produced semen after several days and after successive transformation through blood, flesh, fat, bone and marrow, and that its loss threw the physical and mental system out of gear. In Hindu folklore, seminal loss in the act of copulation is roughly equal to an energy expenditure of twenty-four hours of concentrated mental activity or seventy-two hours of hard physical labour. Gandhi held a similar view. Like most Hindus, he also believed that when accompanied by appropriate spiritual practices, semen moved upward through the spinal cord into the brain and got transformed into *ojas* or spiritual energy, the source of spiritual power. The *ojas* sharpened the intellect, increased powers of concentration and generated *pratibhā* (knowledge in a flash) and *prajñā* (refined and enlightened reason). According to Gandhi, 'All power comes from the preservation and sublimation of the vitality that is responsible for the creation of life'.[7] And again, the 'hidden strength that God has given us should be rigidly self-disciplined and transmuted into energy and power—not merely of the body but also of the mind and the soul'. *Ojas* was the *telos* of semen. The sexual act interrupted the latter's natural evolution and impeded the generation of psychic and spiritual energy.

In addition to the loss of semen, the sexual impulse also involved a loss of psychic energy. It gave rise to fancies, fantasies, idle daydreaming, 'disorderly and unwanted thoughts', all of which led to often unnoticed but persistent seepages of energy.[8] Furthermore, unlike all other impulses, the sexual impulse was indiscriminate in the sense of not being tied to a specific class of objects. A hungry man did not eat leaves or grass; if he was a vegetarian, he preferred to die rather than eat meat; and once he had eaten, he was at peace with himself. The sexual impulse knew no such restraints. Sisters, brothers and even parents and children did not escape its reach. Since it consciously or unconsciously attached itself to all manner of people, it used up considerable energy in the necessary acts of self-restraint.

For Gandhi, the sexual act was profoundly selfish, exploitative and a form of self-inflicted violence. It was selfish because one organ appropriated a large amount of energy depriving the others of their due share, and exploitative because the energy used up was produced by their cooperative efforts to which its own contribution was nil or minimal. The body's ecological rhythm required that the energy it produced should be recycled within it and used to maintain its internal balance and integrity. Gandhi quoted several British and French biologists in support of this view and was particularly impressed with William Lottus Hare's 'theory' that sexual reproduction used up excessive energy and beyond a certain point damaged bodily regeneration or 'internal reproduction'.[9] Since semen was a life-giving substance, he also thought that with every sexual emission, man permanently lost something of himself. Gandhi knew well enough that the body constantly reproduced semen, but insisted that every loss of it weakened the body, wore it down and diminished its capacity to replenish the stock. The sexual act was thus partial suicide and a form of self-inflicted violence. He quoted William Hare's view that the sexual act in the male and parturition of the offspring in the female were 'katabolic' and represented a 'movement towards death'.[10] Gandhi's association of sexuality with death is a recurrent theme in several schools in the Hindu and, indeed, many other religious traditions with the possible exception of Islam.

Gandhi's final objection to sexuality derived from his view that it permanently bifurcated the human species and stood in the way of human unity. Although he was unclear on this point, he seems to have thought that this happened in two ways. First, it encouraged the division of human qualities into masculine and feminine, to which the two sexes were respectively required to conform. Men were expected to be rational, tough, competitive, aggressive, strong, and women to develop opposite qualities. Each sex thus remained only 'half' a human being, systematically excluding qualities associated with the other. Since these qualities were interdependent and formed an organic unity, their separation damaged them so that each sex not only remained incomplete and one-sided but also became distorted. For Gandhi, an individual aspiring to be 'whole' or 'complete' should endeavour to overcome such moral and social bifurcation by internally appropriating the 'other' sex and the qualities associated with it.

Second, Gandhi contended that like greed and ambition, sexuality was necessarily associated with aggression and subtle psychological violence. It involved an attempt to overcome the otherness of the 'other sex' by such means as drawing it into a sexual act, making it desire one's company and infatuating it with thoughts and fantasies about oneself. All this involved manipulation, aggression and a struggle for domination and power, however subtle and subdued their manifestations might be. Since complete non-violence implied total absence of aggression, it involved elimination of the sexual impulse. As we shall see later, this was one of the central inspiring principles of Gandhi's sexual experiments.

The unity of the male and female principles is a recurrent theme in many religions, especially Hinduism and Christianity.[11] In Hindu religious thought, the unity of the two principles has been conceptualised and sought to be achieved in several ways of which two are relevant to our discussion. For the *advaita* tradition, it involves recognising that *qua* spirit, a human being is *neither* male nor female and that sexual differentiation is really a form of *māyā*. The Tantric tradition stresses the complementary principles of *purusha* and *prakriti* and seeks unity or rather union through passionless sexual acts. By remaining detached and 'unengaged' in moments of sexual intimacy, the agent both recognises and denies the sexual duality, affirms it at one level and rejects it at another.

Gandhi's thought gestured in both directions. In the early years he subscribed to the *advaita* view and talked about 'transcending' bodily consciousness. Though he never stated his reasons, he seems to have been unhappy with it largely because it denied the male-female distinction and offered only an abstract and formal unity. His later thought shows the influence of *Tantrism* about which he read during his internment in 1931. Since he held that the sexual act necessarily reinforced the sense of duality, he thought that, however passionless, it could never become a vehicle of unity. For Gandhi, the crucial thing was *both* to recognise the man-woman distinction and to deny it by overcoming the attendant sexual impulse so that the opposite sex no longer remained the 'other' constantly to be sought, appropriated and possessed. Explaining his position on the subject, he wrote to a colleague: 'The idea is that a man by becoming passionless, transforms himself into a woman, that is, he includes the woman into himself. The same is true of a passionless woman'.[12] On another occasion he observed: 'When one achieves complete control over one's thoughts, 'man' and 'woman' include each other.... I still continue my strenuous efforts to become such a *brahmachāri*'.[13] Gandhi sometimes described himself as 'half a woman', as someone who had developed and integrated the feminine principle into his personality.[14] He once asked Sarojini Naidu if she had 'missed the woman in me', and told Manu Gandhi that while he had been a father to many, he wanted to be a mother to her. Many of his European and Indian female associates observed that they could relate to him as they would to other women and felt totally secure and relaxed in his presence.[15]

For these and related reasons, Gandhi concluded that ideally the sexual act should be avoided altogether. Since that would affect the survival of the species, he suggested that while a few should avoid it, the rest should only engage in it for reproductive purposes. It was, therefore, justified no more than once or twice in a lifetime. For the rest of the time the married partners should live 'like brothers and sisters' and 'as if they were not married'.

Gandhi was convinced that the eradication or at least the conquest of sexuality generated enormous energy.[16] Negatively, it avoided both the psychic seepages and the physical loss of semen; positively, it accumulated and transformed semen into psychic and spiritual energy. A man enjoying complete mastery over his senses thus, not only had a vast reservoir of physical and psychic but also spiritual energy. As Gandhi put it, a *brahmachāri*:[17]

> will find that he requires very little food to keep his body in a fit condition. And yet he will be as capable as any of undertaking physical labour. Mental exertion will not tire him easily nor will he show the ordinary signs of old age. Just as a ripe fruit or an old leaf falls off naturally so will such a *Brahmachāri* when his time comes pass away with all his faculties intact. Although with the passage of time the effects of the natural wear and tear must be manifest in his body, his intellect instead of showing signs of decay should show progressive clarity.

Gandhi pointed to his own example as proof of this. He worked nearly nineteen hours a day, lived on an extremely frugal diet, rarely fell ill, was free from moods, intellectually ever alert and capable of sustained concentration for hours. He concluded:[18]

> Many people have told me—and I also believe it— that I am full of energy and enthusiasm, and that I am by no means weak in mind; some even accuse me of strength bordering on obstinacy.... It is my full conviction, that if only I had lived a life of unbroken *Brahmacharya* all through, my energy and enthusiasm would have been a thousandfold greater and I should have been able to devote them all to the furtherance of my country's cause as my own. If an imperfect *Brahmachāri* like myself can reap such benefit, how much more wonderful must be the gain in power—physical mental, as well as moral—that unbroken *Brahmacharya* can bring to us.

Gandhi was convinced that a few score *brahmachāris* like him would be capable of transforming the face of India.[19] They would possess the enormous physical, psychic and spiritual energy required to 'ignite' the Indian masses and to 'fire' them with enthusiasm. Being unmarried and without private attachments, they would also be able to 'rise to the height of universal love' and to give their undivided attention to national regeneration. Gandhi looked upon such a cadre of spiritual elite as his 'army for *swarāj*', which was to settle in the remotest villages, educate and energise the masses and to create a nation of energetic, proud, public-spirited and spiritually disciplined citizens. Gandhi could not train such a band of *brahmachāris* without first becoming one himself and developing the 'science of *brahmacharya*'. Accordingly, he decided to embark upon a series of remarkable and almost daredevilish experiments.

III

Before turning to Gandhi's experiments, a few remarks on his theory of sexuality are in order. First, strange as it may seem in someone who aimed to unite man and woman, he discussed sexuality almost entirely from the masculine point of view. His preoccupation with semen had no relevance for women, and he said nothing about how their physical energy was transformed into spiritual energy. His examples of the 'blinding' character of the sexual passion and the momentary lapses of the great ancient sages were also male. This was not accidental but had deep roots in his attitude to women. He was convinced, perhaps on the basis of his personal experience, that female sexuality was not as intense and powerful as the male, that women were generally better able to cope with it, and that in all sexual encounters, whether in marriage or outside it, the male was the aggressor. In taking this view Gandhi radically departed from the major Indian traditions which took the opposite view on all three counts. His apparently more charitable view of female sexuality had less charitable implications. Since he expected her to be more virtuous and disciplined than man, he was less tolerant of her sensuality. That men should act like animals did not surprise him; that a woman should show carnal interest and be less than 'one hundred per cent' pure pained him. Not surprisingly, his attitude to the lapses of some of his female colleagues and followers was harsh and uncompromising. Since he set up the de-sexualised woman as his ideal and considered her 'too sacred for sexual love', he was only able to see her as a mother, sister, daughter or a dutiful and sexually uninterested wife. Gandhi granted her moral superiority at the expense of her sexuality and even sensuality.

Second, Gandhi's theory of sexuality rested on a primitive approach to semen. Much of what he said about its production and accumulation is obviously untrue. By itself, semen has no 'life-giving power' either and Gandhi was wrong to mystify it. He was also wrong to see it as the ultimate source of all forms of physical, psychic and moral energy. His belief that it could be transformed into spiritual energy had no basis in facts either. There is no evidence, and Gandhi produces none, to show that the celibate clergy has a sharper intellect or greater powers of concentration, let alone unusual cognitive and spiritual powers. Indeed, the very idea of *ojas* or spiritual energy is largely mystical and almost certainly false. Jesus, Gandhi's exemplar, could not cast a spell over Judas, the Roman Pilate or any of the orthodox Jewish priests.

Third, Gandhi postulated a false contrast between love and sex. For him, love had to be unconditional and independent of a desire for reward. When it became associated with sex, it came to depend on desired sexual satisfaction and weakened or even died if the latter was unavailable. As Dada Dharmadhikari, one of his perceptive students, put it 'as love increases, sex decreases'.[20] It is striking that Gandhi rarely talked of sexual *love* and even thought the expression a contradiction in terms. For him, it was always *love based on sex* and, therefore, not love at all. It never occurred to him that it could also be *sex based on love*, that is, not an 'essentially' physical but spiritual act in which two mutually committed spirits affirmed and confirmed their deepest bonds by physical means. As Gandhi himself said, love is a spiritual emotion. There is no obvious reason why it should cease to be such when sexually mediated. Indeed, insofar as it communicates mutual commitment, expresses affection, cements relationships and gives them emotional depth and intensity, sexual activity has an unmistakable spiritual dimension.

Fourth, it is possible to draw opposite conclusions to Gandhi's from his theory of sexuality. Since the sexual impulse on his own testimony is powerful and unpredictable, it requires unceasing vigilance, and the battle against it is never conclusively won. The constant struggle to conquer and eliminate it, therefore, gives it precisely the kind and degree of prominence he says it should not be given. Sexuality can obsess a monk as much as a Don Juan, although of course for wholly different reasons. Gandhi wants to conquer it in order to conserve energy. And yet the very struggle to do so involves anxiety, tension, fear, frustrations, emotional emptiness, irritability, lack of intimacy and warmth, all of which take up an enormous amount of energy often far exceeding what one hopes to save. The point is not that the sexual impulse should not be regulated, but rather that declaring war on it, as Gandhi does, is largely counterproductive. A person who assigns it its proper place in life and gratifies it within limits is far more at peace with himself or herself than one locked in a moral battle with it.

Fifth, although Gandhi's attempt to link sexuality with the regeneration of India was not original, he gave it some unusual twists. Unlike much of the nineteenth century European nationalist literature which is either silent on the subject or celebrates sexuality, the emphasis on sexual self-discipline—at times bordering on puritanism—is a recurrent theme in its Indian counterpart. Several nineteenth century Indian leaders contended that their countrymen had fallen prey to waves of foreign rule because they had become passive, effete and devoid of energy as a result of their sensuous and self-indulgent lifestyle. They married very young, became physical and mental wrecks and lost interest in life by the time they reached adulthood, filled their empty lives with idle fantasies and were only fit to produce 'weaklings'. Some leaders even argued that the 'racial stock' had become degenerate and needed a radical eugenic programme. The terrorist literature at the turn of the century condemned homosexuality, masturbation and sexual excess and required young recruits to lead chaste lives. Swami Vivekananda gave particular importance to sexual discipline as part of a comprehensive syllabus of India's moral and social regeneration. The ideas that India was 'dead' and that loss of semen implied partial death were a standard refrain in his important writings. He was also one of the first to suggest that an organisation of *brahmachāris*, such as the Ramakrishna Mission, should act as a social and religious catalyst. In the twentieth century Swami Shraddhanand spoke for most when he said that modern India had only one 'sacred cause—the cause of sexual purity and true national unity'. The fact that he should have highlighted only these two 'problems' and seen them as part of a single 'sacred' project is striking. He was convinced that 'sexual purity on the ancient Aryan lives', by which he meant sexual self-discipline within the *varna* system rather than total abstinence, was indispensable for 'national self-realisation'.

Gandhi shared these concerns. As we saw, he too was keen to harness sexual energy for political purposes and to transform the 'fire' of sexual passion into a 'fiery spirit' capable of 'igniting the masses'. However, he differed from the other leaders in several important respects. He placed far more emphasis on *brahmacharya* than almost all of them, and his prohibition of non-reproductive sexuality within marriage had no counterpart in any of their writings. His insistence that those who had devoted their lives to social and political work should not marry or, if married, eschew sexual contact was also unique to him. With the exception of a few religious leaders, none of his contemporaries shared his mystical faith in the irresistible spiritual power of a *brahmachāri* either. Gandhi's concern to integrate man and woman and to become a 'whole' person was also unique to him. Most nineteenth century religious reformers stressed 'masculine' virtues and wanted Indians to become 'manly' in the manner of their colonial masters.[21]

Finally, if we ignored the ascetic tradition, Gandhi's theory of sexuality has no support in Hindu thought. For Hindus, sex is a necessary and beautiful impulse and occupies an important place among the four *purushārthas*. It is not just a means of procreation, nor a biological and psychological need, but a legitimate source of pleasure to be enjoyed without guilt during a particular stage in life. Far from reducing it to mere sexual contact or even intercourse, Hindus celebrate it as a sacred activity in which time, space and duality are temporarily transcended. In the *Gitā*, Krishna declares on two occasions that the sexual impulse is divine. Almost all Hindu gods, including divine incarnations, are married and the *Purānas* narrate the sexual adventures of some of them with considerable relish. The Vedic gods had consorts and Indra was a notorious seducer of women. Prajapati, the lord of creation, split himself into two because he found no joy in being alone and desired company.

The *Kumarasambhavam* of Kalidasa, the greatest Indian dramatist, celebrates the union of Shiva and Parvati with great tenderness and offers moving descriptions of the sexual act. The *Gitagovinda* of Jayadev and the devotional poetry of the Vaishnavites offer the most sensitive analyses of the structure and mechanism of the sexual impulse. In the absence of such cultural and religious legitimacy, Hindu writers would not have produced a large body of literature on the subject of sexuality for over two millennia, called some of their authors sages, and assigned their works a status comparable to the *Dharmashātras*. Indeed, had the Hindus not perceived a close relationship between sexuality and religion, their artists would not have thought it proper to decorate some of their most sacred temples with erotic paintings and sculptures. Gandhi's asceticism represented a relatively minor strand within the Hindu cultural tradition.

IV

Gandhi took a decision to practise sexual abstinence in 1910, apparently without consulting his wife.[22] For the first few years he was only 'more or less successful'. As was his wont, he decided to stiffen his resolve by taking an unbreakable vow to observe complete *brahmacharya* in 1906 when he was thirty-seven years of age and about to launch his first *satyāgraha* in South Africa. He did not find his task easy. As he later admitted to Rajkumari Amrit Kaur, the 'sexual passion is the hardest to overcome in my case. It has been an incessant struggle. It is for me a miracle how I have survived it.[23] He made his vow even more difficult by continuing to sleep next to his wife and refusing to follow the 'cowardly' practice of avoiding contact with other women.

Gandhi experimented with his diet, habits and lifestyles to ascertain what stimulated the sexual impulse and how it could be weakened and eventually mastered. He 'discovered' that the senses fed off each other and that none of them could be mastered without conquering the others as well. He found that there was a particularly close connection between food and sexuality and that a rich, heavy and spicy diet as well as milk had a strong tendency to stimulate it. He 'discovered' too, that the 'idle' mind was particularly vulnerable to the solicitations of the sexual desire, and kept himself busy all his waking hours. He thought that a cold shower, chanting the name of Rāma and frequent prayers facilitated self-control. At a different level, he 'discovered' that the sexual impulse derived much of its intensity from a mistaken approach to the human body. So long as one perceived the body as an instrument of pleasure, one expected every organ to yield its distinct mode of gratification and could not avoid feeling that not to seek sexual pleasure was to 'waste' an important organ. Gandhi contended that the battle against sexuality became easier when one altered one's approach to the body. As he put it: 'If one is convinced that the genital organs are not intended for sex gratification, wouldn't one's attitude change completely?'

On the basis of these and other 'experimental' findings, Gandhi evolved a rigorous code of discipline, and his 'thinking process' began to undergo a 'process of cleansing'. Evidently, his conquest of sexuality was not yet complete and he needed to remain watchful. As he said in 1926, though his 'physical celibacy' was 'fairly safe', he had not yet acquired a complete mastery over the mind and was vulnerable to 'insidious invasions' of 'undesirable thoughts'. In a letter to an unknown young correspondent two years later, he described his state of mind with characteristic frankness and without worrying about how his letter might be used.[24]

> I had involuntary discharge twice during the last two weeks. I cannot recall any dream. I never practised masturbation. One cause of these discharges is of course my physical weakness but I also know that there are impure desires deep down in me. I am able to keep out such thoughts during waking hours. But what is present in the body like some hidden poison, always makes its way, even forcibly sometimes. I feel unhappy about this, but I am not nervously afraid.
>
> I have always been vigilant. I can suppress the enemy but have not been able to expel him altogether. If I am truthful I shall succeed in doing that too. The enemy will not be able to endure the power of truth. If you are in the same condition as I am, learn from my experience. In its essence, desire for self-pleasure is equally impure, whether its object is one's wife or some other woman. Its results differ.

Since Gandhi felt fully confident about his physical self-control, he continued to maintain close physical contacts with his female associates. Many Indians disapproved of this, especially his practice of putting his hands on their shoulders, and some even raised the matter with him both publicly and in private. He responded by taking a vow in September 1935 to stop the practice 'for the sake of public good', but broke it in Sevagaon a couple of years later saying that it was not intended to include his wife, Sushila Nayar, Manu and the other girls who were 'like daughters' to him. When accused of casuistry, he rejoined that the spirit of the vow was far more important than the letter and that he alone knew its spirit.

The year 1936 proved particularly trying for Gandhi. Throughout the preceding year he had worked extremely hard and slept no more than four or five hours a day. He fell ill in December 1935 but continued his punishing routine until he finally collapsed in the first week of January in 1936. While he was convalescing in Bombay, he felt an intense sexual desire. He described it with amazing frankness in a letter to a female colleague[25]:

> The experience which tormented me in Bombay was a strange and painful one. All my discharges so far had occurred in dreams and they had never troubled me. I could forget them. But the experience in Bombay occurred while I was fully awake and had a sudden desire for intercourse. I felt, of course, no urge to gratify the craving, there was no self-forgetfulness whatever. I was completely master of my body. But despite my best efforts the organ remained aroused. This was an altogether strange and shameful experience. I have already explained the cause. As soon as that cause was removed the state of remaining aroused came to a stop, that is, during the waking state.
>
> .... I have been striving to attain to Shukadeva's condition. I have not succeeded in that aim. If I succeed, I would become a eunuch though possessed of the vital fluid and discharges would become impossible.

Gandhi had little doubt about why the desire had 'invaded' him after all these years. He wrote to a colleague:[26]

It had its origin in my pampering the body with food while doing no work.... I understood the cause and from that time stopped taking rest as prescribed by the doctors.

Gandhi summed up his feelings in a fascinating and brutally frank article in *Harijan*.[27] When he recovered from his illness, he resumed his earlier heavy routine and regained his self-confidence. Two years later, he had another crisis. On 14 April, 1938, he had a 'bad dream' involving a 'desire to see a woman' and an ejaculation. Evidently, he was completely shattered. As he wrote to Madeleine Slade: 'The degrading, dirty, torturing experience of 14th April shook me to bits.'[28] He was in a 'well of despair', 'obsessed by a feeling of self-guilt' and did not know what had gone wrong. He lost all self-confidence, became moody and his political work began to suffer. He had to see Jinnah for long and difficult negotiations, and he did not feel up to it. Although he met him and worked out important proposals, he felt unsure of himself and looked to Nehru to provide the lead.[29]

Gandhi discussed the 'April Incident' with his close colleagues and, despite their advice to the contrary, wrote an article about it in *Harijan*. He thought that since he was a public figure and his experiments had important lessons for others, he had a duty to share his experiences with them. They came up with all kinds of advice.[30] Both Miraben and Amrit Kaur advised him to avoid *all* contact with women, not merely touch but also 'proximity, speech, look, letter', and not just with some but *all* women, including his wife and doctor. Miraben told him that the April incident was not an isolated one, for she had once seen him put his arm around a female colleague's neck in sleep.[31]

Gandhi decided on 2 June, 1938, that he 'would not touch any woman ever so lightly and even out of sheer fun', the only exception being his doctor Sushila Nayar. The April incident had 'awakened' him to the fact that although he might not consciously feel sexual desire, it could 'unknown to him' lurk around in the dark recesses of his mind. More than ever before, he became alert to its unconscious operations and felt the need to devise new strategies to track down and subdue it. A few months later, he felt sufficiently confident and resumed the old practice of maintaining close physical contacts with his female co-workers. Sometimes they slept next to him and Sushila Nayar even 'slept with' him to keep him warm. She also gave him 'massage and medicated baths' lasting over an hour and a half, during which he often dozed off or transacted business with such male colleagues as his secretary Mahadev Desai and Sushila Nayar's brother Pyarelal.

Gandhi's lifestyle gave rise to considerable gossip both in India and abroad. The gossip became vicious when Prema Kantak, to whom he had written some brutally frank letters about his sexual struggles, published their correspondence with his approval. The first public reference to Gandhi's lifestyle appeared in October 1939 in *Bombay Chronicle* whose Allahabad correspondent reported 'startling revelations' about his private life. A provincial Hindu fundamentalist paper carried more lurid stories, named Sushila Nayar and accused him of 'gross sensuality' and *adharma*. Some of the American journals, which had hinted at his 'improper' relations with Madeleine Slade during their visit to London in 1931, indulged in even wilder speculations. Gandhi was not in the least ruffled by all this. He published in *Harijan* both the *Bombay Chronicle* report and the charges levelled by the Indian and American papers.[32] He repudiated the charges, asked his critics to produce evidence and offered a detailed explanation of his conduct. He contended that the 'campaign of vilification' was inspired by the orthodox Hindus angered by his vigorous national movement against untouchability. That was why it had begun in Maharashtra, been spearheaded by the Brahmins and given greatest publicity in the Marathi papers run by them.

Undeterred by the campaign, Gandhi not only continued his close associations with women but also embarked upon a most unusual practice. For the past few years he had slept with them in the same room at a respectable distance, and of late he had begun to 'sleep together' with some of them. He now decided to take the next step of sleeping naked with his naked female colleagues as part of a new experiment.[33] He seems to have started doing this after his wife's death on 22 February, 1944. His reference to 'women or girls who have been naked with me' in his letter to Birla in April 1945 indicates that several women were involved. It would appear that in addition to Sushila Nayar, Prabhavati Narayan, Abha Gandhi and Manu Gandhi also formed part of the experiment.[34] Lilavati, Rajkumari Amrit Kaur, Antussalaam and several others also seem to have been involved, although it is not clear whether they simply 'slept together' with him or did so as part of the experiment. When some of Gandhi's close friends and colleagues came to know about it, they expressed strong disapproval. While acknowledging that his experiment was 'innocent' and inspired by the highest of motives, they were worried that it would set a bad example, alienate public opinion and bring him into disrepute. Gandhi remained unconvinced. He said that all his life he had insisted on doing what he thought was right 'in utter disregard of social customs'. He had cultivated Muslim and Harijan friends and incurred the wrath of his family; he had insisted on crossing the seas and suffered the penalty of excommunication; he had attacked untouchability and admitted an untouchable woman into his *āshram* and patiently borne the execration of orthodox Hindus. He was not, therefore, going to bow to social pressure on an issue to such vital importance as his sexual experiment. However, since his close colleagues held strong views, he was prepared temporarily to discontinue the experiment and think again. As he wrote to Munnalal Shah in March 1945:[35]

> Thus I am what I am. There is no point in talking about the welfare of society ... I cannot give up thinking. As far as possible I have postponed the practice of sleeping together. But it cannot be given up altogether .... If I completely give up sleeping together my *brahmacharya* will be put to shame .... Such restrictions should not be imposed on me.

Over a year later, Gandhi decided to resume the experiment. Manu Gandhi had for sometime expressed a strong desire to work with him, and he decided to send for her in the October of 1946.[36] She was his grandniece and had served his wife with great devotion during her final illness. Just before her death, his wife had entrusted her to Gandhi who agreed to become her 'mother'. In a letter inviting her to join him, he wrote, 'I am not sending for you to make you unhappy. Are you afraid of me? I will never force you to do anything against your wish.'[37] The last cryptic remark seems to refer to Manu's participation in an earlier experiment and perhaps to her unwillingness to repeat it. Manu's father readily agreed to her joining Gandhi but expressed worry about the 'impure' atmosphere in his *āshram*.[38] He seems to have in mind Pyarelal, whom N.K. Bose later accused of 'shadowing' women in Gandhi's *āshram*. Gandhi assured him that Pyarelal's eyes were 'clean' and that he was 'not likely to force himself on anybody'.

Gandhi's experiment of sharing his bed naked with the nineteen-year-old Manu began on 20 December, 1946. He did not mention it to her father himself, but asked her to do so. The day it began, he wrote a note to her:[39]

> Stick to your word. Don't hide even a single thought from me. Give a true answer to whatever I ask. The step that I took today was taken after careful thinking. Give me in writing what effect it had on your mind. I shall certainly reveal all my thoughts to you.

And he wrote in his diary:

> Got up at 12.30 a.m. Woke up Manu at 12.45 a.m. Made her understand about her *dharma*. Told her to have a talk with Jaisukhlal (Manu's father). She could still change her mind, but once having taken the plunge she would have to run the risk. She remained steadfast.

Gandhi asked her to keep a diary and daily secure his signature of approval.[40]

Though Gandhi first referred to the experiment in a letter to Krishnandas Jaju on 8 January, 1947, just under three weeks after it had begun, it is unlikely that others did not know about it or that he himself had not mentioned it to them earlier.[41] Gandhi's small hut had no privacy and was accessible to the public almost all hours of the day and night. And since this was not the first time he had embarked upon such an experiment, his close colleagues, especially the women in his entourage, must have known about it. Not even his worst enemies, and he had many, and not even the vigilant British officers, ever thought that he was engaged in anything other than an innocent experiment.

Contrary to his general practice, Gandhi made no prior public announcement of his experiment, nor did he take his followers into confidence about his real reasons for undertaking it. Perhaps that would have defeated its purpose, or perhaps he was worried that he might not be allowed to launch it. Anyway, word got around leading initially to a wave of what he called 'small talks, whispers and innuendoes' and eventually to an extremely strong public reaction. Fully aware of the way Vishvāmitra, Vyāsa and other great *rishis* had been defeated by the sexual impulse even after hundreds of years of penance and self-mastery, many of his colleagues and friends began to suspect the worst. Some of his followers, mostly Gujarati, broke off relations with him; two editors of *Harijan* resigned in protest; some started 'non-cooperation' with him; Sardar Patel was 'very angry' and refused to speak to him; Vinoba Bhave wrote to him a letter of disapproval; his son, Devdas, wrote a highly emotional and critical letter; his devoted stenographer, Parsuram, left his service; Kishorelal Mashruwala and others, who had remonstrated against a similar practice earlier, were implacably and noisily hostile; Pandit Nehru was disturbed; and several friends demanded to see him for a satisfactory explanation.[42]

Criticisms of Gandhi's conduct were broadly along the following lines.[43] First, it set a bad example to others. Second, it threatened to weaken the foundations of social morality, outraged public opinion and represented *adharma*. Third, he had begun the experiment in secret. Fourth, he had a duty to submit his 'advanced' ideas to public discussion before acting on them. Fifth, his experiment had no sanction in Hindu religious tradition. Sixth, it was wholly pointless as it did not seem to have beneficial effects either on his immediate surroundings or on the nation as a whole. And finally, it involved emotional and spiritual exploitation of innocent and gullible women and implied that women were inferior. This last point was stressed by Professor N.K. Bose, Gandhi's interpreter-secretary, in his resignation letter. In his view, Gandhi had taken no account either of its deleterious effects on Manu or of the jealousy and 'hysteria' it aroused in the other women around him who all felt possessive about him and feared rejection. He also reminded Gandhi of Freud's view that human beings were often motivated by deep unconscious desires at variance with their conscious intentions and which even the most searching introspection often failed to uncover.

Gandhi was unrepentant. He acknowledged that his actions had cost him his dearest associates, but insisted that the 'whole world may forsake me but I dare not leave what I hold is the truth for me'.[44] He could be making a mistake but 'must realise it myself'. His action might disillusion his followers who might now think badly of him and wonder if he was really a *Mahatma*. 'I must confess the prospect of being so debunked greatly pleases me,' Gandhi rejoined.[45] He recognised the need to explain his behaviour and discussed it in great detail with a number of people, including Swami Anand, Kedar Nath, Khan Abdul Gaffar Khan and especially the wise septuagenarian Thakkar Bapa.[46] Later, he wrote a series of articles on the subject in *Harijan*.

V

Gandhi's explanation of his conduct was complex, not easy to follow and articulated in different idioms on different occasions.[47] It would appear that he had not carefully thought out the nature and basis of the experiment and was himself unclear about its rationale and significance. Sometimes he said that it was in the nature of an 'experiment' designed to probe the limits of celibacy in general and his own self-mastery in particular. Sometimes he said that it was not at all an experiment but a 'sacred duty'.[48] On yet other occasions, he argued that it was a part of his *yajna* involving the 'final oblation of the senses'.

Disregarding these and other inconsistencies, Gandhi's defence of his action was along the following lines. First, it was an integral part of his search for *moksha*. All his life he had endeavoured to master his senses and desires. He had conquered the desire for possession and neither owned nor had the slightest wish to own anything in life. He had more or less conquered anger, a very difficult thing for someone as hot-tempered as he was, and felt nothing but goodwill even towards his enemies, including the orthodox Hindus who had viciously maligned him and threatened his life. He had mastered the fear of death and went about unprotected amongst his violent and sometimes ill-disposed countrymen. He had subdued the palate, a difficult discipline for one who loved food, and lived happily on a simple concoction of milk and raw vegetables. He had conquered his tongue, spoke nothing but the truth, and observed silence once a week even in the midst of complex negotiations. He had mastered the sense of smell and was fully at ease cleaning latrines.

The sexual impulse had given him the greatest difficulty. Even so, he had managed to master it for years until the two incidents in 1936 and 1938 revealed to him the distance to be covered. He had intensified his efforts and was fairly certain that he had succeeded in eliminating all traces of sexuality. However, on 'the lonely way to God on which I have set out', he needed to examine most minutely all his innermost thoughts and impulses, including those too deep for consciousness. The sexual impulse might escape detection by introspection but not the intense and merciless light of practice. Like small children, desires were unable to resist temptations. The best way to flush them out of their hiding places, Gandhi thought, was to offer them a chance of gratification. He had, therefore, decided to subject himself to the 'severest test' of sleeping naked with carefully chosen female associates to ascertain for himself whether he had at the deepest level of his being reached that state of 'absolute purity' in which not only did he not feel the sexual urge himself but they did not do so either. Gandhi's experiment was intended both to 'probe' and 'cleanse' the unconscious.

Evidently Gandhi was pleased with the results of the experiment. As he wrote to Manu: 'I have successfully practised the eleven vows undertaken by me. This is the culmination of my striving for the last sixty years. In his *yajna* I got a glimpse of the ideal truth and purity for which I had been striving'. He went on, 'I do feel that I have come nearer to God and truth'.[49] He could not be sure whether or not he had actually attained *moksha*, for the unconscious was unfathomable and in any case, as long as the body lasted, perfection was impossible. The only conclusive proof was the manner of his death. 'The success of my attempt depends solely on how I meet death. One can say nothing till the moment of death comes'.[50] If he died with the name of Rāma on his lips, 'it should be taken as a proof of the success of my attempt.' According to most but by no means all observers, Gandhi did die this way. Since it was a clue to whether or not he had attained *moksha*, the controversy about his last words was not unimportant for his followers.

It is striking that right until his death Gandhi never really got over his almost Calvinist anxiety about whether or not he would attain *moksha*. As early as 1896 when he first experienced a religious crisis, he had written a long letter to Raichandbhai, the only man who came close to being his guru, asking twenty-four questions over a third of which related to the nature and criteria of progress towards *moksha*. Although rather surprisingly he rarely talked about the subject later, he seems to have remained deeply exercised about it. As he grew older, his anxiety became acute and he looked for 'proof' of his success, thus showing both how much he remained within and departed from his religious tradition. No great Hindu sage shared Gandhi's spiritual nervousness and anxiety, largely because they were all deeply rooted in the tradition and accepted its criteria and methods of attaining *moksha*. Since Gandhi had radically redefined the concept of *moksha* in active and social terms, he lacked its navigational guidance in his uncharted journey.

According to Gandhi, the second reason for his experiment with Manu had to do not with why he started it at all but did so in 1946. The independence of India, to which he had dedicated his life, was looming large on the political horizon, but Hindus and Muslims were busy butchering each other in a climate of intense hatred. He feared for the integrity of the country he deeply loved and wanted at all cost to avoid its impending Partition. He had spent over a quarter of a century training his countrymen in the culture of non-violence, and now found that they were not only rejecting but losing their faith in it. With his life's work in ruins, Gandhi felt deeply sad and frustrated, could not sleep for days, almost lost his will to live and was heard murmuring to himself, 'What shall I do? What shall I do? There is darkness everywhere'. He had thought that he had a message for the world intensely weary of violence, but evidently it had proved impotent even in his own country under his own leadership. He was, however, a tireless fighter not given to admitting defeat. Since he was convinced that his message was true, he thought that there must be something wrong with himself. If he was absolutely pure, with not a 'particle' of impure desire or the slightest element of egoism and violence left in him, he should be able to mobilise his spiritual *shakti*, activate the spirit in others and conquer the madness raging all around him. He had long held that all violence ceased in the presence of pure love and that the principle of good ultimately triumphed over the inherently parasitic and ultimately fragile principle of evil. As he put it:[51]

> Ever since my coming to Noakhali, I have been asking myself the question 'What is it that is choking the action of my *ahimsā*? Why does not the spell work? May it not be because I have temporised in the matter of *brahmacharya*?'

Gandhi's use of the words 'choking' and 'spell' is striking and indicates some of his hidden assumptions. He went on:[52]

> There *must* be some serious flaw deep down in me which I am unable to discover . . . . Where could I have missed my way? There *must* be something terribly lacking in my *ahimsā* and faith which is responsible for all this.

It is hardly surprising that he should have looked upon Noakhali, where evil and violence reigned supreme, as the place where he had 'to know the measure of my strength and let myself be tested.' Since it was not responding to his spell, Gandhi obviously needed to do yet more 'penance', embark upon an yet more fierce *yajna* and become a vehicle fit enough to incarnate the all-powerful cosmic spirit:[53]

> Alas, I am far as yet from that state. At the same time I am hastening towards it. If I attain that state or even come near enough to it (and probably that is all that a human being can reach) this *problem* of Noakhali will be *easily solved*.

Accordingly, he decided to plunge into the 'sacred fire . . . and be burnt or saved'.[54] His sexual *yajna* was a way of mobilising the capital of his spiritual *shakti* and making it yield vitally necessary political dividends. For him, personal purity and political success 'hanged together', especially when the politics was based on non-violence. Non-violence relied on winning over others by evoking their higher impulses, and obviously its efficacy depended on the degree of his spiritual accomplishment. As he put it: 'In non-violent conduct . . . there is an indissoluble connection between private, personal life and public.'[55] Whenever he saw corruption and brutality among his followers, he tended to blame himself. When asked in 1938 why the Congress had deteriorated, he replied:[56]

> There must be power in the word of a *satyāgraha* general ... the power that purity of life, strict vigilance and ceaseless application produce. This is impossible without the observance of *brahmacharya*.... If my non-violence is to be contagious, I must acquire greater control over my thoughts. There is perhaps a flaw somewhere which accounts for the apparent failure of my leadership.

That was why Gandhi had to run his personal and political life in a tandem. The former generated the energy and power he desperately needed to succeed in his momentous political struggles. The more intractable his political problems became, the greater was the moral struggle in his personal life. It was hardly surprising that his finest political experiment of successfully controlling violence in Noakhali should have been conducted alongside his heroic sexual experiment. This was not a coincidence but a logical necessity within his philosophical framework. On the eve of India's independence, when the country was in a terrible state, he wrote important articles on politics *and* a series of five on *brahmacharya*. His readers were, in N.K. Bose's words, 'deeply puzzled why such a series suddenly appeared in the midst of the intensely political articles'. The puzzle was misplaced, for the two were inseparable in Gandhi's thought.

Gandhi said that his third reason for the experiment had to do with his 'researches' in the 'science of *brahmacharya*'. As a spiritual 'scientist', he was anxious to 'test, enlarge and revise the current definition of *brahmacharya* in the light of my observation, study and experiment', and assured his colleagues that 'as soon as my research is complete, I shall proclaim the result to the world'.[57] In almost all religious traditions, *brahmacharya* had been equated with 'physical' celibacy and secured by scrupulous avoidance of all contact with women. For Gandhi, that was a 'narrow, hidebound and retrograde' view. *Brahmacharya* was not merely the suppression but eradication of the sexual impulse. One who had attained it transcended the consciousness of gender altogether and saw no difference whatever between man and woman. He did not need to avoid women any more than men and should be able to enjoy normal contacts, including sleep naked with them 'without either party being in any manner sexually excited'.[58] Gandhi said that he wanted to explore the 'outermost limits' of *brahmacharya*, to find out how far the human body and mind could be pushed and to ascertain what obstacles were likely to be encountered on the way and how they could be overcome.

Finally, Gandhi argued that as a spiritual 'scientist', he was concerned with developing not only a new science of *brahmacharya* but also a 'new system of ethics and morals suited to the present age'.[59] He was convinced that the traditional practice of separating boys and girls from an early age onwards was most harmful. It shrouded sexuality in mystery and encouraged both a morbid fear of and excessive preoccupation with it. He wanted to explore an alternative. He said he was 'deeply influenced by modern thought', especially the ideas of Bertrand Russell, Havelock Ellis and such other 'thinkers of eminence, integrity and experience'. His own 'research ran somewhat in that direction' and he felt persuaded that if ways could be found to raise men and women in a mixed and relaxed environment, the sexual impulse would lose much of its intensity and mystique. When Gandhi's critics argued that developing a new system of ethics or *yugadharma* in such an important area was too great a task to be left to an isolated individual, however eminent he might be, and should be assigned to a panel of wise men, he rejoined that this had no sanction within Hindu tradition and that no panel of moral experts could deprive him of his right to form his own judgement.

Although Gandhi himself did not put the point this way, his thought during this intensely agonising period reveals a tendency latent in his earlier years but not fully manifest until now. He was determined to control the violence raging all around him. He was convinced that, as a national leader, he must accept responsibility for it. He was also convinced that all violence ceased in the presence of non-violence. He, therefore, concluded that if only he could eliminate all traces of violence and aggression within himself, he would be able to exert a quiet and 'contagious' force and send out vibrations that would conquer the violence of his countrymen. Accordingly, he turned his attention inward and probed his psyche. He seems to have concluded that though he had eliminated all traces of violence within himself, one still remained. As we saw earlier, he associated sexuality with violence and aggression. So long as he was conscious of himself as a male, elements of aggression and violence were bound to remain, even if he was not conscious of them. The only way out was to cease to be a male, to become a woman. His final sexual experiment with Manu was an attempt to become, and to test that he had succeeded in becoming, a woman. This was why he said that he wanted to become a 'mother' to Manu. This was also why, unlike his earlier experiments, he now asked her to keep a diary and show it to him every day. He was convinced that if he had really become a woman, she could not feel sexually stimulated in his presence, and wanted to be sure that that was how she felt. N.K. Bose put the point well:[60]

> Personally, I have had the *feeling* that the question which he asked those who shared in his 'experiment' was whether they did not feel the same about him as they felt in respect of their mother. In such experiments, sex, which had so long acted as a barrier to that complete identification which exists between a mother and child, was laid low and the experimenter became free to enter upon a new relationship with men and women which was completely pure and therefore spiritually elevating.
>
> Gandhi's concern about the private, personal life of individuals was the by-product of his attempt to conquer sex by becoming a woman.

Hitherto, Gandhi had talked about becoming half a woman; it would seem that he now wanted to become a complete woman. That was the only way he could eliminate all traces of aggression and violence inherent in sexuality. That was also the only way he could develop pure love, utterly untainted by any thought of possession or power. He believed that he had developed pure love for all men; he now wanted to be sure that he had it for all women as well. It would seem that Gandhi's earlier equation of violence with masculinity became even more pronounced in his old age. Unlike the world of domination, self-assertion, aggression, hatred and brutality created by man, the woman exemplified the opposite principle of non-violence and was tender, gentle, giving, soft, loving, non-assertive and devoid of self-interest. It was only these qualities that would ultimately save the world. Gandhi wanted to move away from the male-dominated world and to reconstitute it on the feminine, especially the maternal principle. He put the point well in an important article in *Harijan* in 1940:[61]

> My contribution to the great problem lies in my presenting for acceptance truth and *ahimsā* in every walk of life, whether for individuals or nations. I have hugged the hope that in this woman will be the unquestioned leader and, having thus found her place in human evolution, will shed her inferiority complex.
>
> I have suggested that woman is the incarnation of *ahimsā*. *Ahimsā* means infinite love, which again means infinite capacity for suffering. Who but woman, the mother of man, shows this capacity in the largest measure? She shows it as she carries the infant and feeds it during nine months and derives joy in the suffering involved. What can beat the suffering caused by the pangs of labour? But she forgets them in the joy of creation. Who again suffers daily so that her babe may wax from day to day? Let her transfer that love to the whole of humanity, let her forget she ever was or can be the object of man's lust. And she will occupy her proud position by the side of man as his mother, maker and silent leader. It is given to her to teach the art of peace to the warring world thirsting for that nectar.

Gandhi's experiment also linked up with another powerful strand in the Hindu, especially the *Vaishnavāite* tradition. He had striven all his life to become a beautiful soul worthy of divine *anugraha* or grace. He had eliminated all 'impurities' and become as perfect as it was within his power to become. He had even surrendered his male identity and the last residual source of violence. He could go no further and had to await divine grace. If God thought him a fit vehicle, he would do His work through him. Otherwise, he stood helpless. That might perhaps explain why, having himself earlier described his experiments as *prayog*, he now called them *yajna*. Unlike a *prayog*, a *yajna* signified total self-surrender, a plaintive prayer and a desperate cry for help.

Having explained his reasons for his experiment, Gandhi went on to deal with the criticisms. Far from setting a bad example, it set the highest standards of *brahmacharya* and dared people to put their virtue to the severest test. It did not weaken the moral basis of society as it was not at all an invitation to promiscuity but the opposite. He had not intended to be secretive about the experiment. The secrecy was entirely 'fortuitous' and a 'serious flaw' which he regretted. He conceded that he should have placed his ideas before the public for discussion, but insisted that they were already known to his colleagues. He denied that they had no basis in Hindu religious tradition, for 'even amongst us there is the Tantra school which has influenced the Western savants like Justice Sir John Woodroffe'. Though Gandhi did not say that his experiment was inspired by the *Tantra* tradition, it is worth noting that it began only a few years after he had read Woodroffe's writings in prison. He also contended that his experiment was in harmony with Hindu religious tradition, which not only permitted but encouraged rare and courageous individuals to explore new areas of experience and extend the boundaries of available knowledge.

Gandhi did not think much of the other criticisms either. He rejected the charge that his experiment had no beneficial effects on his surroundings and asked his critics to be patient. He denied that it involved exploiting women and treating them as inferior. The experiment had been done with their consent, and there could be no exploitation where lust was absent. He had exploited his wife when she was an instrument of his lust. 'She ceased to be that when she lay with me naked as my sister.'[62] As for Bose's 'Freudian' criticism, he asked for evidence and suggested, rather surprisingly, that some of the women involved were perhaps emotionally unhinged long before the experiment had started. He told Bose that he knew nothing about Freud and would like to read him and that he had evolved his own unique ways of uncovering and conquering unconscious impulses.

It would seem that most of Gandhi's critics were persuaded by his arguments. They restored their relations with him and said, both privately and in public, that they had done him a grave injustice. Some of them, however, thought that it was inadvisable to conduct the experiment in the current climate. Thakkar Bapa privately put the matter to Manu. She agreed and raised the question with Gandhi who readily acceded to her wish.[63] The experiment was discontinued on or just after 14 February 1947. As Gandhi wrote to Vinoba Bhave two weeks later: 'Nowadays, Manu does not sleep in my bed. It is her own wish and is due to a pathetic letter from Bapa'.[64] It seems that after due notice to his critics, Gandhi resumed the practice in Delhi in May 1947 and continued it almost until the end of his life.[65] He later wrote a series of remarkably frank articles on the subject which, as usual, elicited fascinating comments from his readers.

VI

Gandhi embarked upon the experiments in celibacy in order to acquire, among other things, the kind of spiritual power he thought he needed to arrest the tidal wave of violence raging all around him and to win over his opponents. Judged by the results, they must be considered a failure. Intercommunal carnage continued unabated: Hindus who were his primary target and could be expected to respond to his appeal were just as brutal as the rest; three attempts were made on his life during the period of his experiments; he gained no privileged insight into the messy political situation; his lifelong friends, including Nehru and Maulana Azad, deserted and even deceived him on the question of the Partition of India;[66] and none of his close associates or any of the women involved in the experiments showed greater courage than before.

This is not to deny that Gandhi performed what amounted to secular miracles in Calcutta, Noakhali and Delhi. However he had exercised such a power over his countrymen long before he had thought up his experiments. And even after undertaking them, he sometimes failed and had to resort to fasts in Calcutta and Delhi. The experiments increased his self-esteem, enabled him to overcome his growing sense of helplessness, and gave him the courage to bear the tragedies of India with considerable equanimity. They had, therefore, an enormous psychological value for him and added to his moral and political self-confidence, but this was not their purpose. He was seeking a kind of mystical power that would silently but irresistibly subdue the violent impulses of his countrymen. Such a power eluded him until his death, not because he did not try hard enough as he thought, but because there is little reason to believe that such a thing exists.

Gandhi's experiments in celibacy were a good example of how he both remained within and radically departed from Hindu religious tradition. They had no sanction within the *advaita* tradition which required scrupulous avoidance of all contact with women. The *Vaishnavāite* tradition to which he belonged is ambivalent. Chaitanya, the father of north Indian *Vaishnavism*, urged ascetics to eschew all contact with women for 'even the wooden image of a woman has the power to steal the mind of a sage.' Other *Vaishnavite* leaders were less rigid. The Sahajiya cult in Bengal stressed the 'homeopathic' principle of purifying desire by intensifying it, and the discipline of *sahaja* involved passionless adoration of young and beautiful girls as a path to salvation. Rāmānanda, a close follower of Chaitanya, bathed and rubbed the bodies of two beautiful *devakanyās* as a way of acquiring self-control. Vishwanath, a philosopher, is reported to have slept with two women with a similar objective in mind. However these and other practices bore only a limited resemblance to Ganhi's experiments. Although they too had a spiritual orientation, they were largely one-off tests of self-control and not at all intended to *acquire* spiritual powers, explore the unconscious, or to assess the responses of the women involved.

Some strands within the *Tantric* tradition, with which Gandhi was familiar, come closer to his experiments. Like him, they too linked sexuality with a search for spiritual power, valued moral athleticism, and aimed to integrate the complementary principles of *purusha* and *prakriti*. However their methods and concerns were totally different to Gandhi's. They aimed to generate spiritual power through passionless sexual acts, an enterprise to which he was violently hostile. They relied on the dialectical technique of raising the sexual impulse to the highest pitch and then restraining and sublimating it, quite the opposite of what Gandhi did. And they saw this not as an experimental test of the already acquired self-control but as a *means* of acquiring it.

Gandhi's experiments were too daredevilish and activist by the traditional, and too sedate and conservative by Tantric standards. Since they had *some* analogues within the Hindu tradition and enjoyed a measure of cultural legitimacy, Hindus, unlike

Christians and Muslims, were not puzzled and outraged by them. Since, however, their goals and manner of execution had *no* parallel within the tradition, they were also unsettled and bewildered by them. Although Gandhi's experiments represented a new departure, they were inconceivable outside the Hindu religious tradition.

There is also another respect in which Gandhi's experiments both remained within and departed from the Hindu religious tradition. In several respects his attitude to his closest female associates is reminiscent of the traditional description of *Krishna*, at least until the last few months of his life when, if our interpretation is correct, the desire to become a woman dominated his thought. For the *Vaishnavāites* and several other Hindu sects, Krishna represents a complete man. He was a great *yogi*, a most wise and skilful statesman, a great thinker, a remarkable warrior and a man of enormous energy and power. He freely associated with the milkmaids who were passionately attracted to him and enjoyed their adoration, but avoided any kind of intimate physical contact with them. When carefully analysed, the colourful stories and legends surrounding him were intended to highlight several important themes lying at the heart of *Vaishnavite* Hinduism, of which two are relevant to our discussion.

First, surrender to God sometimes involves violating established social conventions. Most of the milkmaids, including Rādhā, were married and their love of Krishna involved turning their backs on all that society valued and demanded. When he received them, he told them that he was grateful to them for coming to him 'like the *vairāgi* who has renounced his home'. They had not allowed their social obligations, prestige, social standing and moral traditions to stand in the way of surrendering to their love of him. All this is, of course, allegorical, but it makes the vital point that religion may involve social rebellion and that when the call comes, the world and its conventions forfeit their authority. It is not often appreciated that the apparently sentimental and romantic *Vaishnavism* expresses and encourages a powerful spirit of rebellion and social non-conformity.

Second, *Vaishnavism* establishes a complex relationship between sensuality and spirituality. When the passionately attracted milkmaids got close to Krishna, they discovered that he was not a physical being at all but a pure spirit and lost all desire for physical intimacy. Krishna appealed to their femininity and intensified their sexual self-consciousness, and then helped them to acknowledge and sublimate it into a relationship of spiritual love. Unlike the non-physical Platonic love, what I might call Krishnite love represents a dialectical unity of the sensuous and the spiritual, of body and spirit. Although predominantly physical, the milkmaids' initial fascination with Krishna contained elements of surrender to a universal principle, and thus had a spiritual *telos*. As they got close to him, the spiritual element became infinitely stronger, but even in the ultimate union with him the sensuous element never entirely disappeared. It was transformed, *aufgehoben* (transcended), and retained as a necessary moment.

Although otherwise quite different, Gandhi's relations with his closest female associates had some elements of Krishnite love. Some of these women were strongly attracted to him and felt intensely possessive about him. Madeleine Slade showed her feelings in her letters and behaviour and even told him that she found their separation 'unbearable'. Gandhi assured her that he fully appreciated her feelings but urged her not to 'squander' her 'love' on him.[67] It was striking that he should have given her the highly suggestive name of Mirā and called her letters 'love letters'. When he once decided to avoid all physical contact with his female colleagues, he soon changed his mind because he could not 'bear the tears of Sushila and the fainting away of Prabhavati'.[68]

Gandhi knew very well that his female associates deeply craved his proximity and competed with each other for the opportunity to 'serve' him. He welcomed them, but once they got close to him he subtly transformed their relationship and put it on an altogether different plane. Over time, Madeleine Slade became his daughter whom he addressed as 'dear child' and deliberately gave distant assignments involving long separation. The other women too became his sisters and daughters and, with the exception of Sushila Nayar, were not allowed to stay with him too long. In a manner perceptively described in some of the *Vaishnavāite* literature, Gandhi recognised their sexual self-consciousness and subtly got them to acknowledge and overcome it. When the women involved in his experiments saw him naked, he wanted them to appreciate that his male identity meant nothing to him and should not mean anything to them either. When they stripped in front of him, he similarly wanted them to realise that their femininity had no physical and emotional significance for him and should have none for them either. Their mutually exhibited nudities were at once intended to affirm and deny, to display and transcend, their sexual differences.[69]

Gandhi knew that his experiments involved a gross violation of social conventions. As we saw, he felt fully justified in breaking them himself. However he had to satisfy himself, his associates and the world at large that the women involved were also right to disregard them, and that meant showing that like the milkmaids in the Krishna legend they had joined in the experiments freely and *out of their love* for him. This was why Manu became part of the experiment *only because* and *only after* she had expressed a strong desire to be with him. The references to Sushila Nayar's tears and Prabhavati Narayan's fainting too were intended to stress their *voluntary* participation. In his own way, Gandhi gave a wholly new meaning and significance to the dialectic of the Krishnite love and affirmed or 'validated' some of its central insights.[70]

Chapter Seven

Discourse on Untouchability

As a social reformer Gandhi was used to being attacked by both conservatives and radicals. On no other issue, however, was he as viciously attacked as that of untouchability. When he mounted a systematic campaign against it, the *sanātanists* were deeply alarmed. They feared his powerful hold over the Hindu masses and, since he attacked it from within the Hindu religious framework, they thought him a particularly dangerous enemy. Initially they argued with him, trying to convince him that untouchability was an integral part of Hinduism and that an attack on it threatened the very survival of the Hindu religious and social order.[1] When that did not work, they published leaflets and wrote or inspired articles impugning his political integrity and dropping dark hints about his private life. As we saw, what he called a 'campaign of vilification' coincided with and was designed to frighten him away from his anti-untouchability work. Organised protests with the *sanātanists* waiving black flags and shouting slogans greeted him in major cities during his all-India anti-untouchablity tour in 1934. A bomb was thrown at what was mistakenly believed to be his car, injuring seven persons. Pandit Lalnath tried to break up one of his meetings. In Karachi a man wielding an axe rushed towards him, but was apprehended in time. In Benares Baba Kalabhairav burnt his portrait and published scandalous and inflammatory leaflets against him.

While the *sanātanists* denounced Gandhi for subverting the Hindu social order, Ambedkar accused him of seeking to prop it up by making only token concessions to the untouchables. In his perceptive but uneven *What Congress and Gandhi Have Done to the Untouchables*, he observed:[2]

> Do the untouchables regard Mr. Gandhi as being in earnest? The answer is in the negative. They do not regard Mr. Gandhi as being in earnest. How can they? How can they look upon a man being in earnest who, when in 1921 the whole country was aroused to put the Bardoli programme in action, remained completely indifferent to the anti-touchability part of it? How can they believe in the earnestness of a man who is prepared to practice *satyāgraha* for everything and against everybody but who will not practise it against the Hindus for the sake of the Untouchables? How can they believe in the earnestness of a man who does nothing more than indulge in giving sermons on the evils of untouchability?
>
> Do they regard Mr. Gandhi as honest and sincere? The answer is that they do not regard Mr. Gandhi as honest and sincere. At the outset of his campaign for Swarāj, Mr. Gandhi told the Untouchables not to side with the British. He told them not to embrace Christianity or any other religion. He told them that they could find salvation in Hinduism. He told the Hindus that they must remove untouchability as a condition precedent to Swarāj. Yet in 1921, when only a paltry sum out of the Tilak Swarāj Fund was allotted to the Untouchables, and when the Committee to plan the uplift of the Untouchables was unceremoniously wound up, he did not even raise a word of protest.

Referring to Gandhi's fast against the Macdonald Award of 1931 granting a separate electorate to the untouchables, which the Hindus regarded as one of his noblest and greatest, Ambedkar remarked:[3]

> There was nothing noble in the fast. It was a foul and filthy act. The fast was not for the benefit of the Untouchables. It was against them and was the worst form of coercion against a helpless people to give up the constitutional safeguards of which they had become possessed under the Prime Minister's Award and agree to live on the mercy of the Hindus. It was a

vile and wicked act. How can the Untouchables regard such a man as honest and sincere?

After having gone on a fast unto death, he signed the Poona Pact. People say that Mr. Gandhi sincerely believed that political safeguards were harmful to the Untouchables. But how could an honest and sincere man, who opposed the political demands of the Untouchables, who was prepared to use the Muslims to defeat them and who went on a fast unto death, in the end accept the very same demands—for there is no difference between the Poona Pact and the Communal Award—when he found that there was no use opposing, as opposition would not succeed? How can an honest and sincere man accept as harmless the demands of the Untouchables which once he regarded as harmful?

Lest Ambedkar's criticism be attributed to his personal animus against Gandhi, it should be pointed out that they were echoed by many Harijan leaders, and were recently reiterated by Kanshi Ram, a leader of the Harijan party, the Bahujan Samaj Party:[4]

What has Gandhi done? He fought tooth and naif against the interests of the downtrodden people. In September 1932, he went on fast against reservations. Later it was propagated that Gandhi was responsible for reservations. He was a great hypocrite, to my mind. He lived in a sweepers' colony and he told them: 'Your job is a very good job, you are doing a very good job. If I am to be born again I would like to be born as a sweeper.' He was told: 'If you want to be a sweeper, we can fulfil your desire in this life. Come on.' But he never came. He was a hypocrite just fooling innocent people.

In this chapter I intend to explore the internal logic of Gandhi's campaign against untouchability and to examine the reasons why his conservative and radical critics reached contradictory conclusions. I shall argue that the manner in which he formulated his critique and planned his campaign was a source of both his success and failure. It enabled him to undermine the *moral* basis of untouchability but prevented him from dealing with its *economic* and *political* roots.

I

The practice of untouchability is deeply embedded in the Hindu social structure, has existed for several centuries and is of obscure and controversial origin. It was enforced with varying degrees of rigidity in different areas and had reached the most degrading level in some parts of the South where the untouchables were even forbidden to walk along certain roads or required to make noises in order that caste Hindus could move out of their shadow. Throughout India they were confined to the outskirts of villages, denied access to commonly used wells, rivers, temples, markets and other public places, systematically exploited and brutally punished for giving the slightest offence to caste Hindus.

Though the practice of untouchability was differently justified in different parts of the country at different times, the most common justification was in terms of the three basic concepts of *varna, dharma* and *karma*. Schematically it was along the following lines:

(i) Hindu society consisted of four castes, each with its characteristic occupation, *dharma* and place in the social hierarchy. To be born into a particular caste was to be a bearer of specific rights and obligations and to be involved in a specific pattern of relationship with members of other castes.

(ii) Untouchability was an integral part of the Hindu social order. Those engaged in occupations involving dead animals and the removal of human dirt occupied the lowest place in the social hierarchy and any contact with them was a source of pollution. Hindu religious thought was deeply ambiguous about their social status and remains so till today. For some, untouchables fell outside the caste system, and were not Hindus. For some others, they were *atishudras*, belonged to the lowest rung of the *shudra* caste, and hovered over the boundary of Hindu society with one foot in it and the other out. For most, they were outcastes *within* the Hindu social order, that is, outside the mainstream caste structure but *not* outside

Hindu society, and hence subject to its moral discipline. Unlike the Christians or Muslims, who were all non-Hindus, they had their prescribed *dharma* specifying, if not their social practices, at least their pattern of relationship with the rest of Hindu society.

(*iii*) Birth in a particular caste was not an accident but a just dessert for the agent's *karma* in his previous life. Individuals were born into castes commensurate with the kinds of lives they had led in their earlier lives.

(*iv*) Each individual was the sole cause of and, therefore, uniquely responsible for all his actions. Those born as untouchables deserved their predicament and had none but themselves to blame for it.

(*v*) It was open to the untouchables to improve their lot in the next life and be born in higher castes by doing good deeds in this one. Good deeds included accepting their present condition in the spirit of humility and conscientiously discharging their prescribed duties and obligations.

(*i*) and (*ii*) articulated the Hindu social order and the rights and obligations of different castes. (*iii*) explained why individuals belonged to certain castes, and (*iv*) explained why they had no moral right to complain. (*v*) offered a hope of release and explained why the release could not be found in this life.

During its long history, the practice of untouchability was never without its critics. The dominant *advaita* tradition, which stressed the unity of all men and indeed of all existence, could have provided a powerful critique of it. But apparently it did not feel embarrassed by it and not only connived at but positively justified it. Rāmānuja, one of the greatest philosophical critics of *advaita*, was also one of the first to condemn it. He accepted both the caste system and the law of *karma*, but insisted that untouchability had no religious basis and that social inequality did not imply moral inequality. He threw open several temples to the untouchables and called them *thirukkulathars* or a holy community. The Bhakti movement, too, attacked untouchability on similar grounds. And though it did not campaign against it or do much to integrate the untouchables into the Hindu social order, it encouraged the spirit of social equality and inspired courageous individuals to found sects welcoming them. The Tantric and other schools went further and rejected the caste system itself. Some even rejected the doctrine of rebirth, and actively campaigned to bring untouchables within the mainstream Hindu society. Several *Vaishnavāite* leaders such as Ramananda, and several reformist movements such as those led by Kabir and Nanak, also rejected the caste system and campaigned against untouchability. Though these and other movements had varying degrees of success in different parts of the country, untouchability continued to be practised fairly widely.

Since untouchability aroused strong feelings among the Hindus and many of them believed in it themselves, most early nineteenth century Hindu reformers took little interest in it and concentrated their energies on such largely high-caste practices as *sati*, child marriage, ban on widow remarriage and overseas travel. Bankim Chandra Chatterjee's *Samya*, a powerful attack on inequality published in 1864, did not include untouchability among the 'four great social evils'. The Indian National Social Conference at its first meeting in 1885 did not list it among the 'five great evils' against which it urged educated Indians to campaign. Though criticised by isolated writers and movements from about the second half of the nineteenth century onwards, untouchability did not become a subject of active national campaign until the early years of the twentieth century.

This was not an accident. As we saw elsewhere, from the 1870s onwards Indians had begun to complain bitterly against the authoritarianism and racism of the colonial government and to demand a share in the conduct of public affairs. The irony of demanding social and political equality while denying it to large masses of their own people was not lost on Hindu leaders, and the government never missed an opportunity to embarrass them. As one Indian leader put it, 'With what face will we approach the British democracy or any other power if we are unable to uplift our own brethren'[5] Another argued that Hindus did not 'deserve' equality because they were themselves 'so little mindful of the legitimate rights of others under them'.[6] Yet another thought was that the Hindu treatment of the untouchables was even more racist than the British treatment of Indians. After all, the British did not mind touching Indians or sharing basic facilities with them! Hindu leaders complained of British insensitivity to Indian public opinion, but could not answer the criticism that their own insensitivity to lower caste feelings was just as pronounced. Obviously, if they were to avoid the charges of 'hypocrisy' and 'grave inconsistency', Hindu leaders needed to put their own house in order.

They had another political reason as well for tackling the question of untouchability. Once they began to press their political demands, they found that their internal divisions and disunity were their greatest handicap. Not only did Hindus, Muslims, Sikhs and others remain separated by deep historical differences, the different castes, sects and linguistic groups among the Hindus could not unite either. That was why for several years the Congress insisted on the artificial but unavoidable distinction between social and political matters and excluded the former from its deliberations. Hindu leaders began to realise that unless the entire country was united, the colonial government would continue to rule over their vast and increasingly restless country by intensifying their divisions and successfully playing off one group against another. Untouchables became particularly important in his context. Having once willingly embraced the egalitarian Islam, they were now responding to the tempting overtures of Christian missionaries and striking up dubious alliances with the government. They claimed to prefer the 'inhumane British rule' to the 'tyrannical Brahmin rule' and wanted the former to continue until such time as they secured full social and political equality. Once the Muslims were granted a separate electorate, the untouchables too began to press for it. In order to reduce the proportionate representation of the Hindus, the Muslims began to argue that since the Hindus themselves did not consider untouchables a part of their social order, the latter should not be counted as such. The political dangers of all this were not lost upon Hindu leaders. Unless they abolished untouchability, not only was their political strength likely to be considerably reduced, they were also confronted with the spectre of an alliance of alienated minorities reducing them to a permanent minority in 'their own' country.[7]

The majority of the Hindus, who had for centuries remained relatively opaque to the moral critique of untouchability, could no longer ignore the political argument. Not surprisingly, a number of them began to mount campaigns against it. Dayananda Saraswati denied that it had a scriptural basis and repeatedly warned against its *political* dangers. His Arya Samaj, which had long been content to criticise it, began to cultivate the untouchables and to promote schemes for their social and economic welfare. Vivekananda denounced the 'morbid no-touchism' of the Hindus, and the Ramakrishna Mission went about actively campaigning against it and encouraging welfare activities.[8] Even the socially conservative Tilak observed, 'If God were to tolerate untouchability I would not recognise Him as God at all'. The Congress, which had hitherto studiously avoided social questions, began rather tentatively to criticise untouchability from the early years of the twentieth century onwards. However, it was so afraid of dividing its ranks that it dared not pass an explicit resolution condemning it until 1917.[9] And it did so only because the increasingly vocal untouchables had at their two meetings earlier that year pressed it for 'a distinct and independent resolution' on the subject and passed several resolutions declaring 'loyalty' to the colonial government, 'praying' for its continued rule and asking for separate legislative representation.[10]

Once Hindu leaders decided to attack untouchability, they had to work out an effective intellectual strategy. They developed three lines of criticism which they deployed either singly or in varying combinations.[11] First, some argued from within the Hindu religious framework and attempted to refute the orthodox on their own grounds.[12] They insisted that untouchability had no scriptural basis, at least not in such authoritative sacred texts as the *Vedas*, the *Upanishads* and the *Gītā*, that it was not practised in ancient India, and that it was a 'corruption' or perversion of the fundamentally sound *jāti* or *varna* system. Second, some stepped outside the Hindu religious framework altogether and appealed to the fundamental principles of European liberalism.[13] They argued that untouchability was inhuman, unjust, offended human dignity, violated the fundamental equality of all men and denied basic human rights. Third, some Hindu leaders concentrated on the political dangers of untouchability.[14] They were not interested in discussing either its scriptural basis or its morality, but were only concerned to show that it had become a moral embarrassment and a political liability. So long as it continued, Indian demands for equality and independence sounded hollow. Furthermore, the untouchables were threatening to leave the Hindu fold, and were striking up alliances with the Muslims and the colonial government. Unless the caste Hindus did something, their political future was doomed.

Each intellectual strategy had its advantages and disadvantages and appealed to a specific constituency. The first, which we might call an internal or textualist critique, had the great merit of addressing the Hindus in traditional idioms and appealing to an authority acceptable to them. However, it had obvious disadvantages. Some support for untouchability could always be found in one of the scores of Hindu religious texts. In the absence of a clearly established canonical hierarchy among them, it was always possible to disregard an inconvenient text. And interpreting even an agreed text such as the *Manusmriti* was an inherently inconclusive exercise and invariably left room for doubt.

The second strategy, which we might call an external or modernist critique, had opposite advantages and disadvantages. Since it bypassed the scriptures, it avoided endless and boring textualist debates. It took its stand on general and unambiguous principles. It had the further advantage that these principles were endorsed by the colonial government and respected by the growing body of Westernised Indians. Its advantages were also its disadvantages. Since it ignored the scriptures, it had no appeal for the orthodox and their followers. European liberalism was an alien doctrine and the arguments based on it carried no conviction with them. It was also tainted by its colonial associations, and its champions were vulnerable to the charge of betraying their ancestors and undermining Hindu tradition.

The third strategy, which we might call a political critique of untouchability, had several advantages. It avoided interminable and inherently inconclusive debates about the scriptural basis and morality of untouchability, appealed to vital Hindu interests, and provided a common platform on which the champions of all three strategies could unite. However, it had obvious limitations. It did not refute the case for untouchability and appeared to orthodox Hindus to be a form of political blackmail. Besides, many of them took a very different view of Hindu political interests. Some did not agree that the untouchables would leave the Hindu fold. Some did, but did not think that that would necessarily damage India's struggle for independence. Yet others agreed that it damaged the struggle, but considered the price worth paying in the interest of preserving the integrity of the Hindu social order.

II

When Gandhi appeared on the Indian political scene, the campaign against untouchability had been under way for about two decades. It was confined to a few areas, spearheaded by some religious groups and national leaders, genteel in tone and articulated in terms of the three idioms noted earlier. Gandhi was quick to see its political importance. He put it high on the national agenda and gave it unprecedented momentum.

Though Gandhi had long disapproved of untouchability, he first began to criticise it publicly in South Africa. During the course of his campaign against its racist policies, he was repeatedly told by the whites that men in glass houses were better advised not to throw stones at others. The fact that for centuries Hindus had been treating large masses of their own people as untouchables showed that equality was not a value for them. Since they did not believe in equality, it was inconsistent of them to ask for it and hypocritical of them to blame the whites for denying it to them. Gandhi rejoined that Hindus believed not only in equality and brotherhood but also in the higher principle of the unity of all life. The deeply regrettable practice of untouchability was not an integral part of their religion but a corruption that had entered into it during their years of degeneration and decline. Since Hindus believed in equality they were entitled to demand it from the whites. However, since they did not practise it, they had no moral right to criticise white racism unless they were also prepared to condemn their own treatment of untouchables. Their hypocrisy lay not in demanding equality but in refusing to fight against both kinds of inequality. Accordingly, Gandhi began to attack untouchability in South Africa. He continued the attack on his return to India and repeatedly reminded his countrymen that so long as they treated some of their own people as untouchables, they could not consistently blame the Canadian,

South African and other foreign governments for treating them as 'pariahs of the empire'. Though Gandhi's argument was not new, the international dimension that he brought to it was.

When Gandhi became leader of the independent movement, he discovered yet another and far more important reason for abolishing untouchability. Like his predecessors, he saw that the deeply divided Indians were an easy prey to the British policy of 'divide and rule' and that their demands were never taken seriously. He began to explore ways of uniting the two major communities of Hindus and Muslims and saw a golden opportunity in the Khilafat agitation. He realised that he could not placate the Muslims while ignoring the untouchables, especially as the latter were becoming increasingly vocal and complaining against the favoured treatment the Muslims were receiving at the hands of Hindus. The Non-Cooperation Movement he launched in 1920 had no change of success unless a substantial number of Indians stopped cooperating with the government, and that, too, required him to win over the pro-government untouchables. As Gandhi put it in 1920:[15]

> The Hindus must realise that, if they wish to offer successful non-cooperation against the government they must make common cause with the Panchamas, *even as* they have made common cause with the Musalmans.

Two months later, he made the point even more clearly:[16]

> Non-cooperation against the government means cooperation among the governed, and if Hindus do not remove the sin of untouchability there will be no *Swarāj* whether in one year or in one hundred years.... *Swarāj* is unattainable without the removal of the sins of untouchability as it is without Hindu-Muslim unity.

Two important features of Gandhi's attack on untouchability during this period deserve to be noted. First, he criticised it on the ground that its continued existence hindered national unity and harmed the cause of Indian independence. That is, he did not challenge its scriptural or moral basis and attacked it on political grounds. Second, in the two remarks cited earlier and in many others, he repeatedly compared the untouchables to the Muslims and asked the Hindus to make common cause with them *in the same way* that they had done with the latter. That is, Gandhi was *primarily* interested in Muslims and he cultivated untouchables largely in order to ensure a measure of fairness. At this stage of his career, political considerations weighed far more with him than moral and social reform.

Though Gandhi continued to argue against untouchability on political grounds, he increasingly began to feel that this was not enough. The political argument made only a limited impression on the orthodox Hindus, who neither believed that the struggle for independence required the abolition of untouchability nor cared for one bought at such a 'heavy' price. It made no impression on the illiterate masses either, who were more concerned with religion than with independence and considered untouchability an integral part of it. For reasons to be discussed later, Gandhi wanted caste Hindus to agree to its abolition not for 'ulterior' political reasons but out of genuine conversion. He also felt that untouchability was not an integral part of Hinduism, and that he owed it to his religion to show that it possessed the resources to mount a successful critique of it. For these and other related reasons, Gandhi decided to debate with the orthodox on their grounds.[17]

III

The *sanātanists* had long argued that untouchability was enjoined by the scriptures. Gandhi asked for evidence. When they produced passages from different texts, including the *Manusmriti*, he rejoined that these were interpolations or open to different interpretations. They denied this and the resulting debate was either inconclusive or to his disadvantage. Since the contents and origins of many of these texts were subject to dispute and historical scholarship was still fairly primitive, he could not show that the passages in question were interpolations. And since the passages could be read in several different ways, no interpretation of them was conclusive. If anything, the *sanātanist* interpretation was nearer the mark. When challenged to a public debate by Shankaracharya and some Hindu pandits, Gandhi wisely declined saying he was prepared to explain to them his position on untouchability but not to enter into an exegesis on religious texts.[18]

At this point, he shifted the debate to a different level and raised the larger question of how to read scriptures. For reasons discussed earlier, he insisted that a religious text was not a theoretical treatise composed by a philosopher or a pandit given to weighing every word, but the work of a spiritual explorer containing insights too deep and complex to be adequately expressed in a discursive language. As such, it had to be read over and over again, meditated upon, creatively interpreted, and its overall message sensitively teased out. 'The letter killeth, only the spirit redeemeth.' To concentrate on its isolated passages was to reduce it to the profane status of a 'mere' intellectual construct.[19]

Since a religious text was a work of profound wisdom, interpreting it required other qualifications than textual scholarship. 'Learning there must be, but religion does not live by it'.[20] Just as only a scientist was capable of interpreting a scientific text, only a man who had undertaken the spiritual journey himself was equipped to decipher the deeper meaning of a religious work. A learned but 'dissolute' and sinful Brahmin had neither the *adhikār* nor the necessary competence. Gandhi observed: 'I do most emphatically repudiate the claim (if they advance any) of the present Shankaracharya and *shāstris* to give a correct interpretation of the Hindu scriptures.'[21] Though too modest to say so, Gandhi implied on several occasions that as life-long spiritual seeker he was better qualified to interpret them than almost all his adversaries.

Gandhi went on to argue that religious texts were necessarily articulated at two levels. They propounded eternally valid values and principles and were intended to guide all men everywhere. They were also, however, written in a unique society at a specific time, and recommended practices and institutions most likely to realise these values in the specific circumstances of that society and age. Religious texts, thus, both transcended and were conditioned by time. While their values were eternally valid, the practices they recommended had only a limited validity. A commentator on a religious text, therefore, had a duty to distinguish and separate the two. As Gandhi put it:[22]

> *Shāstras* are ever growing . . . . Each grew out of the necessities of particular periods, and therefore they seem to conflict with one another. These books do not enunciate anew the eternal truths but show how those were practised at the time to which the books belong. A practice which was good enough in a particular period would, if blindly repeated in another, lead people into the 'slough of despond.'

The *sanātanists* were not persuaded by Gandhi's hermeneutic techniques. They contended that sacred texts were composed with infinite care by learned *āchāryas* and required literal interpretation. The creative reinterpretation recommended by Gandhi involved the blasphemy of making the commentator superior to the original author. They argued, further, that the spirit of a sacred text could not be dissociated from, and must be elicited by means of, a diligent study of its letter. They also questioned Gandhi's claim to offer an authoritative interpretation of the sacred texts. While admitting that he was a noble soul, they insisted that his knowledge of them and of the language in which they were written was disgracefully inadequate and that he was too much under the influence of 'Christian religious literature' to appreciate the finer points of his religion.

As the textualist argument was leading nowhere, Gandhi moved the debate to a yet more abstract level and appealed to the 'spirit of Hinduism'.[23] Hindu scriptures, he argued, were an integral part of Hindu tradition and could not be read in isolation from it. A commentator should first determine its central principles or spirit and read the texts in their light. Unlike almost all other religions, Hinduism was not a religion of the book but a continuing and creative spiritual quest undertaken by its great sages and seers. Some of them left behind texts describing their experiences and discoveries; others did not. Though of great importance, the texts were necessarily inadequate records of their profound insights. Their lives spoke far more clearly and authentically than the formal word and were the true

Hindu scriptures. The spirit of Hindu religious tradition had to be teased out of the way the sages lived, the sacred texts having only an instrumental and heuristic value.

For Gandhi, the spirit of Hinduism consisted in its 'three fundamental precepts', namely *satyān nāsti paro dharma* (there is no religion higher than truth), *ahimsā paramo dharma* (non-violence is the highest religion or duty), and *brahma satyam jagat mithya* (*Brahman* alone is real, the world is trivial or inconsequential).[24] Sometimes he added such others as the unity of man, of life and of all creation, *karunā* and *dayā*. They had all not only been stressed by a long line of sages but also cherished by the Hindu masses. These and other related values, which constituted the 'spirit of Hinduism', provided the hermeneutical canons of principles of Hindu scriptures. Sacred texts must be read and interpreted in their light, and those at odds with them discarded or suitably reinterpreted. Untouchability was clearly incompatible with them. A religion which preached the unity of life, non-injury and universal compassion could hardly be expected to sanction it. Indeed it was grotesque to suggest that a religion which enjoined tender concern for animals and even plants could ever wish to subject human beings to such a degrading treatment. Untouchability was and had to be an excrescence, a corruption, a perversion of the true spirit of Hinduism.[25]

Gandhi's appeal to the spirit of Hinduism attracted a few followers but had little influence on the orthodox. They found the concept elusive and irrelevant, and could not see why one needed to appeal to it when the sacred texts were unambiguously clear. They had little difficulty noticing that he had introduced the concept only because some of the texts did not support his case against untouchability, and accused him of deviousness. Many of them argued that since on his own testimony the spirit of Hinduism enjoined the caste system, he must accept that it also sanctioned untouchability which was an integral part of it. And they also repeated the charge that a man who had lived abroad for so long and confessed profound reverence for Christianity was hardly equipped to understand the spirit of his own religion.

Gandhi's increasing frustration with the *sanātanists* came to a head during his most exasperating three-hour debate with the Brahmins of Travancore on 10 March 1925. They had long barred untouchables from passing along a road adjacent to a temple and practised not only untouchability but also unapproachability. When the untouchables launched a *satyāgraha* in 1924, they met fierce resistance lasting over a year. Gandhi decided to visit Vaikkam and 'convert' the Brahmins. The debate between them contained fascinating exchanges and deserves to be quoted at length. It showed how the traditionalists defended untouchability and why Gandhi's critique of it was hampered by his acceptance of some of their basic beliefs.[26]

Gandhi: I say that it is wrong on our part to prevent a single person from passing through that road simply because he is born in a particular caste....

Indanturuttil Nambiatiri: Does Mahatmaji believe in the divinity of the Hindu *shāstras*?

Gandhi: Yes.

Nambiatiri: Does Mahatmaji believe in the Law of *karma*?

Gandhi: Yes.

Nambiatiri: Does he believe in reincarnation?

Gandhi: Yes.

Nambiatiri: According to our faith, according to our Acharya, we believe that they are born in the unapproachable caste by their bad *karma* in their previous birth. We have been enjoined by our Kerala Acharya to treat them in this manner....

Gandhi: Let us grant that. But I ask, who is to punish them—we animal beings?

Nambiatiri: In worldly matters, it is man who punishes man for wrongs done by him. We believe it is the ordinance of God to have them punished by having them born in this caste.

Gandhi: True, true. Let divinity punish them; but how can human beings punish them?

Nambiatiri: God acts through man. Similarly, as a punishment, these people are in the unapproachable caste....

Gandhi: I say that there is no warrant for it in the Hindu *Shāstras*. I know of no Acharyas who will tell me like that.

Nambiatiri: What the Acharyas have done are contained in the Granthas which we have been following from time immemorial.

Gandhi: I understand that and I appreciate that. All my argument is that this is not universal in Hinduism. If you put before me certain books or certain authorities you will find that they will not be of universal acceptance. Therefore you will be able to defend it only on the ground of being custom. What I am referring to is, do not tie yourself down to some authority or some book which cannot be defended by reason. I ask you therefore to adduce reason and do not appeal to authority or custom.

Nambiatiri: In this matter we are not prepared to leave aside customs and sentiments based on religion and faith.

Gandhi: If you set up a plea of that character and say that in matters of sentiment and religion, reason has no place, will you at least show that this is the universl custom in Hinduism or will you show at least that this is the custom in Malbar or Vaikkam that you stand by?

Nambiatiri: There are several Acharyas in the Hindu religion. There is Madhwa Acharya and Sankara Acharya. Both belong to opposite sides. We follow Sankara Acharya. We will accept only what he says and not what the other Acharya will say in regard to customs.

Gandhi: Therefore you would not even seek the aid of reason or justice in connection with its custom which is only peculiar to a few people?

Nambiatiri: We do not want our Acharyas to be revised by ordinary people. There are the Avatars who are well-educated to revise them. Whenever any revision is necessary, an Avatar will take place and these things can be done very easily.

Gandhi: Do you want a divine preceptor even for revising local customs?

Nambiatiri: Yes.

Gandhi: Oh, No!

Raman Pillai: May I ask Mahatmaji whether there is not a class mentioned in the Hindu *Shāstras* who are called the polluted classes?

Gandhi: There is a class called Chandalas.

Pillai: May I further ask whether Mahatmaji believes in births and rebirths?
Gandhi: Oh, Yes.
Pillai: If so, may I not believe that these Chandalas whom we call Panchamas or Ezhavas are born in that section on account of their past *karma*?
Gandhi: It is the fruit of his own past action. I admit that. But Hinduism does not teach you to consider one man low and another man high.
Pillai: But we know that a man who has been born in a particular caste enjoys certain privileges and undergoes certain disabilities. We say that he is put to those difficulties on account of those past *karma*. If that is my belief according to my religion, may I not be allowed to shun him as a human being?
Gandhi: If you speak as a human being and not as a Hindu, then I will have to give further reasons.
Pillai: As a Hindu.
Gandhi: No. As a Hindu you cannot treat him differently.
Pillai: Then to what other reason shall we attribute the differences of births we see in this world?
Gandhi: I have granted to you that the differences of births are due to differences of action. But that does not mean that you can consider one man low and another man high.
Pillai: I do not say he is low. He is equally entitled to enjoy the privileges of the world. But if you want to go away from him you are permitted to do so. I should be allowed to go away from him so that by my approach I may not be polluted.
Gandhi: You are entitled to go away from anybody you like.
Pillai: In the case of this temple, the facts were these. We came away from them, removed ourselves to a certain corner so that we may avoid the unapproachables. We have the surroundings of this temple as our own place.

Gandhi was deeply disturbed by the debate. Realising that it was getting nowhere, he offered the Brahmins three compromises, namely a referendum among the caste Hindus of the area, arbitration by a committee of three of whom two were to be Brahmins, and a critical examination of the canonical status of the text in question by the learned pandits of Benaras or even Madras. The Brahmins rejected all three. Gandhi summed up his feelings in a speech at a public meeting held immediately after the debate:[27]

> I have come, therefore, to reason with my orthodox friends; I have come to plead with them; and by their courtesy and goodwill, I was able to wait upon them this afternoon. They gave me a patient hearing and listened to me. I appealed to their reason. I appealed to their humanity. And I appealed to the Hinduism in them. I am sorry to confess to you that I was not able to produce the impression that I had expected that I would be able to. But despair is a term which does not occur in my dictionary. I shall despair when I despair myself of God and humanity.

The Vaikkam *satyāgraha* and Gandhi's frustrating debates with The Brahmins there and elsewhere led him to reconsider his mode of discourse on untouchability. He had almost for the first time in his life come face to face with orthodox Brahmins and experienced the intensity of their prejudices. He saw that though they were wrong and confused, they felt strongly about their beliefs and sincerely held that these had a scriptural basis. Gandhi seems to have thought that if he was to win them over, he had to earn their confidence and reassure them that he was as much concerned to preserve Hinduism as the most orthodox among them. Ever since his return to India in 1917, he had frequently talked about reforming Hindu society and religion and expressed his great admiration for some of the basic tenets of Christianity. He now realised that his reputation as a reformer and as a man 'in love with Christianity', mischievously exploited by the *sanātanists*, alienated him from many a caste Hindu, cast doubt on his loyalty to his religion and weakened his claim to speak in its name. Gandhi, therefore, decided to reiterate his Hindu credentials, proclaim his allegiance to his religion and to underplay his reformist intentions. As he put it: 'In dealing with the problem of untouchability during the Madras tour, I have asserted my claim to being a *sanātanist* Hindu with greater emphasis than before'.[28] He began to insist far more than he had hitherto done that he was a 'Hindu of Hindus saturated with the spirit of Hinduism' and that he 'loved his religion more than his life'.[29] While asserting his loyalty to Hinduism, Gandhi did not wish to go soft on reform. He knew that reforms were necessary, including the eradiction of untouchability. His problem, therefore, was how to justify reform in the language of tradition and make change synonymous with continuity.

As we saw elsewhere, he solved the problem by interpreting religion in general and Hinduism in particular in scientific terms. Hinduism, he argued, was not so much a religion as a science of the spirit constantly making new discoveries and reinterpreting its central insights in the light of the new *yuga*.[30] During its history, it had frequently suffered degeneration and decay and had been saved from extinction by the timely reforms of courageous individuals. Gandhi said that he was doing no more than follow in their footsteps. He was not interested in reform for its own sake. He sought reform only because and only when it was necessary to preserve the religion he dearly loved. Far from preventing him from criticising it, his love of Hinduism *required* him to criticise and reform it lest it should decay and die. He wished to reform some aspects of it not because he was in love with some other religion to which he was anxious to see it conform, but because he needed to prune the noxious undergrowth so that its essential values could reassert themselves and bring forth historically appropriate forms. In contrast to the self-styled *sanātanists* who, by uncritically idealising existing practices invited the doom of their religion and were, therefore, its enemies, he was a 'true' *sanātanist* reaffirming its central values in a manner relevant to the new *yuga*. He said:[31]

> I call myself a *sanātanist* Hindu because I believe in the *Vedas*, *Upanishads*, the *Purānas*, and the writings left by the holy reformers. This belief does not require me to accept as authentic everything that passes as *Shāstras*. I am not required to accept the *ipse dixit* or the interpretation of Pundits.

And again:[32]

A *sanātanist* is one who follows the *Sanātana Dharma*. According to the *Mahābhārata* it means observance of *Ahimsā, Satya*, non-stealing, cleanliness and self-restraint. As I have been endeavouring to follow these to the best of my ability, I have not hesitated to describe myself as a *sanātanist*.

These extraordinary remarks beautifully capture Gandhi's polemical strategy of using his opponents' weapons against them. The term *sanātanist* had a conservative connotation in popular parlance and referred to someone who uncritically accepted established beliefs and practices. Gandhi used it to describe a person who upheld values Gandhi approved of and who stood up against whatever practices diverged from them. On Gandhi's definition a *sanātanist* was necessarily a social critic! He went even further and turned reform into a religious activity. For him, all desirable reforms were 'holy' and the Hindu tradition was full of and, indeed, only kept alive by a long line of 'holy reformers' including the authors of the *Vedas* and the *Upanishads*! The anti-reform traditionalist was not only a traitor to but utterly ignorant of his religion! The learned Brahmins who had spent their lives studying the *shāstras* could not have been hit harder. Since Gandhi had found a way of reforming tradition by traditionalising reform, he felt able to stress the need both to preserve and to reform it. After all, they amounted to the same thing! Not surprisingly, Gandhi's post-Vaikkam discourse on untouchability was at once more traditional and more reformist than before.

The *sanātanists* were unimpressed by Gandhi's arguments. In their view, he played fast and loose with their tradition and wholly misinterpreted its nature and history. He had no understanding of the canonical status of the sacred texts as no knowledgeable Hindu would have placed the *Vedas* on par with the *Purānas*. He did not grasp the central Hindu values either and put dubious interpretations on them. The *sanātanists* accused him of ignorance and even downright dishonesty. Gandhi remained unmoved. In his view, he understood his religion better than them; unlike them, he sincerely tried to live by its highest values; his knowledge of it was based on *vijnāna* not just *jnāna* and he had nothing but its good at heart. Since he saw no way to convince the *sanātanists* by argument, he concentrated on putting moral pressure on them by mobilising the Hindu masses, the only constituency that really mattered.

IV

Like many other national leaders, for a long time Gandhi saw no internal connection between untouchability and the caste system. For him, it was not an integral part but a regrettable corruption of it and could be eradicated without attacking it. Although untouchability was evil, the caste system was based on 'scientific principles' discovered by Hindu sages after years of 'research' and 'experiment' and was a great monument to Hindu ingenuity and wisdom.

Gandhi defended the caste system on several grounds.[33] First it ensured the continuity of hereditary occupation, for him 'the soul of the caste system'. Hereditary occupation eliminated 'corrosive' competition and class war, was easier to learn and thus saved energy and time, and built up a reservoir of traditional skills. Since Gandhi believed in rebirth and the law of *karma*, he thought that the characteristic occupation of an individual's caste corresponded to his natural abilities and dispositions and represented a necessary moment in his spiritual evolution. Second, caste was 'another name for control'. By requiring each individual to observe specific norms of conduct and follow a specific occupation, it encouraged self-restraint and developed powers of self-discipline.

Third, caste was a self-governing social unit performing legislative, executive, judicial and other quasi-governmental functions and catering to the educational, social, welfare and other needs of its members. As such, it reduced the role and power of the state, fostered habits of self-government and nurtured the spirit of democracy. Fourth, as India's long history showed, the caste system had saved it from total disintegration during periods of oppressive foreign rule and political instability, and preserved intact its religious and cultural tradition. It had thus proved its value and deserved to be retained. Finally, caste ordered and structured human relationships, provided a ready and easily mobilisable network of emotional, moral and economic support, and constituted an effective safeguard against atomisation and anomie. Gandhi concluded: 'These being my views, I am opposed to all those who are out to destroy the caste system.'

Increasingly Gandhi came to realise that although good in principle and its original conception, in its current form the caste system left a good deal to be desired. It divided the Hindus, bred hostility and suspicion, and hindered concerted action. It was excessively rigid and limited the range of social contacts. Above all, it was closely bound up with and, indeed, led to untouchability. Though he was rather vague on this last point, he seems to have taken this view for two reasons. First, the caste system was based on moral inequality. One's dignity varied with one's caste so that the lower one's caste, the lower was one's status as a human being. The most degrading treatment meted out to untouchables was but a concentrated expression of the spirit of inequality inherent in the system. Second, the idea of pollution lay at the heart of the caste system. Untouchability was the most acute manifestation of this pervasive ethos of pollution.

Gandhi began to advocate a reformed caste system, especially after his Vaikkam visit.[34] He was still in favour of its basic principles of functional differentiation and hereditary occupation, but thought that the social groups involved need not be exclusive and hierarchical. As was his wont, he insisted that this was how the caste system was practised in ancient India and that he was concerned not so much to reform it as to return to the original *varna* system. He proposed that the countless castes into which Hindu society had become divided should be regrouped on the basis of their occupational similarity and 'the old system of four *varnas* should be reproduced'. All *varnas* were to be treated as equal; interdining and, in some cases, even intermarriage were to be permitted; and no *varna* was to be considered unclean. While advocating these and other reforms, Gandhi was uncompromising on what he had called the 'soul' of the caste system. Though they were at liberty to learn and practise whatever occupations they liked, all Hindus should earn their living by following their parental occupations. As he put it:[35]

> The *varna* system is connected with the way of earning a living. There is no harm if a person belonging to one *varna* acquires the knowledge or science and art specialised in by

persons belonging to other *varnas*. But as far as the way of earning his living is concerned he must follow the occupation of the *varna* to which he belongs, which means he must follow the hereditary profession of his forefathers.

Gandhi went on:

> *Varna* means the determination of a man's occupation before he is born.... In the *varna* system no man has any liberty to choose his occupation. His occupation is determined for him by heredity.

Gandhi presented the moderately modernised version of the ancient *varna* system as his answer to the agonising Hindu research for a new social order. In his view it united the Hindus, eliminated class war, preserved traditional skills, avoided atomisation, formed the social basis of a plural and uncentralised polity, institutionalised and nurtured the new *yugadharma* and solved the problem of untouchability. It also enabled the Hindus to make common cause with the Muslims and other minorities who would not now be alienated by their obsession with pollution and hierarchy.

Though hereditary occupation was the basis of Gandhi's new social order, he gave little thought to the problems raised by it. Human activities and occupations are too diverse and complex to be amenable to his fourfold classification. This was true even when the *varna* system allegedly prevailed in ancient India; it was especially so in a modern industrialised society. Civil servants, lawyers, engineers, clerks, typists, journalists, members of parliament, diplomats and others belong to none of his four occupational groups. Even teachers and professors cannot be classified as Brahmins as he argued, for the latter devoted themselves not to teaching and learning *per se* but to studying sacred texts and spiritual pursuits. Furthermore, most modern occupations involve competition and selection and have nothing to do with heredity. Indeed, Gandhi himself favoured the system of open competition without realising that it contradicted his advocacy of hereditary occupation and subverted the *varna* system. In short, in a modern industrialised society, occupations are so varied and professionalised and subject to such constant change that they can never provide the basis of a stable social order. Gandhi's attempt to solve the acute moral and social problems of an industrialised society by means of an institution derived from a primitive agrarian society showed how little he understood the modern age.

Strange as it may seem, while Gandhi kept hankering after the ancient *varna* system, his moral theory undercut its very basis. As we saw elsewhere, he equated religion with spirituality, the latter with morality, and defined morality in terms of self-purification and active social service. The highest human activity consisted in total dedication to the service of mankind as a way of attaining *moksha*, and only those engaged in it were true Brahmins. Gandhi had nothing but contempt for the pedantic study of scriptures, religious ceremonies and *karma-kānda*. Since he undermined their traditional occupations, there was no room for a distinct class of Brahmins in his society. Again, he disapproved of violence and wanted the police and the army to be replaced by citizens trained in the art of non-violent *satyāgraha*. The separate class of *kshatriyas* thus disappeared and its radically redefined traditional occupation became the general responsibility of all. Since Gandhi wanted everyone to 'earn' his living and no one to depend on *dāna* or charity, every man became a *vaisya* and thus, again, the *vaisyas* as a separate class disappeared. He insisted that everyone should engage in manual labour, for him the only true form of socially acceptable productive work. Since all citizens performed the work of *shudras*, they too ceased to exist as a separate class.

Gandhi so radically redefined the four categories of traditional occupations underlying the ancient *varna* system that the latter no longer made sense. His well-rounded or fully moral man engaged in all four activities. He served his fellow-men, fought against untruth and injustice, earned his living and engaged in manual labour. Thus, he belonged to all four *varnas* and hence to none alone. At one level, Gandhi tried to revive an irretrievably lost past; at another, he sketched the outlines of a very different future. His social thought pointed in several directions and provided its own best critique, the hallmark of a truly creative and transitional figure.

V

Ever since untouchability was placed on the national agenda, Hindu public opinion was deeply divided concerning the best way to eradicate it. For some, it was a moral and social problem which Hindu society must solve by means of moral persuasion and social pressure alone. For others, the state had a right to intervene in matters of social reform and they urged the colonial government to enact appropriate legislation. Yet others recognised the need for state action but pointed to the obvious dangers of turning to the colonial government and proposed that the problem should be shelved until India became free. Gandhi's position was a mixture of the first and the third. He was, in principle, opposed to state-imposed and even state-initiated reforms, be the state foreign or indigenous, and wanted it to intervene only after society had by means of its own resources created the necessary consensus and climate.

Gandhi's opposition to state-initiated reforms was derived from several sources.[36] As we saw elsewhere, he argued that every person was constituted and perceived the world in his or her own unique way. His integrity, one of the highest values for Gandhi, consisted in being true to himself, in living by his truth. To force him to behave in a manner contrary to his sincerely held beliefs was to violate him at the very core of his being and thus, to be guilty of one of the most unacceptable forms of violence. If others thought him wrong, they were at liberty and, indeed, had a duty to argue with him, persuade him and put moral pressure on him to rethink his position, but they were never justified in compelling and coercing him. Though uneasy about the very institution of the state which he took to be nothing more than concentrated and organised violence, Gandhi was prepared to accept it as an instrument of *order* but not as an agency of social change or *reform*. Restraining people from harming one another in the interest of the universally accepted value of human survival was one thing; compelling them to behave in a manner they sincerely abhorred was altogether different.

He also advanced other arguments against state-initiated reforms. They treated men as 'donkeys compelled to carry a load' against their will and dehumanised them. They encouraged moral inertia and a culture of dependency. Rather than explore ways of mobilising their own and others' moral energies, citizens got into the 'lazy' habit of rushing to the state everytime they felt uneasy about a social practice. Over time, their capacity for initiative and moral resourcefulness dried up and they lost their sense of social responsibility. Gandhi thought, too, that when reforms were externally imposed and did not grow out of the community's own internal moral struggle, they lacked roots and remained fragile and were ignored at the first available opportunity.

For Gandhi, social reform must remain the sole or at least the major responsibility of the community concerned. Every community had several powerful means at its disposal to influence the 'heads' and 'hearts' of its members. These included public discussion, rational persuasion, informal moral pressure, organised pressure by educated public opinion, examples set by leaders, non-violent protest and, when all else failed, the spiritual surgery of the heart in the form of well-planned *satyāgrahas*. By suitably mobilising and combining these and creating a 'moral churning' in their society, reformers should be able to bring about desired reforms. Though Gandhi often insisted that a society's organised moral energies had the power to eradicate every undesirable practice, he was realistic enough to admit that sometimes they proved inadequate and required state assistance. A society might lack men and women of high moral calibre, its members might be illiterate, confused and unused to rational persuasion, or an evil practice might have gone on too long and struck too deep roots to be discussed in a dispassionate manner. He conceded that in such situations the state might play an active role. Even then, however, it should only act as a facilitator and do nothing to forestall vigorous campaigns and struggles vital for a society's collective moral evolution. A brief discussion of his views on various items of social reform would indicate the kind of cooperation he envisaged between the moral resources of society and the coercive pressure of the state. Needless to say, his position was not always consistent and often influenced by the importance he assigned to a reform.[37]

Gandhi was a strong advocate of the prohibition of alcohol. Apart from implying a lack of self-discipline and a futile search for artificial stimulants, its widespread consumption, especially among the lower castes, was largely responsible for their poverty, ill-health, domestic violence and the break-up of families. In the early years he favoured extensive mass education and peaceful agitation, including picketing of liquor shops. When he found these ineffective, he insisted on a total legal ban on the sale of alcohol. Alcoholism had become a 'gigantic problem and was constantly growing'. If nothing was done to stop it now, it would soon be too late to do anything about it. Indians were now in the habit of drinking and one needed to act before it became common and respectable. The level of literacy in India was too low to allow education and agitation alone to have much impact. Gandhi argued, too, that as long as alcohol was freely available, addicts were exposed to constant temptations, like an 'ailing child with a box of sweets in front of him', and the reformers had no chance of success. A law was, therefore, needed to create a propitious climate for moral persuasion. When reminded of his deeply held conviction that men could not be made moral by law, he replied 'You will not be deceived by the specious argument that India must not be made sober by compulsion'. After all, no one thought it wrong to prohibit and punish theft. If the law required drunkards to be whipped, that would be an act of 'pure violence'. Closing down liquor shops was 'only a form of restraint'. Being actuated by a desire to help drunkards lead better and happier lives, it was 'really' an act of non-violence and love. Gandhi did not notice that his argument sanctioned almost all forms of moral authoritarianism.

He thought that the practice of hand-drawn rickshaws carrying two or more adults was 'shameful' and 'inhuman'. While he was prepared to recommend popular education, he was convinced that a law prohibiting them from carrying more than one passenger was fully justified, largely on the ground that it was too inhuman to be allowed to continue until all concerned were persuaded. He thought that insanitary practices, too, required legal intervention: 'I regret to have to confess that ingrained bad habits handed down from generation to generation do not yield to persuasion. Legislation seems to me to be the only effective remedy.' Rather strangely, Gandhi took very different views on other matters. He did not think that smoking should be banned. He was convinced that it dulled the intellect, damaged health, caused cancer, polluted the environment, fouled breath and wasted money, and was, in general, an unmitigated evil. However, since it had attained 'alarming respectability' and was 'difficult' to eradicate by law, education and agitation were the 'only' answer. If they failed, we must regretfully put up with it. He felt the same way about gambling which, too, had become 'a fashion and even a virtue', and was best left to 'long' and sustained education. He did not think that prostitution should be banned either. 'Man cannot be made good by law', and public opinion was not wholly behind the ban.

The fight against untouchability caused Gandhi considerable difficulty. He refused to use the 'Western method' of asking the government to legislate against it on the ground that all the arguments he had advanced against state-initiated reforms applied to it with particular poignancy and force. Millions of caste Hindus sincerely believed that it was an integral part of their religion. So long as they held that belief, they were bound bitterly to resent its abolition, and an unpopular reform was either likely to be fiercely resisted or deviously circumvented. By requiring them to act against their belief, it also violated their integrity and created a lie in their souls. Again, state intervention implied that Hindus had become morally so degenerate that they were incapable of recognising the inhumanity of untouchability and mounting a campaign against it, or even of throwing up a few determined men and women prepared to lay down their lives for the good name of their religion. Gandhi did not think that this was the case. He was prepared to devote his own life to fighting against untouchability, and felt sure that he could both organise a committed cadre and mobilise the moral energies of the Hindu masses.

From the very beginning of his campaign, Gandhi so defined the 'problem of untouchability' that it both helped and limited its success.[38] First, he insisted that untouchability was essentially and exclusively a problem for caste Hindus and not for the untouchables who were merely their helpless victims. It was a matter of 'shame' and 'guilt' for caste Hindus who were 'on trial' and who must find ways of redeeming their collective honour and retrieving their sense of humanity. Second, it was not an ordinary evil but a 'sin', a gross violation of the human spirit. Since it had been perpetrated in the name of Hindu religion, the latter had to be 'thoroughly cleansed' of this 'abominable blot'.

The struggle against untouchability was, therefore, not an ordinary political or economic campaign intended to secure equal rights and economic betterment respectively, but religious and spiritual in nature. As such, it called for a grand and sacred national *yajna* requiring prolonged and painful collective *tapas* to be performed in the spirit of collective repentance and remorse. Every Hindu owed it to his religion to examine his conscience and weed out all traces of inhumanity, of which untouchability was the most outrageous expression.

Since he defined the problem of untouchability in this manner, Gandhi worked out a bipartite strategy. First and most important, he sought to convince and convert the caste Hindus and mobilise their energies by means of moral and religious appeals. He aimed to awaken them to the moral enormity of untouchability and to inspire them both individually and collectively to do all in their power to eradicate it. Second, he encouraged them to undertake welfare activities among the untouchables in a spirit of remorse and guilt. He thought that this would have desirable effects on both. It would 'cleanse' the caste Hindus, redeem their guilt and draw them physically, morally and emotionally closer to the untouchables. It would also give the latter a measure of pride and dignity, increase their self-confidence and improve their habits and ways of life, thereby removing some of the causes of caste Hindu prejudices against them.

From 1920 onwards, Gandhi launched a systematic campaign against untouchability. He denounced it on every available occasion and debated with the orthodox along the lines discussed earlier. He started a weekly paper which regularly exposed its evils. He built up a small but committed cadre of high-caste Hindus who fanned out into different parts of the country to work in a 'true missionary spirit and leaven the Hindu mass'. He challenged the distinction between political and social questions and asked the Congress to take up socially controversial matters. Under his leadership, the 1920 Congress session passed a resolution demanding that the untouchables be admitted to Hindu temples. National schools and colleges set up during the Non-Cooperation Movement were required to admit them and to campaign actively against untouchability. Under Gandhi's guidance, the 1921 Congress session in Ahmedabad passed a resolution requiring, among other things, that everyone participating in the Non-Cooperation Movement should sign the following pledge: 'As a Hindu I believe in the justice and necessity of removing the evil of untouchability and shall on all possible occasions seek personal contact with and endeavour to render service to the submerged classes'.[39] The 1922 Congress Working Committee meeting in Bardoli directed Congressmen to 'organise the Depressed Classes for a better life, to improve their social, mental and moral condition, to induce them to send their children to national schools and to provide for them the ordinary facilities which other citizens enjoy.' Gandhi also prescribed for every Congress worker an eighteen-point Constructive Programme of national regeneration which included campaigning against untouchability.

As a way of emphasising Hindu guilt and the helplessness and innocence of the untouchables, he started calling them *'harijans'*. The name was suggested to him by one of them in preference to the term *'asparshya'* he had hitherto used.[40] Although some of them found it patronising, almost all of them, including Ambedkar, preferred it to the available alternatives. Gandhi set a personal example by admitting a harijan woman in his *āshram* despite the opposition of some of its members, including his wife. He cleaned latrines and required his fellow-*āshramites* to do so as well. He made it a point to stay in harijan colonies, and later in life he only attended marriages in which one of the partners was a harijan. Though relatively trivial, these and other activities had a great symbolic value and helped weaken irrational and deep-seated prejudices.

For several years Gandhi concentrated on an educational campaign among the caste Hindus and welfare work among the harijans. Although his efforts were sincere, they achieved little. He had other priorities and the anti-untouchability campaign did not receive his undivided attention. Many high-caste Hindus were not keen or even sincere, and some tended to subvert his work. Though the Congress had decided to spend a minimum of two lakhs of rupees on harijan welfare work, it spent, on average, just over a fifth of it. Under one pretext or another, harijans were not admitted to some of the national schools. Atrocities continued to be committed against them in several parts of the country with only a minimum protest by high-caste Hindus. When these and other matters were brought to Gandhi's attention, he rebuked the Hindus and urged the harijans to avoid confrontation but did little else.

He was acutely aware of the fact that his educational campaign was making little impact. When some of his followers decided to force the issue and launched the 1924 *satyāgraha* in Vaikkam, he gave it his approval. Though he took sustained interest in it and frequently commented on it, he decided not to intervene directly and allowed it to run its course. It lasted a year, provoked fierce resistance and caused considerable hardship to the *satyāgrahis*. Gandhi finally decided to visit Vaikkam. The slow progress of the *satyāgraha* and his debates with the Brahmins convinced him how much work still remained to be done. As we saw, he modified his language of discourse, intensified the educational campaign and increased the harijan welfare work. However, he neither reconsidered his strategy nor mounted a new initiative.

In the meantime the untouchables were getting impatient.[41] The Mahars of Maharashtra marched to Chowdar tank at Mahad in 1927 and drank water in defiance of the traditional social ban. This led to serious clashes between them and the caste Hindus. Later during the year, they ceremoniously burned a copy of *Manusmriti* in whose name untouchability was widely justified. They launched a temple entry *satyāgraha* in Poona in 1929 which lasted for nearly four months and achieved little. Many local Congressmen disapproved of it and even attempted to defeat it. The Kalaram temple *satyāgraha* in Nasik in 1930 was even more bitter and subverted by a number of local Congressmen. In the same year Swami Satyananda led the Munshigani Kali temple entry *satyāgraha* in Bengal which also encountered hostility from local Congressmen, attracted little upper caste support and only succeeded after considerable hardship.[42] These and other *satyāgrahas* resulted in no more than about half a dozen out of several hundred temples being thrown open to harijans. Confronted with the rash of *satyāgrahas*, the national Congress leadership criticised harijan militancy and urged patience. Some of the frustrated untouchable leaders pressed the old demand for a separate electorate only to be told by the Motilal Nehru Committee in 1928 that it was 'unsound and harmful'. Gandhi was acutely aware that the harijans were getting restless and that caste Hindus remained opaque to his appeals.

When the British government decided in 1932 to grant the harijans a separate electorate and raised the spectre of a major split within the Hindu community, Gandhi knew that he had to do something. If he had made appropriate concessions to Ambedkar at the Round Table Conference, he would most certainly have avoided the Communal Award. Perhaps he underestimated the intensity of Ambedkar's feelings; perhaps he overestimated his hold over the harijans; perhaps he was looking for the right moment to launch a dramatic and decisive attack on untouchability and shake up the Hindus. Whatever his reasons, he announced a 'fast unto death' on 20 September 1932. In a widely circulated statement, he made it abundantly clear that the fast was primarily directed *not* against the separate electorate alone but the practice of untouchability itself:

'No patched-up agreement between caste Hindus and rival depressed class leaders will answer the purpose. The agreement to be valid has to be real. If the Hindu mass mind is not yet prepared to banish untouchability root and branch, it must sacrifice me without the slightest hesitation.'[43]

Gandhi's fast, which lasted for six days, was condemned by Ambedkar who reluctantly gave in under the strongest pressure, and has been subject of much recent criticisms by *dalit* and other writers. A separate electorate would certainly have mobilised the harijans, created a distinct and self-conscious harijan constituency, and elected representatives of their choice rather than those acceptable to a socially conservative Hindu majority. It was also, however, fraught with great disadvantages. It would have alienated the Hindu majority, and encouraged them to wash their hands off harijans and continue with their social apartheid. It is worth remembering that several groups of orthodox Hindus were happy for harijans to leave the Hindu fold rather than accept them as their social equals with all the moral, political and economic price that this entailed. Unlike Muslims and other religious minorities, harijans were also not easy to define, and the separate electorate could have created most acrimonious demarcational disputes. It could also have intensified collective *dalit* self-consciousness as the separate electorate had done in the case of Muslims, and both complicated and weakened the struggle for independence. The separate electorate thus raised highly complex issues that did not admit a simple-minded answer. On balance the compromise reached in the Poona Pact, which gave harijans almost twice the number of seats given by the Award, a promise of extra resources and the Congress commitment to launch a vigorous campaign against untouchability, seemed the best compromise. In retrospect, it is worth noting that after independence Ambedkar himself preferred reserved seats rather than a separate electorate, and that too rather optimistically for a short fixed period.

Gandhi's fast triggered off a public debate and forced the Hindus to concentrate on the issue they had hitherto not taken very lightly.[44] On the day of the fast, the Kalighat Temple of Calcutta and the Ram Mandir of Benaras— the citadels of Hindu orthodoxy—were thrown open. In Bombay, where a nationalist women's organisation conducted a poll of worshippers in front of seven big temples, 24,797 voted for and 445 against the admission of harijans. Thousands of prominent Hindu women accepted food from the hands of the untouchables, and at the Benaras Hindu University, the principal and scores of Brahmins dined publicly with them. Such scenes were repeated in many villages and cities. Many Hindus took pledges not to practise untouchability themselves or to allow it to be practised in their families. Although many of these gestures were largely symbolic, they reflected a deep moral stirring within the Hindu psyche. Thanks to Gandhi's fast, untouchability was now placed at the top of the national agenda and its champions were thrown on the defensive.

Gandhi and his followers kept up the pressure. He concentrated his efforts on the anti-untouchability campaign. Untouchability Abolition Week was observed throughout India from 27 September until 2 October. In February 1933, he started *Harijan Weekly* to publicise the good work done in different parts of the country and to expose lapses. Gandhi thought the progress slow and uneven and embarked upon yet another fast of twenty-one days in April 1933. From November 1933 until July 1934, he undertook an all-India Harijan tour of 12,500 miles, travelling from village to village, mobilising students, women and even children, and carrying the battle to the bastions of orthodoxy.

Gandhi's renewed campaign was conducted at two related, but different, levels. He continued to attack untouchability in moral and religious terms and mobilise Hindu feelings of guilt and repentance. He also, however, began to stress its political dangers far more strongly than he had done during the Non-Cooperation Movement and to which he had made only scant subsequent references. He told caste Hindus how close they had come to losing a fifth of their number and how much such a split would have damaged their political future. He made cryptic references to the dangers posed by a possible alliance of alienated minorities and warned Hindus against becoming a minority in their own country. The political argument injected a much-needed sense of urgency in the debate and made Hindus realise that they could no longer treat untouchability as a marginal issue. As usual Gandhi appealed both to their guilt and fears, self-respect and self-interest, and ran moral and political arguments in tandem. Contrary to what he and his associates maintained, it was not a wholly moral campaign and owed a good deal though by no means all of its success to Hindu self-interest.

During this period, Gandhi helped set up the All-India Anti-Untouchability League as an integral part of his campaign. Having hitherto argued that untouchability was an exclusively Hindu problem, he now changed his mind and suggested that the League should include both caste Hindus and untouchables. Its nine-member board of management had three harijans and it was explicitly committed to fighting untouchability. Its objectives were as follows:[45]

> Carrying propaganda against untouchability and taking immediate steps to secure as early as practicable that all public wells, dharamshalas, roads, schools, crematoriums, burning ghats and all public temples be declared open to the Depressed classes, provided that no compulsion or force shall be used and that only peaceful persuasion shall be adopted towards this end.

Soon differences arose. Ambedkar, one of the three harijan members, wanted it to launch a nationwide civil rights movement.[46] He acknowledged that this might lead to 'social disturbance and even bloodshed', but considered it a better policy than the 'current line of least resistance'. He also demanded that the League should attack not just untouchability but the caste system itself and vigorously campaign against the taboos on inter-caste dining and marriage. When his proposals were turned down he resigned, followed by the other two harijan members. It would seem that not just ideological differences but also personal pique, vanity and misunderstanding had influenced their decision.

Gandhi and his colleagues seem to have felt that they had made a mistake in setting up a joint Hindu-harijan body explicitly devoted to a frontal attack on untouchability. They changed the League's character, objectives and name. They reconstituted it as Servants of Untouchables Society or Harijan Sevak Sangh and decided not to include harijans in its management. When the harijans demanded to be associated with it, Gandhi replied:[47]

> The welfare work for the untouchables is a penance which the Hindus have to do for the sin of untouchability. The money that has been collected was contributed by the Hindus. From both points of view the Hindus alone must run the Sangh. Neither ethics nor right would justify untouchables in claiming a seat on the Board of the Sangh.

Unlike the League, which had removal of untouchability as its main objective, the Sangh concentrated on the less controversial task of harijan welfare and went out of its way to reassure the *sanātanists*. The joint statement issued by the President and the Secretary of the Sangh on 3 November 1932 showed the shift of emphasis:[48]

> The League (Sangh) believes that reasonable persons among the *sanātanists* are not as much against the removal of untouchability as such, as they are against inter-caste dinners and marriages. Since it is not the ambition of the League to undertake reforms *beyond its own scope*, it is desirable to make it clear that while the League will work by persuasion among the caste Hindus to remove every vestige of untouchability the *main* line of work will be constructive, such as the uplift of

Depressed Classes educationally, economically and socially which itself will go a great way to remove untouchability. With such a work *even a staunch sanātanist* can have nothing but sympathy. And it is for such work *mainly* that the League has been established.

The Sangh, an 'organisation of penitent sinners' as Gandhi called it, gave scholarships to harijan children, set up hostels, ran industrial schools, sank wells and provided clean water. It maintained a cadre of itinerant medical and para-medical staff, organised cooperative societies and pressurised local bodies to provide the harijans with basic welfare services. Although it had a well-motivated staff, its severally limited resources made it extremely difficult for it to reach out to the villages. The allegedly penitent Hindus refused to part with their money, and Gandhi had to write repeatedly to a couple of wealthy friends for assistance.

Though Gandhi's educational and moral campaign and the two fasts had gone a long way towards discrediting untouchability, he was acutely aware of pockets of resistance among high-caste Hindus. This may partly explain his ambiguous attitude to Ranga Iyer's Untouchability Abolition Bill introduced in the Legislative Assembly in March 1933.[49] He urged the Government of India to 'facilitate [its] progress and passage', asked Congress members to support it, appointed Rajagopalachari and Birla to canvass support among non-Congress members and urged the *sanatanists* not to campaign against it. While the Bill was going through the various stages, the government announced elections. Fearing that it might lose them the votes of caste Hindus, Congress members withdrew their support. During the election campaign, the *sanatanists* demanded undertakings from them that, if elected, they would not support any such Bill. Congress candidates either gave the undertaking or fudged the issue. After the election, the Bill was never taken up. Gandhi remained more or less silent throughout the election campaign and tended to blame Ranga Iyer for not fully taking the Congress into his confidence.

Overtaken by the Second World War and the Partition of the country, and desperately anxious not to divide and weaken the independence movement, Gandhi decided to leave untouchability alone. He was convinced that he had succeeded in creating the necessary moral consensus for its abolition and that the government of independent India should be able to enact appropriate legislation without fear of popular resistance. He wanted it to ban untouchability and punish those found guilty of practising it. He also wanted it to introduce a massive social, educational and economic programme of harijan uplift, including giving them land for resettlement and necessary financial grants. He proposed that all elected bodies should reserve seats for them in proportion to their number in the population as a whole, but was against reservations in employment and in school and university admissions where merit alone was to count. He asked political parties to actively encourage harijan participation, and hoped that the Congress would give a lead by rotating its higher offices among the minority communities, especially the harijans, and by assigning them proportional representation on its district and working committees.[50]

Gandhi was keen that the Constitution of independent India should lay down the basic framework of such a programme. He took considerable interest in the proceedings of the Constituent Assembly and kept in close touch with its leaders. When Article 11, declaring untouchability a cognisable offence, was unanimously passed, the entire Assembly cheered his name and expressed its deepest gratitude to him. It would seem that it was Gandhi who had been largely instrumental in encouraging Nehru to magnanimously appoint Ambedkar as Law Minister in his 1946 Cabinet. The Congress had won the bulk of harijan seats in the 1946 elections and routed the Scheduled Castes Federation, thereby ending the fear of harijan separatism. It had no reason either to invite Ambedkar to join the Cabinet when he was not even a member of the Congress party. Ambedkar drafted large parts of the Constitution and successfully piloted it through the Constituent Assembly. A great historical justice was done and a moving drama enacted when a harijan abolished untouchability and became the Manu of modern India, giving it a far more humane political *smriti*.

VI

We began this chapter by referring to two conflicting assessments of Gandhi's contribution to the eradiction of untouchability. In the light of our discussion it should be clear that each contains a measure of truth.

Gandhi's contribution was considerable and greater than that of any other Indian leader. No one before him had mounted a frontal attack on untouchability and launched a vigorous national campaign. Though his campaign initially lacked energy and a sense of direction, he soon grasped its importance and put it at the top of the political agenda. He took on the orthodox and by means of sometimes disingenuous intellectual manoeuvres mocked, marginalised and eventually discredited them. By a skilful combination of moral, religious and political appeals and personal example, he shamed and mobilised the Hindu masses, stirred their consciences, awakened their sense of responsibility, and created a powerful body of public opinion demanding and willing to carry through an anti-untouchability programme. Unlike many socialist and secular leaders, who vigorously championed the cause of harijans but studiously avoided close personal contacts with them, Gandhi lived in *bhangi* colonies, adopted a harijan girl and mixed, lived and shared his meals with them. Though trivial at one level, these sincere expressions of compassion and personal commitment touched deep nerves and helped weaken irrational and deepseated prejudices. He gave the harijans a measure of dignity and self-confidence and the courage to stand up for their rights. It is doubtful that, without his efforts, independent India would have had the confidence to abolish untouchability at a stroke and to embark upon a policy of massive compensatory discrimination. The *sanatanists* were right to see him as their most deadly enemy, and Ambedkar was wrong to question his commitment and enormous contribution.

Gandhi's contribution, however, had its limits. Though he discredited and undermined the intellectual and moral basis of untouchability, he failed to shake its social, economic and political roots. The facts speak for themselves. Untouchability continued during his lifetime and does so even now, fifty years after Indian independence. Harijans remain socially ostracised, inter-dining with them is still uncommon, and intermarriages are rare. The policy of reservation and compensatory discrimination arouses considerable hostility and is often half-heartedly implemented. Gandhi's own Gujarat has seen several high-caste agitations against it. In the villages, the harijans are subjected to a daily diet of insults, attacks and atrocities with the connivance and sometimes support of the agencies of the state. They are systematically discriminated against in private sector education, employment and housing. The bulk of them remain extremely poor and hardly any of them has been able to break through the closed world of trade and commerce. Even the limited economic progress they have so far made has been confined to the public sector and is largely a result of state patronage. They remain clients of the state and helpless without its continuing support. They also lack powerful political presence and a sophisticated national leadership capable of articulating their grievances and fighting for their basic rights. Such political power as they enjoy is a result of the inevitable electoral arithmetic of democracy and far less than what their number requires.

No individual, however great, can eradicate a practice that has gone on for centuries and is deeply rooted in his community's way of life. However, the catalogue of harijan hardships remains long and frightening and Gandhi cannot escape part of the responsibility for this. As we saw, he took a long time appreciating that the roots of untouchability lay deep within the caste system and continued to attack it while vigorously defending the latter. His attack, therefore, failed to tackle the roots of untouchability and lacked a cutting edge. Since the caste system was allegedly good, he could only argue that the untouchables should become touchables, not that their lowest social and moral status should be ended. The principle of hereditary occupation upon which his *varna* system rested not only confined them to their lowly traditional occupations but also blinded him to the very need to do something about them. Gandhi's contention that a degrading occupation need not necessarily lead to social and moral inequality took little account of the enormous weight of tradition. His belief in rebirth compounded his difficulties for, if a man deserved to be born into a specific *varna*, he also deserved to be confined to the relevant occupation.

As we saw, Gandhi took a religious view of untouchability and made its eradication an exclusively Hindu responsibility. While this had the great advantage of focusing attention on the centuries of Hindu oppression, it also had the great demerit of treating the harijans as passive objects helplessly waiting for their masters to get off their backs. Like the cow, they were a 'poem of pity', a tragic symbol of Hindu tyranny about which they were themselves expected to do little. They were, therefore, never involved in the struggle for their liberation and failed to develop a collective organisation, a corporate identity, an indigenous leadership, a tradition of struggle and memories of collective action. It was striking that Gandhi's campaign threw up extensive Hindu literature *about* them but little *by* them, reflecting their own experiences, thoughts and feelings about themselves and the Hindus. Gandhi spoke for them, but did not allow, let alone encourage, them to speak for themselves. Thanks to his mistaken strategy, his love kept them almost just as dumb as had the centuries of humiliation.

Gandhi's style of campaign not only prevented them from developing their own organisation but also denied them an opportunity to work and constantly interact with the caste Hindus. Take the Harijan Sevak Sangh. In its earlier incarnation as the Anti-Untouchability League, it was intended to be a forum for both groups and explicitly aimed to eradicate untouchability. Once it was changed into an all-Hindu organisation working for but not with the harijans, the two communities lacked a common platform. Devoid of meaningful contacts at the social level, the two communities remained separate at the political level as well. By taking a narrowly religious view of untouchability, Gandhi not only reinforced harijan passivity but also betrayed his own profound political insight that no system of oppression could be ended without the active involvement and consequent political education and organisation of its victims.

The Sangh's exclusion of harijans would not have mattered much had the Congress provided a common public space to the two communities. It did not, largely because it, too, shared Gandhi's belief in *serving* harijans. Though it recruited them to its membership, it did little to get them elected to positions of power. Gandhi kept insisting that he would like a harijan to become a Congress President, but neither he nor the other

Congress leaders made any efforts in that direction. They did little to get harijans nominated or elected to its Working Committee or even to its regional and local committees. In this respect, Gandhi was far more hospitable to the vocal and well-organised Muslims. The message was not lost on the caste Hindus. It was striking that a man who created scores of great leaders was unable to create a single harijan leader of national stature.

The lack of active harijan involvement in the Congress and other organisations had unfortunate consequences. In the absence of an organised and vocal harijan presence, Gandhi remained surrounded by caste Hindus enjoying direct and constant access to him. Subjected to their daily pressures and skilful manoeuvres, he exaggerated their fears and anxieties and was insufficiently sensitive to harijan feelings and opinions. He could not rely on the organised power of the harijans to counter the caste lobby, and not having encouraged their mass movement, he was unable to mobilise the grassroots pressure either. His daily mail, too, brought scores of letters from angry and bitter caste Hindus but almost none from the illiterate harijans. Gandhi, therefore, tended to take the latter for granted and spent far more of his time and energy reassuring caste Hindus. Indeed, it is worth noting that the more vigorous his anti-untouchability campaign became, the more vigorously he disclaimed any intention of fighting against the restrictions on inter-dining and intermarriage. It is striking, too, that while he was prepared to insist on a spinning franchise, he never thought it proper to insist that no one should occupy a high position within the Congress unless he had participated in the anti-untouchability campaign, dined with a harijan or had a harijan servant.[51] The pledge required during the Non-Cooperation Movement mentioned earlier was never revived.

Since Gandhi was surrounded by high-caste Hindus, his conscience remained his only protection against their constant and powerful pressure. Though his conscience was strong and sharp, it had its obvious limits. Operating in a biased political context and subjected to one-sided political pressure, it often lost direction and sense of urgency and fell prey to easy rationalisation. Gandhi's conscience was anguished by *both* the harijan degradation and the passionate protestations of hurt feelings by the caste Hindus. Since he was far more exposed to the latter, it was finely tuned to and liable to be swayed by exaggerated Hindu fears. Furthermore, Gandhi was involved in several battles, that against untouchability being only one of them, and political exigencies inevitably dictated their order of importance. In the absence of organised harijan pressure, Gandhi found it politically neither necessary nor possible to place anti-untouchability high on his political agenda. It was, therefore, hardly surprising that he gave it his undivided attention only when the restless untouchables clamoured for action and threatened the unity of the independence movement. This was not because he did not genuinely abhor or intend to eradicate untouchability, as Ambedkar suggested, but because his passionate *moral* commitment could not generate an equally strong *political* commitment within a politically imbalanced context created by his style of campaign.

In addition to the absence of organised harijan pressure, it would seem that Gandhi's own analysis of the situation led him to adopt a highly cautious approach. He seems to have been deeply worried about the growing harijan militancy. As he observed on many occasions, the harijans were justifiably bitter, angry and full of hatred. He could not be sure what new pressures and demands their massive entry into public life and their consequent rise to power would generate. His fears were aroused when Ambedkar presented an extensive programme of action in his Memorandum to the Minorities Committee of the Round Table Conference, demanding punitive measures against those preaching untouchability, a separate ministry and adequate representation in all branches of government. Gandhi became even more disturbed when the three harijan members on the board of management of the All-India Anti-Untouchability League resigned in protest against its conservative agenda and approach.

Gandhi, therefore, decided to proceed with extreme caution, beginning with temples, the places most likely to reconcile the two communities, and gradually moving towards the highly contentious social, economic and political issues. Once the question of temple-entry was more or less settled and Gandhi began to move towards the other issues, he ran into powerful political opposition. Guided by both the need to preserve the precarious unity of the independence movement and his own deep political and social fears, he adopted an extremely cautious approach. He discouraged *satyāgrahas*, urged the harijans not to press for a faster pace of change, and pinned his hopes on the cumulative impact of the new moral climate he had created, the policies of independent India and the social logic of industrialisation. Although caution was justified, he carried it much further than was required by his moral commitment and permitted by the Indian political reality. As he well knew, political possibilities are never given; they have to be created. Had he actively mobilised the harijans and innvolved them in his campaign, he would have changed the political equation in a manner that would have enabled him to take greater risks.

Untouchability was both a moral and a political problem: the former because its eradication involved undermining its moral legitimacy and changing, or at least softening, Hindu attitudes; the latter because it was deeply rooted in the highly unequal structure of power relationship between the upper castes and the harijans and could not be removed without restructuring it. It had, therefore, to be fought at *both* levels. Gandhi's campaign was conducted only at the moral and religious level. Hence he concentrated on caste Hindus rather than the harijans, appealed to their sense of duty and honour, mobilised their feelings of shame and guilt, and succeeded in achieving his initial objective of discrediting untouchability and raising the level of the Hindu and, to a limited extent, harijan consciousness. Since he did not organise and politicise the harijans, stress their rights and fight for a radical reconstruction of the established social and economic order, Gandhi's campaign was unable to go further. It gave the harijans dignity but not power; moral and, to some extent, social but not political and economic equality; self-respect but not the self-confidence to organise and fight their own battles. It integrated them into the Hindu social order but did little to release them from the cumulative cycle of deprivation. It softened the arrogance and hostility of high-caste Hindus but did not put sufficient pressure on them to make it in their interest to share their power and privileges. In other words, Gandhi's campaign won the crucial first round against untouchability and permanently discredited it, but it did not and could not enter the equally crucial second round against the high-caste economic and political domination.

Chapter Eight

Indianisation of Autobiography

But for men like me you have to measure them not by the rare moments of greatness in their lives but by the amount of dust which they collect on their feet in the course of life's journey.[1]

I

Autobiography is a complex genre of writing. In the broad sense of individuals writing about themselves, it goes back several thousand years. In the strict and narrow sense of what Auden called 'serious and truthful self-study' directed at self-understanding, it is relatively recent and goes back no further than the eighteenth century.

As long as five thousand years ago, Egyptian kings left behind descriptions of their achievements to be inscribed on their carefully planned tombs. Solon's elegiacs and iambics referred to the great reforms in which 'I made free men' and to the way he resisted temptations that would have 'destroyed a lesser man'.[2] Plato's Seventh Epistle described an important period in his life. Lutatius Catulus, Scarus, Rutilius, Rufus, Sulla, Caesar and other Roman statesmen left behind accounts of what they regarded as their great achievements in order to create among their contemporaries and especially posterity a 'favourable opinion' of themselves. Epictetus, Marcus Aurelius and other Roman philosophers and philosophically inclined statesmen wrote about their deepest thoughts on life with only minimal references to themselves and their achievements.

The practice of writing about one's life rather than achievements was begun by the early converts to Christianity. St. Augustine's appropriately entitled *Confessions* (written in A.D. 397–98) is the best known but not the only one. It was preceded by dozens of similar works by such men as Justin the Martyr, Hilarius, the Bishop of Poitiers and Gregory of Nazianzus. Bishop Synesius of Cyrene was probably one of the first to call his book *'Dio or my own Bios'*. Most of these works had a common structure and orientation largely derived from their novel content. Under the impact of Christianity, their authors had undergone intense and unusual experiences involving a sense of dramatic transition from ignorance to truth, from Fall to Grace, from a life of sin to one of virtue. Since their ruptured and transformed lives could not be described as coherent stories gradually unfolding in time, their accounts took the form of passionate and emotionally charged confessions suffused with the spirit of self-discovery and self-pity. Having embarked upon an exciting spiritual journey and seeing their lives as metaphors of universal significance, they were anxious to share their joys and agonies with others and to urge them to undertake the journey themselves. Not surprisingly, their confessions had a didactic and evangelical orientation and concentrated on a general message rather than the details of their lives.

St. Augustine spoke for most when he said that his *Confessions* was intended to be a 'lengthy record' to be laid before God, not because there was anything in it that He did not know but in order to 'confess my miserable state' and to 'fire my own heart and the hearts of my readers with love of you'. His deeply moving book contains the barest personal details. He condemned his carnal life without mentioning any of the women involved. With the exception of Faustus of Mileve, he made only passing references to the people who had influenced him. And he did not even refer to his domestic surroundings until the ninth chapter.

Once Christianity became an established religion and lost its earlier novelty, confessional writing underwent important changes and became more reflective and detached. During the late middle ages and especially during the Renaissance, non-confessional and secularly-oriented accounts of life began to appear. Diaries, memoirs, chronicles, journals and other forms of writing became popular and paved the way for autobiography in the modern and narrow sense. The term autobiography itself seems to have been first used in Germany in 1796. Commenting on the new kind of writing that was then beginning to appear, Herder distinguished between *Confessionen* and *Lebensbeschreibungen* (life-stories). It is striking that he called autobiography life-story and distinguished it from confession. His contrast between autobiography and confession was intended to suggest that the former was a new and autonomous form of writing not to be confused with its more familiar predecessor. He divided confessions into religious and 'humanly philosophical', the former referring to the early Christian and the latter to late medieval writings, and insisted that autobiographies or life-stories should only be written by 'remarkable men'.

At Herder's suggestion, Seybold published in 1796 a collection of writings entitled *Selbstbiographieen beruhmler Manner* (self-biographies of famous men). Like Herder, Seybold thought that famous and remarkable men alone were entitled to write about themselves. The term self-biography implied that the autobiographical genre was subsumed under the much older biographical form of writing and deemed to be basically of the same kind. Instead of others writing about them, famous men wrote about themselves. From Germany the term autobiography travelled to Britain where it was first used by Robert Southey in 1809. In the course of reviewing contemporary Portuguese literature, he referred to a book by a Portuguese painter as a 'very amusing and unique specimen of auto-biography'. Southey's remark is triply striking. He hyphenated the term autobiography thereby implying that for him, too, it was a form of biography, considered it a novel and unusual form of writing, and found it amusing to read about the details of its author's life.

Over time autobiography developed into a unique and autonomous genre of writing governed by its own distinct requirements. It was expected to provide not only the details of its author's life, which any good biography of him could do, but also, and more importantly, a privileged form of self-understanding. Dilthey put the point well when he observed that the 'new' autobiographical form of writing represented the 'highest and most instructive form in which the understanding of life comes before us'. It was both historical and 'meditative', both narrative and reflective, a history of a life recollected, interpreted and reflected upon from the calm vantage point of the present. As a reflective personal history, an autobiography was a way of appropriating and making sense of one's life. It is interesting that unlike Herder, Dilthey contrasted autobiography not with confession but with memoir. Unlike the latter, in which the author merely described the events of his life as an external observer, the autobiography represented an attempt to comprehend them from within and to give them a coherent personal meaning.

It was not an accident that the modern form of autobiographical writing first appeared in the late eighteenth and especially the early nineteenth century. Like other literary forms such as the epic, narrative poetry, drama and the novel, autobiography presupposes certain cultural conditions in the absence of which it cannot emerge, acquire a firm structure and become socially respectable. We might mention four by way of illustration. First, as the story of a unique self, autobiography presupposes a culture in which individuality is valued and cultivated. Unless a culture encourages men and women to make their own choices, form their own views, take risks, look upon life as a journey and, in general to fashion their lives as they please, one man's life is not significantly different from another's. It is not distinct and interesting enough to constitute the subject matter of a story, and there is no obvious reason why anyone should wish to write about himself or others should wish to read about it.

Second, autobiography rests on the assumption that the self is a product of its past choices and decisions, that it has a history and is only intelligible in historical terms. As a form of reflective personal history in which the author traces and seeks to understand himself in terms of his gradual development in time rather than some transcendental source or naturally endowed properties, the autobiography is only possible in a society with a well-developed historical manner of thinking.

Third, unlike a diary which one writes primarily for oneself and has a deeply subjective orientation, and unlike a chronicle and even a memoir which are primarily written for others, an autobiography is written for *both* oneself and others. As a pursuit of self-understanding by means of a silent and constant dialogue with oneself, it springs from a desire to make sense of oneself.

There is, however, no obvious reason why anyone should wish to write down, let alone publish his self-reflections unless he has others in mind. An autobiography is the story of a social being sharing his thoughts about himself with others and seeking to explain his life both to himself and to them. As such, it presupposes both a body of commonly shared meanings and values, and a unique individual definition and articulation of them. Insofar as it has *others* in mind, it is vulnerable to self-glorification and even exhibitionism and liable to miss out the crucial element of self-reflection. Insofar as it is written for *oneself*, it is prone to self-obsessed brooding and likely to lack the capacity to render the self intelligible to others. An autobiography properly so called must hold the self and society together, seeing each in relation to and emphasising neither at the expense of the other.

Fourth, as a reflective and reasonably detached account of a life, an autobiography presupposes a self at peace with itself and its environment. A person at war with his past, as was the case with the early Christian converts, or with society, as was the case with Rousseau and many eighteenth century romantic writers, lacks the stability and detachment necessary for self-examination and reflection. He is too nervous to face himself and cannot resist suppressing or distorting large areas of his life. Or he is too combative to look at the world around him with a measure of disinterestedness. He is no more able to compose a coherent and reflective narrative of his life than is a historian able to write with detachment about a subject matter he deeply hates or with which he is passionately involved. His strong feelings and restlessness find an adequate expression only in a moving but unstructured confession, a personal testament or a manifesto.

II

Some of these and other preconditions of autobiography did not obtain in India as indeed in many other civilisations. The dominant Hindu metaphysic does not grant ontological dignity to individuality or uniqueness. The body is subject to change and dissolution, and the mind is little more than an unending stream of uniform and basically trivial desires and passions. Since the *ātman* alone is real and is identical in all men and women, Hindu philosophers argue that all human beings are ultimately one. Individuality, selfhood, ego-consciousness or particularity, the terms used interchangeably by them, are therefore *māyā* or inconsequential. All forms of self-assertion, including the desire to perpetuate one's name after death and to claim originality for one's thoughts, are generally frowned upon. Almost every great Indian thinker, including the Buddha, linked himself to a series of real and sometimes imaginary predecessors and presented his view as an extension or reinterpretation of an established tradition.

Like the dominant Hindu metaphysic, Hindu social structure too places only limited value on individuality. The socially prescribed *varnāshrmadharma* lays down the duties of each individual during each of the four stages of his life. From his birth onwards, he is cast in a particular social mould and sees himself largely as a bearer of specific roles and obligations. His caste specifies what is proper for him to do or not to do, and many of his important decisions such as the choice of a marriage partner are generally made for him. Though different castes and ethnic groups follow different lifestyles, there is little diversity *within* each of them. Not individuality but plurality, not individual but group diversity, is the central feature of Hindu society.

As we saw elsewhere, the modern historical manner of thinking did not develop in India either. Since transience or change was equated with illusion, historical details were dismissed as mere gossip devoid of value and significance. Historical truth was important only as an exemplification of universally valid moral truths. Historical understanding, therefore, never occupied an important place in Hindu epistemology. This meant that the details of an individual's life, his habits, idiosyncrasies, moods, feelings and responses to events—in short, the raw material of autobiography—were deemed to be trivial and unworthy of being recorded or written about. Hindus, do of course, have a strong sense of the past and believe that an individual is a product of his choices and decisions in his previous lives. However, since the previous lives are unrecorded and unremembered, they do not and cannot form the basis of historical self-understanding.

Since some of the preconditions of autobiographical writing were absent in India, it is conspicuous by its absence. Ananda Coomaraswamy put the point well:[3]

> Hinduism justifies no cult of ego-expression, but aims consistently at spritiual freedom. Those who are conscious of a sufficient inner life become the more indifferent to outward expression of their own or any changing personality. The ultimate purposes of Hindu social discipline are that men should unify their individuality with a wider and deeper [sic] than individual life, should fulfil appointed tasks regardless of failure or success, distinguish the timeless from its shifting forms, and escape the all-too-narrow prison of the 'I and mine.'
>
> Anonymity is, thus, in accordance with the truth; and it is one of the proudest distinctions of the Hindu culture. The names of the 'authors' of the epics are but shadows, and in later ages it was a constant practice of writers to suppress their own names and ascribe their work to a mythical or famous poet, thereby to gain a better attention for the truth that they would rather claim to have 'heard' than to have 'made.' Similarly, scarcely a single Hindu painter or sculptor is known by name; and the entire range of Sanskrit literature cannot exhibit a single autobiography and but little history.

Unlike autobiography, biography was common in India and is perhaps older than in the West. In its oldest form, it consists of quasi-historical writings about the lives of Vedic *rishis* and such men as Veda Vyāsa, the *Buddha* and Mahavira. A little later, the *Carita* literature began to appear giving rise to such works as Bana's *Harshacarita* and Bilhana's *Vikramānk-deva-carita*. These were largely *prashastis* or eulogies commissioned by kings and generally published after their death. They were not primarily concerned with historical facts and aimed to glorify their subjects' deeds, legitimate their social status and to trace their real or fictitious genealogies. From about the eleventh century A.D., those copying the manuscripts of the *Purānas* and the *Dharmashāstras* began to write their own, their ancestors' and gurus' names and to provide basic details about themselves, occasionally referring to some important events in their lives. From about the thirteenth century onwards, quasi-autobiographical works began to appear. In a somewhat similar manner to early Christianity, the *bhakti* movement triggered off profound changes in the religious lives of its adherents. Not surprisingly, a long line of such saint-poets as Basava, Akkama, Chaitanya, Mira, Kabir, Tulsidas, Tukaram, Akho and Narasinha Mehta wrote quasi-autobiographical poetry, providing details about their parents, brothers, relatives, wives, domestic quarrels and personal frustrations, but little directly about themselves. A few of them did describe some of their traumatic experiences, but largely with a view to drawing out important moral lessons. Almost every one of them saw his or her life as an illustration of human life in general, and his or her trials and travails as those of all men and women everywhere. For the most part, their writings were didactic sermons, illustrated and enlivened by occasional and freely interpreted personal examples. Unlike the early Christian writings, these were not confessions or passionate outbursts of self-pity but devotional works laced with touches of self-mocking irony and self-deprecating humour. Since they were socially meaningful, they became immensely popular and were widely memorised, recited and used as a common currency of moral intercourse.

Islam came to India through Persia and brought with it the Persian penchant for historical details. It encouraged a tradition of writing history, memoirs, diaries and records of royal achievements. Court poets and official record-keepers were engaged to write royal biographies and histories of their periods. It would seem that the Muslim tradition had only a limited influence on Hindu India, for there are only a few instances of such writing by or about Hindu kings and eminent personages. Nana Phadnis, an astute administrator during the last decades of Peshwa rule, Dada Pandurang, and a few others left behind diaries and memoirs containing fascinating personal and political information. However, these were too selective, patchy and impersonal to be called autobiographies in any sense of the term.

During British rule, some of the cultural preconditions of autobiographical writing came into existence. Thanks to the work of British and Indian archaeologists and historians, a chronologically coherent picture of pre-Muslim India was constructed and history as an autonomous and distinct mode of inquiry became respectable. In the early years, history was widely feared and resented. British historians presented an unflattering and distorted picture of India's past, and Indians had little difficulty noticing that history was used to legitimise and to brainwash them into accepting British rule. They were also worried that the new discipline challenged not only the authenticity of the epics, the *Purānas* and the myths but also their traditional and largely pragmatic mode of dealing with the past. But over time, Indian attitude to history underwent a radical change. Indians realised that the only way to counter a bad history was to write a good history themselves. They saw, too, that even as science need not threaten religion, there were ways of safeguarding traditions and myths from the invasion of history. More importantly, they saw that history was a *political* discipline capable of contributing to the growth of their sense of nationhood and fostering patriotism. Once history was accepted as a legitimate and indispensable discipline, such ideas as historical truth, autonomy of the past and explaining the present in terms of it began to strike roots in India.

British rule also introduced modern individualism and rationalism. Indians began to question traditional values and practices and to experiment with new forms of life and thought. Unwilling to fully embrace the new and unable to break with tradition, they became puzzles to themselves. This heightened their self-consciousness and stimulated self-reflection. They were anxious to share with others the excitement of their newly-found freedom and the problems it had brought in its train. Since Hindu society was generally hostile to them, they sought each other's approval and good opinion. For these and other reasons, there grew up a new subculture conducive to autobiographical writing. A group of people were anxious to write about themselves; a well-developed constituency was interested in reading them; and the newly-acquired access to Western literature offered the necessary intellectual tools for writing autobiographies.

While British rule created some of the preconditions of autobiography, it also created others that militated against it. Thanks to British political and cultural domination and the sense of racial inferiority it inspired, those writing autobiographies found it difficult to resist the temptation to please and impress their masters. The result was often a good deal of inauthenticity, play-acting and exaggeration. Furthermore, Westernised Indians enjoyed an ambiguous existence. Though critical of their society, they were also heavily dependent on it for social, moral and emotional support. They had only a limited understanding of the Western ways of life and thought and retained far more of the traditional Indian habits and values than they realised or cared to admit. Not surprisingly, their lives lacked coherence and consistency, and their self-perceptions were often at odds with who and what they really were.[4] Nervous about the continuing presence of the past they thought they had overcome, they were afraid to look at themselves closely lest that shattered their comfortable illusions. Not many of them, therefore, had the courage to write about themselves. Such autobiographies as did appear often lacked structure and displayed an unstable mixture of self-pity and self-assertion, of despair and defiance.[5]

Once British culture lost its novelty and became integrated into the Indian ways of life and thought, and once the Indians, no longer awed by their masters, began to write for each other, autobiographical writing began to acquire a coherent character.[6] It was still an exotic and alien genre and aroused considerable curiosity and a measure of hostility. Authors were not clear either about their reasons for writing autobiographies or about their audience. Thanks to the Hindu disapproval of self-assertion, they felt uneasy and nervous talking about themselves and searched for an impersonal entity around which to weave the stories of their lives. They were not certain about what they should include in or exclude from it, or how much they should reveal about their dead ancestors, parents, brothers, wives, children, friends and, above all, their innermost thoughts and feelings. Since many of them had grown up and continued to live in joint families, their lives substantially overlapped with those of other members raising delicate questions about the morality of talking about them. Conventional Hindu notions of modesty, propriety and privacy also raised disturbing questions concerning how to be interesting and informative without appearing self-indulgent, boastful or exhibitionist. Each writer made his own judgement and took the risk.

Let us take two autobiographies by way of illustration.[7] Damodar Hari Chapekar, a terrorist freedom fighter and a Hindu militant, wrote an interesting autobiographical fragment.

In the preface, he observed that only a person worthy enough to have a biography written about him had a right to write an autobiography, and that it should only include either 'fascinating episodes' likely to interest others or righteous deeds likely to guide and 'save' mankind. Chapekar conceded that he was an obscure Indian with no claim to fame and no right to write about himself. However, he was about to engage in a 'great deed'— shooting a British officer—and wanted to write about it so that the 'patriotic friends who will come after me will take care to avoid the mistakes I may have committed'. Since he was a traditionalist opposed to 'importing' foreign practices including writing an autobiography, he wondered what his ancestors would have thought of his attempt to write one. He solved the problem by arguing that the autobiography was not really new to India and that Vyāsa, Vālmiki, Parāshara and Manu had written 'their own histories'. He did not provide a single reference and invented a non-existent tradition to legitimise what he was determined to do anyway. Although he talked about himself, he was rarely at ease and made his deeds, not his life, the centre of his autobiography. It avoided all unflattering details and was largely a story of his terrorist activities punctuated by general statements of his views on India.

In the preface to his autobiography, Sir Surendra Nath Banerjee tackled the question differently.[8] As we saw elsewhere, he was deeply worried about the fact that since Indians had no tradition of writing history books, they never remembered or cherished the struggles and sacrifices of their ancestors. His autobiography was intended to rectify the situation. Inevitably, as its very title indicates, it took the form of reminiscences of the great Indians he had encountered. As he said: the 'need for reminiscences such as these has become all the more pressing in view of recent developments in our public life when unfortunately there is a marked, and perhaps growing, tendency among a certain section of our people to forget the services of our early nation-builders'. Names of these great men had remained buried in newspapers, and no historian had bothered to write immortal accounts of their deeds. Banerjee wanted 'to do some justice to their honoured memories', and hoped that his reminiscences 'will not have been written in vain if I am able even in part to accomplish this object'. Not surprisingly, he dedicated the book to those 'whose achievements the present generation is apt to forget'. For Banerjee, the autobiography had no other purpose than to remember, cherish and express gratitude to the illustrious contemporaries one was privileged to know. It was an act of both grateful remembrance and pious homage. Whether he would have taken this view if Indians had been in the habit of writing history is difficult to say. His autobiography contained a wealth of personal details but these remained marginal to the narrative. Not he but modern India was its subject and provided the principle of coherence and continuity. It was really the biography of modern India as reflected in the life of one of its most distinguished citizens. Like Chapekar, Banerjee felt uneasy talking about himself and could only do so in the name and under the protective shelter of an impersonal entity.

III

Gandhi's autobiography, written at a time when the tradition of writing one was just beginning to develop, reveals many of the doubts and anxieties of his predecessors. He said in the Preface that the idea of writing it was not his, but pressed upon him by some of his colleagues. He did not immediately accede to their proposal and decided to think further. When he was in prison and had considerable free time, they renewed the request. When he eventually agreed to comply, a close friend raised two objections which made sense in the Hindu cultural context sketched earlier.[9]

First, writing autobiographies was a Western practice and no one in pre-modern India was known to have written one. This was not an accident because it was a form of self-assertion and involved self-display and self-glorification. The West admired these qualities whereas India had always condemned them. Gandhi's colleague asked to know why he, a fervent champion of Indian civilisation, wished to 'borrow' and legitimise an alien and apparently immoral genre of writing.

Second, autobiography was fraught with grave dangers. Indian culture disapproved of people writing about themselves and gave the *adhikār* to do so only to those who had attained great moral and spiritual heights and had something wise and worthwhile to say. Such men only expressed their mature and well-considered views which were widely accepted as authoritative. Since Gandhi was a *Mahātmā*, his autobiography was bound to be taken as a morally definitive text. That was bad enough. To make matters worse, he was also a scientist constantly experimenting with truth and revising his ideas. His readers were, therefore, bound to feel confused and even likely to be misled. His colleague observed:[10]

> What if you stop believing in what you take to be true today? Or what if you later interpret your principles differently and reconsider your earlier actions? Many men take your writings to be authoritative and conduct themselves accordingly. Will they not be misled? Would it not therefore be better to be cautious and for the time being at least refrain from writing something like an autobiography?

Gandhi was 'impressed' by these objections, but thought that they could be met by suitably revising the Western method of writing autobiography. As for the first objection, he rejoined that unless they were patently evil, there was no harm in adopting and indigenising foreign institutions and practices. He agreed that the Western manner of writing an autobiography was essentially self-centred and egoistic. Even when its author was self-effacing and self-critical, his very preoccupation with his transient thoughts, feelings, moods and achievements involved self-assertion and heightened his self-consciousness and sense of particularity. However, Gandhi contended that this was not inherent in the genre and that it was possible to write one in a 'morally innocent manner'. The Western autobiography was vulnerable to the 'vices' of self-assertion and self-glorification because it took the *self* as its subject matter. There was no reason why the *soul* could not be made its centre. As a spiritual aspirant, he had devoted his life to realising Truth or God and conducted all manner of experiments. If he were to describe these, the difficulties he had faced, the lapses he had suffered, the way he had overcome them and the lessons he had painfully learnt, he could easily avoid the characteristic vices of autobiography. It was true that he could not describe his experiments without mentioning the relevant details of his life. However, since his primary purpose was not to tell the story of his life and write an autobiography in the Western sense, he could legitimately exclude all personal details which did not bear upon his experiments and describe those that did solely from the standpoint of the experiments. The 'I' was not to be the subject of his autobiography and would enter it only as the agent or bearer of experiments. His autobiography would thus be concerned not with him but with his experiments; not with his psychological feelings and moods but with his spiritual struggles; not with the transient trivia of his life but with the abiding discoveries he had made in the laboratory of life; not with his self but with his soul.

Gandhi argued that since the kind of autobiography he intended to write was very different from its dominant Western form, the term autobiography was misleading and gave rise to wrong expectations. Accordingly, he distinguished between *jivanvritānta* (description of a life) and *ātmakathā* (the story of a soul) and insisted that his autobiography belonged to the second category. In order to make his point clearer, he sometimes said that he was not 'really' writing an autobiography but a history of his experiments 'in the name of' or 'under the pretext of' an autobiography. On yet other occasions, he said that he was writing an 'autobiography confined to his experiments with truth' (*satyanā proyogo purti ātmakathā*) or an 'autobiography of experiments with truth' (*satyanā proyogoni ātmakathā*).[11] At several places in the preface and in the text, Gandhi used the term *kathā* to describe what he was doing. This old and evocative term connotes a story told with a view to drawing out and emphasising important moral lessons.

Gandhi contended that far from strengthening egoism and self-assertion, an autobiography written along these lines was bound to have the opposite effect. Moral and spiritual achievements were inherently fragile and secured and shadowed by humiliating lapses. He could not describe them without confessing his limitations and recognising the vast moral distance still waiting to be traversed. To write about them was to 'grow in humility' and to see the self as nothing more than a mere vehicle for the discovery of truth. Gandhi asked his readers to read his autobiography *only* in order to learn from his experiments and to ignore and 'condemn' him for every intrusion of egoism.

Since Gandhi intended to write an 'autobiography of his experiments', he said that his reasons for doing so and the constituency he had in mind were very different from those generally associated with Western autobiography.[12] He did not write it to come to terms with his past, for that was of no concern to others; nor to tell the story of his life, for that only titillated idle curiosity and had no moral meaning for them; nor to justify himself to others and earn their good opinion, for the only opinion that mattered to him was the approval of his own conscience. He wrote it in order to share with others his moral and spiritual aspirations, struggles, lapses and discoveries, and thereby to offer them 'some useful material' for their spiritual journey. His autobiography was a scientist's manual and intended to offer to the world the supreme gift of inevitably partial and tentative truths. He wanted to encourage others to conduct similar experiments in the hope that such experimentally-based and reflective autobiographies would contribute to the creation of a collective pool of moral and spiritual knowledge. One lamp lit others, and together they generated the light needed to illuminate the journey of life. Gandhi said that he had, therefore, written his autobiography for the benefit of his fellow-seekers 'who form my world'. As an advanced explorer himself, he owed it to them to write about his journey. And his fellow-explorers would know how to read his autobiography with requisite care and sensitivity.

Gandhi had so far dealt with his colleague's first objection. He now briefly turned to the second, namely, that his autobiography ran the risk of being regarded as morally authoritative. He said that he was writing it for his fellow-seekers who, being themselves engaged in experiments, could not possibly treat it as definitive. Furthermore, since his autobiography was a story of his experiments, he was bound to say that some had proved abortive, that some others had unexpected consequences, and that yet others were inconclusive. No one reading it could, therefore, conclude that it was anything but tentative and exploratory. Indeed, he hoped that his readers would go away charged with the scientific spirit of experimentation and humility.

Having discussed how he proposed to 'purge' Western autobiography of egoism and self-assertion and adopt it to the central values of Indian civilisation, Gandhi went on to explain how he intended to write it. Like scientific experiments, moral and spiritual experiments had to be conducted with clinical precision and described with utmost accuracy. He, therefore, hoped to write his autobiography in a simple, lucid and measured language, a spicy and ornate language being 'as foreign to truth as hot chillies to a healthy stomach'. He also intended to write at a slow pace, lingering on every important experiment and carefully describing all its relevant features. Gandhi knew that the story of his experiments did not coincide with the chronology of his life. Since most of his experiments were incomplete and threw up unsuspected problems, he kept returning to them at different periods of his life. They had, therefore, their own chronology and a distinctly circular time structure. As a result his autobiography had two separate but criss-crossing chronologies. The narration of his life was brisk and unilinear, whereas that of his experiments was circular and had an air of timelessness about it.

Since Gandhi intended to write the story of his experiments, his autobiography was expected to be a *kathā* and not an *itihās*, a didactic discussion of selected experiments rather than their complete and impartial account. The two, however, could not be easily separated. The experiments did not take place in a social vacuum. They involved others either directly, as in the case of his wife, children and close friends, or indirectly, as in the case of his colleagues and associates. As such, they could not be discussed without detailed references to their nature and degree of involvement in them, the way they interpreted and reacted to them, the lessons they learned, and so on. Gandhi said that he necessarily saw his experiments from his own point of view and that his description of them was bound to remain biased and one-sided unless accompanied by detailed statements of the views of those involved. He only wanted to write a *kathā* but found that it also involved an *itihās* and that the two were subject to different, even conflicting, criteria. A *kathā* could be selective and subjective whereas an *itihās* was necessarily objective and many-sided. Gandhi was in a 'moral quandary'. It was interesting that he faced no such dilemma when discussing his wife and children. Apparently he thought that he was at liberty to be brutally frank about them and that he could offer an objective and truthful account of their involvement in his experiments. It was his relations with his European friends that worried him, so much so that he even changed the title of the relevant chapter. Gandhi observed:[13]

> I understand better today the meaning of what I had earlier read about the imperfections and difficulties of autobiography as history. I know that I am not even offering all I remember in the autobiography of the experiments with truth. Who knows how much I should offer in order to present the truth of the matter? And what is the value of the one-sided and incomplete evidence in a court of law? If someone with plenty of free time were to cross-examine me on the previous chapters, would he not throw a flood of new light on their content? And if he were to examine them as a critic, would he not entertain the world by gleefully exposing the hollowness of my account? When sometimes I think like this I cannot help asking myself whether it would not be more proper to stop writing these chapters?

Gandhi did not resolve the dilemma and was tempted to abandon his autobiography. Since writing it was itself 'perhaps a dubious activity', he said that he could afford not to be too finicky about historical accuracy and objectivity. Trying truthfully to describe his experiments was itself one of these experiments, and he would let his readers form their own judgement.

Given his conception of a morally innocent autobiography, it is hardly surprising that Gandhi's autobiography should be intensely moralistic and display an unusual structure. As we saw elsewhere, he conducted different types of experiments in his personal, social, professional and political life. After a prolonged moral struggle, he succeeded in becoming a noble soul, a *Mahātmā*. As he himself said, it was these experiments and what he gained from them that earned him that title. His autobiography is thus really a story of how he evolved into a *Mahātmā*. With serene detachment, the *Mahātmā* narrates the way Mohandas Karamchand Gandhi had tried to live his life according to certain principles. He describes Gandhi's moments of achievement and failure and how he had felt about these at the time. The *Mahātmā* then reflects on Gandhi's reflections, and the hero and the narrator, the subject and the object, become one. The *Mahātmā* finds

Mohandas Karamchand Gandhi both familiar and unfamiliar. He recognises himself in him, for the moral struggle is not yet over and the experiments with the soul are not yet complete. The *Mahātmā* has also, however, overcome many of Gandhi's limitations and even outgrown him and retains only a non-emotive memory of him. Being a story of the fascinating and extremely complex encounter between Gandhi and the *Mahātmā*, Gandhi's *Autobiography* does not remain an autobiography in the Western sense. It is basically a biography of Gandhi written by the *Mahātmā*. As an intriguing combination of the related but logically distinct biographical and autobiographical genres of writing, it should perhaps be called an autobiographical biography.

Gandhi presents his life as a coherent and constantly evolving whole. Although marked by several painful experiences each of which gave a new turn to his life, he sees in it no radical ruptures or discontinuities. He suffered many lapses but learned his lessons and came out the better on each occasion. His *Autobiography* is, therefore, free from the penitential outbursts of Augustine and the nervous exhibitionism of Rousseau, and is less brooding and introspective than either. It shows neither self-pity nor moral conceit and is suffused with the spirit of self-confidence and self-reconciliation. The emotionally charged memories of an early and lustful marriage still unsettle him, largely because his sexual self-discipline is still incomplete, and his references to it show an abiding feeling of guilt and remorse. By contrast, he has come to terms with his ill-treatment of his wife, childhood theft, hot temper and early attempts at playing an English gentleman, and his descriptions of them are remarkably non-emotive and tinged with self-mocking irony.

Since Gandhi was primarily concerned to describe his experiments, his life fell into two broad stages. His early life was marked by a constant struggle to fashion a satisfactory form of life and involved a series of experiments. His later life was largely devoted to living according to the truths he had already discovered and involved few new experiments. This is clearly reflected in the structure of his autobiography. The early parts which describe his years of struggle and the eventual attainment of *Mahātmāhood* are more personal, reflective and self-critical and read like a *kathā*; the later parts which deal with his mature public life are largely descriptive and read like an *itihās*.

Gandhi had hoped to write a morally innocent autobiography, one exclusively concerned with his moral experiments and free of egoism. He was not wholly successful. As the autobiography progressed, he tended to get carried away by its momentum and introduced several details that had no bearing on the experiments. He also began to describe his moods, fears, feelings, hopes and anxieties, and his autobiography was sometimes little different from its Western counterpart. On occasions he even 'fell prey' to egoism. Compare, for example, his description of his years in South Africa in *Autobiography* with that given in his *History of Satyāgraha in South Africa*.[14] His account of his reasons for deciding to stay on there is nearly five times as long in the *Autobiography*; he uses the first person singular three times as often; and he places much greater emphasis on his apparent indispensibility in the struggle against racial discrimination. Even the determined *Mahātmā* found it beyond his powers completely to overcome the inherent logic of autobiographical writing.

Gandhi could not Indianise autobiography without Westernising the Indian cultural tradition. The very fact that he wrote it and the manner in which he wrote it had important consequences. The fact that he, a champion of traditional India, was prepared to turn his hand to a distinctively Western genre was a highly symbolic and radical act and showed to his nervous countrymen how to respond to foreign values and practices. In writing an autobiography, further, he lent his considerable moral authority to the growing practice of talking and writing about oneself in public and helped weaken the traditional hostility to self-disclosure and self-assertion. By describing in detail how he, a timid young man who had once eaten eggs in order to be as strong as an Englishman, eventually overcame his colonial sense of inferiority and regained his racial self-respect and pride, Gandhi showed his countrymen how to come to terms with the menacing reality of colonial domination. In the contemporary context, his autobiography, therefore, had a great therapeutic and inspirational value and was a profoundly political act. Again, unlike almost all Indian autobiographers before him, Gandhi discussed his personal limitations, failures, and moral lapses with remarkable frankness. By revealing that even a saint had a regrettable past and still a long way to go, he introduced the badly needed elements of honesty, moral humility and social courage in Indian life. Not that he said things his countrymen did not know. A culture whose epics and *Purānas* are replete with tantalising references to the moral foibles of gods and goddesses is well-insulated against claims of moral perfection. Gandhi's contribution lay in encouraging a frank and honest discussion of moral issues, including sexuality. As he once put it: 'A person who has realised his or her own error has changed into a new body. Why should he or she feel ashamed of talking about the old one?'[15] For a constantly evolving self, an error or a lapse once recognised and corrected was no longer a living part of him. It belonged to his dead self which he should be able to criticise without emotional involvement. This was an important and relatively novel view in the Indian context.

Although Gandhi chose to write about his experiments rather than himself, the two were not as distinct as he imagined and his autobiography had opposite implications to those he intended. It showed that life was not a diligent discharge of inherited roles and obligations but a romance in self-creation; not a journey along a prescribed route but an adventure in self-enactment. Compared to the great spiritual explorations of the Buddha, Mahavira and other Indian sages, some of Gandhi's experiments were dull and conservative. However, his refusal to accept traditional values without first trying them out and his insistence on seeing life as a laboratory in which the restless individual explores new ideas in his unending quest for self-knowledge introduced an essentially modern though suitably Indianised conception of the self in Indian culture. Once experimentation with life became an acceptable practice, the door was opened to different and unconventional experiments.

Compared to many of his predecessors and contemporaries, Gandhi's autobiography had wholeness and integrity. While the autobiographies of Damodar Chapekar, Surendra Nath Banerjee, Subhas Chandra Bose, Narmada Shankar and others began as descriptions of their lives but soon turned into commentaries on political events, Hindu society, contemporary India or on life in general, Gandhi's never ceased to be one until the end. By and large, he never lost sight of the fact that he was writing about himself and his experiments, and that he had an *adhikār* and indeed a *dharma* only to talk about his struggles and discoveries.

Since he had a clear conception of what he intended to do and was determined to remain within its bounds, his autobiography contained very few digressions and had a remarkably economical structure.

This had its price. Gandhi's gaze remained fixed on his inner world and nothing was allowed to disturb his intense introspection. He had, therefore, little to say about the wider social and political world he dominated for just under three decades. Unlike Banerjee, Bose, Nehru and others, he nowhere outlined his views on the larger issues of the day, entered into a debate with his colleagues and opponents, analysed their triumphs and failures, commented on their physical appearances, mannerisms and political styles and skills or even described the physical surroundings in which he worked. In this respect Nehru's autobiography presents a remarkable contrast.[16] He located and attempted to understand himself in the context of the wider world; he said so in the introduction and remained faithful to it until the end. He analysed his social background, bourgeois upbringing, conflicting influences of India and Europe, his desperate and unsuccessful struggle to integrate the two, his habits of thought and ways of looking at the world and his hopes and fears for his country. He described in detail his surroundings and the places he had visited, offered insightful analyses of his colleagues including Gandhi, discussed his differences and disagreements with them and outlined his vision of independent India. Gandhi could never have written the following paragraph:[17]

> I have become a queer mixture of the East and West, out of place everywhere, at home nowhere. Perhaps my thoughts and approach to life are more akin to what is called Western than Eastern, but India clings to me, as she does to all her children, in innumerable ways; and behind me lie, somewhere in the subconscious, racial memories of a hundred, or whatever the number may be, generations of Brahmins. I cannot get rid of either that past inheritance or my recent acquisitions. They are both part of me, and, though they help me in both the East and the West, they also create in me a feeling of spiritual loneliness not only in public activities but in life itself. I am a stranger and alien in the West. I cannot be of it. But in my own country also, sometimes, I have an exile's feeling.

Gandhi's and Nehru's autobiographies represented serious attempts at self-understanding. While Gandhi hoped to arrive at it by means of an intense and introspective self-analysis, Nehru sought it in the larger social and political forces that had structured and moulded his personality. Like a yogi, Gandhi sat still and immovable with his gaze turned inward; Nehru saw himself from the outside and kept stepping back and forth to find an appropriate vantage point. We might say that Gandhi was concerned to *analyse* and Nehru to *explain* himself, and that Gandhi's autobiography was *introspective* whereas Nehru's was *reflective*. In any case, they were informed by different modes of self-analysis and offered different *forms* of self-understanding. Of the two, Gandhi's seems to have a distinctively Indian orientation and flavour.

Chapter Nine

Gandhi and the Bourgeoisie

On the face of it Gandhi's economic thought appears strange, even self-contradictory, and difficult to classify. He rebelled against many aspects of modern industrial civilisation, advocated self-contained villages and a simple and austere way of life, and appears archaic and pre-modern. However, the Indian National Congress under his leadership pursued policies that promoted capitalist interests and laid the foundations of a bourgeois-liberal state. Yet, he also denounced capitalism, including the very institution of private property, advocated nationalisation of basic industries, and claimed to be a socialist. Like his thought, his practice too seems contradictory. He championed the cause of the poor, lived like one, and was one of the first to place their economic and social uplift on the national agenda. He also, however, enjoyed close relations with the capitalists, lived from time to time in the house of one of them, and depended on them not only to finance the Congress and the independence movement but also his constructive programme.

It is, therefore, hardly surprising that Marxist commentators on Gandhi have had considerable difficulty in coming to terms with him. For M.N. Roy, his first Marxist critic, he was a 'reactionary' leader, the champion of a 'patriarchal or feudal civilisation' and a hierarchical and rurally-based social order. In Roy's view, Gandhi was not unique to India; 'there are Gandhis in every country' embarking on the path of industrialisation.[1] He agreed that Gandhi was genuinely concerned about the poor and the oppressed, but insisted that his preferred society was inherently incapable of promoting their interests. As he put it:

Gandhism is nothing but petty-bourgeois humanitarianism hopelessly bewildered in the clashes of the staggering forces of human progress. The crocodile tears of this humanitarianism are shed ostensibly for the undeniable sufferings of the majority in capitalist society, but they are really caused by grief over the end of the old order, already destroyed or about to be so. It pines for that ancient golden age when the majority were kept in blissful ignorance in order that a few could roll in idle luxury, undisturbed by the revolt of the discontented, the spiritual culture of which was based on the barbarism of the people at large, the simplicity of which was the sign of its backwardness. This ignoring glance backwards is due, in some cases to the consummate intrigues of the forces of reaction, and in others, to voluntary subordination to the influence of the same agency. Its tendency towards a sort of religious or utopian socialism proves that Gandhism, as well as its source Tolstoyism, belongs to the latter category. Or in other words, the services rendered by it to reaction are involuntary.[2]

Lenin had argued that since Gandhi had inspired and led a mass movement, he was a political revolutionary or had at least prepared the ground for revolutionary politics. Roy disagreed. As a religious and cultural revivalist, Gandhi 'was bound to be a reactionary socially, however revolutionary he might appear politically'. There can be no revolution without a 'revolutionary ideology', whereas Gandhi's was a 'reactionary ideology' that systematically emasculated the radical potential of mass mobilisation. As to why Gandhi was a reactionary, Roy pointed to, among other things, his emphasis on social harmony, his desire to 'run from the machine age back to the stone age', and his 'cult of non-violence'. This last tenet, the 'central pivot' of his thought, meant that Gandhi had no answer to and implicitly acquiesced in capitalist exploitation and violence.[3] Roy's view that violence was central to revolution and that a rejection or even a strong moral disapproval of it symbolised political conservatism influenced many a subsequent Marxist commentator on Gandhi. It was doubly flawed. It misrepresented Marx's views on the role of violence in social change, and misunderstood the aggressive thrust of Gandhi's non-violence as well as his willingness to condone certain types of violence.

The Comintern and its Indian allies were more damning of Gandhi than Roy was, but less clear. For them, the Congress under Gandhi was 'a class organisation of the capitalists', working against the interests 'not only of the workers and peasants but also of wide sections of the town petty bourgeois'.[4] Indian capitalists were not really interested in independence because their interests were linked to those of both 'British imperialism' and Indian feudalism. As their spokesman, Gandhi was 'a police agent of British imperialism in India'.[5] Following the Popular Front strategy of the Comintern, the communists did a somersault in the mid-thirties. They now acknowledged their 'left sectarian error' and argued that the Congress represented 'the united front of the Indian people in national struggle'.[6] Though conservative in its orientation, it was capable of transformation by internal pressures from left wing forces. Rather than avoid it, the communists were asked to join or at least work in close cooperation with it. Gandhi was now called a great nationalist leader who had played a 'progressive role' in turning the Congress into an anti-imperialist movement. Though he remained an 'ally' of the capitalists and exerted a reactionary economic and social influence on the Congress, his political and historical influence was warmly commended. Once, however, the Second World War became a 'people's war', the communists changed their view yet again. Gandhi and the Congress were now attacked for not supporting the struggle against Nazi barbarism and taking a reactionary, narrowly nationalistic and politically naive view of the nature, causes and the likely outcome of the war.

In *Why Socialism?* written during his Marxist days, Jayaprakash Narayan offered a somewhat different analysis of Gandhi. Unlike Roy, who could not make up his mind whether Gandhi's thought was feudal or petty bourgeois and dismissed it as reactionary, Narayan thought that it was 'reformist' and represented the interests of the big bourgeoisie. In his view, the 'essence' of Gandhi's 'curious philosophy' consisted of such 'naive' ideas as class collaboration, austere lifestyle, reliance on gentle persuasion to secure large-scale economic changes, and an ineffective theory of trusteeship which made 'the shark a trustee for the minnow.' These and related doctrines had long been advocated in the West by 'smug bourgeois professors, thinkers and churchmen', and were neither uniquely Indian as Gandhi claimed nor original to him. Gandhi was not interested in securing social justice but in 'covering up the ugly fissures of society', and gave his 'open and avowed' approval to the largescale organised theft and violence' inherent in capitalism. Narayan observed: 'Gandhism may be a well-intentioned doctrine. I personally think it is. But it is ... a dangerous doctrine ... because it hushes up real issues and sets out to remove the evils of society by pious wishes. It thus deceives the masses and encourages the upper classes to continue their domination.'[7]

A.R. Desai in his classic *Social Background of Indian Nationalism* took a far more subtle view of Gandhi. He saw Gandhi as a spokesman not so much of a particular bourgeois faction as that of the capitalist mode of production, and thought that although Gandhi attacked the evils of capitalism, he remained trapped within the bourgeois social consciousness. As Desai put it:

> The bourgeois consciousness of Gandhi should not ... be confounded or identified with the sordid consciousness of an ordinary bourgeois. Gandhi was a bourgeois only in the sense that he sincerely believed in the validity of the existing society based on capitalist property system, alternative to which he saw social chaos. Gandhi recognized and denounced in burning words the barbarities of capitalist exploitation but could not transcend his essential bourgeois outlook. Gandhi loved the masses but also believed in the bourgeois social system.[8]

Later Marxist commentators such as Hiren Mukerji, E.M.S. Namboodiripad and B.T. Ranadive have broadly endorsed Desai's view. In recent years, Marxist scholars have adopted a much more sophisticated approach. They concentrate on the entire body of Gandhi's thought rather than his early *Hind Swaraj* and pay close attention to the way in which it changed in response to the exigencies of the nationalist struggle. They also see Gandhi's ideas not as a homogeneous whole but as a cluster of different, and sometimes, contradictory tendencies. And they devote far greater attention to his actions than did the earlier generations of Marxist commentators, and examine his programmes and policies, the groups he favoured, his stand or silence on controversial matters, and the overall political role of his ideas in the consolidation of the nationalist movement. Partha Chatterjee's work is one of the best examples of this new approach.[9]

Chatterjee's argument is articulated at several different levels and is not easy to follow. Like M.N. Roy, he argues that Gandhi's *Hind Swaraj* idealised pre-capitalist economic and social relations, and represented a backward-looking petty bourgeois utopia, but insists that it was not the 'fundamental core' of what he calls 'Gandhism', a conveniently reified term which allows Chatterjee to essentialise Gandhi and ascribe to him only such views that support his interpretation of Gandhi. For Chatterjee, Gandhi's economic ideas are inextricably tied up with his moral theory, especially his doctrines of non-violence and moral purity, and should be understood not so much in terms of his subjective intentions as the way in which they were objectively interpreted and appropriated by the Congress.

For Chatterjee, the Indian nationalist movement was dominated by the champions of the bourgeoisie and furthered the latter's interests. It had no hope of defeating the colonial rulers without mobilising the masses, especially the peasantry, the largest single class in India. The unique historical role of 'Gandhism' consisted in achieving this vital task. It articulated the views and forms of consciousness of the peasantry, and mobilised and brought it within the nationalist movement. Thanks to his emphasis on non-violence and the concomitant moral elitism, he organised the peasantry on a local not national basis, concentrated on its individual grievances rather than the larger question of property rights, and prevented it from developing its own organisation and leadership. Under Gandhi, the peasantry, therefore, played an active but subordianate role within a struggle 'wholly conceived and directed by others', and subserved bourgeois interests. It was true that Gandhi was critical of capitalism, the modern state, the bourgeois representative democracy and so on, but since he had no viable alternatives he kept compromising with them and allowed them to develop and acquire legitimacy. Chatterjee observes:

> It is only by looking at it in that historical context that it becomes possible to understand the unique achievement of Gandhism: its ability to open up the possibility for achieving

perhaps the most important historical task for a successful nationalist revolution in a country like India, viz., the political appropriation of the subaltern classes by a bourgeoisie aspiring for hegemony in the new nation-state. In the Indian case, the largest popular element of the nation was the peasantry. And it was the Gandhian ideology which opened up historical possibility for its appropriation into the evolving political structures of the Indian state.[10]

He goes on:

While it was the Gandhian intervention in elite-nationalist politics in India which established for the first time that an authentic national movement could only be built upon the orgnized support of the whole of the peasantry, the working out of the politics of non-violence also made it abundantly clear that the object of the political mobilization of the peasantry was not at all what Gandhi claimed on its behalf, 'to train the masses in self-consciousness and attainment of power'. Rather the peasantry were (sic) meant to become willing participants in a struggle wholly conceived and directed by others.[11]

For Chatterjee, M.N. Roy and others, Gandhi's emphasis on non-violence and *satyāgraha* was responsible for curtailing and disciplining the peasant movement and allowing the bourgeoisie to harness its energy for their own purpose. Gandhi's 'passive revolution' gave the nationalist movement all the benefits of a mass following while scrupulously avoiding the revolutionary dangers consequent upon such mobilisation.

Chatterjee's perceptive and partially persuasive analysis leaves many a question unanswered. He does not explain why the mobilised peasantry remained passive and allowed itself to be so easily controlled, nor why other leaders and political parties, including the communists and socialists, failed to counter Gandhi by exploiting the political space opened up by him. Furthermore, Gandhi was committed to non-violence as much as to truth and social justice, and Chatterjee does not explain why Gandhi chose to privilege the former. What is more, although Gandhi was committed to non-violence, he condoned violence in several cases, and Chatterjee does not explain why he thinks that

Gandhi was not prepared to do so in the case of the peasantry. Again, Chatterjee assumes that there was a large-scale nationwide peasant unrest which Gandhi and the Congress emasculated; there is little evidence to support this view. One might, of course, legitimately argue that Gandhi should have radicalised the peasantry and turned it into a powerful anti-bourgeois force. However, since that was not how he imagined the nationalist struggle and since it went against his social philosophy, he could not be attacked for 'failing' to do what he did not set out to do in the first instance.

My intention in this chapter is not to comment on these and other Marxist interpretations of Gandhi, nor to trace the significant methodological, epistemological and other shifts in the Marxist discourse on him, but to assess the validity of the central Marxist thesis. The thesis asserts that although Gandhi passionately championed the cause of the poor and the oppressed, and mobilised the masses on a scale unprecedented in Indian history, both his ideas and especially his actions reinforced the bourgeois hegemony of the nationalist movement and helped consolidate the capitalist mode of production. He may or may not have intended the outcome, but its roots lay deep in his thought and actions. His hopelessly unrealistic alternative to capitalism, his theory of non-violence, his largely impotent theory of trusteeship and his naive belief in class harmony not only undermined his criticisms of capitalism but allowed it to flourish without a serious challenge. His failure to organise the peasantry on an all-India basis and challenge the bourgeois hegemony of the nationalist movement meant in effect that the Congress and the new Indian state were taken over by the bourgeoisie.

Since the Marxist thesis draws support from a particular reading of Gandhi's ideas and actions, I shall discuss them in that order in the first two sections. In the third, I shall analyse the ideologically and organisationally complex structure of the Congress under Gandhi's leadership, and in the final section, I shall assess the validity of the Marxist thesis.

I

All his life, Gandhi remained highly critical of the capitalist economy. His critique was fourfold. First, capitalism, socialism, communism and all such 'economically' orientated ideologies rested on the 'materialist' view of man,[12] which equated the human being with the body and saw him as an essentially self-centred being who found his fulfillment in the gratification of his ever-increasing and inherently insatiable wants. Capitalism was based on the belief that most men were most likely to satisfy most of their desires most of the time under a system of private property. Communism rested on the opposite belief that such a goal could only be realised in a state-controlled economy. For reasons too well known to need reiteration, Gandhi rejected the 'materialist' view in favour of the 'spiritual' view of man. Since capitalism and communism rested on a dubious philosophical anthropology, he insisted that they were both morally flawed.

Second, Gandhi argued that the concept of private property underlying capitalism was logically incoherent. It was based on a misguided notion of self-ownership. The individual owed his existence, survival, intellectual and moral capacities, character, skills, ambition, motivation, in short his very humanity to others. Since his capacities, etc., were socially derived, they were not his private property but a social trust, a collective asset of which he was only a custodian. Their products belonged to society and were not a matter of exclusive personal possession to be used as he pleased. Furthermore, the efforts of countless men and women flowed into one another to produce an object, rendering it impossible to demarcate the distinctive contribution of each. Their cooperation occurred within the context of the established social order, whose silent and unnoticed but vital contribution could not be ignored either. Even as an event was caused by a number of factors operating against the background of a given set of conditions such that none of them could be arbitrarily abstracted and called its cause, no human activity could be shown to be the sole cause of and to deserve a particular reward.

Third, for Gandhi, capitalism was an exploitative system propelled by greed and based on the survival of the fittest. Not surprisingly, it caused an enormous moral havoc in society. It created largescale unemployment and condemned millions to miserable lives. Even the employed were poorly paid, worked under inhuman conditions, found neither joy nor fulfillment in their jobs and were constantly haunted by the fear of unemployment and poverty. Since they were treated and even referred to as commodities, they behaved and lived like one, and developed neither self-respect nor self-discipline. They were rightly consumed by anger and hatred against their employers and seethed with the spirit of revenge and violence. In Gandhi's view, capitalists led equally empty and inhuman lives devoted to the pursuit of mindless pleasures. Fearful of losing their privileges and acutely aware of the smouldering violence of their victims, they remained anxious and tense and required a heavily-armed state for their protection and security. Since human beings in Gandhi's view found it difficult to live in affluence in the midst of poverty and degradation without somehow convincing themselves that they were right to do so, the privileged classes built up and propagated a self-serving system of justification that was full of falsehoods and blunted their moral sensibility. In such a climate, truth, morality and human well-being were the inevitable casualties.

Finally, Gandhi thought that the economic order should be embedded in and subordinated to the civilisation of the wider society. Indian civilisation was historically unique and different from the Western. Rather than copy the West or indigenise imported ideologies, India should evolve its own 'humane' and 'spiritual' economy based on the values, motivations and self-understanding characteristic of its people.

Gandhi's 'spritual' alternative to capitalism rested on the following principles.[13] First, every adult had a right to work. Human beings needed to work in order to acquire such basic human qualities as a sense of self-respect, dignity, self-discipline, self-confidence, initiative and the capacity to organise their energies and structure their personalities. Welfare payments by the state sustained the body but impoverished the soul and dehumanised them. Furthermore, since the social order was sustained by the spirit of *yajna* or spontaneous cooperation of all its members, an individual lacking the opportunity to work was denied the privilege of participating in it, and this cut him off from the moral and spiritual life of his community and involuntarily reduced him to the demeaning status of a social parasite.

Second, economic life should be in harmony with and create conditions necessary for moral and spiritual development. For reasons we need not consider here, Gandhi thought that human beings could only realise their full moral potential in small, relaxed, self-governing and interdependent communities. Since the latter lacked vitality without an autonomous economic base of their own, he argued that production should be decentralised and each community should become relatively self-sufficient in its basic needs. As he imagined it, the village land was to be owned in common, farming done on a cooperative basis, the produce equitably divided, and only the surplus land was to be used for cash crops. The villages were to encourage locally-based industries and crafts and to import only what they could not produce themselves. Full employment or the right to work was the necessary requirement of man's spiritual nature, and Gandhi could not see how it could be secured except in such self-sufficient communities.

Third, since village communities were to form the basis of the Indian economy, the nature, pace and scale of industrialisation were to be determined by and subordinated to their requirements. Large-scale industries were necessary, but they had to be restricted to the minimum, located in the cities, and only allowed to produce what the self-sufficient communities themselves could not. Since competition between the two necessarily led to the latter's destruction, a national plan was to lay down what share of the market was to be reserved for each. That was the only way to avoid the rise of huge and inhuman cities and the urban exploitation of the countryside.

Fourth, the means of production of the basic necessities of life should be collectively owned. They affected human survival and could easily become instruments of the most dangerous forms of exploitation. Industries of vital national importance should also be owned by the state, which should either set them up itself or nationalise 'without compensation', for 'if you want the government to pay compensation it will have to rob Peter to pay Paul and that would be impossible'. Fifth, since all socially useful activities were equally important, their wage differentials should be reduced to the minimum. And finally, since a healthy moral community was impossible in a grossly unequal society, the state had to embark on a programme of levelling up the poor and the oppressed and levelling down the rich. The resources needed to help the poor were to be raised by taxing the rich at a 'much higher figure' than the 70 per cent then obtaining in Britain.

Concerning the form of ownership, Gandhi proposed his well-known theory of trusteeship, an economic extension of his philosophical concept of human beings as trustees of their capacities. The theory was intended to avoid the evils and combine the advantages of capitalism and communism, and aimed to socialise property without nationalising it. As he imagined it, every industrialist employing more than a certain number of workers was to look upon his industry not as his property but as a social trust. He was to work along with his employees, take no more than what he needed for a moderately comfortable life, to look upon them as 'members of his family', be responsible for the management of the industry, and to provide healthy working conditions and welfare schemes for them and their families. Part of the moderate profit he made was to be devoted to the welfare of the community, the rest used to improve the industry. The owner was free to bequeath his industry to his children or whoever he liked *only if* the latter agreed to run it in the spirit of trusteeship.

Gandhi acknowledged that capitalists were unlikely to become trustees of their property and urged sustained pressure of educated and organised public opinion, including *satyāgraha*. If that did not work, he was reluctantly prepared for the state to impose trusteeship by law. It would prescribe the amount of remuneration to be paid to the trustee 'commensurate with the service rendered and its value to society'. The trustee was free to choose his heir, but the choice had to be 'finalised' by the state. Gandhi thought that such a cooperative decision checked both. The trustee retained formal ownership subject to state control. As Gandhi put it, 'I desire to end capitalism almost if not quite as much as the most advanced socialists and even communists. But our methods differ, our languages differ'.[14]

Professor Dantwala and other socialists had a long discussion with Gandhi about the nature and implications of his theory of trusteeship. They summed up his views in a draft which he endorsed after making a few changes, all designed to strengthen its egalitarian thrust. The final version read as follows:

1. Trusteeship provides a means of transforming the present capitalist order of society into an egalitarian one. It gives no quarter to capitalism, but gives the present owning class a chance of reforming itself. It is based on the faith that human nature is never beyond redemption.
2. It does not recognise any rights of private ownership of property except insofar as it may be permitted by society for its own welfare.
3. It does not exclude legislative regulation of the ownership and use of wealth.
4. Thus, under *state-regulated trusteeship*, an individual will not be free to hold or use wealth for selfish satisfaction or in disregard of the interests of society.
5. Just as it is proposed to fix a decent minimum living wage, even so a limit should be fixed for the maximum income that would be allowed to any person in society. The difference between such minimum incomes should be reasonable and equitable and variable from time to time so much so that the tendency would be towards obliteration of the difference.
6. Under the Gandhian economic order, the character of production will be determined by social necessity and not by personal whim or greed.[15]

The draft was a fairly accurate statement of Gandhi's mature economic views. Since the early thirties, he had increasingly begun to turn radical, partly in response to political pressure by discontented groups, partly because of his experiences with the Indian capitalists, and partly because he saw more clearly than before the economic implications of his moral and political thought. He insisted that a fundamental revolution in property relations was both necessary and inescapable. 'Without a material revision of vested interests', he observed, 'the condition of the masses can never be improved.'[16] He was concerned that the exploited masses lacked an awareness of their rights, and wondered how to radicalise them without letting them turn violent. 'Land and all property is his who will work for it.

Unfortunately, the workers are or have been kept ignorant of this simple fact.'[17] He was convinced that if nothing was done in time the 'desperate peasants would take the land. We would not have to tell them to take it'.[18]

Gandhi appreciated more than ever before the redistributive role of the state and assigned it a wide range of functions. He was prepared to impose trusteeship by law, raise the level of taxation, nationalise vital industries and establish a programme of positive discrimination for the poor and the oppressed. He repeatedly warned the Indian bourgeoisie of the 'inevitable' violence of the workers and peasants, and urged the latter to stand up for their rights, including launch *satyāgrahas*. He announced that after independence, he might himself lead *satyāgrahas* against vested interests, and thought that they were likely to be 'more bitter' and protracted than those against the British. Though he was opposed to violence, he was prepared to put up with the 'defensive', 'legitimate' and 'pardonable' violence of the 'desperate and frustrated' masses. In 1942, he gave several important interviews to Louis Fischer in the course of which he argued that the landless peasantry should stop paying taxes and even seize the land they cultivated. He acknowledged that this might lead to violence by the landlords but insisted that it was bound to be limited and could be easily brought under control.[19]

Gandhi's ideal society then was semi-industrialised, economically more or less self-sufficient, substantially egalitarian, based on cooperative production and ruled out extensive international trade. It involved medium size agro-industrial residential units, nationalisation of basic industries, heavy taxation, death duties, state regulation of ownership, and workers' participation in the management of industries. Needless to say, Gandhi's vision of the good society is neither communist nor capitalist and nor is it feudal or premodern. The centrality of the state, extensive government control of the economy, large-scale industrialisation, bureaucracy and so on, which characterise communism, are absent in Gandhi's society. The pursuit of profit, the more or less unlimited right to acquire and dispose of property, competition, integration of the national economy into the world market, unregulated mechanisation and the ever-increasing scale of production, which constitute the basic preconditions of the capitalist economy, are also absent. Since Gandhi cherished personal autonomy, equality and social justice and was not opposed to mechanisation and several other aspects of modern civilisation, he was not feudal or reactionary either. His economic thought drew upon and cut across the familiar ideological polarities and was in a class by itself.

II

Having briefly considered Gandhi's economic ideas, we shall now examine his actions, decisions, and the groups he favoured, ignored or opposed or see if they support the Marxist thesis.

When Gandhi became the unquestioned leader of the Indian independence movement, he had to work out a coherent strategy of struggle. He was convinced on the basis of his South African and Indian experiences that moral appeals, petitions and constitutional pressures upon which the Congress had hitherto relied were impotent against a determined opponent. He also ruled out violence on the grounds that it was both morally unacceptable and politically ineffective in the context of a divided, disarmed and demoralised nation facing a united and well-armed government. He was also worried that once violence became respectable and organised, the masses would want to use it against their native exploiters, thereby dividing the nationalist movement and playing into the hands of the colonial rulers. In his view, the method of *satyāgraha* as he had developed and tried out with some success in South Africa was the only acceptable course of action. Its non-violence was, of course, a major factor in its favour, but not the only one. In Gandhi's view, *satyāgraha* involved all classes of men, brought in women, built up habits of concerted action and organisational skills, developed moral and social courage, and fitted in with what he took to be India's cultural traditions. It also went hand in hand with his constructive programme of national regeneration, opened up countless public spaces, could be applied to non-political areas of life as well, and gave Indian independence a firm moral and popular basis. Although it involved non-violence, it had nothing to do with the traditional doctrines of pacifism, turning the other cheek, or pursuit of social harmony at all cost, a point ignored by

M.N. Roy, Chatterjee and others. It was aggressive and unyielding in its pursuit of justice, did not shy away from situations of conflict, and had all the urgency, determination and tenacity of violence, which was why many Christian pacifists felt deeply uneasy with it and thought that although it was not violent, it was not truly non-violent.

Gandhi's *satyāgrahic* method of struggle, which he more or less successfully persuaded the bulk of the Congress Party and even the country to accept, shaped the nature and limits of his political strategy. It required that the Congress should cease being a merely debating body and become an effective tool of collective action with an extensive national network linked to the central leadership by a clearly established chain of command. Accordingly, Gandhi set up Congress branches all over the country, introduced a system of public accountability, vetted and trained local and regional leadership, established a clear structure of authority stretching right down to the villages, and turned the annual Congress session into something like a national parliament of delegates representing regional interests and views. The Nagpur session of 1921 had a distinctly Gandhian look not only in its dress, language and manner of conduct but also in its agenda and political self-confidence.

The *satyāgrahic* method also required mass participation for its success. When Gandhi appeared on the scene, a large number of social groups were outside the Congress and available for recruitment—for example, the poor, the unemployed, the different strata of peasantry, landless labourers, industrial workers, merchants, traders, sections of big bourgeoisie, rising industrialists, women and the untouchables. He selected and set about cultivating some of these but not others. This was not an accident, nor a matter of personal political preference, nor a question of their political accessibility, but inherent in his *satyāgrahic* method of struggle. The method could succeed only if those participating in it met certain conditions. Gandhi, therefore, recruited and mobilised those social groups that did and ignored those that did not satisfy them.

First, *satyāgraha* involved *hartal*, boycott of foreign cloth, and above all non-cooperation with the government, defined widely to include not only the withdrawal of essential services without which it could not function but also refusal to pay land revenue and taxes. This meant that only those groups were capable of contributing to its success who owned shops, traded in foreign cloth, provided services essential to the conduct of government, and paid taxes.

Second, *satyāgraha* involved adherence to non-violence even under grave provocation. Those social groups who had a tradition of non-violence or stood to gain from it were, therefore, ideal whereas those with a high propensity to violence were risky. Third, *satyāgraha* invited government repression and brutality, which the participants could not bear for long unless alternative sources of moral and social pressure were available to strengthen their resolve, dissuade the waverers from capitulating, and to sustain a spirit of mutual help. Well-organised and long-established social groups bound by strong moral and social bonds were obviously better equipped to undertake it than those of relatively recent origin or held together by tenuous ties.

Fourth, *satyāgraha* required mass mobilisation, concerted action and effective local leadership. Those groups that had a tradition of organised action, readily available channels of communication, and a well-established network of leadership were likely to prove more effective than those without them. Finally, since *satyāgraha* involved suffering and sacrifice, people were unlikely to want to engage in it unless they found protest more to their advantage than acquiescence. Those groups who had grievances against the government, or suffered from its policies, or were forced to bear a disproportionate share of the economic burden of colonial rule were, therefore, its ideal constituency. By contrast, those pampered by or privileged under the Raj, standing in an ambiguous relationship with it, or confident of looking after themselves under foreign or native rule would either not participate in *satyāgrahas* or remain unreliable allies.

These and other related considerations explain why Gandhi recruited merchants, traders, the middle and upper strata of peasantry, especially those belonging to common castes and forming stable communities, and the professional classes. Surprising as it may seem, he attached considerable importance to the morally and politically regenerative role of the last group. Though the professional classes in his view suffered from the disadvantage of being culturally alienated from the masses, they had the great advantage of having imbibed such progressive western ideas and values as the scientific spirit, social service, concern for the poor and the capacity to take a fresh and critical look at their society. Gandhi thought that once they were persuaded out of their 'infatuation' with modern civilisation, they represented a happy 'synthesis' of Western and Indian values and were capable of acting as a powerful social catalyst. Gandhi, a London-trained lawyer, himself belonged to that class.

Unlike the above-mentioned groups, the poor, the unemployed, the landless labourers, the industrial workers, big business, the industrial bourgeoisie and the large landlords—in short, the major groups at either end of the economic spectrum—were least equipped to participate in the struggle for independence as Gandhi conceived and conducted it. The first four groups did not pay taxes to the government, render it vital services, own shops, or use foreign cloth. They lacked organised communities and well-established structures of discipline and effective leadership, and had little stake in society. As he repeatedly pointed out, they had long been oppressed and brutalised and were 'rightly' anxious to settle old scores. He knew from experience how easily they tended to resort to violence and diverted the independence movement into a struggle against local landlords, moneylenders and employers. The Chauri Chaura incident convinced him that a 'prematurely' launched and centrally uncontrolled non-cooperation movement was likely to lead to mob violence. The peaceful agitation led by the U.P. Kisan Sabha also turned violent in January 1921 when a large number of low-caste peasants looted the property of their landlords and moneylenders. When the Congress leaders called off the Civil Disobedience Movement in the Midnapore and Hughli districts of Bengal after the Gandhi-Irwin pact of 1931, the poorer peasants turned their agitation against the zamindars and the police had to intervene.[20]

Not surprisingly, almost all of Gandhi's *satyāgrahas* took up only local issues, avoided explosive questions of land-ownership and control, were led by his trusted lieutenants, and withdrawn when they threatened to become violent. This was not because he was uninterested in removing social and economic injustices, for he constantly kept attacking them in the strongest possible terms. Rather, he felt that since the unjust Indian society was seething with discontent and since violence was just below the surface, any attempt to solve India's economic and social problems before independence was bound to set organised groups against each other, which the colonial rulers were likely to exploit, thereby either indefinitely delaying independence or securing it under most inhospitable conditions. When we remember the hundreds of thousands who died in Hindu–Muslim violence alone and the colonial government's relative indifference to it, Gandhi's fears do not appear too unrealistic.

Just as Gandhi's *satyāgrahic* struggle for independence had no effective role for the poor, the unemployed, the landless labourers and the industrial workers, it had little political role for those at the other end of the economic spectrum either. He knew that the interests of some sections of the big bourgeoisie and large landlords were tied up with those of the colonial government or foreign capitalists, and that they had only a limited and essentially instrumental interest in independence. He also knew that most of the rest were anxious not to alienate the government, which had the power to damage their commercial interests by such means as the exchange rate, taxes, trading arrangements and the import policy. He was acutely aware that they generally disapproved of his *satyāgrahas*, both because these created an economically harmful climate of uncertainty and because they raised the expectations of and gave the mobilised masses a sense of power. That was why they preferred the Swarāj Party's policy of council entry and even encouraged it to take over the political leadership of the Congress, leaving Gandhi with his humanitarian programme. This was also why they brought pressure on him not to launch the Civil Disobedience Movement, to settle it quickly after it had begun and attend the Round Table Conference, and had even tried to subvert its second phase.

Though Gandhi, thus, neither needed nor expected the active political support of the big bourgeoisie, he needed their money to run the Congress organisation, to help those who had suffered in *satyāgrahas* and, above all, to finance his constructive programme. To be sure, his financial needs were not very large. The Congress did not have a large bureaucracy and was mainly manned by volunteers. The constructive programme was run by dedicated volunteers, many of them middle-class women brought into public life for the first time. It was striking that the Indian capitalists were unwilling to meet even the limited Congress expenses. Most contributed nothing or very little or did so on a one-off basis. When asked by Gandhi to raise money from the caste Hindus to provide higher education for Harijans, G.D. Birla replied:

> In Delhi, I walked from door to door for two days and I got only Rs. 1500 after great difficulty. One big contractor, who is supposed to be a great reformer and a Congressman ... promised to pay, but never paid. Ahmedabad is also helpless. In Bombay, four Marwari firms, after having promised subscription, are withholding payment. I do not think this is because people do not like the work. But everybody wants to evade payment, if it is at all possible.... I confess that I cannot bring money from others.[21]

Only a few such as Birla, Bajaj and Ambalal Sarabhai were generous with their help. Even that was irregular and modest, and Gandhi often had to write plaintive letters to Birla to help out organisations threatened with bankruptcy. Birla made sure that none of the money went to finance Gandhi's political work. Some of the Indian capitalists were so timid that they kept their contributions secret and sometimes withdrew them under government pressure. Even Birla felt the pressure when Lord Linlithgow, whom he had diligently cultivated, cut him off from his social circle for allegedly financing the independence movement in 1940. Birla reassured the Viceroy's secretary that he was a 'Gandhi-man' not 'a Congressman', but to no avail.[22] He sadly noted, 'this brings to an end my relations with the Viceroy. What wooden minds these men have got'.[23]

The meanness of the Indian capitalists was not lost on a man as shrewd as Gandhi. He knew that they were only interested in their profits, had no social conscience, and used him and the Congress to extract economic concessions from the government. He knew too that during the two World Wars, especially the Second, they had created an artificial scarcity of consumer goods, engaged in black marketeering and used the emergency regulations to repress their workers. What Gandhi really thought of the Indian capitalists is evident in his attitude to Birla, who was like a son to him and whose relations with him arouse strong Marxist suspicions.

In spite of their close friendship and the considerable financial help he had obtained from him, Gandhi remained deeply suspicious of Birla and said so both in private and public. He regretted that Birla had taken no steps to become a trustee of his property and had let him down. When Birla set up a mill in the princely state of Gwalior, the government obtained the land for him without paying adequate compensation to its poor owners. Gandhi pursued the matter with him in a series of letters, and told him to drop the project rather than harm the 'just and legitimate interests of the poor'. When Gandhi received complaints about the mill, he asked Birla for an explanation. Birla blamed local 'agitators' for stirring up trouble. Gandhi wrote back, 'The dispossessed class is today full of rancour. There is no denying the fact that they have been sinned against and as a class we have a lot to expiate for, not necessarily our sins but of the system with which we are identified'. The attempt to exonerate Birla as an individual but to inculpate him as a member of his class was typical of Gandhi. He asked Birla to show understanding and generosity 'not in a spirit of virtue but as a simple discharge of debt overdue'.

When Tata, Birla and Kasturbhai Lalbhai led an industrial delegation to Britain just before independence, Gandhi feared that they might compromise India's vital interests by establishing unacceptable links with their British counterparts. He issued a public statement warning them against a 'shameful deal'. Birla was most upset and cabled Gandhi from Cairo asking why his integrity and patriotism were being doubted. Gandhi reiterated his view in a telegram, and to rub salt in the wound, blessed him in the name of 'famishing and naked India'. He followed it up with a letter saying that Birla and his associates had no reason to be upset 'provided they are sincere in their protestations of injured innocence', and pouring scorn on Tata's alleged concern for the poor. The distraught Birla assured him that Tata was a 'genuine article', and asked to know once again why his patriotism was impugned. Gandhi's reply is not traceable.[24]

III

The Congress under Gandhi's leadership, then, was a middle-class organisation enjoying the support and loyalty of small traders, merchants, the middle and upper peasantry and the professional classes. They were at the centre of the struggle for independence, went to jail, shed their blood, lost their property, suffered domestic and other privations, and, in general, formed Gandhi's 'army for swarāj'. Since they formed the social basis of the Congress, they shaped its ethos, ideals, language of discourse and manner of debating and resolving differences, and created and sustained a distinct Congress culture. The big bourgeoisie at one end of the economic spectrum and the poor, the unemployed and the rural and urban proletariat at the other were not an integral part of the Congress. They neither shared its dominant ethos nor thought of it as their political home, and some of them had their own separate organisations and parties.

Gandhi, however, did not and indeed could not afford to ignore these groups. The Congress was a national party, aiming and claiming to represent all Indians and confronting the colonial government in their name. He knew that by ignoring them, it risked driving them into the arms of the government all too willing to 'divide and rule' its subjects. He was also anxious to evolve a broad national consensus among the country's different groups and communities in order to give the independence movement a broader social and ideological basis and to bequeath independent India a measure of ideological coherence. Since the Congress under him had captured and consolidated the middle ground of Indian politics, he thought it was well-equipped to mediate between the social and economic extremes. It could provide a public forum where all the major groups could meet under its stewardship, debate their differences, get to know one another and evolve a widely acceptable consensus.

Without losing its distinct social basis, the Congress under Gandhi's leadership, therefore, sought to become a broad-based anti-imperialist movement and evolved a complex network of relationship with groups falling outside it. Though it did not mobilise and recruit them, it maintained a constant dialogue with them. It invited them to make representations to it on important issues, sometimes succeeded in persuading their spokesmen to join it, and, in general, remained a relatively open organisation. Such an arrangement also suited those outside as it enabled them to influence Congress policy without risking government displeasure, compromising their ideology or losing their political independence. They, therefore, took full advantage of it, with the result that no major social group was without its sympathisers in the Congress.

Over time, the Congress became a broad 'church' accommodating individuals and organisations representing a wide variety of views and interests. The Swarājists occupied important positions within it and were allowed to speak in its name. Until the communists were barred from holding office because of their position on the 'people's war', they too participated in its elections at all levels and held high offices, including membership of the All India Congress Committee (AICC). For years, the Socialist Party functioned as a ginger group within the Congress, and Gandhi went out of his way to ensure that its views were heard and its members adequately represented at various organisational levels.

In all this, Gandhi played the skilful role of head of the 'national family'. He presided over the internal debates within the Congress, often acting as a kind of conduit through which different groups spoke to one another. He sensitised peasants and landlords, capitalists and workers, intellectuals and illiterate masses, communists and conservatives, caste Hindus and untouchables to each other's expectations, hopes and fears, and urged them to settle their differences in the spirit of justice and goodwill befitting the members of a 'common family'. He threw his weight behind different groups at different times and ensured that none felt neglected. He repeatedly attacked Indian capitalists, held them under check on many occasions, made sure that they did not take over the Congress, alerted the country to their machinations, and instilled in it a healthy suspicion of them. While chiding the poor and the landless peasants for their impatience, lack of discipline and 'immoderate language', he pleaded their cause and kept their concerns before the national consciousness. Although his constructive programme was a woefully inadequate answer to India's appalling problems and had an extremely limited practical impact, its symbolic and pedagogical value was considerable. It stressed the interdependence of political and economic issues, encouraged a sense of solidarity with the poor, helped create a dedicated group of grassroots workers capable of mobilising the masses, and fostered a tradition of social service.

Though organisationally the Congress had a narrow social base, its ideological and political orientation was much broader. That was why it could legitimately claim to be and was widely accepted as a national organisation entitled to speak in the name of all or at least most Indians. M.N. Roy felt compelled to conclude on the basis of his assessment of the communist experience between 1920 and 1934 that 'no movement can be organized separately and in opposition to the movement led by the Congress'. As B.T. Ranadive put it later, all those who pitted themselves against it were inevitably routed. Once we reject the naive view that the masses were victims of false consciousness or mesmerised by the Mahātmā's mysterious magic, their varying degrees of loyalty to the Congress can only be explained in terms of their belief that it represented, however inadequately, some of their basic interests and aspirations.[25]

The Congress under Gandhi then had an intricate and ingenious structure. It had a middle-class or 'petty bourgeois' core, around which it gathered a wide variety of groups. It offered its hospitality to different views and interests, but it was a home only for the middle classes. It provided a public forum for and sought to arbitrate between all Indians, but it had a definite structural, ideological and social basis that set limits to its national character and to the kind of consensus it evolved. Basically it was wedded to the politics of accommodation and compromise, avoided extremes of all types, and sought to occupy the middle ground. It was concerned about the poor and informed by a spirit of social service, but it remained deeply fearful of their 'extremism' and propensity to violence, and did not encourage or even allow them to lead the movement for their liberation. It had a healthy suspicion of the rich and was critical of the evils of capitalism, but it was committed to the defence of private property. Thanks to its distinct middle-class bias, it had a fairly firm identity, an inner point of balance, a measure of autonomy and resilience which saved it from being hijacked by either the right or the left. From time to time, it did swing towards either extreme, but always within a limited range and eventually returned to its normal state of accommodation and compromise.

Although the Congress had a middle-class social basis and bias, it also aspired for a truly national consensus based on the reconciliation of the interests of all major social groups. The hiatus between its composition and aspirations, its social base and ideological consciousness, created problems. The excluded groups had to rely on their sympathisers within the Congress and access to its influential leaders, especially Gandhi, to ensure that their interests received adequate attention. Though all major groups had these advantages, the big bourgeoisie had a considerable edge over the rest. They were politically more skilful and had their professional lobbyists within the Congress; some of them also controlled and many of the rest enjoyed unhindered access to the media; and some others had strong social and familial ties with the Congress leadership. There was also a broad similarity of views between them and many a middle-class group active within the Congress. Some industrialists acted as intermediaries between the Congress and government and were politically important. Some of them financially helped out Congress leaders, as when Birla regularly sent *hundis* to Rajaji, Dalmia financed the provincial elections in Bihar, and several industrial houses offered investment and other opportunities to politically-friendly leaders. The poor, the industrial workers, the agricultural labourers, the poor farmers and others had no such ideological, political, financial, organisational and other advantages. They had to rely largely on periodic riots and agitations and the support of the socially conscious sections of the middle, especially the professional classes, to ensure that they were not forgotten.

Since the weaker sections of society had no real role to play in the struggle for independence as Gandhi conducted it, they were barely visible within it. Hardly any of their leaders was ever elected or appointed to a local or regional Congress committee, let alone to the AICC or as Congress president. Thanks to Gandhi, they were a pervasive *moral* presence within the Congress but, since they lacked an organised and effective voice of their own, they had no *political* presence. Being nowhere near its centre of power, they were not involved in shaping its agenda and priorities. Unlike the middle classes and the spokesmen of the big bourgeoisie, they lacked constant access to him and were unable to put moral and political pressure on him. The largely westernised middle-class radicals led by Jawaharlal Nehru were the only spokesmen the poor had within the Congress. Though they were generally sincere, their pressure lacked urgency, passion, defiance and tenacity. Within such a politically unbalanced context, Gandhi's deep moral concern for the poor and the oppressed could not find adequate institutional articulation.

Not surprisingly, the Congress, which intended to be and generally remained a more or less evenly balanced coalition of classes and interests under middle-class leadership, tended on some occasions to tilt towards the big bourgeoisie. Though Gandhi's 'simple but vital' 11-point programme presented to the Viceroy before the Civil Disobedience Movement in 1930 included such items as reduction of land revenue by half and abolition of the salt tax, it included several others that were designed to promote the interests of the Indian bourgeoisie. The Gandhi–Irwin Pact had a similar thrust. Gandhi knew that the constructive programme was desperately starved of resources, but did little save rebuke the rich for their meanness. When he saw the condition of the agricultural labourers in Bardoli, he bitterly accused the Patidars of 'swadeshi Dyerism' but again, did not launch a movement against them. In the thirties, he pressurised the government to protect Indian textile industries against Japanese competition, but did not demand then or on similar other occasions later that the industrialists in return should support his pro-poor causes.[26]

Gandhi could have avoided the periodic Congress tilt towards the big bourgeoisie and developed a truly national consensus by mobilising the weaker sections of society and giving them an effective political presence within it. He did not do so largely because of the constraints of the struggle for independence. He knew well that the poor were angry and frustrated and seething with the 'spirit of violence'.[27] He was also aware of their role in the Russian and Chinese revolutions, to both of which he was a contemporary witness. He was, therefore, deeply afraid that once they were mobilised and their expectations aroused, large-scale violence was bound to result which neither he nor the Congress would be able to control and of which the colonial government was likely to be the sole beneficiary. Not surprisingly, he strongly disapproved of their spontaneous movements and did not allow even the Congress to lead and organise their campaigns beyond a certain point and without his consent.

Gandhi, therefore, decided to proceed with extreme caution. He repeatedly warned and attacked the rich in the hope of encouraging a conciliatory attitude. He urged the middle classes to take up the cause of the poor and the oppressed and provide a 'responsible' leadership. At the same time, he repeatedly urged the latter to be patient and eschew violence. He hoped in these and other ways to create a moral and political climate in which independent India could embark upon an effective anti-poverty programme. As long as India was fighting for its independence, he was not prepared to risk social violence. Once it became free, he was convinced that the poor and the oppressed would 'justifiably' launch *satyāgrahas* in a more propitious climate and with greater chances of success. As we saw, he was not opposed to their violence either. He was prepared under certain circumstances to put up with their 'defensive' and 'understandable' violence, and to rely on the state to put down the counterviolence of the rich. In other words, Gandhi's theory of nonviolence did not undermine or emasculate his economic radicalism as his Marxist commentators have argued. Rather, he was not prepared to permit violence during the course of the struggle for independence.

IV

In the light of our discussion, we can conclude that though the Marxist interpretation of Gandhi contains important and valid insights, it is oversimplified, and that the picture is complex and messy. The Congress under his leadership was *not* a party of the big bourgeoisie. Although it did not reject the institution of private property, it assigned the state a considerable regulative and redistributive role, stressed the pursuit of social justice, and was not an advocate of unrestrained capitalism. To say, as some Marxists do, that *since* the Congress did not advocate abolition of the capitalist mode of production, it was, *therefore*, its spokesman is to take too simple-minded a view of the range of political possibilities open to radicals. The Congress was essentially a middle-class party, constantly reaching out to new groups and interests on both sides of the economic spectrum and aiming to evolve a broad and fluctuating economic consensus that was neither wholly capitalist nor fully socialist and not heavily biased towards a particular group. Right-wing and left-wing ideas grew up around its 'petty-bourgeois' core and both shaped and were in turn shaped by it. Nehru put the point well: 'Even our more reactionary people are not so rigid in their reactions as they are probably in Europe and America. And even our most advanced people are somehow influenced by Gandhiji. He created connecting links between conflicting interests'.[28]

The flow of political influence and the process of moral sensitisation between different groups proceeded in both directions. The big bourgeoisie did influence the Congress and enjoy a measure of political power as the Marxists argue, but they were also required to recognise the legitimate demands of the poor and the oppressed. The middle and upper peasantry did from time to time link up with the big bourgeoisie, but it also retained its independence, threw up leaders of status and class loyalty, and influenced Congress policies on important matters. Many of these leaders were not created by or in any way indebted to the big bourgeoisie, and had come to power on the basis of their personal sacrifices and leadership of peasant struggles. They had constituencies which they could not lightly ignore and whose interests they could not subordinate to those of some other class. The Marxist commentators exaggerate the situation when they claim that Gandhi delivered the peasantry to the capitalists.

Thanks to the logic of the nationalist movement under Gandhi's leadership, the Congress contained mutually regulating pro-bourgeois as well as pro-poor, pro-industrialist as well as pro-peasantry tendencies within its overall middle-class framework. Since Gandhi failed to mobilise the poor, the pro-capitalist tendency was stronger; but the anti-bourgeois tendency was neither absent nor too weak to offer strong resistance. Thanks to its middle-class bias, the Congress did not allow itself to be taken over by either tendency. From its relatively secure and autonomous ideological point of balance, it arbitrated between them.

It knew that it could not pursue pro-capitalist policies for long without feeling morally troubled, provoking internal resistance, and losing its inner point of balance. As Bipan Chandra puts it: 'Indian National Congress was a popular, multi-class movement. It was not a movement controlled by the bourgeoisie, nor did the bourgeoisie exercise exclusive control over it'.[29]

Any interpretation of Gandhi must also take full account of his complex personal and political relationship with the Left. Although some of his beliefs and actions were strongly and rightly criticised by the intellectuals of the Left, it is striking that most of them never left him, that some of those who did such as J.P. Narayan eventually returned to him, and that even his fiercest critics such as M.N. Roy later changed their view of him. It is, of course, true that his hold over the Indian masses was so great that no one dared challenge him, and in any case he was shrewd and determined enough to outsmart anyone who did, as Subhas Chandra Bose and even Jawaharlal Nehru painfully realised. Many Left-wing leaders with political ambitions, therefore, thought it prudent not to fall foul of him. The Left also knew that its best hope of propagating its relatively unfamiliar radical ideas and policies lay in securing his patronage by means of quiet persuasion and persistent pressure.

All this, however, represents only part of the story. Although Gandhi and the Left needed and used each other, they were also bound by deeper bonds. The bonds were not entirely personal and emotional, for many on the Left did not enjoy the kind of intimacy with Gandhi that Nehru, Narayan, Rajkumari Amrit Kaur, Aruna Asaf Ali and others did. It would seem that many of them were morally overwhelmed by the fact that while they were content to preach their doctrines Gandhi actually lived by his, and that his concern for the poor and the oppressed was no less sincere and deep than theirs. They also seem to have felt that he had raised basic questions about the nature of modernity, the dangers of revolutionary violence, and the character of Indian society which they had long ignored and with which they needed to come to terms. Even as Marx discovered a radical kernel underneath Hegel's apparently conservative vocabulary, many on the Left seem to have thought, rightly in my view, that Gandhi's apparently conservative form of thought had a strong radical content which they should tease out and build upon.

Though Marxist commentators rightly point out that Gandhi did not provide a realistic *alternative* to capitalism, they are wrong not to appreciate that his thought had enough resources to criticise and transform it fairly radically. His endorsement of the Dantwala draft is a good starting point. Its proposals for a socially regulated and accountable system of production, minimum income differentials, the severely restricted right to property, a minimum decent wage, war on poverty, etc., have a genuinely radical thrust. This is also the case with Gandhi's ideas of a heavy death duty, a national plan that gave agriculture its due importance and did not exploit the villages, and nationalisation of key industries. Even his otherwise elusive concept of trusteeship opens up new possibilities if creatively reinterpreted on the basis of Gandhi's own remarks. It is widely accepted that the government is a trustee of the interests of society and may be legitimately disobeyed or removed if it violates its trust. In many other areas of life too, we appoint trustees and hold them accountable for the way they run their organisations. Once we challenge the moral basis of the right to property in the means of production, there is no obvious reason why industries and businesses should not be conducted along similar lines. That would involve such things as denial of the absolute right of ownership, the owner's accountability to his or her workers and the society at large for the way he or she runs his or her business, workers' councils, and industrial democracy. All this is, of course, vague but it indicates how Gandhi's thought could be interpreted and applied in practice. Thanks to the constraints of the nationalist struggle, he did not fully exploit the radical tendencies of his thought.[30] No such constraints existed in independent India. Had his followers mobilised these tendencies, creatively reinterpreted them in the light of the country's needs, mounted a carefully planned campaign of peasants' and workers' *satyāgrahas*, and in these and other ways compelled the Nehru government to adopt a more egalitarian and just path of development, Gandhi would have been the patron saint of a very different India and the Marxists would then have most probably read him differently.

The question as to why Gandhians did not mount a radical movement does, of course, remain. Since it is too large and complex to answer here, a few words should suffice. The answer to the question would seem to lie in a combination of such factors as the Nehru government's unwillingness to harness the radical component of Gandhi's moral and economic thought in its battle with the conservative forces within the Congress, Gandhians' failure to rethink their role and strategy in independent India especially the place of *satyāgraha* in a democratic state, their early acquiescence in Nehru's attempt to turn Gandhi not just into the father of Indian independence but of the nation itself and use him to legitimise the kind of state he was busy creating, and their inability to throw up leaders with the skill and patience to build up a nationwide alternative to Congress and mobilise the excluded groups around clearly-defined issues.

Gandhi's own ambivalence and confusions also played a part. Nehru was rightly his chosen political heir, and Gandhi spent the last few months of his life urging his followers to leave Nehru and his colleagues alone in their task of designing and consolidating the Indian state. When, for example, they complained that the Constituent Assembly had made no provision for Panchayat Raj, he urged them to be patient, stay away from political activity, and concentrate instead on the constructive programme. He intended the programme to encompass much more than its conventional content and to include encouraging voter registration, highlighting local grievances, and even peaceful *satyāgrahas*.[31] However, he did not have the time or the energy fully to spell out all this, with the result that many of his followers took his advice to imply a neat division of labour between politics and social work, one to be left to the government and his 'political' heir, the other to his *āshrams* and voluntary workers led by his 'spiritual' heir Vinoba Bhave. Since Gandhi drew no distinction between politics and spirituality, this was an understandable but wholly misguided interpretation of his post-independence project.

The consequences of the misinterpretation for which Gandhi bears at least some responsibility soon became obvious. Since the Nehru government was naturally unsure as to how Gandhians would respond to its actions and policies and could not afford to risk a direct confrontation with them, it was anxious to neutralise some (for example, J.P. Narayan), marginalise some others (for example, Dr Lohia) and to win over and even incorporate the rest into the Indian state. It did so partly for obvious political reasons and partly because it genuinely believed that rebuilding India required the cooperation of all available talents and political and non-political organisations. Its beliefs was correct but wrongly articulated. Rather than seek their cooperation on state's terms and within the limits set by it, Gandhian and other organisations should have been left alone, as they were best able to make their vital contribution if allowed and even encouraged to act as the state's critic, conscience and unofficial opposition. Since, thanks to its statist approach, the Nehru government did not see things this way, it took over the constructive programme as part of its political project, gave it financial support, even helped raise public funds for it, and patronised Vinoba and his associates. Over time, most of the Gandhians involved in Vinoba's movement built up embrassingly close alliances with the local Congress leadership, worked closely with the government at state and national levels, remained confined to the reformist task set by the state, and virtually lost their identity, autonomy, and radical impulse.

There was still the awkward question of *satyāgraha*, a critical constituent of Gandhi's legacy. Vinoba obligingly redefined it to exclude all forms of conflict and to mean nothing more than gentle moral appeals to the government and vested interests. When urged by some of his colleagues to turn his campaign into a mass movement rather than restrict it to his chosen workers by mobilising landless workers and peasants and leading their marches from one village to the next, he rejected the idea as a recipe for 'class war'.[32] Even within his self-imposed limits, his movement could have been radical if, as advised by his colleagues, he had not distributed the land but used it for model cooperative farms,[33] or concentrated on developing select villages in each district and setting examples to the rest of the country rather than dissipate his energy by falling prey to the 'quantification complex' and counting the amount of land donated to him as opposed to the quality of work done on and with it.[34]

When the Gandhians realised how much they had become an appendage of the state and how little economic and social impact they made on India's appalling problems, they felt deeply confused and disorientated. Vinoba had no answer. He went into a year of silence and then told his followers to do what they liked. Some left his movement, some others half-heartedly continued with it, a few fell for J.P. Narayan's desperate and misguided revolt against the Indian state itself. Since the revolt was conducted in the name of a naively moralistic and politically unrealistic idea of an ill-defined 'total revolution', by means that bore little relevance to Gandhi's *satyāgraha*, and with the support of such groups as the R.S.S. and Jan Sangh who shared nothing in common with Gandhi and who or whose likes he had bitterly fought most of his active life, J.P.'s movement was as un-Gandhian as Vinoba's, albeit for very different reasons. It is difficult to say which of the two did the Gandhian heritage more damage.[35]

What I have said so far is only intended to indicate broadly how we might go about explaining the Gandhians' failure to live up to his legacy and not to provide a full explanation, which would have to include such factors as the politics of post-independence India, the social groups that were available for mass mobilisation, the available space for Gandhian intervention, the constraints of India's mixed economy, and the quality of Gandhian leadership. Whatever the full explanation might turn out to be, the fact remains that there is far more to Gandhi than what his followers have done with him. 'Gandhism' is not an abstract, static, and historically frozen body of thought but a cluster of tendencies, some conservative, others radical, yet others a dialectical blend of both. It is nothing more or less than how we read Gandhi and what we do with him, a product of *our* praxis. By continuing to read and treat him as a bourgeois apologist, Marxist commentators reject a valuable ally and waste a vital political and rhetorical resource. Paradoxical as it might seem, by using his still considerable moral authority to legitimise and propagate their project of a long overdue radical transformation of India, Marxists might do more justice to his legacy than his self-proclaimed followers.[36]

Endnotes

Preface

1. I thank Amalendu Misra for his considerable help with the revised edition, and Professors Benjamin Barber, Guy Welbon, Michael Sandel, Seyla Benhabib and Paul Thomas for sharing their thoughts on Gandhi.
2. Since Chatterjee's book came out just before I had completed mine, I was unable to discuss it at length. Ronald Terchek's excellent *Gandhi: Struggling for Autonomy* (Lanham: Rowman and Littlefield Publishers, 1998) only came to my attention while I was correcting the proofs of this revised edition, and hence I have not been able to discuss it here.
3. Although they are highly suggestive, I have some difficulty with Cox's general approach to Gandhi and his wider theory of the individual's relation to culture. Since my book does not deal with these questions, it has not been possible to incorporate a detailed discussion of Cox in this revised edition.
4. Although I use the terms nationalist movement and thought, I do so only because of the unavailability of better alternatives. Many so-called 'nationalists' leaders did not think of India as a nation and even want it to become one. Furthermore, the terms 'nation' and its cognates or their local equivalents did not become current in India until the 1880s or thereabout, and cannot be used without adequate qualifications to describe earlier writers. The same caution needs to be exercised in talking about the history of Indian independence movement. Until it become a serious political possibility and demand, those who challenged this or that aspect of colonial rule cannot be said to be fighting for or even precursors of the struggle for 'independence'.
5. F.J. Blum, who left Germany in 1938 because of Nazi persecution and settled as an academic in the United States, spent some time with J.P. Narayan and Vinoba Bhave in the 1960s and 1970s. He interviewed over a dozen of Gandhi's close associates at some length in 1973 and 1978, asking them questions about the man, his philosophy, impact, legacy and experiments in celibacy. He died

before he could complete his book. The transcripts of his interviews are happily available at the Abbey in Sutton Courtnay near Oxford. I am grateful to Arna Blum, Barbara Vellacott and the Community at the Abbey for giving me the permission to consult and quote from the transcripts. Among the interviewees Achyut Patwardhan, who showed strange but understandable nervousness when interviewed in February 1978, insisted that his interview should remain anonymous. With one solitary and innocuous exception on Ch. 9, fn. 34, I have respected his wishes. Blum's transcripts are hereafter cited as Blum Papers.

6. In his interview with Blum, Pyarelal insists that they were not experiments but intended to 'put a theory to test' in 'the course of performance of duty', the theory being that a fully non-violent and sincere person is able to evoke a similar response from others. Since putting a theory to test is an experiment in its conventional sense, I fail to see Pyarelal's distinction. He was also interviewed on this subject by Ved Mehta for his *Mahatma Gandhi and his Apostles*. He complains bitterly about the book, saying that Mehta 'has put into my mouth over fifteen statements and each of them is either a caricature or is the reverse'. He claims that the *New Yorker*, where Mehta's article had first appeared, even refused to publish his rejoinder. In these matters, misunderstanding is easy and neither side is likely to be above reproach.

7. I am particularly grateful to Usha Mehta, Himmat Zaveri and Gopal Gandhi who in personal conversations, and to Manju Zaveri and Pravin Sheth who in long and kind reviews, pointed out these two mistakes. P.C. Upadhyay's long, confused and tendentious review in *Economic and Political Weekly* (2.10.1989), to which I replied (*EPW*, 23.10.1989), rightly criticises me on this point as on a couple of others.

8. For somewhat exaggerated contemporary accounts, see *The Sunday Times*, London (22.10.1989) and *The Economist* (28.10.1989). The support of Sir Richard Attenborough, who said that his film 'would have needed twenty minutes to set Gandhi's celibacy experiments into context', was particularly helpful in diffusing the situation. I was also privileged to have the unstinting support of C.B. Patel, the late I.K. Patel, and Amit Roy.

Chapter One

1. J.C. Heesterman, *The Inner Conflict of Tradition* (Delhi: Oxford University Press, 1985), pp. 23, 41, 43 f, 177.
2. For a good discussion see John Pocock's 'Time, Institutions and Action: An Essay on Traditions and their Understanding' in Preston

King and B.C. Parekh (eds.), *Politics and Experience* (Cambridge: Cambridge University Press, 1968).
3. For perceptive discussions, see Paul Younger, *Introduction to Indian Religious Thought* (Philadelphia: Westminster Press, 1972), ch. 5; Pratima Bowes, *The Hindu Religious Tradition: A Philosophical Approach* (London: Routledge & Kegan Paul, 1977), ch. 1; Lloyd and Suzanne Rudolph, *The Modernity of Tradition* (Chicago: Chicago University Press, 1966); and Heesterman, op. cit., ch. 1.
4. P.V. Kane, *History of Dharmashāstras* (Poona: Bhandarkar Oriental Research Institute, 1973).
5. Ibid., Vol. III, p. 31.
6. Ibid., p. 862.
7. Ibid., p. 867.
8. For useful material see Benoy Ghose (ed.), *Selections from English Periodicals of Nineteenth Century Bengal*, Vol. I to VI (Calcutta: Papyrus, 1980). Ordinary Hindus wrote letters to newspapers and journals protesting against social rigidity and condemning the orthodox. One widow pleaded for the right to remarry and debunked 'silver-headed Brahmins and big-bellied baboos,' ibid., Vol. III, p. 209.
9. P.V. Kane, op. cit., Vol. III, pp. 890 ff.
10. For a critical evaluation see ch. 3. Gandhi remained a marginal man all his life. After nearly twenty-four years abroad, three in London and twenty-one in South Africa where he spent a good deal of his time with his Jewish and Christian friends, he was and all his life remained something of an 'insider–outsider' in India. Even in India he spent many years in prisons and thus at its inner margins. His background and development also had several unusual features. His mother belonged to the Punami sect which, though Hindu, had several Islamic features. As a child he was exposed to Jain influence. His best childhood friend and later his employer and clients were mostly Muslims. His closest friends in South Africa with some of whom he lived on a communal farm were Jews and Christians. The impact of Judaism on his thought is often not fully appreciated. As Fred Dallmayer puts it, 'seen from this angle . . . Gandhi emerges as a figure critically inhabiting the margins of cultures—one employing his marginality precisely in order to tease out novel ways of cultural interaction or of reciprocal challenge and response'. See his unpublished paper, 'Gandhi as Mediator between East and West' presented at a conference on Phenomenology and Indian Philosophy in Delhi, 1988.
11. 'Every one of the Indians who has achieved anything worth mentioning in any direction is the fruit, directly or indirectly, of Western education. At the same time, whatever reaction for the better he may have had upon the people at large was due to the

extent he retained his eastern culture.' Quoted in T.K. Mahadevan, *Dvija* (Delhi: Affiliated East-West Press, 1977), p. 178.
12. Gandhi himself said that he had acquired some of the basic insights into the nature of *ahimsā* from Tolstoy. 'I have nothing to be ashamed of if my views on *ahimsā* are the result of my Western education', ibid., p. 179. For a stimulating discussion of the interplay between Christianity and Hinduism in Gandhi's thought, see M.M. Thomas, *The Acknowledged Christ of the Indian Renaissance* (London, SCM Press, 1969). The book is a perceptive account of a dialogue between the two religions from Ram Mohun Roy onwards.
13. The best discussion of the subject still remains Eric Stokes, *The English Utilitarians and India* (Oxford: Clarendon Press, 1959).
14. Quoted in Tapan Raychaudhuri, *Europe Reconsidered* (Delhi: Oxford University Press, 1988), p. 155 (emphasis added).
15. Ibid., p. 315 (emphasis added).
16. For excellent discussions see Lloyd and Suzanne Rudolph, *The Modernity of Tradition* (Chicago: University of Chicago Press, 1966) and Heesterman, op. cit., ch. 11.
17. *The Collected Works of Mahatma Gandhi* (Ahmedabad: Navajivan, 1958), Vol. 35, p. 123. This work is hereafter referred to as *CW*.

Chapter Two

1. The ranks of traditionalists included Bhudev Mukhopadhyay, Rajnarayan Basu, movements led by Sasadhar Tarkachudamani and Krishnabihari Sen, and the journal *Bangabasi* which had a circulation of nearly fifty thousand. Damodar Chapekar declared in his *Autobiography*, 'We like all the Hindu customs . . . . There is no necessity for innovation'. He went on, 'We have taken a vow to treat even our father as our enemy if he infringed the *shāstras*'. He and his brother went about breaking up reformist meetings and even burnt down the pandal of the Social Conference. The traditionalist influence was so strong in some parts of India that there was no demand for British-established schools and colleges.
2. Quoted in Raychaudhuri, *Europe Reconsidered*, (Delhi: Oxford University Press, 1988), p. 70.
3. The usual reference was to *sholkas* 13 to 15 in ch. 16 of the *Gitā*.
4. Raychaudhuri, op. cit., p. 92.
5. Ibid., p. 73.
6. For a good discussion see Dennis Dalton, *Indian Idea of Freedom* (Gurgaon: The Academic Press, 1982), pp. 35 f.

330 Colonialism, Tradition and Reform

7. Sri Aurobindo, *The Foundations of Indian Culture* (Pondicherry: Sri Aurobindo Ashram, 1959), p. 29.
8. Raychaudhuri, op. cit., pp. 153 f.
9. See his *Swaraj, The Goal and the Way* (Madras: Upendra, 1921) and *The Spirit of Indian Nationalism* (London: Hind Nationalist Agency, 1910).
10. V.C. Joshi (ed.), *Lala Lajpat Rai: Writings and Speeches* (Delhi: University Publishers, 1926), Vol. 1, pp. 37 f. See also ibid., pp. 56 f and 132 f.
11. Ibid., pp. 93 f.
12. See the remarks by Ram Mohun Roy, K.C. Sen and other Hindu leaders cited in J.K. Majumdar, *Indian Speeches and Documents on British Rule: 1821-1918* (London: Longman, Green & Co., 1937), pp. 15, 16, 88, 134, 152 and 156.
13. For good discussions see W.H. Forbes, *Positivism in Bengal* (Calcutta: 1975); Bimanbehari Majumdar, *History of Indian Social and Political Ideas: From Ram Mohun Roy to Dayananda* (Calcutta: Bookland Private Ltd., 1967); and M.M. Thomas, op. cit.
14. William Jones was one of the first Europeans to compare classical India to classical Athens.
15. J.K. Majumdar, op. cit., pp. 47, 84, 93, 134, 136 and 152.
16. Ibid., p. 156.
17. K.D. Nag and D. Burman (eds), *The English Works of Ram Mohun Roy* (Calcutta: 1958), Part IV, p. 83.
18. J.K. Majumdar, op. cit., p. 41, where Victor Jacquemant reports his conversations with Ram Mohun Roy.
19. For good discussions see Thomas Pantham and Kenneth L. Deutsch (eds.), *Political Thought in Moderrn India* (Delhi: Sage, 1986) and Donald Bishop (ed.), *Thinkers of the Indian Renaissance* (Delhi: Wiley Eastern Ltd., 1982). These and other such anthologies have a strange habit of missing out such important thinkers as Dadabhai Naoroji: Bipan Chandra Pal, Lala Lajpat Rai and Jayaprakash Narayan.
20. Referring to his father, Jawaharlal Nehru wrote: 'He was, of course, a nationalist in a vague sense of the word, but he admired Englishmen and their ways. He had a feeling that his own countrymen had fallen low and almost deserved what they got'. *An Autobiography* (London: Bodley Head, 1936), p. 5.
21. Bimanbehari Majumdar, op. cit., p. 200.
22. J.K. Majumdar, op. cit., p. 93. (emphasis added).
23. Ibid., p. 151. (emphasis added).
24. Ibid., p. 174. (emphasis added).
25. R.C. Majumdar, (ed.), *Struggle for Freedom* (Bombay: Bharatiya Vidya Bhavan, 1969), pp. 447 f. Referring to the rabid writings in such Anglo-Indian journals as the *Englishman* and the *Civil & Military*

Gazette, Henry Nevinson on a short visit to India wrote: 'It must have been difficult for any thoughtful Indian who loved his country to read them during 1907 without cursing our race'. He referred to their 'deliberate attempts to stir up race hatred and incite to violence' and their 'obvious instigation to indiscriminate manslaughter'. Even the Prince of Wales told Morley, the then Secretary of the State, how much he was upset by the behaviour of Europeans towards Indians. Lord Ampthill found it 'most painful' to see and to hear of insolent racist behaviour by the English, especially army officers, but did little. Ibid., pp. 450 f. Many such incidents are recollected by some of the eminent Indians in Zareer Masani, *Indian Tales of the Raj* (London BBC Books, 1987). See also Kenneth Ballhatchet, *Race, Sex and Class under the Raj* (London: Weidenfeld and Nicolson, 1980), and Reginald Reynolds, *The White Sahibs in India* (Connecticut: Greenwood Press, 1937), ch. XIII. The last book carries an interesting Foreword by Jawaharlal Nehru.

26. J.K. Majumdar, op. cit., p. 155. Most Indian leaders described the British government in India as 'despotic' or 'autocratic'. For some of them this was unavoidable in the Indian context, a view the British fully shared.
27. For a useful discussion see Anil Seal, *The Emergence of Indian Nationalism* (Cambridge: Cambridge University Press, 1968).
28. See Ravinder Kumar's excellent 'The New Brahmans of Maharashtra' in D.A. Low (ed.), *Soundings in Modern South Asian History* (Canberra: Australian National University Press, 1968). For their own reasons, lower castes welcomed British rule. Jyotiba Govinda Phule wrote, 'The creator has puposely sent the English people to this country to liberate the disabled sudras from the slavery of the crafty Aryas.' In his *Gulāmgiri* (1872) dedicated to American negroes, he argued that the Brahmins were 'worse exploiters' than the British. See Bimanbehari Majumdar, op. cit., pp. 165 f. The Raj was the lowest common denominator between the contending groups and seemed to most of them to be a lesser evil than the available alternative. No wonder it met little concerted opposition for long.
29. J.K. Majumdar, op. cit., p. 158.
30. Ibid., pp. 134 f.
31. In Bankim's *Anandamath*, Satyananda asks, 'Will the Muslims return?,' to which the divine voice replies: 'No. The English will rule.' For the fear of a Russian invasion see, J.K. Majumdar, op. cit., p. 152.
32. There is an understandable tendency among some Indian historians to condemn many of the nationalist leaders for not being more anti-British. The tendency arises from the failure to appreciate the deep

fears, hopes, a sense of hurt and humiliation, anxieties and calculations of the nationalist leaders. A good phenomenological account of their consciousness exploring their perceptions of India's predicament is long overdue.
33. I owe this point to a conversation with Professor B.R. Nanda.
34. For personal reminiscences of those involved see Zaheer Masani, op. cit., pp. 15, 27, 46, 47, 51, 89, 94, 110 and 111.
35. Modernists covered a wide group ranging from Young Bengal, radical writings in *Gyanvesan* and the *Enquirer* to M.N. Roy, the Hindustan Republican Association and the Communists. Dadabhai Naoroji, Pherozeshah Mehta, Motilal Nehru and the early Jawaharlal Nehru show a pronounced modernist tendency.
36. Cited in Dennis Dalton, *Indian Idea of Freedom* (Gurgaon: The Academic Press, 1982), p. 41. This excellent work contains many useful references to the views of the critical modernists and critical traditionalists.
37. For an illuminating discussion of Bankim, see Partha Chatterjee, *Nationalist Thought and the Colonial World* (Delhi: Oxford University Press, 1987).
38. See Dalton, op. cit., pp. 49 ff.
39. For interesting attempts to combine Indian and European ideas, see Sri Aurobindo, *The Ideal of Human Unity* (Pondicherry: Sri Aurobindo Ashram, 1950).
40. Sri Aurobindo, *The Foundations of Indian Culture* (Pondicherry: Sri Aurobindo Ashram, 1959), p. 389. For Bipan Chandra Pal, see his *The Spirit of Indian Nationalism* (London: Hind Nationalist Agency, 1910) and *Swaraj, The Goal and the Way* (Madras: Upendra, 1921).
41. Ibid., p. 388.
42. Ibid., pp. 322 ff. This chapter remains one of the best statements of the Indian search for an alternative to the modern state.
43. Dayananda Saraswati's reforms were extensive and radical. He was avoided 'like a leper' by orthodox Brahmins, and frequently accused of the 'spirit of hypercriticism' for his attacks on Hindu society. Sawarkar, a critical traditionalist, was an atheist.
44. Cited in Raychaudhuri, op. cit., p. 314.
45. Ibid., p. 267.

Chapter Three

1. Raghavan Iyer (ed.), *The Moral and Political Writings of Mahatma Gandhi* (Oxford: Clarendon Press, 1986), Vol. 1, p. 215.

2. For further discussion, see my *Gandhi's Political Philosophy* (London: Macmillan, 1989), ch. 4.
3. Iyer, op. cit., Vol. I, pp. 215 ff and 231 ff.
4. Ibid., pp. 291 f. Gandhi formulated the distinction in this way in South Africa.
5. *Harijan*, 9 May 1936; *Young India* 17 November 1920, and *Harijan*, 2 November 1947.
6. *Young India*, 11 August 1927; Iyer, op. cit., Vol. I, pp. 232 f.
7. Iyer, op. cit., Vol. I, p. 455 and pp. 471 f.
8. Christianity 'has shocked us into setting our own house in order', ibid., p. 455.
9. *CW*, Vol. 90, p. 125; for Gandhi's comprehensive critique of Indian character, see Iyer, op. cit., Vol. I, pp. 307 f.
10. *CW*, Vol. 14, pp. 444, 469, 475 and 510.
11. *CW*, Vol. 15, p. 2; *Harijan*, 29 August 1936; *Young India*, 20 December 1928.
12. *CW*, Vol. 24, p. 211.
13. *CW*, Vol. 7, p. 67; *Harijan*, 4 April 1936.
14. *CW*, Vol. 14, pp. 260 ff.
15. Ibid., p. 261.
16. *Young India*, 8 Januray 1925; 26 January 1921; 7 October 1926 and 11 August 1927.
17. *Young India*, 7 October 1926.
18. *CW*, Vol. 37, p. 167. The attack on 'dead' traditions is a recurrent theme in Gandhi's thought. He frequently talks about breaking out of their 'fetters' and 'tearing' and 'prising' open their 'hidden' meaning. See Iyer, op. cit., Vol. I, pp. 502 f.
19. *CW*, Vol. 87, pp. 90 f.
20. Iyer, op. cit., Vol. I, p. 504.
21. Ibid., pp. 289 f, 310 ff and 502 f; see also Preface to his *Autobiography*.
22. For Gandhi, moral truths are discovered by great religious leaders. Every society therefore depends on religion for its periodic regeneration.
23. Iyer, op. cit., Vol. I, p. 477. See also ibid., p. 502, where he says that every faith gets 'petrified' and needs 'a living reformation', and ibid., p. 517, where he calls theology an enemy of religion.
24. The idea that Hinduism is not so much a religion as a spiritual science is common among many Hindus.
25. The scriptures 'grew out of the necessities of particular periods' and could be revised in the light of new experiences and insights. Ibid., p. 502.
26. I have vivid recollections as a child of frequently hearing about my father, senior Gandhian leaders of my caste and teachers trying out 'experiments' in matters relating to diet, sleep, daily routine and personal relationships.

27. Iyer, op. cit., Vol. I, p. 88.
28. Ibid., pp. 137 f.
29. For a fuller discussion upon which I rely here, see ch. 4 in my *Gandhi's Political Philosophy*, op. cit.
30. Iyer, op. cit., Vol. I, pp. 13 f. and *Harijan*, 8 September 1940.
31. *CW*, Vol. 50, p. 237.
32. *CW*, Vol. 50, p. 194; *Harijan*, 29 August 1936 and Preface to *Autobiography*.
33. *Harijan*, 30 December 1939, 1 September 1940, 25 January 1942 and 28 July 1946. See also R.K. Prabhu (ed.), *Democracy: Real and Deceptive* (Ahmedabad: Navajivan, 1961).
34. Iyer, op. cit., Vol. I, p. 448.

Chapter Four

1. For good discussions of the Indian traditions of *ahimsā*, see Unto Tähtinen *Ahimsā: Non-violence in Indian Tradition* (Ahmedabad: Navajivan, 1976); D. Bhargava, *Jaina Ethics* (Delhi: Motilal Banarasidas, 1968); T.K. Unnithan and Yogendra Singh, *Traditions of Nonviolence* (Delhi: Arnold Heinemann, 1973); S. Radhakrishnan (ed.), *History of Philosophy, Eastern and Western* (London: George Allen and Unwin Ltd., 1952); E. Conze, *Buddhism: Its Essence and Development* (Oxford; Cassirer, 1960 and 1974); A. Schweitzer, *Indian Thought and its Development* (New York: 1936, Bombay: Wilco, 1960); William Theodore de Bary, *et al.*, *Sources of Indian Tradition* (Delhi: Motilal Banarasidas, 1972), 2 vols. Many of the quotations which follow are to be found in Tähtinen's book.
2. Gandhi thought that Tolstoy understood non-violence better than anyone, including the ancient Indian thinkers, and took over his concept of active love. Raghavan Iyer, *The Moral and Political Writings of Mahatma Gandhi* (Oxford: Clarendon Press, 1987), Vol. I, p. 116. To avoid misunderstanding. I am not suggesting that Hindu religious thought does not have the concept of or value love. It is obviously central to Vaishnavism and dominates the Tamil *Tirukural*. I am arguing that it is absent in the dominant *advaita* tradition, and that no tradition, including the Vaishnavaite, understands love in active and social terms.
3. Iyer, op. cit., Vol. II, p. 225.
4. Ibid., pp. 220 f and 325 f.
5. Ibid., p. 237.
6. Ibid.

7. *Young India*, 11 August 1920.
8. Ibid., 9 September 1925.
9. Iyer, op. cit., Vol. I, p. 117.
10. Ibid., p. 116.
11. Iyer, op. cit., Vol. II, p. 220.
12. Ibid., p. 264.
13. Ibid., p. 214.
14. Ibid., p. 352.
15. Ibid., p. 223.
16. *Young India*, 30 January 1930.
17. Iyer, op. cit., Vol. II, p. 274 and 307.
18. Ibid., pp. 234 ff and 270 ff.
19. Ibid., p. 276.
20. Ibid., pp. 213 ff and 276 f.
21. Ibid., pp. 269 f.
22. Ibid., pp. 270 f.
23. Ibid., p. 272.
24. Ibid., p. 282.
25. IBid., p. 280; also *Harijan*, 3 July 1937.
26. Iyer, op. cit., Vol. II, p. 222.
27. *Harijan*, 1 September 1940.
28. Iyer, op. cit., Vol. II, pp. 221 f.
29. Ibid., p. 387.
30. *Young India*, 29 May 1924.
31. Iyer, op. cit., Vol. II, p. 317.
32. *Young India*, 9 September 1926.
33. Iyer, Vol. II, p. 212. For Gandhi not so much the intention as the disposition of the moral agent was crucial to the evaluation of his act. See also M.K. Gandhi, *Non-violence in Peace and War* (Ahmedabad: Navajivan, 1942), Vol. II, pp. 129 f.
34. 'Violence and non-violence are mental attitudes, they concern the feelings in our hearts', Iyer, op. cit., Vol. II, p. 316.
35. Iyer, op. cit., note 2, Vol. II, p. 316.
36. Ibid., p. 274.
37. *Young India*, 18 May 1921.
38. *Young India*, 14 April 1927; and 17 July 1927.
39. *Harijan*, 9 June 1946; 5 May 1946; and 7 July 1946.
40. Iyer, op. cit., Vol. II, p. 432.
41. Ibid.
42. Ibid. p. 307.
43. Ibid., p. 347.
44. *CW*, Vol. 37, p. 270; *Young India*, 13 September 1928; *Harijan*, 5 May 1946; 9 September 1946; and 10 November 1946.

45. Iyer, op. cit., Vol. II, p. 431; *CW*, Vol. 25, p. 168; and *Harijan*, 25 August 1940.
46. For a detailed discussion see my *Gandhi's Political Philosophy*, ch. 4.
47. Louis Fischer, *The Life of Mahatma Gandhi* (Bombay: Bharatiya Vidya Bhavan, 1983), p. 421.
48. *Harijan*, 9 Decmber 1939; 21 October 1939; 8 September 1940; Iyer, op. cit., Vol. II, p. 438.
49. Iyer, op. cit., Vol. II, p. 438.
50. *Young India*, 15 December 1921; 4 August 1920; and 8 May 1941.
51. *Young India*, 16 June 1927; and 11 October 1928. See Iyer, op. cit., Vol. II, p. 451, where Gandhi says: 'A coward is less than man. He does not deserve to be a member of a society of men and women.'

Chapter Five

1. For useful accounts of the terrorist movement see R.C. Majumdar, *Struggle for Freedom* (Bombay: Bharatiya Vidya Bhavan, 1978), ch. VIII; K.K. Gangadharan, *Indian National Congress: Growth & Development* (Delhi: Kalamkar Prakashan, 1972), chs. 7 & 8; Ram Gopal, *How India Struggled for Freedom* (Bombay: Book Centre, 1967), pp. 111 ff, 179 ff, and 208 ff; and Bipan Chandra, *Nationalism & Colonialism in Modern India* (Delhi: Orient Longman, 1979), pp. 223 ff.
2. G.T. Trevelyan, *The Life & Letters of Lord Macaulay* (London: Longman, 1899), p. 655.
3. Raychaudhuri, op. cit., p. 18.
4. Ibid., p. 17; Nemai Sadhan Bose, *Racism, Struggle for Equality and Indian Nationalism* (Calcutta: Firma KLM Private Ltd., 1981), p. 217.
5. Bose, ibid., p. 216.
6. Ibid., p. 218.
7. For a good discussion of terrorist groups in London, see James Hunt, *Gandhi in London* (Delhi: Promilla Publishers, 1978), pp. 133 f. G.K. Chesterton was not much impressed by them. He wrote: 'The principal weakness of Indian Nationalism seems to be that it is not very Indian and not very national. It is all about Herbert Spencer and Heaven knows what. What is the good of the Indian national spirit if it cannot protect its people from Herbert Spencer? . . . . One of the papers, I understand, is called the *Indian Sociologist*. What are the young men of India doing that they allow such an animal as a sociologist to pollute their ancient villages and poison their kindly homes?

'When all is said, there is a rational distinction between a people asking for its own ancient life and a people asking for things that have been invented by somebody else . . .
' . . . If there is such a thing as India, it has a right to be Indian. But Herbert Spencer is not Indian; "Sociology" is not Indian; all this pedantic clatter about culture and science is not Indian. I often wish it were not English either. But this is our first abstract difficulty, that we cannot feel certain that the Indian Nationalist is national.' Quoted in Hunt, p. 151.

8. Nemai Sadhan Bose, op. cit., p. 217.
9. Ibid., p. 219.
10. *Source Material for a History of the Freedom Movement in India* (Bombay: Government Publication Division, 1958), Vol. II. P. 524.
11. Gangadharan, op. cit., p. 121.
12. Cited in R.C. Majumdar, *Three Phases of India's Struggle for Freedom* (Bombay: Bharatiya Vidya Bhavan, 1967), p. 41. As the terrorist Jatin Mukherjee put it, *amra morbo jat jagbe* (we shall die to awaken the nation).
13. Kalyan Kumar Banerjee, *Indian Freedom Movement: Revolutionaries in America* (Calcutta: Jijnasa, 1969), p. 67.
14. Cited in Dhananjay Keer, op. cit., p. 153.
15. Ibid., p. 154.
16. For a useful discussion see Richard Cashman, *The Myth of Lokamanya* (California: University of California Press, 1975). Tilak was not at all defensive about the charge of politicising Hinduism. 'Why shouldn't we convert large religious festivals into mass political rallies?' (*Kesari*, 8 September 1896).
17. David R. Kinsley, *The Sword and the Flute* (California: University of California Press, 1978).
18. See Earl of Ronaldshay, *The Heart of Aryavarta* (London: Constable, 1925).
19. Gangadharan, op. cit., p. 124.
20. Ibid., p. 123.
21. *Kesari*, 15 June 1897.
22. *CW*, Vol. IX, p. 509. See also Iyer, op. cit., Vol. I, pp. 278 f and *Young India*, 26 January, 1921. Gandhi said he wrote *Hind Swarāj* because he could not 'restrain' himself after his four-month long discussions with the Indians, especially the anarchists in London. Iyer, Vol. I, p. 199.
23. James Hunt, op. cit., pp. 133 f.
24. It is striking that *Hind Swarāj* was written in the form of a dialogue. Gandhi said that this was because it grew out of a dialogue whose authenticity he intended to preserve. Iyer, op. cit., Vol. 1, p. 271. The

English text is quite different from the Gujarati original. Gandhi himself said that he 'hurriedly dictated' its translation and that he had difficulty conveying the 'exact meaning' of the original, ibid. The English text is more assertive and dogmatic.
25. For references see Iyer, Vol. II, see. VI and *Gandhi's Non-Violent Resistance* (New York: Shocken, 1967).
26. *CW*, Vol. 19, p. 466; *Young India*, 23 March 1931.
27. *CW*, Vol. 23, p. 27 and Vol. 58, p. 230.
28. *Hind Swarāj* (Ahmedabad: Navajivan, 1939), pp. 28 f and 101.
29. *Gandhi's Non-Violent Resistance*, op. cit., pp. 80 ff.
30. Ibid., p. 97.
31. Iyer, op. cit., Vol. II, p. 262.
32. Iyer, op. cit., Vol. I, p. 455.
33. Ibid., p. 187. Gandhi observed: 'The dividing line between fact and fiction is very thin, indeed, and ... facts are after all opinions.' Gibbon and other historians were 'inferior editions of *Mahābhārata*'. See alo ibid., p. 245.
34. Our ancestors solved the problem 'by building on slight events their philosophical literature', ibid., p. 187.
35. Ibid., Vol. I, pp. 274 and 534; Vol. II, pp. 32, 123, 164, 255, 514, 531 f, and 536.
36. Ibid., Vol. 1, pp. 484 and 485; *Harijan*, 3 October 1936; *Young India*, 21 May 1928, 15 December 1927 and 6 August 1931. Gandhi knew his *Mahābhārata* well. In his early life, he preferred *Rāmāyana*. After he returned to India, *Mahābhārata* became his favourite epic. His jail dairy reveals that during 1922–4 in Yerevada prison, he spent as many as 163 days reading it, devoting nearly a third of the time to *Shāntiparva*. In an interview in February 1924 when he had just been released, he said: 'I have plunged into politics simply in search of truth.... I want to show how to epitomise the *Mahābhārata*.'
37. *Harijan*, 21 January 1939.
38. Quoted in Keer, op. cit., p. 443.
39. Iyer, op. cit., Vol. I, p. 514.
40. Ibid., p. 81.
41. Ibid., Vol. II, pp. 476 f. See also *CW*, Vol. 70, p. 334, where Gandhi contends that the *Mahābhārata* was written to establish the futility of war. He was heavily influenced by Vinoba Bhave's reading of it and greatly respected his classical scholarship.
42. Iyer, op. cit., Vol. I, pp. 81 ff.
43. Ibid., p. 81, *Harijan*, 1 September 1940; *Young India*, 6 August 1931; *Navajivan*, 11 October 1925.
44. It was striking that Gandhi took *anāsaktiyoga* to be the central message of the *Gitā*.

45. Iyer, op. cit., Vol. I, pp. 77 f.
46. Ibid., p. 85.

Chapter Six

1. The concepts of power and energy recur with great regularity in Gandhi's writings since the time of his political involvement in South Africa.
2. *CW*, Vol. 32, p. 2 and p. 10.
3. *Harijan*, 23 July 1938; 12 May 1938; and 1 September 1946; *Young India*, 1 September 1920.
4. *Young India*, 17 November 1921; *Harijan*, 3 August 1947; *Navajivan*, 23 January, 1921.
5. *Harijan*, 28 April 1946. See also *Key to Health* (Ahmedabad: Navajivan, 1948), pp. 46 f. and *Harijan*, 8 June 1947.
6. 'I hold this desire as unnatural in the human species and its satisfaction detrimental to the spiritual progress of human family', *CW*, Vol. 62, p. 361. St. Augustine, whose views bear some resemblance to Gandhi's, offered an ingenious reconciliation between sexual desire, which is bad, and reproduction which is a duty. He wanted the sexual act to be performed with a mind 'free of libido'. Had the Fall not occurred, men would have gone on reproducing as at present but without 'excitement'. See Edwyn Bevan. *Christianity* (London: Oxford University Press, 1932), p. 128.
7. *Young India*, 2 September 1926.
8. *Harijan*, 23 July 1938.
9. *Self-Restraint versus Self-Indulgence* (Ahmedabad: Navajivan, 1933), p. 47.
10. Ibid., pp. 137 f.
11. Every religion has a habit of inspiring its own distinct sexual sensibilities. Origen cut off his genitals because he wanted to follow the Gospel's advice that aspirants for the Kingdom of Heaven should make themselves eunuchs. Bishop Demetrius considered him profoundly mistaken and demanded that he be barred from joining the priestly order. See Richard Hanson, 'Notes on Origen's Self-mutilation', *Vigilae Christianae*, Vol. 20, 1966, pp. 81–82. As far as I know this has no parallel in Hindu thought. Some of the early Gnostics either practised total abstinence or used rather nasty contraceptive practices because they were anxious to stop the divine element from getting 'imprisoned in matter'. Others went to the opposite extreme and practised unrestrained indulgence.

12. *CW*, Vol. 70, p. 307.
13. Ibid., p. 287.
14. *Harijan*, 14 November 1936. Gandhi observed, non-violence is 'the inherent quality of women.... Even since I have taken to non-violence, I have become more and more of a woman'. R.K. Prabhu and U.R. Rao, *The Mind of Mahatma Gandhi* (Ahmedabad: Navajivan, 1967), p. 275.
15. See Mrs Polak's article in C. Shukla (ed.), *Gandhi as We Know Him* (Bombay: Vora and Company, 1945), p. 47.
16. *Young India*, 16 September 1926.
17. *Key to Health*, op. cit., pp. 48 f; *Harijan*, 8 June 1947 and *CW*, Vol. 32, pp. 2 f where Gandhi talks of such a person's *vibhutis*.
18. *CW*, Vol. 85, p. 216.
19. *Harijan*, 7 July 1946; *CW*, Vol. 70, p. 288.
20. See his interview with Blum in Blum Papers.
21. When Pandurang (Senapati) Bapat announced his plan to commit *Jal Samadhi*, his action was criticised for having a 'feminine odour' about it. He replied: 'My proposal ... has certainly a 'feminine odour' about it. I have a woman's heart as well as a man's, as certain women have proved themselves to have a man's heart as well as a woman's. We can never forget Kumaris Shanti, Suniti, Bina and Kalapna and other manly women as we can never forget Mahatma Gandhi and a host of other womenly men.' Quoted in Y.D. Phadke, *Senapati Bapat* (Ahmedabad: Harold Laski Institute, 1981), p. 19. The idea that the woman possesses such qualities as energy, intensity and resilience which man can acquire by 'appropriating' or 'internalising' her is a recurrent theme in Hindu thought. Shiva internalised Parvati and as a result became capable of, among other things, permanent erection. At a more mundane level, stories circulate of such men as N.T. Rama Rao, the Andhra ex-chief minister, going to sleep in a sari. According to the folklore in some parts of India, even Rama is believed to have followed the practice. Traditional fairs in several parts of India attract 'yogis' boasting of unusual accomplishments. Professor Gulam Shaikh informs me that in the annual fair in Junagadh, Gujarat, men are to be found who have after years of practice either 'introjected' their genitals and are little different from women, or elongated them disproportionately.
22. *CW*, Vol. 39, p. 252. Pyarelal says the opposite; Gandhi took the vow 'in consultation with her, with her consent and permission'. See the Blum Papers. Gandhi persuaded Prabhavati Narayan and Sucheta Kriplani to do the same, in each case against their husbands' wishes. See Blum's interviews with Pyarelal and Sucheta Kriplani.
23. *CW*, Vol. 67, p. 69.
24. *CW*, Vol. 40, p. 312; also *CW*, Vol. 67, pp. 117 and 148.

25. *CW*, Vol. 62, pp. 428 f.
26. Ibid., p. 373.
27. Ibid., pp. 210 f. Gandhi wrote: 'Thank God, my much-vaunted Mahatmaship has never fooled me. But this enforced rest has humbled me as never before.' Ibid., p. 212.
28. Ibid., p. 60.
29. Ibid., p. 56.
30. Ibid., p. 118.
31. Her letter is not traceable, but see Gandhi's letters to her dated 3 May 1938 and 12 May 1938 in ibid., pp. 60 and 103.
32. *CW*, Vol. 70, pp. 312 f: Gandhi's article details all the charges levelled against him and patiently refutes them.
33. 'If we distinguish between sleeping together and the experiment, the difference between the two in my view is a big one,' *CW*, Vol. 79, p. 212.
34. Ibid., p. 213.
35. Ibid., 215 f.
36. For a full account see Pyarelal, *Mahatma Gandhi*, Vol. I, Book 2, ch. XI.
37. *CW*, Vol. 86, p. 24.
38. *CW*, Vol. 87, pp. 109 f; Vol. 86, pp. 220 and 221.
39. *CW*, Vol. 86, p. 245.
40. Ibid., pp. 248, 280 and 335. Gandhi took considerable interest in her clothes and hairstyle and who she should talk to. Ibid., p. 280.
41. *CW*, Vol. 87, p. 270.
42. *CW*, Vol. 87, pp. 152 f and Vol. 86, p. 451 which contains Gandhi's reply to the Navajivan Trustees' telegram disapproving of his conduct.
43. Pyarelal, op. cit., pp. 224 f and *CW*, Vol. 86, p. 414 and Vol. 87, p. 533.
44. *CW*, Vol. 87, p. 13.
45. Ibid., pp. 14 f.
46. Pyarelal, op. cit., pp. 224 f.
47. See his *CW*, Vol. 87, pp. 14 f and Vol. 86, p. 476.
48. Ibid., p. 14.
49. *CW*, Vol. 87, p. 384.
50. Ibid., p. 462.
51. Ibid., p. 14.
52. *CW*, Vol. 86, p. 302. (emphasis added).
53. Ibid., p. 414. (emphasis added).
54. *CW*, Vol. 87, p. 62; Vol. 86, p. 302.
55. *CW*, Vol. 86, p. 442.
56. *Harijan*, 23 July 1938.
57. *CW*, Vol. 87, p. 90.

58. Ibid., p. 108.
59. *CW*, Vol. 87, pp. 90 f and Pyarelal, op. cit., pp. 218 f.
60. N.K. Bose, *My Days with Gandhi* (Bombay: Orient Longman, 1974), p. 176.
61. *Harijan*, 24 February 1940.
62. Pyarelal, op. cit., p. 242.
63. Ibid., p. 226.
64. *CW*, Vol. 87, p. 63.
65. Ibid., p. 238.
66. See my *Gandhi* (Oxford: Oxford University Press, 1998), pp. 103 f.
67. *CW*, Vol. 67, p. 5. Also Shirer, op. cit., p. 230.
68. Letter to Balwant Sinha, dated 11 June 1938.
69. In his interview with Blum, Dada Dharmadhikari argues that Gandhi 'had shed all fear of the woman's body'. Sexual abstinence as advocated and practised in all religions springs from that fear; true *brahmacharya* such as Gandhi's, which is qualitatively different from abstinence and even celibacy, 'conquers' and even eliminates the fear. Gandhi thought that it came more easily to women than to men, and encouraged and even gently pressured his close married female associates to adopt it. The story of Sucheta Kriplani is fascinating. As she says in the interview with Blum, Gandhi was opposed to her marriage to J.B. Kriplani for fear that it would affect the latter's wholehearted devotion to India. When she insisted that Gandhi would have two workers instead of just one, he gave in but wondered about the distracting power of sexual intimacy and the likely children. She reassured him that she and her husband would only live as 'close friends'. She observes that although such a restraint could and did destroy some marriages, hers benefited from the absence of sex. The fact that several of the men and women involved were constantly in and out of prison and deeply involved in political and social work made the task of what Sucheta Kriplani calls 'sublimation' much easier.

    Gandhi's experiments find a parallel in the life of Socrates. At the end of *Symposium*, Alcibiades speaks to the august gathering about his having taken into his arms 'this wonderful monster', and talks of Socrates' 'haughty virtue'. He remarks: 'He was so superior to my solicitation, so contemptuous and derisive and disdainful of my beauty ..., nothing more happened, but in the morning when I awoke ... I rose as from the couch of a father or an elder brother'. In his mid-life, Freud decided to become a celibate and thought that it greatly helped 'savants' but not artists. Concerning some amusing details about Gandhi's colleagues, see Ved Mehta, *Mahatma Gandhi and His Apostles* (London: Andre Deutsch, 1977).

For an informative discussion of the Hindu concept of spiritual power, see Philip Spratt, *Hindu Culture and Personality* (Bombay: Manktalas, 1966), pp. 62 ff. and 107 ff. Though full of useful information and insights, the book is deeply flawed by its clumsy applications of rather crude Freudian tools whose relevance to Indian reality is nowhere defended. Poor Indian *yogis* end up having all the sexual hang-ups and paranoia of the modern western man, except that their pursuits of them are considered crude and uncivilised.

70. For stimulating discussions of Hindu theories of sexuality, see Wendy Doniger O'Flaherty's *Women, Androgynes and Other Mythical Beasts* (Chicago: University of Chicago Press, 1980) and *Asceticism and Eroticism in the Mythology of Siva* (Delhi: Oxford University Press, 1973).

Chapter Seven

1. For a good discussion, see Dhananjay Keer, *Mahatma Gandhi: Political Saint and Unarmed Prophet* (Bombay: Popular Prakashan, 1973), pp. 577 and 587 ff. Shankaracharya of Karriv Pitha criticised Gandhi as a dangerous heretic whose teachings 'contradicted' the central tenets of Hinduism, whose *ahimsā* was 'detrimental to Aryan cult' and who 'often' quoted Christ.

   Some of the Shankaracharyas remain as obtuse as those in Gandhi's days. See a most depressing interview with the Shankaracharya of Puri in the *Illustrated Weekly of India*, 1 May 1988, where he vigorously defends *sati* and inequality of women on *Shāstric* authority. The interview with Swami Agnivesh of the Arya Samaj in the same issue presents a very different view. The fierce debate between the two on the question of the Harijans' right to enter the Shreenathji temple in Nathdwara shows how much untouchability still remains a problem. The government's refusal to intervene in spite of the Supreme Court's decision on the matter some years ago shows how little Hindu caste opinion is interested in tackling it.
2. B.R. Ambedkar, *What Congress and Gandhi Have Done to the Untouchables* (Bombay: Thacker & Co., 1946), pp. 266–67.
3. Ibid., pp. 270–77.
4. Cited in Mark Tully and Zareer Masani, *From Raj to Rajiv* (London: BBC, 1988), p. 78.
5. Cited in Ambedkar, op. cit., p. 2.

6. Ibid., p. 3.
7. Referring to the demand for a separate electorate for Harijans, Gandhi observed: 'The separate electorate will create division among Hindus so much that it will lead to bloodshed. "Untouchable" hooligans will make common cause with Muslim hooligans and kill caste Hindus. Has the British government no idea of this? I do not think so.' *The Diary of Mahadev Desai*, Tr. and ed. by V.G. Desai (Ahmedabad: Navajivan, 1953) p. 301.
8. *CW*, Vol. V, pp. 20 f.
9. Ambedkar, op. cit., p. 1.
10. Ibid., pp. 14 f.
11. There was hardly a Hindu leader who did not attack untouchability in all three idioms. The distinction drawn is based on which idiom dominated their discourse.
12. This was the position of such men as Bhudev Mukhopadhyay, Bankim Chandra Chatterjee, Dayananda Saraswati, Vivekananda, B.C. Pal, Tilak and Aurobindo Ghose.
13. For example, Surendra Nath Banerjee, D. Naoroji, Mahatma Phule, W.C. Banerjee and a number of liberal reformers.
14. For example, Lala Lajpat Rai in some of his speeches and writings, Rama Iyer, Bhulabhai Desai and such Hindu nationalists as Savarkar and Lala Shadi Lal.
15. *Young India*, 20 October 1920.
16. *Young India*, 29 December 1920.
17. For detailed references see V.B. Kher (ed.), *Social Service Work and Reform* (Ahmedabad: Navajivan, 1976), Vol. III. This is a useful collection of Gandhi's major writings and controversies on the subject.
18. Ibid., p. 53.
19. *Young India*, 27 October 1921 and 27 August 1925.
20. *Harijan*, 18 July 1936 and *Young India*, 8 April 1926.
21. *Young India*, 27 April 1921 and 4 May 1921.
22. Ibid., 8 April 1926.
23. Keer, op. cit., pp. 71 f.
24. *Young India*, 27 August 1925.
25. Ibid.; 23 April 1925.
26. T.K. Ravindran, *Eight Furlongs of Freedom* (Madras: Light and Life Publishers, 1980), pp. 166 ff.
27. Ibid., p. 193.
28. See Introduction for Gandhi's reasons for doing so.
29. Speech in Trivandrum reported in *Young India*, 20 October 1927.
30. *Young India*, 8 April, 1926 and 20 October 1927; *Harijan*, 5 January 1934 and 3 August 1934.
31. T.K. Ravindran, op. cit., p. 180.

32. *Harijan*, 23 December 1939.
33. Gandhi's clearest statement on the subject first appeared in Gujarati in *Navajivan* and is faithfully translated by Ambedkar, op. cit., pp. 286 f.
34. Gandhi's statements criticising the caste system as a perversion of the ancient *varna* system first began to appear in 1925. See *Young India*, 23 April 1925 and 13 August 1925. Ambedkar, op. cit., makes a similar point on p. 288.
35. Cited in Ambedkar, op. cit., p. 289.
36. Dheer, op. cit., pp. 19 f and 41 f; *Young India*, 20 October 1927 and *Harijan*, 23 September 1939.
37. For references relating to his positions on various reforms, see V.B. Kher, (ed.), *Social Service, Work and Reform* (Ahmedabad: Navajivan, 1976), Vol. 1, Sections IV to VII.
38. *CW*, Vol. 37, pp. 136 ff; *Young India*, 27 April 1921, 1 May 1924 and 26 December 1924 and *Harijan*, 31 August 1934. 'Though the problem is capable of yielding either way enormous economic and political results, it is to me pre-eminently a religious question', *CW*, Vol. 37, p. 136.
39. Zaidi A. Main and Zaidi Shaheda, *The Encyclopaedia of Indian National Congress*, Vols, I to XXIII (New Delhi: S. Chand and Company, 1976-84). Vol. VIII, p. 462.
40. For detailed references to the controversy surrounding the name, see Kher, op. cit., pp. 77 ff.
41. See Zelliot, op. cit., pp. 82 f.
42. Buddhadeva Bhattacharya, *Satyāgrahas in Bengal 1929-1939* (Delhi: Minerva, 1977).
43. Cited in Ambedkar, op. cit., p. 77.
44. For a good account see Keer, op. cit., pp. 584 f.
45. Ambedkar, op. cit., p. 126.
46. Ibid., pp. 133 f.
47. Ibid., p. 142.
48. Ibid., p. 127.
49. Keer, op. cit., pp. 327 ff.
50. See *Young India*, 19 March 1925 and *Harijan*, 29 April 1933, 23 March 1934, 16 November 1935 and, especially, 28 July 1926.
51. Swami Shraddhanand had insisted that every caste Hindu should employ a Harijan domestic servant. Gandhi prevaricated. See *Harijan*, 16 Septermber 1933. For Gandhi's views on employing harijan cooks, see *Harijan*, 25 May 1940 and 19 May 1946.

346 Colonialism, Tradition and Reform

Chapter Eight

1. Gandhi to N.K. Bose, cited in M.P. Sinha, *Contemporary Relevance of Gandhi* (Bombay: Nachiketa Publication, 1970), p. 45.
2. George Misch, *A History of Autobiography in Antiquity* (London: Routledge, 1951), Vols. I and II.
3. Ananda Coomarswamy, *The Dance of Siva* (Delhi: Munshiram Manoharlal, 1982), p. 119.
4. See G.N. Devy, 'Romantic, Post-Romantic and Neo-Romantic Autobiography in Indian English Literature', in Dioranne Mac-Dermott, (ed.), *Autobiography and Biography in the Commonwealth* (Barcelona: University of Barcelona Press, 1985), and the Preface to *CW*, Vol. 36, pp. ix f.
5. For example, Gujarati autobiographies by Narmada Shankar and Hemachandra. The former finds it difficult to decide what to say about himself and ends up writing a series of notes. Vishwanath Bhatt remarks that Narmada's autobiography lacks 'coherence, order and a sense of discrimination about what to write'; cited in Raman Modi, *Gandhijinun Sahitya* (Ahmedabad: Navajivan, 1971), p. 175. See also Devy, op. cit., p. 64.
6. Dozens of autobiographies by Indian writers began to appear from about the middle of the nineteenth century. Most of the early authors were social reformers. Only at the turn of the century did political leaders begin to write about themselves. The novelty of the genre was evident in the fact that their titles showed little variety. For example, Narmada Shankar's was called *Māri-Hakikat* (My life or statement); Narayan Hemchandra's *Hoon Pote* (I myself); Rajnarayan Basu's *Atmajivani* (My life); Dadoba Pandurang's *Atmacharitra* (My life); and Dwarkanath Tagore's *Autobiography*. Most of them said in the preface that they wanted to popularise this 'useful' and 'instructive' genre. Narmada Shankar said that his purpose in writing it was 'not so much introspection as the desire to provide a model so that like the West, Gujarat too could start the practice of writing autobiography.' (*Māri-Hakikat*, p. 2, cited in Modi, op. cit., p. 174).
7. Chapekar's *Autobiography* is included in *A History of the Freedom Movement in India*, (Bombay: Government of Bombay Publication Division, 1958), Vol. II.
8. S.N. Banerjee, *A Nation in the Making* (Delhi: Oxford University Press, 1925).
9. See his 'Introduction' to *An Autobiography: The Story of My Experiments with Truth* (London: Jonathan Cape, 1949). The translation is mine.

In Gujarat, Narmadashankar and Hemchandra were probably the only ones to have written autobiographies before Gandhi. For good discussions of Gandhi's autobiography, see preface to *CW*, Vol. 36; C.N. Patel, *Mahatma Gandhi in his Gujarati Writings* (Delhi: Sahitya Akademi, 1981), pp. 63 ff; and Hyman Muslin and Prakash Desai, 'The Transformation of the Self in Mahatma Gandhi', in C.B. Strozier and D. Offer (eds.), *The Leader* (Chicago: Plenum Publishing Corporation, 1985). For a dramatic rendering of Gandhi's Autobiography, see Asif Currimbhoy's three-act play called *An Experiment With Truth* (Calcutta: Writers Workshop Publication, 1972).
10. Ibid., p. XI.
11. Ibid., pp. xi f. The English translation misses Gandhi's distinction. Even as late as 1946, he insisted that he had 'certainly not written an autobiography' and promised to update his *Autobiography* if he found the time; see *Harijanbandhu*, 1946. Gandhi had a fairly clear idea of how a good biography should be written. See *CW*, Vol. 32, pp. 3 f, where his reminiscences of Raichandbhai are an interesting mixture of biography and autobiography.
12. Ibid. The Gujarati *'Introduction'* is much clearer on this point. See also p. 234.
13. Ibid., p. 234.
14. Compare Part II, ch. 17 of *Autobiography* with ch. VI of his *Satyāgraha in South Africa* (Ahmedabad: Navajivan, 1928). There are also other interesting differences. In his *Autobiography*, Gandhi is preoccupied with himself and says little about his surroundings *Satyāgraha in South Africa* is different.
15. Raghavan Iyer, op. cit., Vol. II, p. 197.
16. See his *An Autobiography* (London: Bodley Head, 1958), pp. xi f and, especially, 595 f.
17. Ibid., p. 596.

Chapter Nine

1. Sibnarayan Ray (ed.), *Selected Works of M.N. Roy* (Delhi: Oxford University Press, 1987), Vol. 1, p. 348.
2. Ibid., p. 347.
3. 'India's Message' in *Fragments of a Prisoner's Diary*, Vol. 2, (Calcutta, 1950). For a good discussion, see Dennis Dalton, *Mahatma Gandhi: Nonviolent Power in Action* (New York: Columbia University Press, 1993), pp. 78–90.

4. 'Draft Platform of Action' in Democratic Research Service, *Indian Communist Party Documents, 1930-1956* (Bombay, 1957), pp. 1-21.
5. See Jairus Banerji, 'The Comintern and Indian Nationalism' in K.N. Panikkar (ed.), *National and Left Movements in India* (Delhi, 1980), pp. 213-65.
6. Gene D. Overstreet and Marshall Windmiller, *Communism in India* (Berkeley, 1960), p. 158.
7. J.P. Narayan, *Why Socialism?* (Varanasi, 1936), p. 47.
8. A.R. Desai, *Social Background of Indian Nationalism* (Bombay, 1948), p. 148.
9. Partha Chatterjee, *Nationalist Thought and the Colonial World: A Derivative Discourse?* (Delhi, 1987), ch. 2.
10. Ibid., p. 100.
11. Ibid., p. 124.
12. For a good discussion of Gandhi's relations with the Indian bourgeoisie, to which I am indebted but which takes a somewhat different view, see Claude Markovitis, *Indian Business and Nationalist Politics, 1931-1939* (Cambridge, 1985). See alo my *Gandhi's Poltical Philosophy*, pp. 134 ff.
13. *Young India*, 13 October 1921, 27 October 1921, and 26 October 1924.
14. *Harijan*, 16 December 1939.
15. *Young India*, 16 April 1931 and 17 September 1931.
16. *CW*, Vol. 55, p. 42.
17. Ibid., Vol. 64, p. 192; Vol. 76, p. 367.
18. Ibid., Vol. 76, pp. 437, 445 f.
19. See p. 149 above.
20. For a useful discussion, see David Hardiman, *Peasant Nationalists of Gujarat: Kheda District, 1917-1934* (Delhi, 1981), pp. 250 f.
21. G.D. Birla, *In the Shadow of the Mahatma* (Bombay, 1968). p. 101.
22. Ibid., p. 277.
23. Ibid., p. 278.
24. G.D. Birla, *Bapu: A Unique Association* (Bombay: Bharatiya Vidya Bhavan, 1977), pp. 361 f, 364, 368, 370, 377-78.
25. Although Gandhi and the Congress were closely identified in popular mind, their tension was also widely recognised. Loyalty to one did not therefore automatically translate into loyalty to the other.
26. D.N. Dhanagre, *Peasant Movements in India* (Delhi, 1983), pp. 91-92.
27. The belief that the Indian society was based on oppressive violence and constantly provoked the violence of the oppressed is a recurrent theme in Gandhi's writings.
28. Tibor Mendus, *Conversations with Mr Nehru* (London, 1957), p. 140.
29. Bipan Chandra, et al., *India's Struggle for Independence 1857-1947* (New Delhi, 1988), p. 26.

30. Richard Fox rightly argues that for Gandhi 'class conciliation was a short term experiment in the interests of achieving independence and that he might himself have organized resistance' to independent India's economic policies. See his *Gandhian Utopia: Experiments with Culture* (Boston: Beacon Press, 1989).
31. See my *Gandhi's Political Philosophy*, pp. 121 f.
32. See Blum's interview with Annasaheb Sahasrabuche in Blum Papers.
33. See Blum's interview with Zaverbhai Patel in Blum Papers.
34. This criticism of Vinoba is made by Achyut Patwardhan in his interview with Blum.
35. For a valuable discussion, see Richard Cox, op. cit.; see also my *Gandhi's Political Philosophy*, pp. 220 f.
36. Parts of this chapter draw on my 'The Marxist Discourse on Gandhi' in Dwijendra Tripathi (ed.), *Business and Politics in India: A Historical Perspective* (Delhi: Manohar, 1991).

Index

Abhinav Bharat, 164, 166
absolute-relative distinction, 144
adhikār, 21, 29, 100, 165, 240, 291
advaita, 48, 69, 199–200, 224, 232
Agnivesh, Swami, 343
ahimsā, 26–27, 86, 89, 94, 108, 111–12, 120–27, 129–30, 132–33, 135–38, 153, 179–80, 217, 248
Akbar, 49, 87
Akho, 278
Akkama, 279
Ali, Aruna Asaf, 321
All-India Anti-Untouchability League, 262, 268, 270
All-India Congress Committee (AICC), 315, 317
Ambedkar, B.R., 228, 230, 260–62, 264–66, 270, 343–45
Ampthill, Lord, 171, 331
Amrit Kaur, Rajkumari, 206, 209–10, 321
Anand, Swami, 214
Anandamath, 57
anāsakti, 26, 186–88
animals, 18, 125, 142, 146, 153, 180, 242–43
Antussalaam, 210
anugraha, 221
Arya Samaj, 47, 167, 235
Arya Samaj: A Political Body, 167
asceticism, 49, 128, 205–06
āshram, 107, 153, 211–12, 258
Asiatic despotism, 31
Asoka, 67
asuri prakriti, 43
ātman, 196, 277
ātmasātkarna, 73

ātmashuddhi, 89, 178
Attenborough, Richard, 327
Auden, W.H., 272
Augustine, St., 273, 289, 339
Aurelius, Marcus, 272
authority, 17–18, 27, 36–37, 75, 96, 109, 138, 154, 159, 236
autobiographies, 274–75, 279, 288–89
autonomy, 56, 73, 76, 122, 127, 157, 175, 193, 280
Azad, Maulana, 153, 223

Bacon, 52
Bahujan Samaj Party, 230
Ballhatchet, Kenneth, 331
Bana, 278
Banerjee, Kalyan Kumar, 337
Banerjee, Surendra Nath, 35, 56, 60, 282–83, 291–92, 344, 346
Banerjee, W.C., 344
Banerji, Jairus, 348
Bapat, Pandurang (Senapati), 340
Barber, Benjamin, 326
Bary, William Theodore de, 334
Basava, 279
Basu, Rajnarayan, 329, 346
Bengalee, 54, 60
Benhabib, Selya, 326
Bentinck, Lord, 59
Bevan, Edwyn, 339
Bhāgavata Purāna, 124
Bhakti tradition, 165, 232, 279
bhaktiyoga, 169
Bhargava, D., 334
Bhatt, Vishwanath, 346
Bhattacharya, Buddhadeva, 345
Bhave, Vinoba, 213, 323–26, 338

Index 351

Bilhana, 278
Birla, G.D., 264, 312-13, 317, 348
Bishop, Donald, 330
Blum, Arna, 327
Blum, F.J. 326-27, 340, 342, 349
Bombay Chronicle, 210
Bose, Khudiram, 169
Bose, N.K., 212-13, 218, 220, 222, 342, 346
Bose, Nemai Sadhan, 336-37
Bose, Subhas, 291-92, 321
Bowes, Pratima, 328
brahmacharya, 90, 101, 114, 130, 200-02, 204-05, 211, 217-19, 222
Brahman, 27, 84, 110, 118, 122, 172, 193, 196
Brahmins, 37, 49-51, 62-63, 234, 240, 242, 245-46, 251-52
Brahmo Samaj, 69
British rule, 38, 58-61, 63-64, 67, 71, 79, 113-14, 234, 279-80
Brown, Judith, 9
Buddha, 97-98, 194, 270, 291
Buddhism, 23, 67, 87, 94, 120, 122-24, 126-27, 179, 181
bureaucracy, 115, 155, 158
Burke, Edmund, 30, 65
Burman, D., 330

Calvinism, 215
Cama, Madame Bhikaji, 162-63
capitalism, 298, 301, 304-05, 316, 319, 322
Cashman, Richard, 337
caste, 45-50, 66, 70, 76-77, 88, 94, 231, 242-44, 249-50, 256-57, 259, 267, 269-71, 312
celibacy, 207, 214, 218
Chaitanya, 224, 279
Chandra, Bipan, 321, 336, 348
Chapekar, Damodar, 77, 281-83, 291, 329, 346
Chatterjee, Bankim Chandra, 33, 44, 49, 56-57, 60, 72, 233
Chatterjee, Partha, 298-300, 326, 332, 348
Chesterton, G.K., 336
child marriages, 21, 43, 50, 233

Chitrol Valentine, 158
Christianity, 19, 23, 26, 28, 44, 53, 62, 69-70, 79, 81, 83, 87-88, 90, 99, 102-03, 112-13, 120, 129, 199, 232, 241-42, 246, 273, 279, 329
citizen, 61, 67, 76, 84-85, 96, 110, 115, 148, 202, 252-53
Civil Disobedience Movement, 310-11, 328
civil society, 32
civilisation, 15, 31-35, 41-45, 49, 53-54, 61, 66, 68, 70-75, 78, 82, 84-85, 88, 90, 92-93, 95, 108, 113-14, 163, 171-72, 175, 180, 191, 276, 294
colonial discourse, 33, 35
colonial rule, 22, 35-36, 40-41, 43-45, 54, 62-63, 65, 68, 72, 82, 91, 94, 116, 159, 161, 175, 298, 309, 311, 314
colonialism, 36, 65, 82
Comintern, 296
Communal Award, 260-61
Communism, 301, 304, 306
Communists, 161
compassion, 89, 113, 126-27
compensatory discrimination, 109
Comte, Auguste, 52, 158
conduct, 19, 21, 37, 145, 154, 174, 217
Confessions, 273-74
Congress, Indian National, 58, 110, 115, 159-61, 218, 234, 257-58, 264-65, 268-69, 294-96, 298, 300, 307-08, 310-24
Congress Socialist Party, 161
conscience, 89, 113, 269
conservatism, 18-19, 23, 91, 228
Constructive Programme, 89, 258
Conze, E., 334
Coomaraswamy, Ananda, 278, 346
cosmic spirit, 84-85, 103, 117, 121, 193, 195, 217
courage, 105, 147, 152, 163, 172, 176-78, 223
cowardice, 133, 137, 150, 162-63, 172, 177, 206
Cox, Richard, 9, 326, 349
creative synthesis, 72-73, 86, 93, 112

critical modernism, 42, 66, 68–77, 79, 92, 112
critical traditionalism, 42, 66, 72–80, 90, 93, 109
critique, 232, 236, 252
cultural synthesis, 72–73, 86, 93, 112
culture, 15–16, 36, 49–50, 52, 70, 75, 104, 115, 275, 281
Currimbhoy, Asif, 347
Curzon, Lord, 160

Dallmayer, Fred, 328
Dalton, Dennis, 9, 329, 332, 347
Darwin, Charles, 52
Decca Anusilan Samiti, 167, 169
defensive violence, 150
degeneration, 15, 39, 45, 48–52, 62, 68, 88–89, 94–95, 103, 105, 237
democracy, 70, 74, 234, 249, 269
Desai, A.R., 297, 348
Desai, Bhulabhai, 344
Desai, Mahadev, 210
Desai, Prakash, 347
Desai, V.G., 344
detachment, 188, 199
Deutsch, Kenneth, 330
Devy, G.N., 346
Dhanagre, D.N., 348
Dhat, B.N., 58
dharma, 20–21, 37, 66, 100, 113, 135, 165, 169–71, 184, 190, 212, 231, 291
Dharmadhikari, Dada, 203, 342
dharmashāstras, 19, 27, 37, 97, 179, 206, 278
dharmayuddha, 128, 168
dhārmic view of violence, 134, 167, 171
Dhingra, Madanlal, 163–64
dialogue, 86, 90, 113
dignity, 114, 116, 128, 149, 152, 193, 235, 250, 266, 302
Dilthey, W., 274–75
Dio or my own Bios, 273
discourse, 22, 38, 40, 188, 248
Disquisition Concerning Ancient India, 51
divide and rule, 81, 87, 238, 314
divine grace, 221

Dufferin, Lord, 159
duty, 139, 188–89, 214, 271

East India Company, 46, 60, 63
Einstein, A., 52
elite, 38, 89, 114, 158, 299
Ellis, Havelock, 219
energy, 39, 42–43, 53, 61, 69–70, 84, 96, 115, 173, 191–93, 197, 200, 218, 302
Enlightenment, 26, 51, 53, 69
epics, 167, 183, 278
epistemological pluralism, 69–70, 87
equality, 15, 30, 34, 43, 45, 69–70, 74, 85, 113, 232–33, 237, 271
Eton, 32
Euclidean view, 143–45
evil, 185–87, 217, 256
experiment, 27, 29, 91, 98, 116–18, 194, 199, 202, 206–07, 210–15, 218, 221–27, 249, 284–85, 287–91

Fall of the Moghul, The, 51
fasting, 26, 118, 260
female sexuality, 202
feminine principle, 199–200, 221, 340
Fischer, L., 149, 153, 306, 336
Forbes, W.H., 330
freedom, 48, 59, 70, 93, 101, 149, 154
Freud, S., 222, 342

Gadamer, H., 26
Gandhi, Abha, 210
Gandhi, Devdas, 213
Gandhi, Gopal, 327
Gandhi, Jaisukhlal, 212
Gandhi, Manu, 200, 208, 210–13, 216, 220, 222–23, 227, 265
Gandhi-Irwin Pact, 310–11, 318
Ganesh, 165–66
Gangadharan, K.K., 336–37
Ghose, Aurobindo, 45, 49, 52, 57, 72–75, 77, 105, 162, 183, 185, 330, 332, 344
Ghose, Barin, 163
Ghose, Benoy, 328
Gitā, the, 75, 168–72, 179, 183–88, 189–90, 205, 235

Index   353

Gitagovinda, 206
Gnostics, 339
God, 76, 79, 89, 107, 119, 168, 170, 186, 188, 197, 215, 221, 243, 246, 273, 284
Gokhale, G.K., 46, 49, 52, 60, 68, 70, 104–05, 111
guilt, 256–58, 262
Gupta age, 54, 85, 94
Gupta, L.C., 49

Hanson, R. 339
Hardiman, David, 348
Hare, William Lottus, 198
Harijan, 209–10, 213–14, 221
Harijan Sevak Sangh, 263, 268
Harshacarita, 278
Hastings, Warren, 41, 65
Heesterman, J.C., 327, 329
Hegel, 49, 77, 321
Hemchandra Narayan, 346–47
Herder, J.G., 274–75
hermeneutics, 241
himsā, 123–26, 130–34, 187
Hind Swarāj, 114, 172, 177, 297–98
Hindu Mahasabha, 161
Hindu nationalism, 160–61
Hindu Patriot, 57
Hindu tradition, 15–17, 29, 117, 197, 219
Hindu view of history, 181–84
Hindus, 15, 22–23, 41–42, 46–47, 49, 50–52, 61, 76, 79–80, 87–88, 112, 117, 120–23, 153, 159–60, 163, 165, 169, 171, 180–81, 195–96, 205, 221, 234–35, 238–39, 247–48, 250, 256–62, 268–69, 277, 279–81, 312, 315
Hinduism, 23–24, 26–28, 47–48, 67, 74, 76, 79, 90, 94, 100, 103, 107–08, 112–13, 165, 169, 171, 179–80, 183, 187, 199, 225, 228, 239, 241–42, 244, 246–47, 278, 329
Hindustan Gadar, 163
historical truth, 181–83, 277
history, 31, 36, 46, 50–51, 62–64, 66, 90, 94, 162, 176, 179, 181–84, 247, 275, 279, 285

Hitler, Adolf, 118–19
Hodson, 156
humanity, 25, 46, 140, 246
Hume, A.O., 159
Hunt, J., 336–37
Hyndman, J., 160

identity, 67, 80, 166, 221, 284, 295
ideology, 31, 36, 51, 62
Ilbert Bill, 59, 65, 57
independence (India's), 115, 152, 155, 161–62, 168, 175–76, 190, 216, 218, 235, 238–39, 307, 310–14, 317, 319, 323, 325
Indian civilisation, 73–74, 80, 82, 85–87, 90, 92–94, 96, 114, 172
Indian National Social Conference, 233
Indian Opinion, 95
Indian Sociologist, 158, 167
individualism, 42, 48, 71, 90, 280
individuality, 275–78
industrialisation, 45, 55, 60, 70–71, 74, 84, 114, 116
injustice, 96,105, 141, 143, 189–90
inner voice, 96
integrity, 121, 152, 175, 190, 219, 253
Islam, 23, 79, 87, 99, 112–13, 165, 198, 212, 234, 279
itihās, 184, 287, 289
Iyer, R., 332–35, 344, 347
Iyer, Ranga, 264

Jain, Mahavira, 97–98, 278, 291
Jainism, 23, 123
Jains, 112, 120, 124–27, 132, 134–35, 137, 153, 181
Jaju, Krishnandas, 212
Jallianwala Bagh massacre, 82, 161
Jan Sangh, 325
Jayadeva, 206
Jesus, 28, 98, 194, 203
Jinnah, M.A., 209
jnānayoga, 169
Jones, Sir William, 51, 53, 330
Joshi, V.C., 330
Judaism, 23, 26, 203
just war, 188

justice, 15, 31–32, 36–37, 45, 62–63, 70, 151–52, 315, 319
justification, 143, 145, 162, 188

Kabir, 97, 233, 279
Kali, 166–67
Kalidas, 206
kaliyuga, 20
Kane, P.V., 328
Kanshi Ram, 230
Kantak, Prema, 210
karma, 79, 184, 231–32, 243, 245, 249
karmayoga, 169, 184, 191
karuṇā, 127, 242
kathā, 184–85, 285, 287, 289
Kedar Nath, 214
Keer, D., 337, 343
Khan, Abdul Ghafar, 214
Khan, Afzal, 170
Kher, V.B., 344–45
Khilafat agitation, 238
King, Preston, 327–28
Kinsley, David R., 337
Koran, 50
Kriplani, J.B., 342
Kriplani, Sucheta, 340, 342
Krishna, 124, 170, 185, 188–89, 205, 225–27
Krishna-Gopi legend, 225–27
Krishnamurti, J., 146
Krishnite love, 226–27
Kshatriyas, 85, 110, 180, 188–89, 252
Kulinism, 21
Kumar, R., 331
Kumarasambhavam, 206

Lala Lajpat Rai, 21, 56–57, 167, 344
Lala Shadi Lal, 344
Lalbhai, Kasturbhai, 313
Lalnath Pandit, 228
law, 32, 36–37, 55, 61, 66, 70, 85, 109
legitimacy, 31, 75, 82, 85, 224
legitimate self interest, 134, 139–41
Lenin, 15, 295
liberal democracy, 70, 84, 115
liberalism, 37, 45, 67, 75, 162, 235
liberty, 31, 69, 74, 85, 166, 177, 253
Linlithgow, Lord, 312

loksangraha, 21–22, 29, 77, 123, 126, 134, 169, 181
love, 87, 103, 108, 117, 124, 126–29, 133–35, 146, 149, 203, 220, 226–27, 247, 268
Low, D.A., 331
loyalty, 24, 28, 48, 246–48

Macaulay, T., 59, 65, 156
MacDermott, D., 346
Macdonald Award of 1931, 229
Madhavacharya, 244
Mahābhārata, 21, 122–26, 168, 170–71, 179, 184–88, 248, 338
Mahadevan, T.K., 329
Mahatma Munshi Ram, 167
Majumdar, B., 330–31
Majumdar, J.K., 330–31
Majumdar, R.C., 330, 336–37
Malaviya, Madan Mohan, 91
malevolence, 131–132
man, 70, 83, 117, 125, 146, 186
mānavdharma, 20, 29
Manicheism, 35, 168, 185
Manu, 19, 282
Manusmriti, 20, 236, 239, 259
Mao, 15
Markovities, Claude, 348
Marx, 162, 295, 321
Marxism, 67, 162, 167
Masani, Z., 331–32, 343
Mashruwala, K., 213
material power, 192–93
maternal principle, 221
Maurya period, 54, 85
Max Mueller, 53
Mazzini, G., 162
Mehta, Narasinha, 279
Mehta, Pherozeshah, 332
Mehta, Usha, 327
Mehta, Ved., 327, 342
Mendus, Tibor, 348
Mill, J.S., 52, 118
Mira, 226, 279
Miraben, 209
miracles, 196
Misch, G., 346
Misra, Amalendu, 326

missionaries, 62, 69, 87, 257
Modern History of Hindustan, 51
modernism, 66–68, 70–73, 76–79, 84, 92, 236
modernity, 66–67, 69–70, 79, 84, 98, 109, 114, 236
Modi, R., 346
Mohammed, 98, 194
moksha, 15, 104–06, 111, 126, 169, 186–87, 214–16, 252
moral colonisation, 175
moral consensus, 52, 253, 265
moral energy, 149, 254
moral order, 15
moral purity, 298
moral theory, 153–58, 187, 298
moral tradition, 117
morality, 16, 22, 45, 88, 94, 96–97, 105, 117–19, 137, 141, 144, 149, 152, 170, 174, 188–89, 219, 235, 252
Moses, 98
Mughal period, 30, 50–51
Mukerji, Hiren, 297
Mukherjee, Jatin, 337
Mukhopadhyay, B., 157, 329, 344
Muslims, 19, 40–41, 45, 47, 49–52, 54, 60, 79–80, 87, 94, 113, 118, 159–60, 166, 216, 225, 232, 234, 238–39, 251, 269
Muslin, Hyman, 347

Nag, K.D., 330
Naidu, Sarojini, 200
Nair, Sankaran, 58
Namboodiripad, E.M.S., 297
Nanak, 97, 233
Nanda, B.R., 330
Naoroji, Dadabhai, 56, 60, 63, 65, 158–60, 330, 332, 344
Narayan, Jayaprakash, 51, 296–97, 323–25, 326, 330, 348
Narayan, Prabhavati, 210, 226–27, 340
nation, 79–80, 85, 88, 152, 162, 202, 323
national character, 88, 92, 156, 159
nationalism, 47–48, 56, 160–61, 167, 176

Nayar, Sushila, 208–10, 226–27
Nehru, Jawaharlal, 51, 209, 213, 223, 265, 292, 318, 320–24, 330, 332
Nehru, Motilal, 57, 332
Nevinson, Henry, 331
new system of ethics, 219
Noakhali, 217–18
Non-Cooperation Movement, 138, 161, 238, 257–58, 262, 269
non-violence, 120–54, 161, 172, 174, 180–83, 186, 188, 217, 219–21, 254–55, 273, 295, 298–300, 307–09, 319
non-violent killing, 135

Oakeshott, M., 30
objectivity, 181
Offer, D., 347
O'Flaherty, W.D., 343
oppression, 152, 178, 268
orthodox, 27, 95, 210–11, 214, 239, 242, 257, 260–61
Overstreet, Gene D., 348

pain, 125, 131, 135, 138
Pal, B.C., 47, 49, 56, 73–74, 77, 105, 330, 332, 344
Pandurang, Dada, 279, 346
Panikkar, K.N., 348
Pantham, Thomas, 330
Parāsharasmriti, 20, 22
Parekh, M.C., 328
Partition of Bengal, 160–61, 177
Partition of India, 264
past, 17–18, 51, 53–54, 62, 181–84, 252, 280
Patanjali, 146, 179, 196
Patel, C.B., 327
Patel, C.N., 347
Patel, I.K., 327
Patel, Sardar, 213
Patel, Zaverbhai, 349
patriotism, 48, 55, 62, 172, 176, 178, 313
Patwardhan, Achyut, 327, 349
penance, 213, 217
Phadke, Y.D., 340
Phadnis, Nana, 279

philosophy, 52, 161
Phule, Jyotiba, 331, 344
Plato, 272
Platonic love, 226
plurality, 152, 176, 277
Pocock, John, 327
political culture, 48, 53, 115
political Hinduism, 161
political morality, 77, 95
political parties, 115, 265
political pedagogy, 35, 57
political philosophy, 54, 70, 152
political virtues, 54, 71
politics, 44, 77, 103-05, 152, 166, 186, 197, 314, 316, 323, 325
polytheism, 21
Poona Pact, 230
positivism, 116, 161
power, 37, 45, 49, 78, 83, 110, 146, 180, 191-92, 194, 197-99, 218, 223-24, 267-68, 271
Prabhu, R.K., 334, 340
principles, 29-30, 36, 42, 52-53, 68, 71, 76-77, 83, 86, 91-92, 117-19, 121, 153, 170, 178, 180, 183, 186-87, 193, 199, 224, 235-36, 302
private property, 301, 306
progress, 35, 61, 95, 144
Protestantism, 53, 99, 313
public opinion, 162, 233, 253, 261, 266
Purānas, 124, 167, 183-84, 247-48, 278, 280
Purani, Ambala, 185
purity, 215, 220
Pyarelal, 210, 212, 327, 340-42

Queen Victoria, 155

RSS, 325
race, 34, 53, 57, 164, 186
racism, 59, 64, 77, 95, 157-58, 204, 233, 290
Rai, Lala Lajpat, 47-48, 330
Raichandbhai, 216, 347
Raj, 31, 61-62, 64-65, 82, 155-56
Rāja Tarangini, 35
Rajagopalachari, C., 264, 317
Rājasuya yagna, 166

Ram Chandra, 163
Ram Gopal, 336
Rama Rao, N.T., 340
Raman Maharishi, 146
Ramakrishna Mission, 235
Ramananda, 224, 233
Rāmānuja, 232
Rāmāyana, 168, 184, 338
Ramkrishna Paramhamsa, 97, 146
Ranade, G., 49, 52, 56, 60, 105, 157
Ranadive, B.T., 297, 316
Rao, V.R., 340
rationalism, 28, 31, 36, 45, 52-53, 61, 254, 280
rationality, 35, 67
Ravindran, T.K., 344
Ray, Sibnarayan, 347
Raychaudhuri, T., 329-30, 332, 336
reason, 28-30
reform, 16, 19, 21-22, 27, 41, 54, 70, 76, 228, 253-55
regeneration, 15, 51, 57, 73, 77, 104, 178, 197, 202, 204
reincarnation, 79, 243
religion, 14, 28, 37, 44-45, 49-50, 58, 61, 69, 76, 79, 86-87, 96, 98-100, 103, 108-09, 128, 181, 183, 237, 241-42, 246, 256, 271, 280
religious text, 240-41
religious tradition, 100, 103, 105, 108-09, 121, 195, 198, 213, 218, 222, 224-25
Renaissance, 51-54, 66, 273
'renouncer', 16
representative, 59-60, 82, 90, 158, 235
revelation, 98-100
revivalism, 66
revolution, 89, 143, 149, 164, 166, 177
Reynolds, R., 331
rights, 59, 68-69, 84, 113, 139, 141, 164, 235, 257, 262, 266, 271
Robertson, William, 51
Roman empire, 44, 58-59
Rousseau, J.J., 276, 289
Roy, Amit, 327
Roy, M.N., 9
Roy, Ram Mohun, 21-22, 40-41, 44, 48-49, 53, 56, 65, 68-69, 112, 329-30, 332

Rudolph, Lloyd and Suzanne, 328-29
rule of law, 32, 61-62
Ruskin, J., 23, 90
Russell, B., 219

sacred texts, 242, 248
sādhāranadharma, 20-21, 29
Sahajiya cult, 224
Sahasrabuche, Annasaheb, 349
salvation, 55-56, 66, 91, 133
Samya, 233
sanātanadharma, 20, 29-30
sanatanists, 228, 242, 246-48, 263-64, 266
Sandel, Michael, 326
Sarabhai, Ambalal, 312
Saraswati, Dayananda, 21-22, 74, 77, 91, 167, 234, 332, 344
Sarkar, Narmada, 49
sati, 21, 43, 50
satya, 86, 130, 248
satyāgraha, 89, 102, 106-07, 110, 112, 117-19, 149, 151-53, 180, 206, 218, 243, 246, 254, 259, 271, 299, 304, 306-11, 319, 322-25
Savarkar, V.D., 91, 164, 332, 344
Scheduled Castes Federation, 265
Schweitzer, A., 334
science, 24, 27, 44, 46, 55, 61, 67, 69-71, 74, 81, 90, 96-100, 103, 116-17, 120, 167, 183, 240, 247, 280
science of non-violence, 145
science of spirit, 98, 100, 116, 310
scientific inquiry, 52, 100-01, 144
scriptures, 239, 241, 252
Seal, A., 331
secular, 61, 69, 75, 161
self-confidence, 302
self-discipline, 302
self-interest, 131, 140, 176, 189, 192, 221, 262
self-ownership, 301
self-respect, 134, 136, 144, 148, 150-52, 163, 195, 271, 290, 302
self-understanding, 272, 275, 277, 293, 302
selfishness, 131, 133, 135, 139, 198
Sen, K.C., 21-22, 56, 68-69, 330
Servants of India Society, 104, 111

Servants of Untouchables Society, 263
sevādharma, 15, 105, 113
sexual energy, 197-98, 204-05
sexual yajna, 217
sexuality, 39, 83-85, 96, 101-02, 157, 197-98, 202-03, 289
Seybold, 274
Shah, Munnalal, 211
Shaikh, Gulam, 340
shakti, 191, 197
Shankar Narmada, 49, 57, 291, 346-47
Shankaracharya, 240, 244
Sheth, Pravin, 327
Shirer, W.L., 342
Shivaji, 166, 170
shudras, 21, 179
Shukla, C., 340
Singh, Y., 334
Sinha, Balwant, 342
Sinha, M.P., 346
Slade, M., 209-10, 226
smritis, 19-20, 22, 37-38, 95, 265
Social Background of Indian Nationalism, 297
social justice, 307, 319
social service, 103, 106, 117, 310, 316
Socialist Party, 315
Socrates, 342
soul, 221, 250, 284, 288, 302
South Africa, 15, 28, 180, 237, 290
Southey, Robert, 274
Spencer, H., 159, 167, 336-37
spirit, 24, 83-86, 302, 309-10, 315-16, 318
spirit of Hinduism, 241-42, 247
spiritual, 26, 66, 68, 74, 83, 85, 103-04, 173, 175, 189, 192, 195, 197, 203, 220, 302, 323
spiritual energies, 194-95, 201, 216-17
spiritual exercise, 106
spiritual experiments, 25, 217, 220, 224-27
spiritual inertia, 173
spiritual power, 193, 195-97, 203, 205, 224-25
spiritual scientist, 98, 116, 193, 218-19, 240
spiritual surgery, 173, 254

spirituality, 49, 128–29, 224, 252, 285
Spratt, P., 343
srutis, 20, 22
Stalin, J., 118
state, 36, 45, 52–56, 66–68, 70–71, 74–76, 80, 84–85, 105, 108–10, 115, 133, 143, 148–49, 176, 180, 192, 253, 267, 302–05
Stokes, Eric, 329
Strozier, C.B., 347
suffering, 30, 137, 173, 221
suffering love, 26
suicide, 133, 147
swabhāva, 43, 90, 93, 175–76
swadeshi, 130, 158, 318
swadharma, 189
Swami Satyananda, 259
Swami Shraddhananda, 167, 204, 345
swarāj, 130, 151, 175–76, 178, 202, 229, 238, 314
Swaraj Party, 311

Tagore, D., 56, 346
Tagore, R., 16, 51, 56, 60
Tähtinen, Unto, 334
Taitreya Samhitā, 122
Tantra, 222, 224, 232
Tantrism, 200
tapasyā, 89, 257
Tarkachudamani, S., 329
technology, 55, 61, 67, 71, 74, 90, 111
terrorism, 61, 155, 158, 162–63, 172, 175, 177–78, 181, 183, 190
Thakkar Bapa, 214, 222
theology, 99
Thomas, M., 51
Thomas, M.M., 329–30
Thomas, Paul, 326
Thoreau, H.D., 23
Tilak, B.G., 49, 56–57, 91, 105, 158, 165–66, 169–70, 235, 344
Tolstoy, L., 23, 90, 129, 334
tradition, 15–31, 35, 38–40, 48–49, 66, 81, 89, 95–97, 100, 106–07, 112, 118, 126–31, 134, 138, 176, 179, 195–96, 199, 216, 222, 236, 247–49, 268, 290

tradition of inquiry, 117, 180
traditionalism, 38, 42–45, 68–69, 72–73, 78, 90, 92–95
Trevelyan, G.T., 336
Tripathi, D., 349
trust, 322
trusteeship, 111, 296, 300, 304, 306, 322
truth, 21, 52, 71, 81, 86, 97, 100, 103, 108, 117–18, 151, 164, 173–74, 183, 195, 214–15, 221, 235, 253, 273, 284, 289, 299
Tukaram, 279
Tully, M., 343
Tulsidas, 279

U.P. Kisan Sabha, 310
Unnithan, T.K., 334
untouchability, 15, 46, 76, 107, 109, 210, 228–71, 308, 315
Upadhyay, P.C., 327
Upanishads, 46, 53, 69, 75, 179, 235–36, 248
utilitarian attitude, 35, 147

Vaikkam *satyāgraha*, 243, 246, 248, 250, 259
Vaishnavism, 206, 221, 224–26, 233
Vallabhacharya, 94
Valmiki, 282
Varma, S.K., 158, 167
varnas, 114, 180–81, 205, 231, 235, 250–52, 267
varnadharma, 20, 45, 190
Vedanta, 69
Vedas, 20–22, 27, 53, 75, 183, 235, 247–48
Vellacott, Barbara, 327
vibhutis, 196
vicarious antonement, 26, 112
Vidyasagar, I.C., 20–22, 49
violence, 77, 84, 101, 109, 122–24, 131–33, 136, 138–43, 146–53, 159, 161–65, 167–69, 172–76, 178–79, 181, 186, 188–90, 198, 214, 216–17, 219–21, 223, 252–54, 297, 302, 306, 308–09, 316, 318–19, 321
Vishvāmitra, 213

Vivekananda, Swami, 20, 34, 46, 49, 70, 72, 77–78, 89, 111, 204, 235, 344
Vyasa, 122, 184, 186–88, 213, 278, 282

Welbon, Guy, 326
What Congress and Gandhi Have Done to the Untouchables, 229
Williams, Monier, 53
Windmiller, Marshall, 348
Woodroffe, Sir John, 222
Wyllie, Sir Curzon, 164

yajna, 85, 89, 107, 214–15, 217, 221, 257, 302

Yoga *Sutra*, 179, 196
Younger, P., 328
Yudhishthira, 184
yuga, 20, 22, 92, 113, 247
yugadharma, 15, 20–23, 26–28, 39, 92, 95–96, 101–03, 105–06, 111, 113–14, 116–17, 119, 154, 219, 251
Yujurveda, Sukla, 122

Zaveri, Himmat, 327
Zaveri, Manju, 327
Zelliot, E., 345
Zoroaster, 98

About the Author

Bhikhu Parekh is Professor of Political Theory at the University of Hull, UK. He has served as Vice-Chancellor of the University of Baroda (1981–84) and Deputy Chairman of the Commission for Racial Equality, UK (1985–90). He has been a Visiting Professor at the University of British Columbia (1968–69), Concordia University, Montreal (1974–75), McGill University (1976–77), Harvard University (1996), the Institute of Advanced Study, Vienna (1997) and the University of Pennsylvania (1998).

Professor Parekh has published six widely acclaimed books in political philosophy, including *Hannah Arendt and the Search for a New Political Philosophy* (1981), *Marx's Theory of Ideology* (1982), *Contemporary Political Thinkers* (1982), *Gandhi's Political Philosophy* (1989) and *Gandhi* (Oxford University's Past Masters Series, 1997). His *A Theory of Multicultural Society* will be published by Macmillan early next year.